CHILD MURDER
BRITISH CULT

1720–1900

JOSEPHINE McDONAGH

CAMBRIDGE
UNIVERSITY PRESS

CAMBRIDGE UNIVERSITY PRESS
Cambridge, New York, Melbourne, Madrid, Cape Town, Singapore, São Paulo

Cambridge University Press
The Edinburgh Building, Cambridge CB2 8RU, UK

Published in the United States of America by Cambridge University Press, New York

www.cambridge.org
Information on this title: www.cambridge.org/9780521781930

First published 2003
This digitally printed version 2008

A catalogue record for this publication is available from the British Library

ISBN 978-0-521-78193-0 hardback
ISBN 978-0-521-05456-0 paperback

For Colin

And for the little infant's bones
With spades they would have sought.
But then the beauteous hill of moss
Before their eyes began to stir;
And for full fifty yards around,
The grass it shook upon the ground.
                    Wordsworth, 'The Thorn'

Contents

Illustrations

Acknowledgements

I began to consider the issues in this book during a period spent at University College Cork, and since then have dropped and revived the topic a number of times before realising the extraordinary wealth of material and ideas to which the grim motif of child murder would lead. I would like to thank my friends and colleagues from that time, especially Mary Breen, Patricia Coughlan, and Ann Fogarty, for pointing me in this morbid direction. Most of the work for this book, however, has been carried out while working in the School of English and Humanities at Birkbeck. I would like to thank my colleagues, especially Stephen Clucas, Esther Leslie, and Mpalive Msiska, as well as students, including those who have taken my 'Narratives of the Body' course, for helping me to think through the issues. Isobel Armstrong and Sally Ledger have in different ways provided rich inspiration, advice, and friendship, and I am warmly indebted to them both.

    The project could not have assumed its present shape without certain kinds of support, and I thank the Arts and Humanities Research Board, the Leverhulme Trust, and the Research Committees of the University of Exeter and Birkbeck College, University of London for research funds. I am fortunate to have spent two periods of research leave at Stanford University, and thank the Institute for the Study of Women and Gender and the Department of English for providing an excellent environment in which to read and think. Throughout I have been most grateful for the assistance of librarians at the Bodleian Library, University of London Library, British Library, Birkbeck College Library, Special Collections, Cecil H. Green Library, Stanford University, Department of Special Collections at UCLA Library, and Huntington Library. Some of the material in Chapter 5 has previously been published in an earlier form in *Nineteenth-Century Literature* (© 2001 by the Regents of the University of California. Reprinted from *Nineteenth-Century Literature*, 56: 2, by permission of the University of California Press).

I have incurred many debts, intellectual and other, over the long period in which I have been working on this book – too numerous to mention each one. I am grateful to Linda Bree and her colleagues at Cambridge University Press for their help throughout. Many people have generously shared ideas and information with me, and often these have led me in unforeseen and rewarding directions. Joe Bristow, Maud Ellmann, Jenn Fishmann, Anne Janowitz, Roger Luckhurst, Laura Marcus, Patricia Moyer, and Ana Parejo Vadillo have, at different times, been resourceful and provocative sounding boards. Margot Finn, Mark Jackson, Vivien Jones, Sally Ledger, Jane Spencer, Jenny Taylor, and Michael Wood all kindly read the manuscript in its final stages and provided invaluable feedback. I am immensely grateful to them all. Any remaining errors are, of course, my own. Finally, my greatest debt is to Colin Jones. The book is for him.

Note on references

Except in cases where the full title is instructive, I have used short titles of eighteenth- and nineteenth-century texts in the notes, and full titles in bibliography. Unless otherwise stated, the place of publication is London.

Abbreviations

DNB	*Dictionary of National Biography*
FB	Bernard Mandeville, *The Fable of the Bees: or, Private Vices, Public Benefits, with commentary critical, historical and explanatory by F. B. Kaye*, 2 vols. (Oxford, 1924)
MP	Jonathan Swift, *A Modest Proposal* (1729) in *Irish Tracts*, vol. 12 of *Prose Works*, 14 vols., ed. Herbert Davis (Oxford, 1955)
NL	*Northern Liberator and Champion*
NS	*Northern Star*
OBSP	*Old Bailey Session Papers*

Introduction: plots and protagonists

On the evening of 2 February 1774, a small, injured body was discovered in the 'necessary' at the home of Paul Cauldwell, a soap-maker of Cow Cross, East London.[1] A carpenter was called, who released a new-born boy from the vault. The baby, whose cries had been heard by the servants, had been dropped in the privy and pushed down with a stick, sustaining a half-inch wound in his belly. Astonishingly, he was still alive. Cauldwell's servants tended him until the surgeon arrived, but the efforts to repair his damaged body were in vain, and, in the early hours of the following morning, the child died. His mother, a spinster named Jane Cornforth who was a maid in the Cauldwell household, was arrested, and held in prison until her trial at the Old Bailey on 21 May 1774.[2] She was found guilty of wilful murder, sentenced to death, and executed a few days later. During the procession to Tyburn, a runaway bullock from Smithfield stormed into the crowd, 'tossing several persons who were much hurt' – an act of random violence that formed the backdrop to Jane Cornforth's sorry end.[3]

From court records and press reports, a little can be gleaned of Jane Cornforth and the events that led her to the scaffold. Character witnesses at the trial attested that she was 'a tender, humane girl', who was 'kind to children'. She had recently purchased new linen, evidence that she was preparing for the birth, facing up to the consequences of her pregnancy. Her employment record – less than a month with Cauldwell – suggests that the shame of her condition had been the cause of her dismissal from her previous employer, Margaret Jarvis, who nevertheless testified to her good character at the trial. Perhaps Cauldwell had not spotted that Cornforth was in the late stages of pregnancy when he took her on. His servants were not so blind: they had no trouble in identifying the source of the miserable deposit in the privy – the new servant girl, who 'in cleaning the grate, could not get up without laying hold of something to help her up'.[4]

Like all such documents, however, the existing records tell only part of the story, leaving much to our speculation. There is nothing, for instance, about the identity of the father, or the circumstances of the child's conception. Should we assume that the father was a member of Jarvis's household, another servant, or perhaps even a family member – Jarvis's husband, or son? Had Jane Cornforth been seduced, or raped? Had she fallen in love? Cauldwell claimed in the trial that he had told her that he 'would have put [her] into the hospital to lie-in if [she] had acquainted [him] of this matter; all the answer she made...was, what could she do?'[5]

Why had Cornforth – by everyone's account a 'tender, humane girl' – perpetrated such a violent deed? Had she acted in cold blood, or through temporary insanity (she claims herself that she was 'out of her senses')?[6] If the latter, was this provoked by the physical trauma of giving birth, or was it a regrettable, yet intelligible, response to the social stigma and destitution that were the likely consequences of an illegitimate birth? In court and in the newspapers, none of these questions are raised, and given the absence of diaries or correspondence, we can only imagine what might have happened, and how Jane Cornforth might have felt. Amid the hustle and the bustle on the discovery of the child, the calling of servants, surgeons, carpenters, and constables, and the shock that each one registers on seeing the terrible injuries of the newborn baby, there is no probing of Cornforth's motives, or the circumstances that might have provoked this act. For today's reader there is something chilling about the apparent ease with which the violent death of the infant bastard seems to be accommodated in the run of everyday events. Our gaze jolts back and forth between the wounded corpse of the infant, and the pathetic culprit named in the reiterated refrain: 'poor Jane Cornforth, who loved children'.[7]

Despite the silences in the records, social historians have used cases such as Jane Cornforth's as source material from which to piece together an understanding of child murder, and the society in which it was committed.[8] Unmarried women, like Cornforth, who would have been subject to the harsh social pressures exerted on illegitimate mothers, committed the overwhelming majority of crimes that came to trial. Extra-marital pregnancies often led a woman to the loss of regular employment, homelessness, being disowned by family and friends, and being cast out of parishes that were unwilling to pay poor relief for illegitimate children.[9] Documentary evidence of child murder cases available from legal depositions, court records, newspaper accounts, and medical records, has allowed the reconstruction of scenarios of illegitimate birth and death, extending knowledge of the lives of single women, their position in the community, and their treatment under the law. We know, therefore, that the discovery of an infant corpse in the privy, or concealed elsewhere – in a box in a servant's bedroom, or thrown into a river – was not a daily event by any means, but neither was it uncommon through the eighteenth and nineteenth centuries.[10] We know, too, that the mothers of these unfortunate infants were likely to be servants like Cornforth, women whose domestic situation made them vulnerable to illegitimate pregnancy, but ill-placed to raise children.[11] We also know, however, that it was usually difficult, if not impossible, to establish whether the child in such cases had been stillborn, had died of natural causes, or was the victim of a violent crime. The very high level of infant mortality shrouded many such cases in uncertainty. So, too, did the shame which was generated by illegitimate pregnancies, as women were often compelled to give birth alone and in secret. The usual defence of a woman accused of killing a newborn was that it had died of natural causes; indeed Jane Cornforth claimed that she thought her baby had been stillborn, although in her case, the cries of the child abandoned to the privy make this difficult to believe. In many cases, however, the cause of death was genuinely uncertain; sometimes, one must presume, even to the parturient mother herself, whose desires and intents in such traumatic circumstances are likely to have been deeply confused.

The level of uncertainty surrounding these crimes presents a particular challenge in the reconstruction of child murders. Even though historians have used the documentary evidence effectively to imagine the events at and around the scene of the crime by using a kind a probabilistic calculus, such endeavours often overlook the extent to which the exact nature of the events was always obscured to contemporary commentators.[12] The law under which most suspicious deaths of new-born infants were dealt with had been set up precisely in recognition of the difficulty of establishing the facts, and did not require positive proof of murder in the way that later courts would require. The 1624 'Act to Prevent the Destroying and Murthering of Bastard Children' (21 Jac. I c. 27) directed attention not to the death of the child, but to whether or not the mother had concealed the death.[13] Under this statute, concealment of the death of an infant bastard established the legal presumption that the mother was guilty of murder, whether or not she could be shown to have caused the death, and reflected the common supposition that the shame of illegitimacy was motive enough to provoke a woman to commit the deed. The law was interpreted differently at various times, but towards the end of the eighteenth century, when Cornforth was tried, the concealment of a pregnancy had come to be taken as evidence of an intention to murder the child. A standard vindication of women facing such charges was, therefore, that they had prepared for the birth, the evidence of which being the purchase of linen. Hence the significance of the claim in Cornforth's defence that she had done just this. The concealment charge also came to mean that, unlike in the treatment of most other crimes, the burden of proof lay on the suspect to establish her innocence, rather than on the prosecution to prove her guilt.[14] The paradoxical but not uncommon result was an unusually severe law, but one under which courts were reluctant to convict. According to Jackson, in the Northern Circuit courts, for example, in the period between 1720 and 1800, only six of nearly two hundred indicted women were found guilty of the crime, and of those, only two were executed.[15] Cornforth's case is unusual in that she was found guilty of murder – but in her case the evidence of live birth was incontrovertible.

The 1624 statute was remarkably long-lived. It was not used in all cases of women convicted of murdering their children – there is no direct mention of the statute, for instance, in Cornforth's trial. As Jackson has shown, however, it dominated the legal discussion of the crime and shaped the kinds of evidence that were presented and verdicts that were reached until the end of the eighteenth century, and arguably beyond. By the time that Cornforth was convicted it was already 150 years old, and despite efforts by reformers, especially in the 1770s, it was not repealed until 1803. Indeed, it was partly the contentious and ambiguous nature of such cases that stood in the way of reform. Nevertheless, by the late eighteenth century the law was widely held to be anachronistic, out of synch with the mores of a changing society: it was considered inefficient by some, on account of the courts' reluctance to convict under it, and inhumane by others, in the harsh treatment of unmarried women it was empowered to mete out.[16]

A series of reforms in the nineteenth century changed the legal definition of the crime and its social ramifications. A new statute enacted in 1803 (43 Geo. III c. 58) put the murder of infant bastards on the same footing as other murders. The burden of proof now fell on the Crown rather than the defendant, and a lesser charge of concealment was created which carried a maximum penalty of two years' imprisonment, and which could be invoked in cases where there was insufficient evidence of murder.[17] In 1828, the Offences Against Person Act (9 Geo. IV c. 31) extended the charge of concealment to married women, thus ending the legal association of the crime with illegitimacy. A change in the law in 1861, the Offences Against Person Act (24/25 Vic. c. 100), made concealment into a separate, substantive crime, which applied to any person, not just the mother.[18]

Despite these changes, consistent notes can be traced in the commentary on the law regarding child murder throughout both centuries. In particular there continues to be a division between, on the one hand, those who saw child murder as a crime committed by sexually deviant, unmarried women, and, on the other hand, those who held it to be a crime provoked by archaic or corrupt institutions, which themselves required reform. By association, people often deemed the crime itself to be a throwback to an earlier state of society, a scratch on the civilised veneer of modern life. The 1624 statute had shaped the ways in which child murder was perceived, as a crime of convenience or necessity committed by unwed mothers, but opinion divided as to whether its ultimate cause was the sexual disorder of unmarried women, or alternatively, the ignominy of illegitimacy, and a failure of sympathy on the part of institutions. The events of child murder were notoriously murky, and they always provoked highly differentiated and deeply contested explanations.

This strong element of doubt and confusion pervades many aspects of the crime and its treatment under the law. For contemporary onlookers, these awful events did not easily, if at all, yield their secrets. At a certain level, the high rate of acquittal is indicative of this. This was not always or only an effect of the courts' sympathy for the plight of unmarried women – part of the more general trend in the eighteenth century in which affective relations within the family, especially between mothers and children, enjoyed heightened significance.[19] It was also an expression of the difficulty of making convictions on the basis of partial and inconclusive evidence, an admission of the inability to know the truth.[20] Indeed, we can often detect a sense in which contemporary society did not *want* to know the truths of these horrible crimes. Legal and other discussions of child murder in the eighteenth and nineteenth centuries register a strong sense of ambivalence: a fascination with, and horror of, its violence, but at the same time a seemingly sympathetic tolerance towards it, a willingness to turn a blind eye. Such ambivalence is witnessed in the newspaper reports of 'poor Jane Cornforth', whose terrible violation of her child is documented at the same time as the pathos of her dismal end. This difficulty of knowing – which constitutes a kind of epistemological shortfall – is registered in many of the representations of child murder prevalent within British culture throughout the eighteenth and nineteenth centuries, and contributes to its peculiarly complex effects.

Although this study draws on the work of social historians, its aims are somewhat different. My purpose is not to establish what happened – the whens, wheres, and whys. I am interested less in individual cases of murder, like that of poor Cornforth junior, who in any case receded from public purview as quickly and as unceremoniously as he entered it, than in the murder of any child, in the *idea* of child murder as it circulated in society and through time, far beyond the scene of the crime. Despite, or possibly because of, the awfulness of the events, child murders left cultural traces across society, vestiges of crime and misfortune that offered ground for anxiety, concern, and reflection. Discussions of child murder frequently seeped into debates on other issues, often providing an example or test case through which society examined its own values and standards of civilised behaviour. Child murder is thus in evidence in a wide array of sources, quite apart from court records and newspaper reports, and, in each case, carries complex and often contradictory meanings. In novels, poems, and plays, in philosophical and polemical works, political and economic tracts, in scientific and medical works, we encounter the unnatural deaths of children of vastly different kinds: violent deaths, deaths from neglect, sacrificial and revengeful deaths, even sympathetic and redemptive deaths. There are babies killed by desperate and destitute mothers, like Jane Cornforth, and their representations in literature – Wordsworth's Martha Ray, or Hetty Sorrel in George Eliot's *Adam Bede*. But there are many other kinds of child murder. For example, babies eaten by greedy gourmets in Swift's *A Modest Proposal*; babies scoffed by hungry beasts in Mandeville, and later Rousseau; babies murdered by primitive fathers in anthropological works of the eighteenth century; babies of slaves, *saved* through murder from an ignominious life, like the child of the 'Runaway Slave' in Elizabeth Barrett Browning's poem; Indian girls slaughtered at birth by their families, according to ancient custom; English children, 'positively murdered' by neglectful and ill-educated mothers, as Mary Wollstonecraft claimed; children forced to starve by cruel Dame Nature in Malthus's shocking account of the natural restrictions of population; children supposedly massacred by an uncaring government, according to critics of the New Poor Law; babies 'killed for a burial fee' by the avaricious poor, according to Tennyson in *Maud*; and children sacrificed by 'Old Father Time' in Thomas Hardy's *Jude the Obscure*, 'because we *are* too menny'.

While the historical record often reveals reluctance on the part of society to confront the full implications of child murder, it is curious that so many texts return repeatedly to scenes of infant killing, to produce a plethora of modes, motives, and meanings of murder. The sheer range of these can be glimpsed when we consider the various child murder plots that were in circulation throughout the period, many of which were inherited from classical and biblical mythology and ancient history: for instance the story of Medea, who killed her children to wreak revenge on Jason; or of Herod, the cruel tyrant whose massacre of the innocents accompanied the birth of Christ; or Brutus, who allowed his sons to be executed under due process of law for

Figure I. Jacques Louis David, *Les Licteurs rapportent à Brutus les corps de ses fils*, 1789

the sake of the Roman Republic. The last was an episode much admired by Jacobins in France, who were attempting to establish a new republic on the model of Rome. Its most famous visual representation is David's 'The Lictors returning to Brutus the bodies of his sons' (see Fig. I), produced on the cusp of the Revolution.[21] Even before 1789, however, within the idiom of civic humanism that was prevalent in the political culture of eighteenth-century England, Brutus's sacrifice is lauded as a model of virtuous behaviour and as a fable illustrating individual sacrifice for a common good.

Each of these stories involving child murder is retold repeatedly in eighteenth- and nineteenth-century contexts.[22] Taken together they demonstrate that, despite the emphasis in the legal records, in eighteenth- and nineteenth-century Britain, not all child murderers were imagined to be mothers – men, too, of varying kinds, were also held to kill children – nor all their victims newborns – in Brutus's case the sons are adult men.[23] Moreover, in these imaginative renderings, acts of child killing had diverse and conflicting associations. They could be invoked to dramatise and explain states of insanity such as Medea's, and ideals of civic virtue embodied by Brutus's sacrifice; and political ideas, from Herodian tyranny to Roman republican democracy.

The purpose of this study is to track motifs of child murder as they circulate in British culture across the eighteenth and nineteenth centuries, accreting layers of meanings that are intricately related to the contexts in which they appear. These motifs take on a life of their own, and are never reducible to a reflection of a particular case, such as Jane Cornforth's, even though their symbolic resonance will often frame the responses to and representations of such deeds. If our own culture is inclined to see child murder as an act devoid of meaning, an expression of nihilism, the earlier period reveals instead that child murder is invested with a bewildering excess of meanings, and it is this that contributes to its particularly potent and unstable character.

As the persistence of plots from classical and biblical mythology indicates, acts of child murder had been a source of imaginative speculation since ancient times. At the beginning of the eighteenth century, however, they appear as a theme in novel and unlikely contexts, and begin to assume new and complex meanings. In a cluster of texts published in the 1720s, child murder is a topic of discussion in both apologias for, and arguments against, the new commercial society. Whether bemoaned or celebrated, the spirit of commercialism was widely experienced at this time as a profound break with traditional forms of social organisation and discussions of it set the terms for later critiques of capitalism and commodity culture that would dominate discourses about society in the later eighteenth and nineteenth centuries. It is here, then, in the midst of heated debates about the social and moral consequences of commercialism – the quest for profit, the desire for luxury, the inexorable circulation and consumption of goods – that child murder embarks on a new career as the focus of critiques and celebrations of the new social organisation. As I will show, in highly influential works by Bernard Mandeville and Jonathan Swift, acts such as that which was later committed by Jane Cornforth became, for the first time, a key motif through which both writers contemplate, albeit to very different ends, the new economic conditions of their society.

The heightened emphasis placed on the violation of children in this period may be seen as an aspect of broader social and cultural trends, a paradoxical symptom of the new value that has come to be placed on the child. The period is often characterised as one dominated by new conceptions of the affectionate family, and by sentimental attitudes towards childhood.[24] Moreover, modes of family relations tended to be taken at the time as analogues for the condition of society as a whole, so that, for instance, standards of childcare were regarded as gauges of a society's civilised values. As a corollary to this, the harm of children is a frequent sign of an antiquated and brutal regime. Some recent commentators have taken this trend at face value: that is to say, that the various changes across the two centuries have been understood as part of a process of modernisation in which society gradually threw off its antiquated, child-murdering ways to become a more child-loving, and hence enlightened society. This view has been articulated most strongly – and controversially – by historian Lloyd De Mause, who in his psycho-historical account characterises the early modern period as a time in which child murder was rife.[25] A similar teleology is at work in much of the more measured historical writing about child murder, in which the legislative reforms of the nineteenth century, including the repeal of the 1624 statute in 1803, but also the enactment of various statutes towards the end of the nineteenth century for the protection of children, are viewed in a strongly progressive light.[26]

A broader array of evidence, I suggest, presents a more complicated and less teleological picture. Indeed, it is precisely because of the new value that is placed on children that accounts of the violation of children carry so much weight. The rhetoric of both Swift and Mandeville, and of subsequent writers, relies for its effect on the existence of sentimental notions of young children. Moreover, a discourse of child sacrifice, in which the murder of a child, or children, in one way or another is valued as a positive or virtuous act, remains in evidence at least until the end of the nineteenth century. In surveying the literature of the period, I have detected no diminution in its usage, and although it is subject to fluctuations, it remains available to writers throughout. More emphatically, even the rhetoric that speaks for the amelioration of infant life is paradoxically entwined with the rhetoric of child sacrifice. This proves efficacious for campaigners for legislation for the protection of infant life at the end of the nineteenth century, who were keen to make distinctions between the relative values of infant lives on proto-eugenic grounds. When we read widely in the literature of the period, rather than encountering a society that is progressively kinder in the attitudes it expresses towards children, less tolerant of infant death or violation, less willing to engage with the rhetoric of child sacrifice, we find, instead, a society that continued to maintain highly complex and ambiguous attitudes to infant death and its symbolic potential.

The discussion of child murder in the eighteenth and nineteenth centuries is too extensive and complex to lend itself to an exhaustive inventory. In order to gain purchase on it, I have chosen, therefore, to concentrate on clusters of texts in which the interest in child murder appears particularly intense: the discussions of commercial society from the 1720s; anthropological debates about the nature of man in the 1770s, which revolve around the spectacle of child murder; debates about social order following the French Revolution in 1798; the explosive responses to the New Poor Law at the end of the 1830s; and the so-called epidemic of child murder in England around 1859. In each of these contexts, child murder emerges as a motif in which debates of a serious nature about key issues in Britain's self-imaginings are conducted.

My emphasis on cultural instantiations of the act leads me to depart from the historical treatment of child murder in two ways. First, I interpret child murder more widely than historians have tended to do, to include not only acts of neo-naticide, but also the violent death of any person who is represented as a child. Second, while most accounts by historians follow a periodisation dictated by legislative reform, and see the repeal of the 1624 statute in 1803 as marking an important break between the treatment of the crime in the eighteenth and nineteenth centuries, from the point of view of the cultural reverberations of child murder, the break comes not at the beginning of the nineteenth century, but at the very end. Although the notion of child murder would continue, in different forms, to haunt British culture well beyond this date, a cycle of debate whose initial terms were set by Swift and Mandeville in the early eighteenth century draws to a close at the end of the nineteenth century. By the 1890s, child murder came to be embedded in discussions of birth control and overlapping debates about eugenics, both of which exploited the rich rhetorical repertoire of child murder that had accumulated over the previous two centuries. As we shall see, advocates for the new technologies of contraception on the one hand, and evolutionary science on the other, saw child murder as a strategy of adaptation, a force for good in a changing world, and used an inherited narrative of sacrifice and redemption in order to justify this interpretation. These themes converge in the controversial figure of the New Woman. The invention of *fin-de-siècle* culture, the New Woman is a fascinating symptom of the times: Janus-like, she is both a scandalous throw back to primeval states, but also the harbinger of change, and the model for the new, autonomous individual. As we shall see, her modernity is sometimes registered through her association with child murder through both her associations with birth control, and the fact that she refuses maternal roles in her quest for autonomy. Equally, it is associated with her embrace of proto-eugenic theories for the amelioration of social problems, and the strengthening of the empire.

In a short, final chapter I revisit a theme that has run throughout the book, from the discussion of Swift's idea that the Irish are killers of their own children in his *A Modest Proposal* (1729). In the complex and politically charged context of 1890s Ireland, I argue, the idea of the Irish child killer is re-inhabited by Irish writers as a powerful yet highly ambivalent sign of a new modernity. As if completing a cycle, the Irish adaptation of the child-murder rhetoric at the end of the nineteenth century repudiates a long history in which accusations of infanticide had sealed Ireland's subaltern status.

This present work sets out to establish both a genealogy of ideas of child murder, and a map of their cultural transmission and diffusion. In each of the chapters, I follow the figure of the murdered child across a broad array of texts: parliamentary debates, legal cases, medical records, scientific tracts, economic theories, political speeches, sermons, newspaper reports, travel literature, the archives of colonial bureaucracy, and, of course, works of imaginative literature. The latter are particularly important in this study, because, more noticeably and symptomatically than other kinds of texts, they act as receptacles for the motifs and preoccupations of the time, and reveal a great deal about both the parameters and mechanisms of the cultural imaginary.

There are a number of features that distinguish the motif of child murder and the cultural work that it performs. These have shaped this project in particular ways, and influenced the methods that I have evolved for seeking to understand the phenomenon. First, child murder is a motif that operates across a range of discursive locations. In this study, I deal with texts of vastly different style and intent, and often draw them into surprising conjunctions. To do so, however, reveals the fluid ways in which ideas are transmitted across a culture, and the interrelationships that exist between divergent kinds of knowledge and forms of expression. Second, child murder carries out its effects not only within a designated moment, but also over time. I argue that one of its most significant characteristics is that it acts as a bearer of meanings from previous contexts, and functions as a mechanism of historical memory. Thus, even though I have organised this study around a series of episodes, one of the points that I wish to emphasise is that the meanings of child murder are not contained within any discrete historical moment, but rather travel across them. In my emphasis on continuities and transformations that occur across time, I depart from the trend in current literary and cultural studies, to focus on a 'moment', however broadly conceived, as the privileged site of historical enquiry.[27]

Child murder, I argue, is a significant figure in British culture for the ways in which it bears within it, enfolded in its surfaces, the accumulated remains of previous usages and earlier contexts. The Freudian term of 'Nachträglichkeit', or deferred action, is useful for encapsulating the way in which it functions: as Laplanche and Pontalis explain, 'Nachträglichkeit' refers to the process by which 'experiences, impressions and memory-traces that may be revised at a later date... fit in with fresh experiences or with the attainment of a new stage of development'.[28] In the following chapters, I explore the ways in which the motif of child murder becomes a site for the recollection and revision of past historical moments and events, the peculiar and yet enduring ways in which child murder operates as a mechanism or bearer of memory. Part of the potency of child murder, especially in the mid nineteenth century, is that it seems to perform the processes of cultural memory that are central to the constitution of a particularly prominent idea of national community at that time. Even in today's society, in certain contexts it continues to carry with it the remnants of a rhetoric of nationhood that is now more or less defunct.[29] It bears the characteristics of what Pierre Nora has called a 'lieu de mémoire', an archive of a national past, a site for the rememoration of the rhetorical networks in which ideas of community would be formulated, tested, and contested.[30]

The term 'Nachträglichkeit' is useful not only for the way in which it highlights the relationship between the figure of child murder and forms of memory. It also underlines the disrupted temporality that this implies. Frequently, the inclusion of child murder in a text is a moment of puncturing that deflates the even contours of meaning and narrative, and the chronology on which they depend. The historical memory borne by the figure of child murder therefore complicates the conventional teleology of historical narrative, and opens the possibility of counter-histories that question the authority of conventional, progressive accounts.[31] The murder of a child ruptures the surface of the text in which it appears by obtruding a narrative of a different kind, introducing the potential for rich interpretive complexity. In this way, I suggest, even though its narrative form differs substantially, child murder's impact is nevertheless comparable with that of an anecdote – those 'little complete stories... that perforate the context of narrative understanding', which have been the staple of New Historicist and cultural historical studies.[32] Catherine Gallagher speaks of the appeal of the anecdote not only in terms of its capacity to undermine the grand narratives of historical truths, but also in terms of its ability to penetrate the boundaries of the received disciplines, and the forms of knowledge that these imply. As she puts it (echoing Joel Fineman), in 'pry[ing] the usual sequences apart from their referents... [anecdotes] point toward phenomena that were lying outside the contemporary borders of the discipline of history and yet were not altogether beyond the possibility of knowledge per se'.[33] The formulation here can usefully be adapted to describe the peculiar operations of the figure of child murder. For in its frenetic and promiscuous journeys across genres, disciplines, and historical moments, the figure of child murder often disavows its most literal referent – the murder of a child – and connotes instead a host of other meanings, all of them suspended beyond the boundaries of positive knowledge, in the much more shadowy domain of the cultural imaginary.

The final feature of the figure of child murder that requires commentary is that it is incorporated into discussions that vary markedly in tone. Many of the accounts that are encountered in this book are deeply sentimental; some morbid; some dispassionate and matter-of-fact; but some are also highly parodic and comedic. It is the last that are perhaps the most startling to the modern reader. Indeed, this study identifies a strong tradition in British radical culture, stretching back to Swift's *A Modest Proposal*, in which child murder is the hub of a macabre joke. Swift is not the only writer to find fun in such a grim topic. In this study I have tried to take the joke seriously, and rather than condemning the humour, followed Robert Darnton's Geertzian observation, that it is precisely by seeking to understand what is historically contingent in the humour of a past society that we acquire an invaluable point of entry into its *mentalité*.[34] In doing so, I hope to confront and come to terms with the obvious disjunction between the unnatural and violent deaths of infants, such as Jane Cornforth's baby – events which demand our most sober regard – and the extraordinarily potent array of traces – tragic, grotesque, trenchant, and ludic – which child murder left in eighteenth- and nineteenth-century culture.

CHAPTER I

Child murder and commercial society in the early eighteenth century

THE SCENE OF EATING

It is early in the eighteenth century. Somewhere in the distance a child is being eaten...[1]

In *The Fable of the Bees*, Bernard Mandeville describes the feastings of a rough type of gourmande – 'an half-starv'd Creature... mad with Hunger'. He asks us to imagine a situation in which we are

lock'd up in a Ground-Room, where in a Yard joining to it, there was a thriving good-humour'd Child at play, of two or three Years old, so near us that through the Grates of the Window we could almost touch it with our Hand; and if while we took delight in the harmless Diversion, and imperfect Prittle-Prattle of the innocent Babe, a nasty over-grown Sow should come in upon the Child, set it a screaming, and frighten it out of its Wits.

But what if, he asks, the creature should 'actually lay hold of the helpless Infant, destroy and devour it'?

To see her widely open her destructive Jaws, and the poor Lamb beat down with greedy haste; to look on the defenceless Posture of tender Limbs first trampled on, then tore asunder; to see the filthy Snout digging in the yet living Entrails, suck up the smoking Blood, and now and then to hear the Crackling of the Bones, and the cruel Animal with savage Pleasure grunt over the horrid Banquet; to hear and see all this, What Tortures would it give the Soul beyond Expression![2]

The sow's appetite and manner of eating contrast markedly with the polite decorum exhibited on the pages of that other account of infant-ingestion from the same decade – Jonathan Swift's *A Modest Proposal* (1729), a dining guide for cannibals of a decidedly *arriviste* complexion. 'A young healthy Child,' Swift advises, 'well nursed, is, at a Year old, a most delicious, nourishing, and wholesome Food; whether *Stewed, Roasted, Baked*, or *Boiled*; and, I make no doubt, that it will equally serve in a *Fricasie*, or

Ragoust.[3] Adaptable, economical, nutritious, and flavoursome, baby meat gratifies the refined palate as handsomely as the savage.

As they suspend our attention between a pig and a polite and refined people, Mandeville and Swift's texts reveal much about the early eighteenth-century fascination with the borders of civilised behaviour – and the visceral pleasures of their transgression – in a society in the throes of cultural change. They also, I suggest, inaugurate a new and distinctive rhetoric of child murder that will persist for a century or more. This is *not* on account of the kinds of death they describe: infant death by the gorging of hungry cannibals or animals tends to slip out of the foreground as the century progresses. Nor is it on account of the voluptuous pleasures that, at some level, each writer associates with the obscene act. Rather, the two texts are distinctive for the way in which both use the unnatural deaths of infants as a vehicle for talking about other matters: the modes and manners of commercial life, the pleasures and pains of luxury, the pitfalls of colonial policies, the corruptions of the state.

Although it is true that cases of new-born child murder had long appeared in the courts, and infanticide had figured as a theme in stories from classical and Christian antiquity, from the beginning of the eighteenth century it is possible to track a much more systematic consideration of the specifically metaphorical usages of infant death than in previous times. Individual acts of child-killing now tend always to be tangled in the interpretative strategies of a society prone to see those acts as signs or metaphors, intelligible in terms of a larger story, the narrative and plot of which will change over time. In the context of this study, Mandeville and Swift are significant for being the first writers to draw child murder into discussions about commercial society and thereby set the terms for subsequent usages of the motif. As will be seen, the tales that each tells about unnatural infant death in the 1720s will be told and retold by different generations. It is thus important first to attend to these early articulations if we are to understand the cultural potency that infanticide will accrue in the later eighteenth and nineteenth centuries.

The fact that in both the instances cited above the child is not merely killed but ingested draws attention to the idea of the appetites. In both of these castings, these are displayed as awful and destructive. At the beginning of the eighteenth century, the appetites of humans – as opposed to those of sows or savages – were deeply fraught concepts in contemporary debates about luxury and commerce. These debates provide an important context in which to consider Swift's and Mandeville's texts. Both writers share the common perception that patterns of everyday life in early eighteenth-century

Britain had been transformed by the expansion of trade, and the widespread consumption of luxury goods by people of all classes. A whole new realm of imported goods – silk, calico, muslins, china, chocolate, tea, coffee, sugar and spices, dyes, drugs, and oils, from the East and West Indies and other distant places – had whet novel appetites: in the bustling urban world that Mandeville describes in *The Fable of the Bees*, and that economic and urban historians have since mapped, everyone, from the richest aristocrat to the humblest servant, was subject in quite new ways to extravagant desires for clothes, food, drink – all kinds of commodities, the daily making, selling, and buying of which were now held to be the essential business of the national economy.[4] Even a 'common Harlot', Mandeville tells us, 'must have Shoes and Stockings, Gloves, the Stay'. Her wants generate business for the 'Mantua-maker, the Sempstress, the Linnen-draper, [who] all must get something by her, and a hundred different Tradesmen dependent on those she laid her Money out with, may touch part of it before a Month is at an end'. (*FB*, I: 88) Each tradesman, in turn, uses his profits to purchase commodities too, participating in an ever-expanding cycle of buying and selling, and wealth generation. Everyone aspires to live like those who are richer than themselves, and in the new world of goods, the consumption of commodities makes such fantasies of social improvement seem realisable – at least for an instant. The labourer's wife wants to dress like the weaver's wife, the weaver's wife like the shopkeeper's, who in turn adopts the fashions of the merchant's wife. The merchant's wife 'flies for Refuge to the other End of Town', and emulates the ladies of the court, alarming them so profoundly that the 'Contrivance of Fashions becomes all their Study, that they may have new Modes ready to take up'. 'It is this,' Mandeville concludes, 'that sets the Poor to Work, adds Spurs to Industry, and encourages the skilful Artificer to search after further Improvements.' (*FB*, I: 129–30) Mandeville describes a world in which the desire for material goods generates wealth and industry. But this desire also engenders a highly theatricalised style of social interaction in which all perform according to their social aspirations as though they were actors on a stage.[5] For Mandeville, then, these appetites are fundamentally productive, and create commercial opportunities for all – not least for Bernard Mandeville himself. A physician who specialised in nervous disorders, the classic symptoms of the new 'diseases of civilisation',[6] Mandeville's *A Treatise of the Hypocondriack and Hysterick Passions, Vulgarly Call'd the Hypo in Men and Vapours in Women* would run to three editions between 1711 and 1730.

Not all were as sanguine about the effects of luxury as Mandeville – especially not Swift. At the time at which the *Fable* was published, it was also widely held that the new fashion for consuming goods was having a demoralising influence on the nation. It was a 'spreading contagion', one commentator objected; consumption was 'the greatest Corrupter of Publick Manners and the greatest Extinguisher of *Public Spirit*'.[7] This great consuming passion that enveloped fashionable city dwellers sapped the entire nation's energies, making everyone effeminate, and distracting them from their higher Christian duties. For many, the new commercial society brought about a pernicious shift in the balance of power, away from landowners, the traditional ruling class, towards an increasingly influential and wealthy class of merchants. Such anxieties about changes in the social order were exacerbated by the new habits of emulation, which were held to diminish traditional distinctions of rank.[8] Indeed, Swift was among those who called for the re-institution of sumptuary laws, to prevent 'Excesses in Cloathing, Furniture and the Like',[9] and in order to help restrict some of the dangerous levelling effects of commercialism. *A Modest Proposal* is informed by this sharply critical view of commercial society, the pernicious effects of which were all the more severe in a colonial nation like Ireland where the markets were dominated by the metropolis which dictated inequitable terms of trade.[10] According to Swift, commerce '*promote[s] foreign Luxury*'; encourages '*Pride, Vanity, Idleness, and Gaming*' in women; discourages '*Parsimony, Prudence, and Temperance*'; makes people act '*like the Jews, who were murdering one another at the very moment their City was taken*'; and relieves shopkeepers of '*a Spirit of Honesty, Industry, and Skill*' (*MP*, 116). All of which, in Swift's eyes, is tantamount to killing babies.

On the issue of the appetites, as much else, Swift and Mandeville hold sharply contrasting views. More striking, then, that both should choose to make the unnatural deaths of infants a pivot around which their contrasting arguments turn. We shall see that the murder of children in particular emerges as a convenient vehicle through which Swift and Mandeville express quite different views not only on the uses and abuses of luxury but on other issues too: for example, the true nature of mankind, the proper organisation of society, and the relationship between human and monetary value. Mandeville will use child murder – specifically the murder of illegitimate newborns by their mothers – as a figure that encapsulates what for him is the wonderful theatricality of modern life itself. For Dean Swift, on the other hand, the notion of child murder is deployed in a deeply moralising discourse, which resonates with biblical accounts of the redemptive potential of sacrifice. If for Swift, child murder is at the heart of a critique of commercial society, for Mandeville it is equally useful in his celebration of commerce's dangerous pleasures – the pleasures of consumption that he renders satirically in the image of the greedy, infantophagous sow.

TWO KINDS OF KILLING IN SWIFT'S *A MODEST PROPOSAL*

Suffer the little children and forbid them not to come unto me, for of such is the kingdom of heaven. (Matt. 19:14)

The unthinkable thought perversely articulated throughout *A Modest Proposal* is that people might profit from the killing of children. This idea is no less shocking today than it was at the time of publication, and, as though trying to dispel its unsettling implications, critics still seem almost transfixed by the attempt to track down its origins, identifying ever more arcane sources for this cannibalistic fantasy: biblical and classical sources, commentaries on Irish history and politics, European romances.[11] Despite all this, Irvin Ehrenpreis was probably close enough to the mark when he wrote that both 'religious indignation' and 'economic theory' lay behind the piece.[12] The injunction in Jeremiah, 'And I will cause them to eat the flesh of their sons and the flesh of their daughters' (Jer. 19: 9), an Old Testament premonition of present decadence, may well have been the motto in Swift's mind when he composed the piece.[13] The work was one of over seventy pieces on Irish affairs written by Swift in the period from 1714 until his death in 1745.[14] In 1714 he had returned to Ireland, the place of his upbringing, as Dean of St Patrick's in Dublin, having already established himself as a literary celebrity in London, a pamphleteer for the Tory administration, editor of the newly established Tory journal, *The Examiner*, and essayist and poet.[15] His return to Ireland was precipitated by the Tory ministry's fall from power in 1714, and was an expedient move for a man who had already swapped party allegiance once before from Whig to Tory, and was now held under considerable suspicion by the new Whig government. When he reached Ireland he witnessed widespread poverty and suffering among the people. Failing crops – when Swift wrote *A Modest Proposal*, Ireland was in the midst of the third famine caused by crop failure since 1708[16] – restrictions on trade instituted by the London government, high taxes, absenteeism among landowners, and the habits of the middle-class consumers: all of these were among the factors that he considered had conspired to reduce the Irish to conditions of abject misery.[17]

Swift's correspondence shows that he was moved by the conditions of extreme poverty he encountered on his return to Ireland. He observed with disgust the degrading conditions to which the Irish had been reduced.

'Three terrible years dearth of corn', he wrote to Pope, 'and every place strowed with beggars... Imagine a nation the two-thirds of whose revenues are spent out of it, and who are not permitted to trade with the other third, and where the pride of the women will not suffer them to wear their own manufactures even where they excel what comes from abroad.'[18] Such scenes rebutted the reports that circulated at the same time by mercantilists who held the high population in Ireland to be an indicator of its wealth. Following the political arithmetician, Sir William Petty, whose survey of Ireland carried out in the previous century continued to shape English colonial responses to Ireland, they enumerated Ireland's resources, including population, and found it to be in a period of 'unprecedented prosperity'.[19]

A Modest Proposal satirises this kind of panglossian economic optimism, mimicking its language of calculation, and ridiculing the idea that size of population in itself was a simple measure of a country's wealth. The proposal that the Irish might enrich themselves by literally consuming their excess population, was an idea that built on documented beliefs to the effect that in previous times, the Irish had shown a peculiar penchant for human flesh. The seventeenth-century writer, Fynes Moryson, had reported incidents of intergenerational, famine-induced cannibalism during Tyrone's Rebellion in 1602: an old woman eaten by her starving children, and others who lured little children to a fire, to murder and devour them – stories that bore all the hallmarks of fairy tales.[20] Swift's friend and collaborator, Sheridan, had referred to these events in an essay published in the *Intelligencer* shortly before Swift produced his pamphlet.[21] According to Claude Rawson, ancient associations between the Irish and cannibalism went even further than this.[22] Swift himself held the Irish to be descended from the Scythians, a people whose cannibalistic ways had been noted by Herodotus. In Swift's *A Modest Proposal*, these signs of a primordial Irish savagery are subverted by a stroke of economic genius: the realisation that the delicate meat of children has a commercial potential that is ripe for exploitation. The baby-banquet envisaged here is no wild, native ritual, no orgy of bestial scoffing, as in the Mandeville account. Rather, baby flesh will be food for the polite and refined – decidedly not fodder for the untamed poor. 'Stewed, roasted, baked or boiled', or more elaborately, French-style, in '*Fricasie*' or '*Ragoust*', baby-meat is 'delicious and nourishing', and economical too: 'A Child will make two Dishes at an Entertainment for Friends; and when the Family dines alone, the fore or hind quarter will make a reasonable Dish; and seasoned with a little Pepper or Salt, will be very good Boiled on the fourth Day, especially in *Winter*.' (*MP*, 112) 'Those who are more thrifty... may flay the Carcase; the skin of which, artificially dressed, will make admirable *Gloves for Ladies*, and *Summer Boots for fine Gentlemen'*. Babies are commodities produced for the lower end of the luxury market, dainties to be sold in Dublin, and to be distributed across 'the rest of the Kingdom': 'I compute that Dublin would take off, annually, about Twenty Thousand Carcasses; and the rest of the Kingdom (where probably they will be sold somewhat cheaper) the remaining Eighty Thousand' (*MP*, 116). In the process of consumption, the refined are made barbarous by the nature of their food. The savage customs of natives are transposed to the consumers of luxury goods, who are barbarised by the very refinement of their palates and by the cold calculations of political arithmetic.

The idea that child-killing was a constituent of savage life is implicit in the accounts of exotic and barbarous people by travellers to the New World who returned to Europe in this period. The Jesuit, Lafitau, for instance, acquainted European audiences with the idea that child murder was extensively practised, in his widely read *Moeurs des sauvages ameriquains* (1724). Later in the eighteenth century, these accounts would be formulated in a more systematic way, as ideas about civilisation and good parenthood became inextricably entwined. I discuss this in the next chapter, but it is useful here to note that Swift's pamphlet can be seen as part of the build up to later pronouncements, reinforcing in the public imagination a vivid link between primitive peoples and their dismal habits of child care. Throughout *A Modest Proposal*, however, Swift draws on the distinctions between savage and civilised peoples only then to undermine them, to throw one back on the other. In matters of cannibalism, he claims, the petty refinements of modern society reduce all to states of savagery. Thus London, the centre of finance and of the trade in luxuries, no less than the most exotic tropical locations, becomes the place for encounters with primitive peoples. It is where the Modest Proposer's friend meets 'the famous *Salmanaazor'*, from the notorious island of Formosa (Taiwan), who reported the practice there of selling the corpses of executed felons, to '*Persons of Quality*, as a prime Dainty'.[23]

[T]he Body of a plump Girl of fifteen, who was crucified for an Attempt to poison the Emperor, was sold to his Imperial *Majesty's prime Minister of State*, and other great *Mandarins* of the Court, *in Joints from the Gibbet*, at Four Hundred crowns. (*MP*, 113–14)

But, he goes on wryly,

if the same Use were made of several plump young girls in this Town, who, without one single Groat to their Fortunes, cannot stir Abroad without a Chair, and appear at the *Play-House*, and *Assemblies* in foreign Fineries, which they never will pay for; the Kingdom would not be the worse. (*MP*, 114)

The barbarous Formosans, with their ministers and mandarins, travesty the customs of civil society; but equally, polite citizens mince and masquerade, just like the primitive Formosans. And both would happily dine off the flesh of children.

The account of savagery in *A Modest Proposal* thus contributes to a wider critique of commercial society and the trade in luxuries. This takes as its central theme the notion that, by exciting the unlicensed passions, luxury and its apologists (which would include writers such as Mandeville) do not civilise people, but, on the contrary, turn them into savages, forcing them to commit awful deeds – like child murder. Underpinning this is a set of terms that are broadly informed by the political idiom of civic humanism, which continued to provide a compelling vocabulary throughout the first half of the eighteenth century. Implicit in the civic humanist lexicon, however, is a figure of infant death that is strikingly different to the licentious child-killing of savages.[24] It is this that makes Swift's satire all the more acute.

Civic humanist ideals opposed virtue to corruption, self-restraint to sensual indulgence, public service to self-interest. These ideas, shaped by the works of Machiavelli, the political ideologue of the Italian Renaissance, had been developed in England during the Interregnum, in the aftermath of the civil wars, in particular in works such as James Harrington's *Oceana* (1656). Harrington's was a programme for a republican state which identified political liberty with landed property; the country, he argued, should be run by a polity of independent freeholders, drawn together in an assembly based on the model of the classical republics. As J. G. A. Pocock has shown, the language of civic humanism underwrote a tradition of political critique, extending into radical republicanism, which continued well into the nineteenth century, and was powerful partly because it was adaptable to different political opinions and programmes. In Swift's time, it was utilised in particular by Tories (the 'country' party) to attack the Whig administration (the 'court' party), for its corruption and support of commerce above the landed interest. Swift himself drew conspicuously on these terms in his critique of the 'monied interest' in tracts and essays written in the years directly preceding his return to Dublin in 1714.[25] The view of human nature and of society implicit in the civic humanist frame is thus in sharp contrast to that proposed by Mandeville and other apologists for luxury and commerce. It provided a conception of an ideal society, based on classical models such as that of Sparta or of the Roman Republic in which individuals restrained their own desires for the sake of the greater public good.[26] The frequent motif through which writers expressed the virtue of individual restraint was the ancients' dispassionate acceptance of the social value of the death of children. The austere Spartans – as opposed to the Athenians – routinely abandoned their children, gathering in only those tough enough to survive; while one of the most widely cited examples of Roman republican political commitment was the gesture of Brutus in ordering his errant sons to be executed for crimes against the republic.[27] For many writers, especially Swift, these practices of child sacrifice resonated with examples found in the Judeo-Christian tradition, most notably God's sacrifice of Christ.

Although Swift's *A Modest Proposal* makes the killing of children a sign of a decadent society and draws on the idea of the child-killing savage, it simultaneously, albeit in a more muted way, evokes this civic humanist motif of the virtuous acceptance of infant death. The satire is thus intensified by the comparison which hovers over the piece, between the profligate slaughter of children for sensory indulgence and monetary gain in decadent commercial society on the one hand, and Roman or Spartan, or indeed Christian self-denial – the death of children for the welfare of society – on the other. The latter view is never stated directly in *A Modest Proposal*, but within the dense texture of the prose there are traces of a standpoint from which it is imaginable that children might be killed as a sacrifice for a greater social good – the merest innuendo that infanticide might be considered an act of redemption.

The closest Swift comes to articulating this idea directly is in the penultimate paragraph where he writes:

I desire those Politicians who dislike my Overture, and may perhaps be so bold to attempt an Answer, that they will first ask the Parents of these Mortals, Whether they would not, at the Day, think it a great Happiness to have been sold for Food at a Year old, in the Manner I prescribe; and thereby have avoided such a perpetual Scene of Misfortunes, as they have since gone through; by the *Oppression of Landlords*; the Impossibility of paying Rent, without Money or Trade; the Want of common Sustenance, with neither House nor Cloaths, to cover them from the Inclemencies of the Weather; and the most inevitable Prospect of intailing the like, or greater Miseries upon their Breed for ever. (*MP*, 117–18)

The idea that a man would rather have been sold for food when a year old than perpetuate the miseries of Irish poverty is of course mired in irony. But it is an irony invigorated by distant evocations of classical and Christian notions of self-denial for the common good, encapsulated in the necessary death of a child. The idea of the sacrificial infant death thus shadows the burlesque of sensual gratification, and pierces the insistent vocabulary of economic calculation – 'Prospect', 'intailing', 'Breed' – with the pathos of human suffering. For an instant, the Irishman who would rather have been killed is transmogrified and ennobled; the brute savage flickers into view as a human saviour, willing to lay down his own life for the good of his 'Breed'.

At the heart of Swift's critique are thus two very different and mutually contradictory figures of child murder. On the one hand, it is the pastime of the idle savage and the product of sensuous indulgence encouraged by apologists for commercial society and colonial policy, and encapsulates the demoralising effects of civilisation. On the other hand, and from a different perspective, child murder is presented as the necessary sacrifice that is forced on people through human need; an emblem of self-restraint and civic virtue.

These opposing terms become the staple of subsequent critiques of capitalism, trade, and commodity culture throughout the eighteenth century and beyond. The complaint articulated in various ways from now on is that the mechanisms of commerce and capital obviate the realities of human need, distracting people with the glistening world of goods, which conjure new and powerful desires; people are enslaved to their passions and appetites, and become no better than child-eating savages. Walter Benjamin will evoke something like this in his famous aphorism, that 'there is no document of civilization which is not at the same time a document of barbarism,'[28] although the underlying assumption here, of a logic of parasitism – that civilisation is made possible by the exploitation of other, colonised peoples, often represented in figures of ingestion, the vampiric sucking of resources from the colonised body – is the insight of a later age, and not clearly evident in Swift's essay. In Swift's case, not only do the colonising English eat the Irish; the Irish eat themselves in mimicry of, and defence against, the neglect shown by the colonising country. But in both cases, civilisation is made degenerate by money, with the result that it is drawn together with barbarity as an identical, rather than a distinct, formation. Coincidentally, however, the position from which Swift argues against the infanticidal tendencies of modern society has implicit within it the idea of a different kind of infant death – the socially useful death, based on the model of Brutus, or the deadly child abandonment of Spartans, or indeed the child sacrifices of Christian tradition. Torn between these figurings of infant death, a critique opens up in which the suffering or dead child stands as the embodiment of human value, in opposition to the demoralising effects of commercialism. Embedded in this is the suspicion that there is some particular connection between the mechanisms of capital and a disregard for infant life: as if to love money – or merely to make money – is to kill children.

CHILD MURDER AND MODERNITY: MANDEVILLE'S
FABLE OF THE BEES

For Swift, as for other eighteenth-century readers, Bernard Mandeville was the most notorious apologist for luxury.[29] In sharp contrast to Swift, Mandeville seemed to celebrate the unlicensed gratification of the appetites, evoking a society in which people are ruled by their passions, driven by their overwhelming quests to gratify their own self-love. While Swift was driven by classical ideals of virtuous restraint, Mandeville on the other hand proffered a more naturalistic account of society, in which it was seen to have developed from a savage state, spurred by the forces of the human passions.[30] 'The Seeds of every Passion are innate to us', he wrote, 'and no body comes into the World without them' (*FB*, I: 281). For Mandeville, then, there was no essential difference between people in their civilised and so-called savage states; on the contrary, he held that civilised society had been formed by the operations of the passions – principally, self-love. While his contemporaries – such as Swift – found this approbation of savagery a matter of disgust, a mark of the demoralisation endemic to modern society, Mandeville's views would influence the development of a strain of primitivist thought that held sway in the later eighteenth century, explored most significantly through the notion of the noble savage, an idea to which Jean Jacques Rousseau gave a significant twist.[31] Of interest here, however, is the prominent inclusion of figures of child murder in *The Fable*, betraying a macabre fascination that matches Swift's own. The scene of the pig's feast, cited at the beginning of the chapter, is just one infant death in a work in which children seem chillingly dispensable. But while Swift's child murder referred back to the mores and values of antiquity, Mandeville presents a version that becomes an influential motif of modernity.

The Fable of the Bees began life in 1705 as a poem entitled *The Grumbling Hive: or, Knaves Turn'd Honest*.[32] In 1714, after he had published many other works, including his medical treatise on vapours, Mandeville revised the poem, and added a series of prose commentaries. The new work was published under the title, *The Fable of the Bees: or, Private Vices, Publick Benefits*. But this was only the beginning of a long process of accumulation and revision. Over the next fifteen years, Mandeville added more and more material. In 1723, two new pieces, 'An Essay on Charity and Charity-Schools' and 'A Search into the Nature of Society'; the following year, 'A Vindication of the Book', responding to two attacks on the work (from the Grand Jury of Middlesex and a writer in the *London Journal*, under the name of

'Theophilus Philo-Britannus') which were also published with the *Fable*; and, in 1729, *The Fable of the Bees, Part II*, a further elaboration and justification of his views in a series of dialogues between two characters, 'Cleomenes' and 'Horatio', mouthpieces for Mandeville and Shaftesbury respectively. The result is a composite work, written over twenty-five years, encompassing poetry and prose, moral commentary, economic theory, parables and fables; Mandeville himself described it as a 'Rhapsody void of Order or Method'.[33]

In its early incarnations, the work attracted little attention, but in 1723, a stream of criticism from philosophers, moralists, and clergymen began to be published, and the following year it was brought before the Grand Jury of Middlesex, under the charge of having caused a 'public nuisance'.[34] Mandeville had caused offence by claiming, in his 'Essay on Charity and Charity Schools', that philanthropists were self-serving hypocrites who aggrandised themselves in the name of doing good works for the poor. Rather than being socially useful, Mandeville held that charity schools actually harmed society, by providing the wrong kind of education, and producing a class of parasites unfit for labour. While the charge brought by the Grand Jury was more than likely provoked by the charity school essay, W. A. Speck has pointed out that *The Fable* was also immured in party political disputes between the Country Tories who constituted the Jury, and the Whig, Mandeville. It is easy to see how Mandeville's celebration of commerce and luxury might offend a party that espoused the civic humanist rhetoric of anti-corruption and self-restraint.[35] The work's capacity to shock, however, transcended its immediate political context, and despite its wide influence in the history of eighteenth-century economic and anthropological thought, it continued to be represented throughout the century as a dangerous defence of licentiousness. Only by the early nineteenth century was its notoriety eclipsed by that of another supposed high priest of licentiousness and alleged child-killer, the Reverend T. R. Malthus.[36]

The notorious proposition of the *Fable of the Bees* that shocked not only the Middlesex Grand Jury but also subsequent generations was that the culture of commerce had created the conditions in which private vices were not counter to, but in fact productive of, public benefits. This was not to say that Mandeville encouraged or condoned vice and immorality; rather that he recognised that vice was unavoidable, and, moreover, that it was not necessarily detrimental to the public good. Instead, the gratification rather than suppression of desires – for fashion, food, and the sundry pleasures of urban life – created all-important markets for the bustling new world of goods, making the nation wealthy, rather than sapping its strength. Mandeville's work was significant for its disaggregation of private and public spheres of action, and in many ways, this was its most influential contribution.[37] Unlike the civic humanist belief in the congruence of public and private virtue, Mandeville portrayed a world in which private morality was at best incidental to public order, and at worst inversely related to it. He thereby posited the idea of a secret world of vice, hidden from the public gaze, but which nevertheless underpinned, or even generated the shape of public life.

Mandeville's account of this paradoxically intimate disjunction between private and public worlds – the secret realm of vice that is constitutive of public order – contributes to an analysis of modernity that continued to hold well into the twentieth century. As historians of political ideas have pointed out, it lies behind Adam Smith's description of capitalism later in the eighteenth century, in which aggressive individualism is seen to be, nonetheless, socially productive, creating the wealth and prosperity of the nation.[38] And it is at the heart of the psychological account of alienation under capitalism that Georg Simmel describes in *The Philosophy of Money* in the early twentieth century.[39] Mandeville draws on various examples to illustrate this complex relationship, but most provocatively, that of child murder. Focusing on the maternal conduct of different types of women, he makes the counterintuitive claim that 'modest' women would not flinch at destroying their unwanted offspring, while 'common Whores', or 'Publick Prostitutes' (*FB*, II: 124) are full of motherly tenderness. The idea is first raised in Remark C of *The Fable*, although he will return to it later in Dialogue Three of Part II. 'It is commonly imagined', he writes in the former,

that she who can destroy her Child, her own Flesh and Blood, must have a vast stock of Barbarity, and be a Savage monster, different from other Women; but this is likewise a mistake which we commit for want of understanding Nature and the force of the Passions. The same Woman that Murders her Bastard in the most execrable manner, if she is Married afterwards, may take care of, cherish and feel all the tenderness for her Infant that the fondest Mother can be capable of. (*FB*, I: 75)

On the other hand,

Common Whores, whom all the World knows to be such, hardly ever destroy their Children, nay even those who assist in Robberies and Murders seldom are Guilty of this Crime; not because they are less Cruel or more Virtuous, but because they have lost their Modesty to a greater degree, and the fear of shame makes hardly any impression upon them. (*FB*, I: 75–6)

In fact, Mandeville was not alone in his view that unmarried mothers would be provoked to kill through shame; this, after all, was the presumption that lay behind the 1624 statute. What is new and striking is the way in which it leads him to a radical re-interpretation of 'virtue'. For him, a virtuous reputation encourages the most heinous crime, its pious surfaces able to conceal a turbulent world of sexual vice and murder. And women, who have a heightened sense of shame, are most susceptible to its perverse effects. It is for this reason, Mandeville argues in the Third Dialogue of Part II, that women need to develop a greater degree of pride than men, for pride is a defence against the weakness of the flesh – a kind of advance guard for shame. Without pride to restrain them, the results will be catastrophic: '[N]otwithstanding the Weakness of their Frame, and the Softness in which Women are generally educated', he goes on, 'if overcome by chance they have sinn'd in private, what real Hazards will they not run, what Torments will they not stifle, and what Crimes will they not commit, to hide from the World that Frailty, which they were taught to be most ashamed of!' (*FB*, II: 124) What crimes indeed!

Mandeville's views on women are developed further in his *A Modest Defence of Public Stews* (1724), a work whose title Swift may have echoed – ironically, of course – in his *A Modest Proposal*.[40] Dedicated pointedly to the 'Gentlemen of the Societies', the very philanthropists that he had attacked in his 'Essay On Charity' the previous year, the work calls for the licensing of brothels as a way of preventing licentiousness and protecting women's virtue. 'The only way to preserve Female Chastity', he writes, 'is to prevent the Men from laying Siege to it';[41] and if men's sexual needs were to be met by 'Public Whores', virtuous women would as a consequence be safe from seduction. The distinction that he establishes between 'Public' and 'Private Whores' has the surprising effect of turning the former into wholesome public servants, who provide a medical and social service to the whole society, protecting men from venereal infection, and, significantly in this context, saving infant bastards from murder.

Of course, not many would agree. Others considered public stews to pose not only a threat to the health of the nation, being a source of infection rather than a protection against it, but also a risk to public morality. Daniel Defoe, for instance, in his 'Some Considerations upon Street Walkers' (1726), held that 'Public Whoring' would infest the whole society with licentiousness, so that 'our lewd abandon'd Women are the Characteristic of the Modest and the Good'.[42] Mandeville, on the other hand, proposed that the debauchery of one woman was in fact a necessary tariff for the preservation of others. 'Private whoring' – or the seduction of modest women – for him, performs a beneficial function as a recruitment exercise for the public stews. In what E. J. Hundert has described as his 'fullest technical account of how vice may lead to public benefit',[43] Mandeville explains that if numbers of prostitutes in the public stews should fall below levels of demand,

> why then the worst Accident that can befall, is a gradual Relapse into our for-mer State of *Private Whoring*; and this no farther than is just necessary to re-cruit the *Stews*, and thereby make them retrieve their former Character: For every Woman that is debauch'd more than is barely necessary, only brings so much additional Credit and Reputation to the *Stews*, and in some measure atones for the Loss of her own Chastity, by being a Means to Preserve that of others.[44]

Overlaying an explicit vocabulary of economic calculation – a kind of political arithmetic of sex – with references to Christian notions of sin and atonement, Mandeville evokes a machinery for subtly balancing the books of moral loss and gain, in which women are reckoned unambiguously as sexual commodities. In the logic of the sexual market, the debauchery of the few is necessary for the greater good of the nation.

In his writings of public stews, therefore, Mandeville makes a case for the social and economic value of debauchery. So, too, with child mur-der. The murder of children by their mothers is another act that para-doxically contributes to the national good by sustaining the economy of public benefit and private vice. As an act that enables the appearance of virtue to be maintained while underneath its empty surface is concealed a clandestine world of private passions and intrigues, child murder allows for the gratification of private appetites that are necessary for the gener-ation of public wealth. It thus assumes a quasi-foundational role, split-ting the stagnant arena of public virtue from its bustling undercurrent of vice.

The self-serving act of child murder as described by Mandeville is utterly different from the sacrificial infant death, which, in the idiom of civic humanism, invigorates Swift's satire in *A Modest Proposal*. Nevertheless, in that Mandeville's child murder also has a larger social and economic function, it replicates the structure of the sacrifice. It almost seems to mimic the civic humanist, Christian discourse: this death of a child is for public benefit too – but public benefit that is derived from luxury and indulgence rather than virtue and self-restraint.

'TO HEAR AND SEE ALL THIS': THE AESTHETICS OF
CHILD MURDER

Mandeville's discussion of child murder as a crime of insidious and
widespread prevalence in modern society was shocking not only in the
way that it impugned 'private' women as opposed to 'public' prostitutes,
but also in its contention that the crime may hold public benefits.[45] His
views were particularly controversial in that the care of neglected infants
was a favoured philanthropic cause in this age of commercialism. In the
context of widely held worries about the diminishing population, the responsibility of saving the nation's children was a highly potent one.[46] For
many philanthropists, the mothers of England's innocents threatened to
destroy the very basis of national prosperity through their incontinence,
incompetence, neglect, or sheer murderousness. Mandeville's suggestion,
therefore, that the public stews would halt the 'dispeopling' of the nation by preserving the lives of infant bastards was, no doubt, satirically
charged.[47] Charitable endeavours to save infant life took more sober forms:
Thomas Coram's Foundling Hospital, established in 1739, was one of
a number of mid-century ventures, including the Lock Hospital (est.
1746) for the treatment of venereal diseases, the British Lying-in Hospital (est. 1749), and the City of London Lying-in Hospital (est. 1750), all
of which aimed to alleviate the medical and social problems of reproduction, and ultimately, protect infant life from the dangerous threats of bad
mothers.[48]

To augment Coram's philanthropic work, artists including William
Hogarth were commissioned to contribute paintings to adorn the walls
of the hospital, depicting Biblical scenes of child abandonment and recovery, especially from the infancy of Moses.[49] The symbolism of the recovered
infant was all the more powerful beside Hogarth's satirical representations of
urban modernity, such as his highly charged engraving, *Gin Lane* (1751).[50]
In this scene, amid the semi-built ruins of the London cityscape strewn
with the debauched victims of luxury, slumps a drunken woman, clothes
ragged, and face ravaged, and slipping from her dissolute arms is a baby,
unwanted and uncared for. Here in *Gin Lane*, then, was a different trajectory of infant loss from the stately scene of Moses' recovery: the child as
debris, the unwanted refuse of luxury.

Mandeville's account of the secret murders of unwanted infants by polite
women, however, was subtler than Hogarth's Swiftian satire – and in some
ways it was closer to the logic implicit in the current legislation on these

matters. Its significance in relation to the law, however, is not as a reflection
of the existing statute, but as an articulation of a new way of thinking and
feeling about infant death that eventually, in 1803, would shape a major
legal reform.[51] The 1624 Act to Prevent the Destroying and Murthering of
Infant Bastards, under which cases of child murder continued to be tried
throughout the eighteenth century, recognised that women were unlikely to
allow their children to die in full public view, as the inebriate in *Gin Lane* was
doing. Rather these were acts more likely to be committed, as Mandeville
had claimed, in secret and alone. Indeed, in view of the difficulties of
ascertaining whether or not a child had been stillborn, the 1624 statute
had made secrecy itself a crime: in the eyes of the law, the concealment
of the death of a child was considered tantamount to murder, and was
itself a capital offence. In effect, it drew a veil over the intricate details
of cases of child murder, and, paradoxically, maintained the secrets of the
mother's fallen past. Mandeville, too, considered child murder to be a crime
committed in secrecy, but while the law implicitly understood concealment
to be a cover-up for murder, Mandeville held the murder itself to be an act
of concealment, a veil hiding the intriguing details of women's private lives.
And if the 1624 law required no further scrutiny of the case, Mandeville, on
the contrary, incites us to probe the concealed realms of passion, to know
the intimate details of female lives.

Mandeville's insight in this respect was in line with new modes of mon-
itoring private vices that emerged in the eighteenth century.[52] The 1624
legislation had placed infanticide in a group of crimes that were remarkable
for their unusual reliance on presumptive evidence.[53] Prominent among
these was witchcraft, a crime that bears interesting similarities to child
murder. In demonological writings, witches were sometimes invoked eating babies on the Sabbath; and like women accused of witchcraft, infanticidal mothers were also liable to stigmatisation and even demonisation.
Moreover, as in witchcraft, where in any case the baby supposedly had been
ingested, the 1624 statute held that evidence provided by the infant corpse
was outside the court's concern, for it was unnecessary to provide positive
proof of murder for a court to reach a guilty verdict. However, while the
statute continued to regulate the legal treatment of child-murder cases in
the early eighteenth century, the conviction rate was surprisingly low, and
in fact its history in the later part of the century is one of its gradual obso-
lescence. Various explanations for this have been proffered, including the
emergence of new standards of evidence and greater sympathy for women.[54]
But it is also the case that a law that operated under the principle of presumption, making scrutiny of the crime unnecessary, was simply rendered

anachronistic in a society that was drawn to know the fascinating details of private vice.

Alexander Welsh has observed that one aspect of the rationalisation and reform of the law that began in this period was the change from a preference for testimonial evidence, to what was known as secondary, or circumstantial evidence,[55] a shift that brought to an end the special category of the 'secret crime'.[56] Faced with the possibility of a witness who lied, courts began to place their trust instead in objects – the testimony of a material world that bore the traces of the acts perpetrated within it. An observer endowed with scientific expertise was able to read these marks and traces, to discover the true history of events. As William Paley wrote in *Principles of Moral Philosophy* (2nd edn, 1786), 'A concurrence of well authenticated circumstances' is 'stronger ground of assurance than positive testimony, unconfirmed by circumstances'.[57] Thus important treatises on evidence published during the second half of the century – influential works such as Gilbert's *Law of Evidence*, written in the 1720s, but not published until 1754 – attempted to systematise evidence on the basis of a more sound epistemological foundation. In child-murder cases, the preference for circumstantial evidence led to a greater emphasis on the specialist opinion of medical witnesses – coroners and doctors. By the 1770s, child-murder cases figured prominently in the new systematic studies of forensic medicine, or medical jurisprudence.[58] Rather than being disregarded as insignificant to the verdict, as the 1624 statute had instructed, the baby's corpse came to be an important piece of evidence. The wounded body of the child was held to display the guilt – or innocence – of the mother.[59]

The signs of causes of death in a new-born baby, however, were notoriously unreliable. Ironically, the violations of birth could easily be confused with the contusions of murder, and, in fact, a peculiar aspect of child-murder cases is that rather than viewing the forensic evidence as a primary source of revelation of the guilt or innocence of the accused, courts often used the very unreliability of medical evidence as the grounds for acquitting suspects. In his influential tract 'Uncertainty of Signs of Death in a New Born Infant' (1784), used widely by courts in making verdicts in the latter decades of the century, the surgeon William Hunter explained the problems inherent in the common forensic test for proving live birth, the hydrostatic test.[60] In this, the baby's lungs were immersed in water: if they floated, the baby was deemed to have been born alive; if they sank, the baby deemed born dead. According to Hunter, the test could not distinguish between cases of murder and those of natural death, and indeed, cases in which air had been breathed into the baby's lungs in an effort at revival. Given the unreliability of the forensic evidence, Hunter presents a different kind of evidence – the moral character of women. In most child-murder cases, Hunter claims, the mother is innocent; rather, 'the father of the child is really criminal, often cruelly so; the mother is weak, credulous, and deluded.'[61] A large part of his short work is filled with seduction narratives, tales of innocent women who fall prey to the debauchery of libertine men. Indeed, the very authority of the forensic evidence seems to be usurped by his revelation of secret plots of seduction and lechery. Faced by the opacity of the material facts and corporeal evidence, inhibited by the sheer unreliability of bodily signs, Hunter turns instead to the more readable 'facts' of women's virtue. The truth of physical matter gives way to the truth of feeling, and science succumbs to sentiment.

The problem with child-murder cases, then, was that when one looked more closely at the evidence, the facts became more and more unclear. Commentators like Hunter invariably referred to a surge of feeling that took over when one scrutinised the facts, although it is often unclear as to whether these feelings obscured rational judgement, or took over when judgement had already failed. Adam Smith epitomised the sentimental approach to infant death when he wrote in his *Theory of Moral Sentiments* (1759) that 'scarce a child can die without rending asunder the heart of somebody'.[62] Although he is not necessarily talking of child murder, Smith encapsulates the visceral response that is evident in many such accounts. There is a peculiar anonymity in his formulation: the response is predicated upon observing infant death rather than on personal attachment or family connection, and moreover, it is almost as though the 'rending asunder' of the heart of the spectator, the nameless 'somebody', exceeds the suffering of the child. The extraordinary intensity of the response perhaps explains the fact that for Hunter and for judges and juries, the feelings felt on the death of a child could be extended to the mother of the child, who in many cases, paradoxically, was the likely agent of death. Remember 'Poor Jane Cornforth', for whom commentators exuded sympathy, even though she had disposed of her child in an ignominious and violent way.[63]

For all his scientific credentials, Hunter's tract, with its graphic and highly sentimental accounts of women's seduction, reads like a novel – but a tale of wounded female honour, like Richardson's *Clarissa* (1748), rather than, for instance, the more Mandevillian plots of feminine guile authored by Daniel Defoe. Curiously, despite their different views on so many matters, Mandeville's account of child murder is similar to that of Defoe's in his novels, *Moll Flanders* (1722) and *Roxana* (1724): both protagonists are brilliant illustrations of what happens to a woman on the slippery slope between modesty and private whoring, and both abandon children – with varying degrees of regret. Moll's extended contemplation on the rights and wrongs of abandoning her child to foster care in order to marry the banker sees her shift from her categorical insistence that the disposal of a child in this way is 'only a contriv'd method for murder; that is to say, a-killing their children with safety', to her realisation, persuaded by Mother Midnight, that a child's life might be preserved for an extra fee.[64] The analogues between Hunter's and Mandeville's work and those of the novelists are revealing because they suggest that for all these writers, despite the obvious variances in their estimations of women's virtue, child murder is an event whose sentimental potency overwhelms its ethical complexity. As Mandeville writes in response to the sow's gorging of the innocent baby, 'To hear and see all that, What Tortures would it give the Soul beyond Expression!' The effects of witnessing, or even just contemplating infant death are nothing less than sublime.

The importance of the grotesque banquet scene cited at the beginning of this chapter is that it presents a kind of allegory of the sentimental response that infant violation and death constantly produce. The spectator is separated from the scene of violation; he is close enough to hear and see the terrible violation; but, being locked in a room, is unable to intervene. He sees the child playing, a sow approach, 'mad with Hunger', and sees 'her widely open her destructive Jaws'; he 'look[s] on the defenceless Posture of the tender Limbs . . . tore asunder', 'see[s] the filthy Snout digging in the yet living Entrails . . .', and 'hear[s] the Crackling of the Bones'. The act inspires an 'ake' that 'no Language has an Epithet to fit' (*FB*, I: 255–6). As in Smith's account, the feelings of the spectator are also expressed on the body itself, and seem to exceed the suffering of the child.

Mandeville uses this scene to present a criticism of the philanthropists. The feelings experienced when watching the terrible death of the infant are of 'pity' – but pity understood as a bodily response rather than a moral one. It is not exactly that pity is self-serving, but rather that it is detached from moral virtue. It 'comes in at the Eye or the Ear', and, he claims, can be felt by anyone regardless of their morals or social standing – a 'Man of Humanity' as well as 'an Highwayman, an House-Breaker, or a Murderer' (*FB*, I: 256). The philanthropists, therefore, have sensibilities that are no more refined than those of common criminals – and, as if to underline the point, Mandeville's ideal spectator is locked in a room, as though a convict himself.

Nevertheless, through this scene, Mandeville sketches out a mode of response that will be central to a tradition of aesthetics that continues through the eighteenth and nineteenth centuries. His somatic, quasi-psychological explanation for the pleasures of pain accounts for the contemporary taste for things gory, such as public executions and the gothic novel, and is developed further in a host of philosophical works which explore the perverse, and frequently isolating pleasures to be elicited from representations of danger and pain, responses that, at the time, were codified under the term, the 'sublime'. Among these, the most famous is Edmund Burke's *Philosophical Enquiry into the Nature of the Sublime and the Beautiful* (1754), but this is just one in a vast body of works from this period which set out to examine and celebrate this particular aesthetic mode.[65] In the nineteenth century, following Immanuel Kant's reformulation of the sublime in his *Critique of Judgement* (1790), a more absolute splitting of aesthetic response from ethical principles will shape a culture of decadence, in which murder, especially the murder of a child, can be, in the words of Thomas De Quincey, considered as one of the fine arts.[66]

Swift and Mandeville thus both use the figure of child murder to explore their different responses to commercial modernity. For Swift, for all his comedy, there is a suggestion that child murder might be a redemptive act, a sacrifice made in the interests of the renovation of society. It is a pretext for political opposition, in a tradition that will play out spectacularly among the Chartists in the 1830s, as we will see in Chapter Four. For Mandeville, on the other hand, the joke is that there can be no redemption: modern society is irredeemably corrupt – but for him, and generations who follow him, that is its source of profit and its pleasure.

These two contrary views place the idea of child murder firmly at the heart of the imaginary realm of eighteenth-century British culture. They ensure that from this point onwards until at least the end of the nineteenth century those who critiqued modern culture would often do so as though they were in mourning for the infants murdered by commerce, capitalism, or other technologies of modern progress.

CHAPTER 2

'A Squeeze in the Neck for Bastards': the uncivilised spectacle of child-killing in the 1770s and 1780s

ROUSSEAU REVISES MANDEVILLE

When Jean-Jacques Rousseau set out to describe the operations of pity, it was paradoxically to Mandeville, the arch-priest of vice, that he turned. In his *Discours sur l'origine et les fondements de l'inégalité parmi les hommes* (1755) (*Discourse on Inequality* or *Second Discourse*), he revisits Mandeville's scene of infant violation. That even Mandeville's heart could soften on seeing a murdered child proved for Rousseau that pity was an enduring human characteristic that could withstand the worst corruptions of modern society.

One sees with pleasure how the author of *The Fable of the Bees*, when forced to acknowledge that man is a creature of compassion and feeling, discards his cold and sophisticated style in the example he gives of this, offering us the heartrending image of a man being compelled to observe, from a place of imprisonment, a wild beast tear a child from his mother's breast, crush the child's frail limbs with its murderous teeth and tear out the living entrails with its claws. What terrible agitation must be felt by this witness of an event in which he has no personal interest! What anguish he must suffer in seeing it and being unable to do anything to help the fainting mother or the dying child![1]

As in Mandeville's version, an onlooker is compelled to witness a child being molested by a wild beast, its desolate mother a helpless bystander. But Rousseau has made crucial changes. Gone are the references to the beast's gargantuan appetite; the sow is now a 'wild beast'; and the infant is murdered in a frenzy of bestial rage. Rousseau has also interposed a mother, from whose breast the child is torn. The mother faints, and with her lapse of consciousness, he presents a picture of feminine passivity and suffering that could not be further from Mandeville's vignette, in which the only female was the greedy pig who gorges on the human child.

That Rousseau should return to Mandeville's scene of infant violation is striking, but the changes that he made are all the more important as they point to the transformations in the discussion of child murder that came to characterise later eighteenth-century debates. Swift and Mandeville had used the idea of child murder for exploring the character of commercial society, and indeed it continued to be used in this way. However, from the middle of the eighteenth century a new context extended the parameters of the discussion. Through the growing interest in travel and exploration, discussions of child murder increasingly assumed a geographical and quasi-ethnographic perspective. The anthropological dimensions of child-murder discussions, which were implicit in Swift and Mandeville, were now empha-sised very strongly, and child murder frequently figured in complex debates about the nature of primitive man. These anthropological discussions lay at the heart of new developmental theories of civilisation, which emerged in the later decades of the century. Opposing accounts of the development of civilisation were current, but whether writers espoused the belief that civilisation was a process of gradual progress and improvement spurred on by the influence of commerce, as was the view of Adam Smith and other writers of the Scottish Enlightenment, or, on the contrary, whether they believed with Rousseau, that civilisation was a process of decline and decay, all subscribed to a stadial model of historical change. Paradoxically, child murder would be important in both versions: on the one hand, it was seen as an event that had been outlawed by civilised society; and on the other hand, it was an event that corrupt civilisation had caused. Its double signi-fication gave it a heightened role in the rhetoric of the time, especially for humanitarian reformers, for whom it would provide a pivot around which to conceptualise the project of reform.

The major structural change that Rousseau made to Mandeville's scene of infant violation, and that humanitarian reformers would replicate, was his insertion into the vignette of the grieving mother. This had a number of effects. By framing the scene with the mother's sorrow, Rousseau not only provided a blanket of sentimentality with which to muffle Mandeville's cynicism, he also drew the scene into the lexicon of Christian ritual, as it evoked the potent exposition of maternal grief at the Crucifixion – the occa-sion of the *Stabat Mater*.[2] In line with changing attitudes to the family, the Stabat Mater became a popular topos in the mid eighteenth century. The great musical settings by Vivaldi and Pergolesi were both composed in the early part of the century, in 1727 and 1736 respectively. More than this, however, it also transformed Mandeville's account of pity, as an emotion driven by self-love that operated primarily on the body of the beholder (it 'comes in at the Eye or the Ear' and produces an 'ake' that no words can express[3]), into a fundamentally social emotion. In the latter version, the addition of the mother opened the scene to a more complex understanding of pity, as an emotion that functioned through an intricate network of identifications. The mother is both a witness to the child's suffering, but also the one who suffers with the child, her lapse of consciousness under-lining the transformation from witness to victim. As the mother slips from spectator to sufferer, a new mobility is introduced to the scene, a chain of doubled identifications, that is the crucial mechanism of pity: the spectator looks with the mother, who feels with the child. And we, as spectators of this scene of spectation, shift our identification from the spectator, through the mother, to the child.[4]

Through frequent repetition, Rousseau's powerful revision of Mande-ville's scenario would be absorbed into the vocabulary of humanitarianism that dominated the later decades of the eighteenth century.[5] The scene was effective in part because it offered the reader multiple points of iden-tification, and thus a variety of emotional gratifications. Indeed, through shifting the position of the mother within the triangle of violator, victim, and spectator, the emotional force of the scene shifts from pity to the sub-jacent responses of disgust and pleasure, terror and desire, and an economy of emotional response emerges around the triangulated scene of infant suffering.[6] In fact, the form of the scene provides something like a gram-matical structure in which these changes of meaning are generated through slight shifts and substitutions.[7] By following them, in a number of instances it is possible to ascertain a stronger sense of both the particularity and the range of usages of the scene of infant suffering within the culture of the time, and the effects of the slippages between them.

In this chapter, I will examine three recurrent variants of the Rousseau-ian scene to be found in the literature of the late decades of the eighteenth century – primarily the 1770s and 1780s. In the first, a child is killed by a tyrannical father, and watched by a desolate mother; in the second, a child is sacrificed by a good mother; and in the third, a child is smothered or stabbed by a debauched mother. As we shall see, the cultural meanings of each are very different. This is reflected in the fact that the spectator plays a different role in each version: in the first, he is a man of reason, seeking knowledge; in the second, a humanitarian, or man of feeling, seeking justice; in the third, the man of pleasure, seeking sexual titillation. Each of the scenes is to be found in broadly similar sources. Instantiated first in travel writing among the observations of either adventurers or missionaries, they are then transmuted and transmitted into the broader culture partly through the synthetic, historical works of the Scottish Enlightenment, but also through poetry and drama. All of them will refer us back to the same story – that of Medea – even though in some important instances, including in Rousseau's version itself, the mother is not even the murderer. And all of them need to be read within the context of contemporary debates on the nature of civilisation. Thus before moving to the first of the three scenes, I will consider the discursive context in which they emerge, which, in passing, will shed some light on the failed attempts to repeal the 1624 child-murder statute – appropriately, one of the causes taken up by the humanitarian reformers whose campaigning zeal shaped the sensibilities of the age.

CHILD MURDER AND PRIMITIVE MAN IN THE SCOTTISH ENLIGHTENMENT

The grammar of emotional response that emerges in the late decades of the eighteenth century relies on the fact that the meanings of child murder are contested, especially in relation to debates about primitive man. The spectacle of the murdered child had particularly strong topical resonance at this time, because a society's treatment of children had come to be viewed as an important arbiter of civilised values, in a context in which these were hotly debated. Thus for Rousseau, it is man in his natural state who was more likely than civilised man to pity the infant child in a state of danger.[8] For him, to be in a state of nature was to be in a condition of plenitude; civilised society, in contrast, was founded on the introduction of various privations, which had caused the moral state of mankind to deteriorate. Pity was thus a response natural to primitive man, 'the pure movement of nature prior to all reflection',[9] which would gradually diminish in developed society.

For Adam Smith, on the other hand, pity for children was the province of civilised man. In his *Theory of Moral Sentiments* (1759) he asked, 'Can there be greater barbarity...than to hurt an infant? Its helplessness, its innocence, its amiableness, call forth the compassion of an enemy, and not to spare that tender age is regarded as the most furious effort of an enraged and cruel conqueror.' Yet, he went on, 'we find, at this day that this practice prevails among all savage nations'.[10] For him, not only would men in a state of nature *not* pity an infant child; it was an attribute of savages that they would actively murder it.

It was with a view to highlighting the controversial nature of Rousseau's position on primitive men that Smith first introduced the *Second Discourse* to a British readership in a letter published in the *Edinburgh Review* in 1756. His critique of Rousseau included the questionable claim that Rousseau espoused Mandevillian views about the nature of man and the persistence of the primitive in civilised society. While Rousseau had 'softened' Mandeville's account of the primitive according to Smith, nevertheless both had mistaken the natural 'wretchedness' of primitives for happiness, and their 'indolence' for natural virtue.[11] For Smith, on the contrary, it was the rough condition of primitive life that caused people to live in isolated and selfish ways; only through the gradual recognition of shared interests had men been able to improve their material conditions and consequently their own moral qualities. Of course, as we have seen, the violation of the child in Mandeville's scene of pity had provided Rousseau with evidence of the strength of man's primitive virtue, and the assurance that even that most corrupt of civilised men, Mandeville, might be susceptible to pity on seeing an infant die. But for Smith, Rousseau's adaptation of the scene proved that Rousseau's virtuous natural man was none other than Mandeville's primitive with his natural vices. This left the way open to Smith to present a case for the civilising impulse of commerce, contrary to the controversial implications of Mandeville's philosophy.

For Smith, social and economic improvements were inextricably entangled with the idea of mutual co-operation and human benevolence. This insight was the basis of his influential account of the progressive development of society: an economically grounded theory of social change, in which society was held to pass through each of four stages, from an early primitive form based on hunting, to the fourth and most advanced stage, based on commerce.[12] Smith's views on the development of society were broadly shared by other intellectuals of the Scottish Enlightenment, and in a cluster of works published between 1766 and 1777, including Adam Ferguson's *Essay on the History of Civil Society* (1766), John Millar's *Observations Concerning the Distinction of Ranks in Society* (1771), William Robertson's *History of America* (1777), as well as Smith's hugely influential *Wealth of Nations* (1776), a powerful case was made for the progressive nature of commercial society. Collectively, they refuted Mandeville's insistence on its foundations in private vice and radically revised the moral script of commerce.

In developing their ideas, these writers drew extensively on contemporary travel literature – as is witnessed in their meticulous and copious footnotes. There were many varieties of travellers' tales in print at the time: adventures of seafarers, and the imaginative works they inspired, such as Swift's *Gulliver's Travels*; the writings of missionaries, in particular French and Spanish Jesuits, and of traders and colonial agents, who had documented their encounters with native peoples on foreign terrains in Asia, Africa, and the Americas. Latterly, they included accounts of a series of scientific expeditions to the South Pacific, sponsored by the British and

French governments in the late 1760s and 1770s, that had fired a renewed enthusiasm for the exotic that spread widely across society.[13] For writers of the Scottish Enlightenment, the various revelations of such works provided important evidence that the different peoples of the world had progressed at variable rates, and had achieved different stages of development.[14] In his letter to William Robertson in 1777, congratulating him on the publication of his monumental *History of America*, Edmund Burke noted that in Robertson's work 'the Great Map of Mankind is unroll'd all at once; and there is no state or Gradation of Barbarity, and no mode of refinement which we have not at the same instant under our view.'[15] The Great Map of Mankind was a means of comparison, a way of plotting and assessing differences between peoples. All aspects of life were compared – forms of labour, the organisation of families, treatment of wives, standards of hygiene, housing, even hairstyles, and of course, standards of child care. It was the very existence of other peoples that allowed the process of comparison. And whether people believed in progress, and accepted that Europeans were innately more civilised than other peoples, or held the opposite view, that Europeans were more corrupt and corruptible, they nevertheless all ascribed to the necessity of comparison: civilisation, it was agreed, could best be evaluated in the contrasts between societies of vastly different structure and habitation.[16]

The revelation that the peoples of the world developed at different rates had fascinating consequences. On the one hand, it meant that the wider world became a living museum in which foreign peoples represented stages of an historical past, as the vestiges of civilisation's unruly origins. But it also introduced a notion of variability into the contours of progress, a variability that could equally be applied to Britain. It is this notion that provided penal reformers, for instance, with an apposite model for understanding the persistence of tyrannical laws or institutions within even an advanced society like Britain – and also justification for their reform. Transferred to Britain, the principle of different rates of development explained how certain institutions might lag behind in the onward march of progress. In this respect, Rousseau's critique of the notion of progress in commerce and civilisation is very important because it provided a powerful counter-narrative that illuminated such moments in which an awareness of uneven development obtruded on people's consciousness. Despite its antithetical relation to the philosophies that were favoured by reformers, in practice Rousseau's work aided their arguments and invigorated the project of reform.

Because of its double signification, then, child murder emerged as a pivotal term around which notions of uneven development revolved. Witness, for example, an influential essay – which in fact pre-dated Rousseau's critique – by the Scottish philosopher, David Hume, 'On the Populousness of Ancient Nations' (1752). In this, he sets out to argue against the current orthodoxy, that ancient societies could not have been more populous than modern enlightened societies, because of the oppressive institutions of ancient societies: the ancients' reliance on slavery, their love of warfare, rough manners, and lack of commerce militated against population growth. By contrast, modern Britain, which, Hume wrote, drawing attention in this case to its precocious youthfulness, is 'a prodigy even in modern times, for humanity, justice and liberty': it presented the ideal conditions for a large, flourishing population.[17] Thus far he provides a familiar account of the tyranny of ancient nations compared with the humanity of modern ones, and to emphasise his point he invokes ancient customs of child abandonment as a marker of the dissolute state of past societies. The practise of exposing infants, he wrote, 'was very common [in classical antiquity]; and is not spoken of by any author of those times with the horror it deserves, or scarcely even disapprobation'.[18]

Hume's views of ancient nations were backed up by evidence provided by contemporary travellers to China and the East, for Hume and his contemporaries believed oriental societies to be the atrophied remnants of ancient ones. At this point in his argument, therefore, the experience of China – a country that even in Hume's time was known both for its huge population, and its proclivity for exposing children[19] – undermines the certainty of his argument, for it suggests that the legality of child-killing is, paradoxically, an incentive to population. According to Hume, the availability of child abandonment in the customs of Chinese society encourages early marriages in a context in which, 'few...would have resolution enough...to carry into execution their former intentions'. Thus, he speculates, 'by an odd connexion of causes, the barbarous practice of the ancients [and orientals] might rather render those times more populous'. The point is that it is the institutions of ancient and oriental nations, not the people, who are barbarous. And if this is the case in oriental China, it is also so in modern Europe. While even the Chinese cannot kill their children, numerous nameless women in the capitals of Europe, including London, regularly hand over their children to the rough care of the foundling hospital, institutions Hume holds to be detrimental to 'health, industry and morals', and ultimately to population. What is this if not infanticide by another name?[20] And which is the uncivilised nation now? This logical impasse presented by the case of child murder opens up the possibility for reform; and it does so by disrupting the historical trajectory of his argument: in relation to child murder, it proposes, ancients are modern, and, in some aspects, moderns are ancient, just as some Europeans are more oriental than the Chinese.

Hume's argument in this essay was very influential among reformers. Indeed, it lay behind a speech made by the parliamentarian Sir William Meredith on introducing his Penal Reform Bill to the Commons in 1770. The Bill marked the beginning of a phase of vigorous campaigning on the part of humanitarians to reform institutions across the spectrum of British society. A central plank of Meredith's cause was the excessive number of capital crimes in the British legal system. The legal historian Radzinowicz writes that between 1765 and 1769 there were 160 capital statutes – a number that over the next fifty years would increase, rising eventually to 220.[21] According to Meredith, the unreformed law was a force of depopulation: as he put it, a 'fertile source of depopulation' – a 'waste of people,' the 'greater part of them . . . very young people'. As such, it was a vestige of a tyrannical past, a remnant of a primitive self, out of step with present modernity, and it turned Britain into an ancient, or even oriental, nation: 'Our criminal codes seem to have been formed on the principles of the Stoics, who deemed all sins equal; or rather they breathe the spirit of Draco, whose laws were all written in blood.' Worse: '[t]urn your eyes to the Japanese. Nothing can be more horrible than their executions. [. . .] they are savagely cruel. The state of other nations justifies the same remark'. Britain's penal laws were no better: punishments were disproportionate to crimes, and 'equal justice' was not 'administered to every delinquent'.[22]

For Meredith, the law, with its injustices and oppressions, killed, if not precisely children, certainly 'very young people'. Implicit here is a critique of institutions that is close to Rousseau's notion of the corrupting influence of institutions – that the law is demoralising, and causes the death of infants. Through the invocation of child murder the temporality of the modern nation is disrupted, so that Britain assumes a partial identification with ancient and oriental societies. In order to assume a truly civilised state, these throwbacks to earlier societies must be eliminated.

The implicit charge, that the antiquated law killed children, was repeated frequently in the rhetoric of the penal reformers, not least in their bid to repeal the 1624 child-murder statute.[23] Following Meredith's initial petition in 1770, a committee was established under the chairmanship of the penal reformer Sir Charles Bunbury, to consider the excessive number of capital statutes, reporting to the House the following year, and again in 1772, with a list of eight for repeal, including the 1624 child-murder law. Speaking specifically to the child-murder law, Meredith and his collaborators, who included Edmund Burke, Charles James Fox, and William Harbord, argued that,

In the case of women having bastard children the common statute laws were inconsistent; . . . that this institution necessarily rendered the having of bastard child infamous; that the dread of infamy necessarily caused concealment; that the statute law . . . made concealment capital; . . . that nothing could be more unjust, or inconsistent with the principles of all law, than first to force a woman through modesty to concealment, and then to hang her for that concealment; . . . that the concealment of the birth of a bastard might proceed from the best causes, from real modesty and virtue; . . . that, while all due praise was allowed to legitimate children, it was not just to give a squeeze in the neck to bastards; and that humanity and justice pleaded strongly for the alteration contended for.[24]

Their case for repealing the 1624 statute, then, was built around the charge of concealment, which, as we have seen in the previous chapter, was usually taken by the courts to be the presumption of murder. The reformers argued that not only was this out of line with the emergent legal principle that a person be considered innocent until proved otherwise, but that it was also unjust, in that the stigma of illegitimacy encouraged women to conceal their unwanted pregnancies.[25] In contrast to the hidden nature of the mother's crime, however, they invited the assembled men of parliament to witness a different assault on an infant body. Attention is drawn first to the executed mother as an object of sympathy, but then in a clever conceit, the spectators' eyes are averted from the mother to the body of the infant, the real site of suffering: 'while all due praise was allowed to legitimate children, it was not just to give a squeeze in the neck to bastards'. It was as if the law as it stands might as well have hanged the bastards itself. In the reformers' eyes, the law's draconian measures eclipse the mother's murderous act, so that in the end we watch while the law kills the child, and the mother is no more than an innocent bystander. This, of course, is a version of Rousseau's topos of infant suffering – the spectacle of the murdered child. The tyrannical and irrational force of the unreformed law kills innocent children, just as Rousseau's wild beast has done.

When parliament came to consider the list – an assortment of capital statutes from laws which made it an offence to call oneself an 'Egyptian' or gypsy, to crimes of disloyalty to monarchs – the 1624 statute was upheld together with a law that allowed 'the benefit of clergy' (that is, the privilege of clerics to be tried in the more lenient, Ecclesiastical Court) to 'those guilty of violently carrying away women with an intention to force them into marriage with the ravisher'. While the Commons was convinced by the rational argument that all men were equal before the law, regardless of race – 'even a gypsy' they agreed '[should not be] hung on suspicion' – appeals to the sympathy of the house for the sufferings of women and children fell on deaf ears. There were, no doubt, political reasons for this, and it would be wrong to impugn the humanitarianism of the Commons for not heeding Meredith's appeal to sentiment. But the failure highlights the ambiguity that was implicit within Meredith's rhetoric. For in the scenario described by Meredith and the parliamentarians, the mother for whom sympathy was sought may also have been the murderer. It is possible that Meredith and his collaborators' invocation of the emotions of their colleagues failed to convince in part because it remained uncertain as to which of the emotions was summoned, and, moreover, on whose behalf. It was difficult to elicit pity for an unmarried, sexually involved woman, even a victim of seduction, when sympathy could so easily be subsumed by the equally potent feeling of disgust, aroused by the thought that she may have murdered her child. The reformers had adapted Rousseau's scene of pity for their own political ends; and the result might have been effective, if the scenario had not reminded the sceptical audience of the very crime for which the mother stood accused. Paradoxically the over-determined and slippery connotations of child murder within contemporary debates meant that they imputed the mother's guilt in the very assertion of her innocence.

Three further attempts to repeal the law were made in bills presented in 1772 and 1773 by the reformer John Lockhart, and by Charles Bunbury in 1776. In each of these subsequent efforts the speakers sought to elicit sympathy only for the child: 'It is respecting the situation of bastard children,' Lockhart claimed, 'which calls aloud for the humanity and interposition of this house'[26] – but there is no mention of the unfortunate mother. It was, however, to no avail: the Lords was to reject all three, and the statute would not be repealed for another twenty years in the very different circumstances of 1803.[27]

The complexity of the issues raised by the practice of child murder seemed to be exacerbated rather than clarified by the rhetoric of infant suffering. Indeed, when we read extensively in the contemporary literature, the range of meanings that it could yield becomes apparent, so that in the end, through its sheer fecundity, the topos of infant violation provokes discomforting thoughts of the uncertainties of human emotion and the proximity of contradictory responses. Compassion, condescension, pleasure, pain, arousal, outrage – all might be generated by Rousseau's primal scene.

CHILD MURDER ON THE WORLD STAGE

Scene 1: The tyrannical father, from Patagonia to the London theatre

For penal reformers of the 1770s, the unreformed law resembled a primitive or savage patriarch, who vented his irrational anger on the body of a defenceless child. That savage peoples might indeed behave in such a tyrannical way was evident from the ethnographic literature of the time. This anthropological anecdote was just one version of an account of paternal tyranny that circulated widely in these decades.

Commodore John Byron, the sea-faring grandfather of the poet, provided one such source in his account of his perilous adventures following a shipwreck off the coast of Patagonia.[28] Byron's voyage had taken place in 1745, but his *Narrative* was not published until 1768, capitalising on the interest in exploration spawned by recent expeditions to the South Pacific – including his own return to the Magellan Straits in 1765 in the *Dolphin*.[29] In fact, it was Byron's second voyage that inspired the British admiralty to sponsor a number of other scientific expeditions, including Cook's three voyages between 1768 and 1780. These expeditions fed a broad popular appetite for scientific curiosities – geographical, botanical, and ethnological: specimens collected in the South Pacific, for instance, were displayed in museums across London to the entertainment of a wide spread of audiences.[30] In his *Narrative*, Byron emulated scientific authority through inclusion of ethnographic evidence: incorporated in his swashbuckling tales of human endurance amid extreme climates, privations of nourishment, threats of sly and bloodthirsty natives, not to mention the treacheries of his crewmembers, are eye-witness accounts of the customs of the people and places he encounters. The inclusion of these is in accordance with his stated intention, articulated in the preface, to act as a scientific observer: 'there is no other way of ascertaining the geography and natural history of a country which is altogether morass and rock, incapable of products of culture,' he writes, 'than by setting down every minute circumstance which was observed in traversing it'.[31]

The following anecdote of infant violation is thus recounted without embellishment or comment in Byron's *Narrative*:

[A man] and his wife had gone off, at some distance from the shore, on their canoe, when she dived for sea eggs, but not meeting with great success, they returned a good deal out of humour. A little boy of theirs about three years old, whom they appeared to be doatingly fond of, watching for his father and mother's return, ran into the surf to meet them: the father handed a basket of sea eggs to the child, which being too heavy for him to carry, he let it fall; upon which the father jumped out of the canoe, and catching the boy upon his arms dashed him with the utmost violence against the stones. The poor little creature lay motionless and bleeding, and in that condition was taken up by the mother, but died soon after. She appeared inconsolable for sometime: but the brute his father showed little compassion.[32]

A little boy is cruelly murdered while his mother watches, the whole scene observed by an impartial observer, whose viewpoint we are encouraged to replicate. The anecdote bears a striking resemblance to Rousseau's scene of infant suffering. This time, however, the observer is not a man of feeling as in Rousseau's account, but an ethnographer, a scientific recorder of foreign customs. There are other differences too: the child is no longer a baby but a toddler; the violator is not a beast, but the 'brute' father; and the mother's grief is transitory and because of this, it suggests, inauthentic. The scene's dramatic mode is difficult to gauge, as it seems to teeter on the border between tragedy and burlesque.

The question of how much power a father should hold over his children had been a point of concern in philosophical and social debate across the century. John Locke's influential *Some Thoughts Concerning Education* (1693) had argued for limiting the powers of the father, in a context in which the family was re-imagined as a social unit made of mutual duties and obligations, rather than domination and authority.[33] In a similar vein, Rousseau would later claim, in *Du Contrat Social* (1762), that the bond between father and offspring was not one of absolute and lasting power, but restricted to a period of childhood; and neither did it include the father's right to kill the child. While such works had had a major impact in shaping educational beliefs and practices during the period, it is also the case that they reflected and extended a reconfiguration of political relations and attitudes towards authority that occurred in England following the Revolution of 1688 – an event that marked the end of absolutism in English history. A perceived symmetry between the concerns of the family and of the state defined a common agenda in a range of debates, from the management of the nursery to affairs of government. The moderation of the father's authority was thus as much a political concern as a social and domestic one. As Jay Fliegelman and others have pointed out, the political language of the period was seeped in metaphors of family relations, to the extent that political conflicts and crises tended to be represented in terms of family traumas, usually focusing specifically on the status of the father. This is dramatically the case from the 1770s, through the period of the American Revolution (1776–83), when relations between England and America were represented in political discourse on both sides of the Atlantic in terms of the strained relations between either an ungrateful son and his enlightened father, or alternatively, a repressive father and his enlightened son.[34] Humanitarian reformers of this period adopted a similar language: the laws on slavery, or the penal code itself, demonstrated that England's own law was a bad father, in need of restraint.

Overlapping with these metaphorical family dramas was the production of works by Scottish intellectuals, in which the bad father was the touch-stone of uncivilised society. In these works of the Scottish Enlightenment, the idea of paternal tyranny – a capricious and wilful violence exerted over children just as in Byron's example – was commonly associated with ancient and foreign peoples. It was at the centre of Hume's example in 'The Populousness of Ancient Nations' already discussed: the ancients and the Chinese abandoned their children because their customs had allowed fathers absolute dominion over their children. This is in contrast to the modern family, in which the father's authority is tempered by love, and is humane and rational. In Hume's example, however, as we have seen, the tyrannical power of ancient and oriental fathers is seen to be an attribute not of individual fathers as such, but of the law that had ascribed them such excessive power over others. Thus Hume turns the discussion away from individuals and the family, to a critique of the law, contrasting ancient and oriental tyrannical laws with modern ideals of justice. The theme is picked up by Adam Ferguson, in his *Essay on the History of Civil Society* (1767), a work shot through with allusions to Hume's essay, including a direct reference to his discussion of Chinese child murder.[35] For Ferguson and others, Chinese child abandonment comes to be a dramatic motif, full of pathos, of the absolute discrepancy between the tyranny of the un-reformed law and the natural beneficence of human love. The necessary process of modernising the law in Britain, then, is seen as a process of realignment, of drawing it into line with the natural contours of human feeling – represented in its most poignant form, as the love of a parent for a child.

Adam Smith, in his *Theory of Moral Sentiments*, had made a similar point. Like Hume, he referred to the 'exposition, that is the murder of new-born infants', which 'was a practice allowed of in almost all the states of Greece, even among the polite and civilized Athenians; and whenever the circumstances of the parent rendered it inconvenient to bring up the child, to abandon it to hunger, or to wild beasts, was regarded without savage barbarity'.[36] Like Hume, he too turns his attention to the processes of law, rather than acts of individuals. Thus the abandonment of a child under the harsh conditions of savage life was an excusable act, as when, for instance, 'in flying from an enemy, whom it was impossible to resist', a man 'should throw down his infant, because it retarded his flight'. But 'in the latter ages of Greece... the same thing was permitted from views of remote interest or conveniency, which could by no means excuse it.' The Athenian law is thus a degenerate law, because it serves only the self-interest of individuals, not the greater good of society, providing Smith with the basis of a comparison with the enlightened standards of modern justice.[37]

In all these examples then, the motif of the too-powerful father killing his child is used as a way of discussing the relationship between the state and its people, as mediated by the law. And it is in this light that John Millar, the Professor of Law at Glasgow University, appropriates Byron's anecdote. *Observations Concerning the Distinction of Ranks in Society*, first published in 1771, was a comparative study of the law in different societies, tracing 'natural progress from ignorance to knowledge, and from rude to civilised manners'.[38] In a chapter entitled 'Of the jurisdiction and authority of a father over his children', Millar surveys the contemporary ethnographic and historical writings, to provide a compendium of tyrannical fathers, including the Chinese child-abandoners. It is here that we find Byron's anecdote, retold verbatim, 'to show the spirit with which the savages of South America are apt to govern the members of their family'. Thus Byron's Patagonian father takes his place within a gazetteer of paternal tyrants all of them exemplifying the degradations of earlier and foreign societies, compared with the reasonable and moderate forms of authority in modern societies. 'The tendency... of a commercial age is rather towards the opposite extreme', he concludes, and the persistence of various tyrannical practices and institutions within modern Britain is merely an anachronism, or an accident of uneven development.[39] For Millar, the unreformed law and slavery are two examples of practices – like the Patagonian father's abuse of his son – that are residues of some former society in need of reform.

Within this context, however, the very urge to soften manners, and restrain paternal authority, ideas that were central to notions of progress and civilisation, and which underpinned the zeal for reform, also assumed a more worrying potential. For what if that softness should go too far, and the very basis of authority and order break down? Throughout the literature that celebrates the modern tempering of paternal power, then, we encounter a repeated expression of this anxiety. John Millar, for instance, having criticised the tyrannies of primitives, noted that parental fondness, on the other hand, sometimes leads a father to treat his children with 'the utmost complacency and indulgence'; and earlier, Adam Smith had warned that 'nature... has rendered [parental] affection so strong that it generally requires not to be excited, but to be moderated'.[40] The subtle dangers of paternal fondness resound throughout Adam Smith's *Theory Of Moral Sentiments* – paradoxically, perhaps, in a work which otherwise can be read as a handbook of the modern sensibility. For him, men's fondness for their children is potentially a feminising tendency – something best safely concealed.

He shows this by presenting another variant on Rousseau's spectacle of infant suffering: 'A parent in private life might, upon the loss of an only son, express without blame a degree of grief and tenderness, which would be unpardonable in a general at the head of an army.'[41] In this version, the point of interest is the grieving parent, who is now a father, not a mother, as in Rousseau's version; and there is no spectator – for Smith's point is that paternal grief is not a fit subject for public consumption. The tone he takes when asking us to consider a father witnessing the scene of infant death is surprisingly chiding: a father's grief is a cause of 'blame' – something to be 'pardoned'. As such it can only be expressed in private. There can be no legitimate spectator of Smith's scene of paternal fondness.

By contrast, however, he points to the noble act of Brutus, who, as we have noted, condemned his two sons to death, for conspiring against 'the rising liberty of Rome'.[42] In doing so, Brutus sacrificed what, if 'he had consulted his own breast only would appear to be the stronger to the weaker affection' – paternal affection for love of country. Brutus's act has for Smith, a 'great . . . noble, and exalted propriety': it accrues a 'new beauty', which raises it above displays of mere sentimentality. This is not the act of a tyrannical and irrational father – the savage patriarch on the beach of Patagonia, the Chinese child-abandoner, or even the Athenian degenerate. Brutus's child murder is a virtuous sacrifice, a rational act for the sake of the republic – an act of a wholly different order. As an act of public virtue, Smith's sacrificial child murder looks back to the long civic humanist tradition of public virtue discussed in the previous chapter. In fact, the virtues of Brutus are yet more impressive in the context of the culture of sensibility when, as Smith himself put it, 'scarce a child can die without rending asunder the heart of somebody'.[43]

Despite this commonly expressed caution about the softening of manners, or possibly even because of it, the idea of the tyrannical father who killed his children seeped into other more popular arenas, as the stock figure of primitive or antiquated authority. His presence was very much in evidence in literature, where displays of violent paternal rage were usually contrasted with scenes of domestic harmony, in which families lived together in mutual love, the father's authority tempered to meet the needs of modern, refined society.[44] The repeated narration of such contrasting scenes may be considered as part of the larger process of the inculcation of domestic ideals. For instance, in a stage version of *Medea* by the playwright and parliamentarian Richard Glover, performed for the first time in 1767, even the archetypal child-murdering mother could be absolved of guilt, as blame is transferred first to Jason, but ultimately to Creon, the tyrannical king, as the true author of their tragedy. *Medea* was performed infrequently on the London stage in this period, its display of maternal passion considered too extreme for contemporary taste.[45] This particular version emphasised not only Medea's madness, but also, and more bizarrely, the enduring love of Jason for Medea.[46] In a sequel, *Jason* (1799), which was never staged, Medea and Jason are reunited in the underworld, and seek revenge on the tyrant king. In the final speech, scenes of domestic bliss are imagined involving Jason and Medea's descendants, as the family triumphs in posterity, its gentler fabric having usurped the tyrannies of an irrational king.

There were performances of Glover's *Medea* at Drury Lane until 1776, but four years later, in 1780, the London theatre saw a yet more outlandish version of the story: the brainchild of George Colman the Elder, the manager of the Haymarket Theatre, this was the highly successful burlesque, '*Medea and Jason*, A Ballet Tragi-Comique by Signior Novestris'.[47] In this version, the parts were to be played as a melange of pantomime characters: Jason as Pierrot, Medea as Mother Shipton, and Creon, 'in the character of Mr Punch'. The authoritarian father – the subject of so much philosophical argument – now assumed his pantomime form as Mr Punch.

While audiences may well have held Glover's *Medea* in their not-so-distant memories, the immediate target of Colman's burlesque was a ballet that had been produced at the rival theatre, the King's Theatre, just a few months beforehand, by the French choreographer and dancer Gaetano Vestris. Vestris's *Medea and Jason* was a revival of a production by the influential choreographer Noverre, whose new style of *ballet d'action* had revolutionised ballet performances across Europe (see Fig. 2).[48] As one commentator remarked, Noverre's ballets were 'no longer strictly speaking dances, they are great happenings represented by movements of the body alone without the use of speech and yet they are very different from ordinary pantomimes.'[49] In Noverre's ballet, movement had become a kind of spoken drama in which words were encapsulated in gesture. The British actor, Garrick, had been so impressed by Noverre's new techniques that he had contracted him for a season in 1755, although strong anti-French feelings in the audiences caused the contract to be prematurely ended.[50] *Medea and Jason* was considered one of the most successful of Noverre's productions,

Figure 2. Ballet design for Noverre's *Jason and Medea*, London, 1781

and it is interesting to note just how different a version of the play it was to Glover's. Medea is presented as a woman incensed by jealous rage, the violence of her passions on full display: she gives a poisoned nosegay to Creusa who dies, after which Medea reappears in a chariot with her children – one of whom she has already murdered, but the other she stabs on stage.[51] Jason, a part that Vestris liked to dance, is a heroic role, which ends in his dramatic suicide. Most significantly, perhaps, Creon is played not as a tyrant, but as a 'majestic' figure.[52] With Glover's version of autocratic tyranny in mind, it is easy to see how in Colman's satirical version, supposedly the work of 'Signior Novestris', a confection of Noverre and Vestris, Creon played as Mr Punch, might transform into a satire on French absolutism – especially at a time when anti-French feelings were strengthened by France's joining the Americans in their war against Britain.

The targets of Colman's burlesque extend beyond this, however. His *Medea and Jason* was performed following two other parodic pieces, including a cross-dressed performance of the *Beggar's Opera*. In the first piece, *Preludio*, it is suggested that the cross-dressing is a 'remedy' to the fact that *The Beggar's Opera* is in English, not Italian – like the Italian operas regularly performed, alongside the French ballets, across the street in the King's Theatre. But the dialogue in the *Preludio* continues: 'the times out Burlesque you', for already 'men are losing their old British character, in dress, paint, red heels and white feathers', while women become 'martial and masculine'.[53] English society has already become like an Italian opera – the men foppish and the women more manly – more educated and independent on the one hand (like the bluestockings), and more sexually adventurous and permissive on the other. The final joke, however, is that whatever they do 'your actress will always come nearer to men than the things who represent Lovers and Heroes on the other side of the Haymarket', so irredeemably effeminate are the actors at the King's. *Medea and Jason* which completes the performance, then, is presented as a corrective to this world of disordered gender, where the actors play exaggerated and satirical versions of masculine and feminine roles: the King as Mr Punch, displaying his machismo in brutal displays of domestic violence; and Medea as Mother Shipton, saving, rather than killing, her children.

Colman's entertainment thus exploits contemporary anxieties about an incipient social disorder, of which irregularities around gender were considered to be both a symptom and a cause. Absurdly, Colman's burlesque performs, in the spirit of pastiche, but nonetheless precisely, the dilemma that emerges in Adam Smith's *Theory of Moral Sentiments*. For the softening of forms of social relations and of authority brought its own particular problems of disorder and social disarray – men displaying grief like only mothers should, or men wearing high heels and makeup – and the social and political problems of indulged children, like America, whose 'ingratitude' to its 'parent' was only too apparent on the 1780s' world stage.

These theatrical versions of the *Medea,* each in its iconoclastic way, play with one of the most common ideas associated with child murder in the period – the idea of primitive paternal tyranny. But there are other versions of the *Medea* to be found embedded in distinct discussions of child murder. While these will not be staged, except in the imaginations of their writers and readers, nevertheless the metaphor of the theatre is a live one, because each scene is set up on the Rousseauian model of the scene of infant suffering: a child is killed, and a man observes. In the next of the scenes, the murderer is a mother – Medea enslaved.

Scene 2: The good mother: republican maternity and slavery in Raynal, More, Barbauld, and Yearsley

In 1779, the physician William Alexander published a two-volume *History of Women*. Like Ferguson, Robertson, and Millar, Alexander based his work on a thorough reading of historical and travel sources, and the resulting volumes are very much in the spirit of these previous natural histories – a celebration of the improvements that their society enjoys. His work, however, addressed the specific issue of the treatment of women, arguing that this was the true gauge of a civilised society.[54] In doing so, it constructed a different historical trajectory: for him medieval chivalry represented the pinnacle of civilisation, a period of perfection from which society had sunk into libertinism, before rising again after 1688 eventually to embrace the values of domesticity and sentimentality in his own time. Addressed to a female readership, Alexander confirms his own chivalric suavity by expressing an intention to include no foreign or technical terms – so as not to confound the ladies. Nevertheless, his accounts of the abuse suffered by women in savage and uncivilised times are surprisingly frank. In a discussion of the condition of savage women, he incorporates a long speech, purportedly the words of an Indian woman, on the banks of the Oronooka, recorded by the missionary, Father Joseph Gumilla. In her lament, she describes the excessive labour, physical violence, and sexual humiliation she has suffered. 'I wish to God, Father,' she complains, 'that my mother had, by my death, prevented the manifold distresses I have endured, and have yet to endure'; 'had she kindly stifled me at my birth', she goes on, 'I should not have felt the pain of death...'; and again, 'I repeat...would to God my mother had put me under ground the moment I was born!'[55] The author of the woman's miseries is her tyrannical husband, a man like the too-powerful patriarch who in the works discussed earlier was represented as the killer of children. In this version, however, the scenario is inverted: in the face of such patriarchal cruelty, a good mother should pre-empt her daughter's suffering, and kill her at birth. Here we have the second variant of Rousseau's scene of pity. Now, the spectator is the humanitarian – in this instantiation, a missionary; and the murderer is the mother herself.

In a work that insists that maternal affections are 'the most powerful of human feelings', and that a woman's true role is as a gentle wife and mother, this manifestation of mother love is shockingly perverse. Alexander claims that it is an 'obliteration' of maternal love, induced by the inhuman oppressions of savagery, but it is easy to see it rather as an extreme expression of this love – an act of salvation rather than one of neglect or harm – and one that draws on the legacy of the civic humanist idea of child sacrifice.[56] In a footnote, he appends a further example which speaks to the universality of the violent passions of motherhood: 'Shocking as this description may appear, it is greatly exceeded by two others exhibited by the Abbé Raynal, in his *History of the European Settlements*'.[57] He then quotes at length from the 1776 English translation of Raynal's *Histoire des deux Indes*. Raynal's work, which in fact had been drafted by several authors, was a survey of the American colonies, and from its first publication in France in 1770 it circulated widely across Europe.[58] The extract reprinted by Alexander was taken from the passages on slavery. This was a vivid and outspoken attack on slavery, and constituted the most radical of anti-slavery writings of the period. It had been drafted by the utopian, Jean de Pechméja, and according to Blackburn, it was 'discrepant with the moderate reformism found in other sections' of Raynal's work.[59] Nevertheless, it is from this that Alexander cites the following example:

Such hard labour is required of negroe women both before and after their pregnancy, that the children are either abortive, or live but a short time after delivery; mothers, rendered desperate by the punishments which the weakness of their condition occasions them, snatch sometimes their children from the cradle, in order to strangle them in their arms, and sacrifice them with a fury mingled with a spirit of revenge and compassion, that they may not become the property of their cruel masters.[60]

Here are two radically different images of aberrant maternity: on the one hand, women who are so weak their children cannot live – passive victims whose suffering is embodied in their dying progeny; and on the other, women who actively murder their children. Both are perverse inversions of the maternal ideal: the first associates female passivity with infant death; the second transforms maternal caresses into murder, as they 'snatch' the children from 'the cradle' to 'strangle' them in their arms. But it is the second image that is so arresting: the sudden burst of energy, the eruption of a baffling cocktail of 'fury mingled with revenge and compassion', as, Medea-like, maternal love turns to hate. Alexander claims that he relegates the example to a footnote on taxonomic grounds, because the miseries described are inflicted by a people 'whom we do not class among savages'.[61] But it seems equally likely that he pushes the example to the margins of his page for its startling and alarming vision of debased womanhood.

In fact, in Raynal's text this image of the murdering slave mothers has a very particular role in a much longer, and politically provocative discussion.

The work goes on to argue, much as Hume had done in his essay 'On the Populousness of Ancient Nations', that slavery is a system that works against population, and that 'the allurements of liberty are the most powerful that can influence the human heart', to turn slave women into good mothers. According to Raynal's text, giving slave women freedom would be an expedient measure, for it would capitalise on the 'extraordinary fruitfulness of the negro woman', swelling the population, and the productive labour force.

Alexander's use of Raynal's example is striking in part for its omission of any direct mention of slavery. Indeed, he curtails the quotation at the very point at which Raynal's polemic begins, and the moment at which the image assumes its extraordinary power. Raynal's text follows the image with a commentary on its uses, the way in which it should be read. He writes:

> This barbarity, the whole horror of which must be imputed to the Europeans, will, perhaps make them sensible of their error. Their sensibility will be roused by paying a greater attention to their true interests. They will learn that they lose more than they get, by committing such outrages against humanity; and if they do not become the benefactors of their slaves, they will at least cease to be their executioners.[62]

For Raynal, the image encompasses the 'whole horror' of slavery; it is a dramatic metonym standing for all its appalling abuses. Its inclusion here is a way of compelling European slave owners to confront the effects of their actions, appealing to their sensibility. A repetition of Rousseau's spectacle of pity, Raynal's is one in which the roles are doubled and inverted. The mother is both the miserable witness to infant suffering, but also its agent; and the spectator, who is also the real violator – the European slave owner – is both the man of feeling, but also the violent brute. In this instance the spectacle becomes something like a mirror, reflecting back to the European the true horror he inflicts. But there is a further inversion, for the mirror will reveal that the sufferings of the Negro are those of the European too: slavery harms 'their true interests', they 'lose more than they get', that is to say, their own humanity is wounded by their oppression of others. In this moment of refraction and fragmentation, the slave owner is thrust into all three positions at once – as spectator, victim, and the violator; shame, pity, and suffering conjoin, as the slave owner performs the abjection of the slave, before his very own eyes.

Raynal was widely read in Britain in this period, but in the works produced for the British anti-slavery cause, there are few examples of this arresting image of the murdering slave mother – possibly because of the likely offence it would cause to standards of decorum.[63] On the other hand, the image of the suffering mother as the passive victim of slavery – the mother whose children are stolen from her by slavers, or the mother whose children die from the privations of the middle passage – is a staple component in representations of the human suffering caused by slavery. These images appear in particular in works that celebrate the achievements of the anti-slavery movement, as pictures of suffering already alleviated. Thus, in 'A Poem on the Bill Lately Passed for Regulating the Slave Trade' (1788), Helen Maria Williams utilises this sentimental lexicon of maternal suffering in a typical way when she writes of the 'Woman...too weak to bear / The galling chain, the tainted air' who following the new legislation,

> No more, in desperation wild
> Shall madly strain her gasping child;
> With all the mother at her soul,
> With eyes where tears have ceased to roll,
> Shall catch the livid infant's breath;
> Then sink in agonizing death.[64]

Thomas Clarkson opens his *History of the Rise, Progress, and Accomplishment of the Abolition of the African Slave Trade* (1808) with a striking vignette of an African mother who has lost her children. As in Raynal's text, this picture of the mother's suffering is presented as a metonymic representation of all the human degradations of the slave trade. And, as in the Raynal text, Clarkson sets up the scene as a spectacle to be observed, inserting within it the presence of an audience, in this case 'ourselves', the like-minded humanitarians who constitute his readership. 'Suppose ourselves on the continent just mentioned' he invites. 'Well then – we are landed – we are already upon our travels – we have just passed through one forest' and so on, until the suffering woman appears as an 'object' that 'obtrudes upon our sight'. 'Who is that wretched woman, whom we discover under that noble tree, wringing her hands, and beating her breast, as if in the agonies of despair?'[65] While we, the humanitarian-explorers, roam freely across the continent, surveying the scene with our panoramic gaze, the African woman, in contrast, is static, beneath a tree, watching for her lost children, who we know will never return. 'Beneath [the tree's] spreading bough they were accustomed to play – but alas! the savage man-stealer interrupted their playful mirth, and has taken them for ever from her sight.' Here is a potent image of devastated domesticity. Clarkson's vignette repeats the pattern and structure of Rousseau's scene of pity: the children have been stolen by a 'savage man-stealer' – Clarkson's pseudo-primitive vocabulary here ventriloquising for the African woman, underlining the brutishness of the slaver, his similarity to Rousseau's wild beast; the mother watches in despair; and 'we', the spectators, we 'men of feeling', look on, and pity. Unlike in Raynal's extraordinary version of the scene of pity, all roles are reassigned and disaggregated, returned to their original order.[66]

In the period between 1788 and 1791, when the anti-slavery movement was invigorated by the events in France, a series of poems by women writers, namely Hannah More, Ann Yearsley, and Anna Barbauld, pursued the complexities of Raynal's violent reconfiguration of the scene of suffering in more acute ways.[67] The shared themes and imagery of the three poets suggest a dialogue between them. By focusing on the role of the spectator of the scene of suffering, a role that in these works shifts uneasily between that of the slaver and the humanitarian, they each explore the complicity of all Britons in the system of slavery. As Barbauld puts it, most explicitly, 'By foreign wealth are British morals changed.'[68] Images of inverted spectatorship abound, as the humanitarian gaze of pity is reflected back as guilt, as in More's 'Slavery, A Poem' (1788):

> Whene'er to Afric's shores I turn my eyes,
> Horrors of deepest, deadliest guilt arise;
> I see, by more than Fancy's mirror shewn,
> The burning village, and the blazing town.[69]

Or more complicatedly in Yearsley's 'A Poem on the Inhumanity of the Slave Trade' (1788), the slaver is feminised, and represented as the Gorgon, the Medusa, who blinds those that look at her (in the poem, the slaver blinds the slave, who is 'A blind involuntary victim');[70] in the course of the poem, the blinding gaze is reflected back, the slaver blinded by his own moral turpitude. Barbauld repeats Yearsley's imagery in her 'Epistle to William Wilberforce, Esq. On the Rejection of the Bill for Abolishing the Slave Trade' (1791), when she represents 'the unfeeling sneer' of Parliament, which 'turns to stone the falling tear' of pity (lines 31, 32). But, she warns, 'injur'd Afric, by herself redressed, / Darts her own serpents at her Tyrant's breast' (lines 45–6) – the slave will return the gaze, and look back in anger and rage.

Yearsley's poem ends with the wish that the slave trader might 'enlarge' his vision, so that paradoxically, the 'fetters of his mind' (line 407), rather than the 'fetters' of the slave (as in More's poem), might be removed. What must be restored to him is the possibility of sympathetic vision, the gaze that will let him 'feel / Another's pang' – as Rousseau's spectator could:

> ... for the lamenting maid
> His heart shall heave a sigh; with the old slave
> (Whose head is bent with sorrow) he shall cast
> His eye back on the joys of youth, and say,
> 'Thou *once* could'st feel, as I do, love's pure bliss;
> Parental fondness, and the dear returns
> Of filial tenderness were thine, till torn
> From the dissolving scene.'   (lines 417–24)

The restoration of sympathetic vision will bring with it the repair of the family relations that have been broken by slavery. The spectacle of the ruptured family pictured here is central to all these poems as the primary scene of the infliction of suffering. The abuse of slavery is expressed as the violent fragmenting of parental bonds: 'The fibres twirling round a parent's heart, / Torn from their grasp, and bleeding as they part' (More, 'Slavery', lines 109–10), or 'Curse / On him who from a bending parent steals / His dear support of age, his darling child' (Yearsley, 'Inhumanity', lines 64–6). And this rupture is repeated in the wresting of the slave from his native land, which is also expressed as a relationship between parent and child – 'heaven-taught fondness for the parent soil' (More, 'Slavery', line 116). Again, the spectacle of suffering is complicated by the fact that in these poems it is often a reflected, and distorted image of the British family and British patriotism. 'Love your own offspring, love your native land', urges Hannah More of the slave owners, 'respect the passions you yourself possess' (lines 114, 112). Yet more knowingly, Yearsley turns the mirror back on the slaver. The slaver, she argues, will justify his actions on the grounds that he does so to support his children; but in supporting his family, she points out, he ruptures another:

> I know the crafty merchant will oppose
> The plea of nature to my strain, and urge
> His toils are for his children: the lost plea
> Dissolves my soul – *but when I sell a son,*
> *Thou God of nature, let it be my own!*
>   (lines 75–9)

Yearsley exposes the slave owner's exploitation of the African family for his own family. She slips from the mode of comparison, into a comment on the form of inter-racial contact that it engenders. The last lines of this passage turn the mirror back on the idea of the family itself, in which person and property are elided. Yearsley, like the other anti-slavery writers, looks to 'social life' as the means of redemption from the slave trade. But in this poem, the idea of 'social life' – based as it is on the notion of the family – itself becomes an uncomfortable notion, riven by complicities of exploitation.[71]

All three poets pick up on the idea of spectatorship that is at the very heart of the Rousseauian topos of infant violation that Raynal has adapted for his own political ends. Implicit in their work is also a critique of the gendering of this gaze: that it is the look of masculine dominion that underpins the degrading relationships of slavery. This is the point to which Elizabeth Barrett Browning will return fifty years later, in 1848, in her powerful anti-slavery poem, 'The Runaway Slave at Pilgrim's Point'.[72] Barrett Browning's poem should be read as a response to the anti-slavery poems of this former generation of women poets, but cast in the particular intellectual concerns of her time, namely the new emphasis on biological inheritance, and an emerging science of race, which would emphasise colour and physiognomy. In 'The Runaway Slave', then, the slave woman's child is the product of her rape by the slave owner, and inherits the colour and eyes of his father. In this mid-nineteenth century version, the slave woman will kill her child not to save it, but rather to avoid *its* gaze: Medea slays the Medusa.

Scene 3: The bad mother: Cook, Hawkesworth, and the erotics of looking

The campaigns against slavery drew attention in a dramatic way to the moral problems endemic to the whole project of travel and discovery, and, in particular, the kinds of relationship to be assumed between people of different colours and customs. There were, however, nobler forms of voyaging. For evangelical writers, such as Hannah More, the recent expeditions to the South Pacific presented an antidote to slavery's inhumanities, and Captain Cook was the golden hero of discovery's better side. Had other travellers possessed Cook's 'gentle mind', his 'love of arts', and of 'humankind', More muses in 'Slavery: A Poem', 'Discoveries had not been a curse to man!':

> Then, blessed Philanthropy! Thy social hands
> Had linked dissevered worlds in brothers bands;
> Careless, if colour, or if clime divide;
> Then, loved, and loving, man had lived and died.
> (lines 236–42)

In a similar vein, the anti-slave trade campaigner, Capel Lofft, celebrates the humanitarian effects of Cook's expedition in a long poem on the glories of science, *Eudosia* (1781). He calls attention to Cook's 'life-preserving arts', and the 'mutual benefit to commerce, and the improvement of human society, with the increase of happiness' brought by scientific exploration, 'if we could quit the unphilosophical and impolitic idea, of a supposed acquisition of such places on the pretended idea of occupancy, which has no foundation where countries are already inhabited.'[73]

When More's poem was published, Cook had been dead for nine years – murdered in Hawaii in 1779 in a scuffle with natives, the exact details of which are still a matter of dispute.[74] His untimely, and in most eyes, heroic, death was an important component in the mythologies that grew up around him: Cook was the good traveller, who had embarked on a process of civilisation, softening the manners of primitives, whose dangerous savagery was demonstrated all too clearly in the mortal attack of the marauding natives. But it was also evident in the accounts of the customs of native people, and not least in reports that Otahetians (Tahitians) killed their new-born children as a form of birth control. At the centre of these accounts of Captain Cook, therefore, lay another instance of Rousseau's topos of infant violation – but one that is markedly different from the versions so far examined. In this new context, child murder becomes an attribute of native exoticism; and the spectator either a defender of moral virtue, or a licentious voyeur. The easy slippage between the two roles made this the most troubling version of the scene to be encountered.

For the most part, Captain Cook is represented as the defender of moral virtue. In a number of hagiographic works written on his death, he figures as the beneficent father of foreign peoples, nurturing them, and inculcating in them civilised values, which are usually represented through images of British domesticity. Scenes of his own domestic context, his 'cherish'd scene of home', watched over by his 'faithful' wife, as Helen Maria Williams writes in 'The Morai: An Ode', are contrasted with the dangerous foreign terrains he braved, the 'raging wave', the 'wild abyss', which in the end proved fatal to the gentle hero. Nevertheless, Williams concludes, 'The ruder nations of the earth / Shall oft repeat thy honor'd name; / While infants catch the frequent sound, / And learn to lisp the oral tale.'[75] Children and savages are deftly drawn together into Cook's large family, all gratefully subordinated to the kindly patriarch. Cook, the discoverer, is the civiliser, and global domesticator.

Anna Seward, in her 'Elegy on Captain Cook', is more explicit about Cook's achievements in this respect. Where Cook has been, she claims, 'chasten'd love in softer glances flows', and 'with new fires parental duty glows'. She explicates further: 'Captain Cook observes, in his second voyage, that the women of Otaheite were grown more modest, and that the barbarous practise of destroying their children was lessened.'[76] Cook, the good father, protects children from the murderous attacks of their own lascivious mothers. The preserver of infant life, he quite literally plays out the metaphorical role of child-loving civilisation. But equally, the very same terms would be used to express misgivings about his moral qualities. The poet William Cowper, once himself an enthusiastic supporter of Cook, became suspicious when he read of Cook's pleasure in the adoration he inspired in the native people. Because he consented to be treated as a god, Cowper reasoned, Cook deserved the same punishment as another usurper – Herod – the archetypal child murderer.[77] From the good father, to the very worst, the moral questions raised by Cook's controversial figure were encompassed by the capacious figure of child murder.

Seward's positive views on Cook's achievements were based on the account of Cook's second voyage. Andrew Kippis, Cook's first biographer, found similar cause to celebrate Cook's achievements, although he puts a different slant on it. For him, it was not that Cook had civilised the natives himself, but that he had corrected a common – and appropriately French – misapprehension about the lascivious lives of Otahetians. The notion that the people of Otaheite lived lives of sexual abandon had become popular in Europe, largely from the reports of recent travellers. The French explorer, Bougainville, who had led a voyage to the South Pacific that coincided with Cook's first voyage, had reported on the sexual licence enjoyed by the native people and extended to the visiting Europeans, an environment of sexual freedom that was the subject of Diderot's *Supplément au voyage de Bougainville* (written in 1772).[78] In Britain, the scandal of Otahetian promiscuity was circulated by John Hawkesworth in his notorious accounts of the South Pacific expeditions, his *Voyages*. In these he reported on the existence of a sexually permissive society known as the Arreoy (*Arioi*), made up of 'the principal people' of Otaheite, 'in which every woman is common to every man; thus securing a perpetual variety as often as their inclination prompts them to seek it...'[79] The Arreoy, according to Hawkesworth, considered children to be an obstacle to pleasure, and smothered them at birth. Kippis claimed that these reports had inflicted an 'injustice... [on] the women of Otaheite and the neighbouring isles,' and one of the 'agreeable effects of Captain Cook's second voyage' was his ability to correct these. According to Kippis: 'Chastity is so eminently the glory of that sex, and, indeed, is so essentially connected with the good order of society, that it must be a satisfaction to reflect that there is no country, however, ignorant or barbarous, in which this virtue is not regarded as an object of moral obligation.'[80] The spectacle of Otahetian licentiousness, therefore, was a fiction designed, in part by the scurrilous Hawkesworth, merely to titillate European readers. Cook's achievement was not to have civilised the natives, but rather to have, in a sense, civilised the British, to have cleaned up their reading material, and restored virtue to the page. Cook himself had been sharply critical of Hawkesworth's account of his voyage, and decided as a result to maintain authorial control over the accounts of subsequent expeditions.

John Hawkesworth, a well-connected and moderately successful writer of miscellaneous works, from oriental tales to oratorios, had been commissioned in 1771 by Lord Sandwich, the first lord of the admiralty, to produce the official account of the expeditions to the South Pacific.[81] Sandwich – a man whose notoriety for debauchery went before him – gave him the journals that had been composed on the various voyages, including John Byron's account of his navigation across the Pacific in the Dolphin in 1765, and Cook's journal from his first voyage on the Endeavour from 1768 to 1771. He also passed on the records of Joseph Banks, who had accompanied Cook in his capacity as a scientific expert. Hawkesworth saw his role as author of the *Voyages* as that of a populariser and entertainer; the resulting work was a massive best-seller and a commercial success for both Hawkesworth, who sold his manuscript for the handsome price of £6000, and for his publishers, Cadell and Strahan.[82]

In constructing the work, however, Hawkesworth showed little circumspection for his sources. He invented a first person narrator, as the protagonist of all four voyages, whom he claimed, would 'bring[] the Adventurer and the Reader nearer together', and 'intersperse[d] such sentiments and observations as my subject should suggest'. The result is an odd compendium of the separate voyages, in which Hawkesworth's sentimental and often prurient sensibility constantly obtrudes.[83] The participants in the expeditions, like Cook, were appalled by the inaccuracies that resulted. Other readers, however, were offended less by its inaccuracies than its indecencies. Hawkesworth, demoralised by the adverse responses, died the following year, reputed by some to have committed suicide with an 'immoderate dose of opium'.[84]

Hawkesworth emphasised the sexual licence of Otahetians throughout. In Wallis's journey, he reports on the 'wanton ladies' who have no virtue. In later sections, the account of the customs of the Arreoy comes to epitomise the tantalising degradation of such a permissive society. The Arreoy is an inverted, almost parodic, vision of domesticity. Should any woman succumb to the 'instinctive affection which Nature has given to all creatures for the preservation of their offspring', he writes, she is only able to 'spare the life of her infant' if she is able to find a man who is willing to 'patronise' her child, and in this case both she and the man would be expelled from the society, and 'forfeit all claim to the privileges and pleasures of Arreoy for the future'. Such is the Arreoy antipathy to the virtues of motherhood, that they possess a 'term of reproach', 'Whannownow, meaning "bearer of children"', 'though', he adds, lest we are swayed by the thought of free love in Otaheite, none but a mother 'can be more honourable in the estimation of wisdom and humanity, of right reform, and every passion that distinguishes the man from the brute.'[85] The Arreoy thus presents Hawkesworth with a compelling image of the negation of the domestic ideals of motherhood: the Arreoy mother who smothers her child so as not to be interrupted in the 'pleasures of her diabolical prostitution'.[86]

The emphasis on the diabolical nature of the Otahetian women is Hawkesworth's contribution to the narrative. Joseph Banks, from whom Hawkesworth had taken his account almost word for word, is no less shocked by the custom 'so devilish, inhuman, and contrary to the first principles of human nature'; but he casts no particular blame on the women. Rather Banks reserves sole blame for the men: 'this custom as indeed it is natural to suppose owes...its existence chiefly to the men'.[87] Excessive patriarchal power is once again the problem; Banks sees in the customs of the Arreoy another instance of the tyrannical father – the very same motif of primitive tyranny exemplified by Byron's Patagonian father. Hawkesworth's recasting of this story, however, shifts the spotlight to the murderous mother and, most importantly, her 'diabolical desires'. The change of focal point is crucial. Hawkesworth presents another refiguring of the Rousseau spectacle of infant suffering: but now it is the mother who kills her own child, and the spectator witnesses not her virtuous pity, but her murderous acts, and her horrible lust. No longer a scene of pity, the spectacle of infant suffering has been transformed into something more like pornography – a spectacle of degraded and violent female desire. No wonder that Kippis would applaud Cook's reports of Otaheitian virtue.

Hawkesworth conveys a strong sense of the illicitness of looking, an anxiety about witnessing these lewd events so strong, that it begins to seem as though *no one* has actually seen them. Banks, in his account, refers to 'one of our gentlemen', who 'saw part of one but I believe very little of their real behaviour tho' he saw enough to make him give credit to what we had been told.'[88] But Hawkesworth omits this passage, not admitting to any of his 'gentlemen' being witness to the show. What he does write follows Banks fairly closely (my emphasis):

It is not fit that a practice so horrid and so strange should be *imputed* to human beings upon slight *evidence*, but I have such as abundantly *justifies* me in the account I have given. [...] [B]oth myself and Mr Banks when particular persons have been pointed out to us as members of the Arreoy, have *questioned* them about it, and received the account that has been here given from their own lips.[89]

The long and short of it is that he has no first-hand evidence. Nevertheless, he affects a solemn tone here and a vocabulary of a judicial investigation that suspends us between the court and the scientific enquiry. He even calls on the authority of Banks – the real man of science. Hawkesworth is in the business of accrediting facts and he will call on whatever means he can. This is partly a defence against the imputation that the events are of his own imagination – his own vile fantasy – an accusation he seems eager to fend off: 'There is a scale in dissolute sensuality which these people have ascended', he writes, 'wholly unknown to every other nation whose manners have been recorded from the beginning of the world to the present hour, and which no imagination could possibly conceive'.[90] 'No imagination' – not even his – could summon these scenes.

This play between the pleasures of witnessing what one shouldn't, and the realm of fantasy, is crucial to the structure of pornography, and while Hawkesworth's account of the Arreoy's sexual practices is mild in comparison with the explicit nature of eighteenth-century pornography – Hawkesworth's lewderies pale in comparison with a work such as Cleland's *Fanny Hill* (1748–9)[91] – it nevertheless draws on the very conventions that pornography exploits. Hawkesworth's anxiety of witnessing is structural here: the various screens through which he presents the sexual material intensify its pleasures, turning the scene of witnessing into a kind of 'peek-a-boo'. He tantalises us with reports of provocative dancing, sexual acts, and cruel murders – possibly witnessed, possibly not.

Hawkesworth's account of the Arreoy spawned a number of poems, which picked up on the themes of debauched maternity in the idyllic island. All of them skated a thin line between titillation and higher purposes. *Otaheite: A Poem*, for instance, published anonymously in 1774, expresses the pious wish for the reform of native people, through the Christian ministry of the British, who will 'rise the Teachers of Mankind', 'pour[ing] radiant Beams' of enlightenment on the fallen race. But what is striking here, especially in the light of Hawkesworth's coyness, is the detail in which the scenes of decadence are described. After 'The wanton dance, the Love-inspiring song', the poet finally brings us to the scene of murder, when 'cruel Passions these calm seats infest, / And stifle[s] Pity in a Parent's breast? / Does here MEDEA draw the vengeful Blade'. Exploiting the conventions of Senecan tragedy, foregrounded in the poem's epigram from Seneca's *Medea*, it focuses on the pain of the baby, and the lust of the mother:

> Ah! see in vain the little suppliant plead
> With Silent Eloquence to check the Deed:
> He smiles unconscious of th'uplifted knife,
> And courts the Hand that's arm'd against his Life.
> Not his last sighs the Mother's Bosom move;
> She dooms his Death, her sacrifice to Love:
> Impatient hastes her am'rous vows to plight,
> And seals with Infant Blood the barb'rous Rite.
> Reclin'd upon her Lover's panting Breast,
> See in his Arms the beauteous Murd'ress prest![92]

Unlike in Hawkesworth's account of the Arreoy, we are invited to watch, not only the innocent child as he faces his executioner-mother, but also the mother embracing her lover's 'panting breast'. Indeed, the scene is striking for the way it shifts from the murder to the embrace, implying that the murder of the child – ritualised as 'sacrifice' – is in itself a sexual act. Sex and violence merge here, the infant's blood becoming the blood of passion.

Otaheite: A Poem is presented as a call for the conversion of native people to British modes of social and sexual propriety. But other poems turn the conceit around, and see the Otahetian customs as the basis for a satire of British corruption. For instance, *An Epistle (Moral and Philosophical) from an Officer at Otaheite to Lady Gr**v*n*r with Notes Critical and Histori-cal* (1774) attributed to John Courtenay, the politician and reformer, and *Seventeen Hundred and Seventy-Seven; or, a Picture of the Manners and Char-acters of the Age in a Poetical Epistle from a Lady of Quality* (1777), attributed to the Irish poet William Preston, the Arreoy customs are summoned as a satirical mirror to the aristocratic coteries of London society, whose various vices and corruptions were the scandal of the day. Lady Grosvenor, invoked in Courtenay's poem, was the unfaithful wife of Earl Grosvenor, who had been involved in a high-profile adultery case in 1770 involving the king's brother.[93] In his poem, Courtenay compares with mock seriousness the women of London to the Otaheitian woman, who 'stab[s] the smiling offspring of her womb'; in England, on the other hand, 'population teems around the land; / As thorn-trees by inoculation bear / The juicy apple, and the luscious pear' as women 'by a *strange* embrace, / Yield to their Lords an unresembling race'.[94] The thorn-tree, a traditional reference to illegitimacy, and a term which is frequently invoked in these poems, un-derlines the message.[95] In Preston's poem, the rapacious sexual energies of the 'Lady of Quality' are summoned through her enthusiastic expressions of the desire to learn from the Otahetians their 'arts of pleasure', including those in which 'Intruding babes shall bleed as soon as burn, / And pleasure's bloom divested of its thorn.'[96]

The latter poem is supposedly addressed to Omiah, an Otahitian native who had come to England with Cook's first expedition. To all intents and purposes, Omiah was a scientific curiosity, to be displayed alongside other trophies that had been collected and brought back to England.[97] Omiah attended London salons, and was a constant guest of the Earl of Sandwich at his country home in Hitchinbrook; Reynolds painted his portrait in oriental dress in 1775, and William Parry painted him with Banks and Solander – Omiah barefoot in classical robes, the others in modern dress – before he was returned to his island home on Cook's next voyage.[98] Many of the satirical poems include references to Omiah, including, for instance, a series of lewd poems on the sexual peccadilloes of Joseph Banks by John Scott.[99] With mock scholarliness they mimic Banks's scientific endeavours, while at the same time pursuing lewd and scatological themes.

Other satirical poems labour the fact that the establishment figures behind the expeditions to the South Pacific were themselves well-known rakes of London society, involved in sexual scandals, and belonging to clubs and coteries not unlike that of the Arreoy in Otaheite. In a footnote to the still un-ascribed poem, *Omiah's Farewell inscribed to the Ladies of London* (1776), a reference to the Arreoy is explained – with a heavy wink – as 'a place or coterie of general intrigue'.[100] A prominent offender in this regard was the Earl of Sandwich. In *Omiah's Farewell* there are covert and satirical references to Lord Sandwich, the 'gallant Peer, the Neptune of this day', and his mistress, the singer Martha Ray (who later lent her name to Wordsworth's famous child-killer in 'The Thorn' [1798]), 'a coelestial Ray' who ravishes him with her song. *Omiah's Farewell* marked Omiah's return to Otaheite in 1776, but before he left he had become entangled with an affair that would lead to the murder of Martha Ray, in 1779. As we shall see in Chapter Three, in a neat piece of role reversal, Omiah would later be remembered not as the object of the British pornographic gaze, but rather as himself the secret witness to Ray's indiscretions.[101]

The reports of the Arreoy filter into British culture as a horrific vision of native debauchery, a pornographic fantasy, and a source of lewd references. As the third of the variants on the Rousseauian scene of infant suffering, it completes the range of variations on this spectatorial event. In the three versions that I have identified, spectacles of infant suffering are used in different ways: as a representation of primitive tyranny within the supposedly objective condescension of the explorer reflecting the superiority of

British modes of government; as the inspiration of humanitarian pity; and to provoke erotic titillation. As these scenes circulate, what is striking is the easy mobility between them. In this light, it is important to recognise that these scenes of infant murder were part of a broader network of related images that drew notions of sexual regulation alongside discussions of political authority on the one hand, and humanitarian pity on the other, exposing the very entangled nature of these themes. Thus, one way in which ideas about Otaheitian debauchery functioned was as a corrective to both the new form of political authority presented through the critique of tyranny conveyed by the primitive child murder, and the destabilising potential of the humanitarian campaigns, their appeal to sympathy for the poor and powerless, and the levelling impact this might have. For what was the promiscuous Arreoy woman, eschewing the delights of motherhood, other than the corollary of the effeminate man, the consequence of the softened manners of fathers parodied in Colman's *Preludio*? And on the other hand, was not the murderous Medea of the South Pacific a vicious version of the Medea slave woman, described so powerfully by Raynal, presenting an effective way of undermining the rhetorical potency of the rhetoric of humanitarian concern?

Given the complexity of meanings that are implicit in the Rousseauian topos, and the very flexible boundaries between them, William Meredith's appeal to the sentiments of the men of parliament through the scene of infant suffering in his 1772 speech for the repeal of the 1624 child-murder statute was probably bound to fail to convince. For the very same scenario that he evoked to raise the sympathies of parliamentarians for innocent babies and defenceless women, the double victims of lechery and vice, could so easily slip into a scene of lechery itself – something closer to Hawkesworth's risqué accounts of women's own licentiousness. Moreover, discussions of child murder in these decades were primarily opportunities to stage a working through of issues of masculine subjectivity that had only a tangential connection to the human dramas of single women and their illegitimate offspring, which criminal cases of child murder evoked.

When the reform of this antiquated statute was finally effected thirty years later in 1803, a dramatic shift in the focus of the discussion of child murder had taken place. As will be seen, at the turn of the nineteenth century, child murder was no longer an act used primarily as a way of exploring the nuances of masculine sentiment. The primary focus of discussions of child murder would become the criminal acts of women.

CHAPTER 3

1798/1803: Martha Ray, the mob, and Malthus's Mistress of the Feast

1798: BLAKE AND THE POLITICS OF CHILD MURDER

In 1790, William Blake included a macabre piece of advice in his notoriously cryptic 'Proverbs of Hell' in *The Marriage of Heaven and Hell*: 'Sooner murder an infant in the cradle than nurse an unacted desire.' Its scandalous implications that seem to teeter on the brink of incitement to murder have puzzled critics ever since its publication. The proverb derives some intelligibility, however, from its context in the 1790s, notably the French Revolution of 1789, and the British response. As we shall see, Blake flags a new area of debate that will be played out through the idea of child murder, which marks a new phase in the history of its rhetoric.[1]

Linda Colley's *Britons* has highlighted the extent to which the formation of British national identity was grounded in an enduring Francophobia throughout the eighteenth century.[2] There was, then, nothing new about the fact of vituperative antipathy to France in the 1790s. A great deal of pre-1789 Francophobia had crystallised around the figure of the foppish libertine man[3] – such as that witnessed in George Colman's irreverent satire on the Frenchman, Noverre's choreography in his *Medea and Jason* discussed in the previous chapter. What was new about Francophobia in the 1790s, the tone of which was set by Edmund Burke's enormously influential *Reflections on the Revolution in France* (1790), was the way in which the figure that emblematised social and political disorder in revolutionary France was now less the foppish male than the sexually voracious woman. Female sexual license, supposedly encouraged by the liberalisation of family laws that took place during the Revolution,[4] became a frequent sign of general political disorder and social mayhem in France. Indeed, revolutionary France came to be represented through various figures of female debauchery: the prostitute, the actress, the unmarried mother, the mob of licentious women. In his *Letters*

68

on a Regicide Peace of 1796, Burke highlights the 'mother without being a wife', a vaunted heroine of revolutionary society, as the most contemptuous figure of French social disorder.[5] Very often these figures of female vice, as we shall see, were associated with child murder. The terms of abuse that associated sexual licentiousness with revolutionary activity were frequently transferred to British radicals too, especially women such as Mary Wollstonecraft, for whom the Revolution did indeed represent new possibilities for female emancipation.

For Blake, another strong counter-voice to the conservative backlash in Britain, the free expression of sexual desire was in itself the articulation of revolutionary spirit, a means of throwing off the repressive forces of the *ancien régime*. Hence his proverb, 'Sooner murder an infant in the cradle than nurse an unacted desire': an admonition against sexual repression, that it is better even to kill a child than to repress a desire. His proverb operates within the same realm of associations as the rhetoric of counter-revolution, but corrects the view that revolution causes child murder. In the voice of the devil, Blake inverts the vocabulary of reaction, and speaks to the revolutionary potential of sexual desire, and the murderous effects of repression.

This background provides a useful context for understanding the change in emphasis in discussions of child murder in Britain that took place in the 1790s. As we saw in Chapter Two, in the 1770s and 1780s, the scene of child murder tended to be used to present a flexible scenario for exploring a range of emotions in male spectators, and to provide a grammar of emotional response. In the 1790s, the focus of discussions of child murder shifted away from the effects of witnessing, and transferred instead to the perpetrator of the deed, who was invariably a woman. In so far as child murder continued to provide a scene of fantasy, the fantasy had solidified around the murderous threat of women – and it is a fantasy that had strong social and political connotations.

Two versions of the female child-killer will emerge in this period. The first of these is that of the unmarried and destitute mother, who kills her child in poverty and emotional despair. Blake possibly had such a woman in mind when producing the engravings that surround 'Holy Thursday', in *Songs of Experience*. Michael Phillips notes that a child found dead in Lambeth marshes in February 1793 may have been Blake's inspiration for his depiction of a woman, standing in a stylised pose, like a gravestone over the body of a dead baby, as an accompaniment to his searing indictment of society:

> Is this a holy thing to see
> In a rich and prosperous land,
> Babes reducd to misery
> Fed with cold and usurous hand?[6]

There is no sense that she herself has committed violence on the child, and her act is not represented in the text either. Instead, the poem encourages us to see the child's death as the responsibility of the 'cold and usurous hand' of society more generally.

Wordsworth's version of a similar figure is a more widely shared one, and in fact, as we shall see, is something of a prototype for subsequent literary representations of child murderers. This is Martha Ray, whose story is told in 'The Thorn', composed in the spring of 1798, and published in the first edition of the *Lyrical Ballads* later the same year. 'The Thorn' is narrated by a character described by Wordsworth, in a note appended two years later, as someone like 'a Captain of a small trading vessel for example', who had retired 'to some village or country town of which he was not a native, or in which he had not been accustomed to live.'[7] In the course of the poem he pieces together Martha Ray's story from local gossip: twenty years after abandonment by her lover, Stephen Hill, Martha Ray sits at the same spot on the moor, by a thorn bush, a muddy pond, and a hill of moss; all these features are thought to mark the grave of her infant, whose birth and death are presumed by the villagers, but never proved. Martha Ray, the probable child-killer, thus becomes a constituent part of a haunted landscape, a terrain that memorialises her loss and longing. A painting by Sir George Beaumont from 1803, based on Wordsworth's work nicely conveys the sense of the eeriness of the landscape, as Martha Ray, in her blood red cloak, crouches, like a 'jutting crag', beneath a brooding sky, confronting the menacing shape of the thorn bush, which here resembles a lightning bolt or an electric charge.[8]

Wordsworth's rendition of the perpetrator of child murder, in which madness, maternity, and elemental nature are woven together, becomes a new and pervasive image of pathetic womanhood, and a determinant in a frequently evoked plot throughout the nineteenth century. The particular combination of insanity, destitution, and rurality comes to prevail in nineteenth-century accounts of child murder. Nevertheless, it is important to bear in mind that Martha Ray appears less a reflection of a social reality than a contribution to an argument about the political effects of women, the social function of the family, and the need to promote reproduction and regulate female sexuality at the end of the 1790s. Indeed, she is another version of the 'mother without being a wife' – elsewhere, by turns, the heroine and the scourge of revolutionary society.

Against a background of extreme political turbulence at home, when fears of a French invasion were exacerbated by the republican rebellion in Ireland in 1798, and government clamp-downs on radical organisations were at their most severe,[9] the invention of the figure of Martha Ray, as the deranged and dispossessed mother who kills her child, is in a curious way a characteristically English response to the politically threatening idea of the sexually independent woman. This is lent weight by the fact that 1798, the year of the *Lyrical Ballads*, also saw the appearance of another response to these same issues, a work of profound and far-reaching influence – Malthus's *Essay on the Principle of Population*. Malthus goes so far as to make the unregulated reproductive female body the origin of all social ills, raising the stakes of feminine sexual unruliness still further.[10] While Burke had seen female illegitimate sexuality as a manifestation of the horrors of revolutionary society, both Wordsworth in 'The Thorn' and Malthus relocate the problem of female sexuality in nature, dissipating its political threat, but generalising its social dangers. Wordsworth and Malthus thus both respond to the political risks posed by women at the end of the eighteenth century by absorbing dissident femininity into nature.

Despite strong differences of opinion on population and political econ-omy, Wordsworth and Malthus had a shared understanding of nature as a regulatory power.[11] Both personify Nature as a female, but one who is neither a mother nor a wife, rather a teacher, nurse, or guardian. For both Malthus and Wordsworth, Nature is custodian of the moral order, regulator of resources, and disciplinarian. And while in Wordsworth's work, Nature is an essentially benign tutelary and admonitory force who 'foster[s] alike by beauty and by fear',[12] Malthus attributes to her a more sinister aspect, especially in the notorious second edition of his essay, published in 1803. Here she makes a dramatic appearance in the person of Dame Nature, the mistress of the feast, who expels all but the deserving poor from her bounties, abandoning her charges to the certain death of starvation.

This is the second of the two child-murdering figures. It is prefigured in Blake's proverb, in the idea of the nurse. While the proverb does not invoke an embodied figure of a nurse, nevertheless, its meanings turn around the verb 'to nurse', which here acts as both a metaphor for repression (as in 'to nurse' or retain 'unacted desires'), and a metonym for murder (the child will be murdered 'in the cradle' where one would otherwise nurse it). As in other works by Blake, the idea of nursing is thus given wholly negative connotations – in this case the act of nursing by association is equated with child murder. In the 'Nurse's Song' in the *Songs of Experience*, for example, the nurse is a sinister figure driven by envy of her charges; and the accompanying image to 'Infant Sorrow' in the same collection depicts a nurse who might be seen to be in a pose of murderous rage over her infant charge. Blake, however, is not the only writer to identify professional women, like the Nurse, as potential child-killers, figures of female authority who are not mothers, but guardians or supervisors, and whose ministry of care is of a professional kind, and implemented with cold passion. Throughout the nineteenth century we will encounter various versions of this figure – the nurse, the foster mother, midwife, abortionist, or baby farmer – all fatal carers for infant lives, and all of whom insinuate themselves, with their cool efficiency and regulatory zeal, in imaginative and other literature throughout the century.

The focus on women in the discussions of child murder in the 1790s introduces a new stability to a discourse that, during the previous decades, as we saw in Chapter Two, had been a flexible arena for the exploration of different forms of masculine subjectivity. Nevertheless, the doubling of the female killer, its split into two contrary personae in the 1790s, means that child murder retains its highly complex and controversial meanings. It also accentuates an unmistakeable misogyny in the discourse of child murder – so that the murder of children, from this point onwards, is usually associated with the horror of femininity.

WORDSWORTH'S 'THE THORN'

We turn first to Martha Ray, Wordsworth's 'wretched' woman who inhabits the wild landscape of the moor, who is:

> . . . known to every star,
> And every wind that blows;
> And there beside the thorn she sits
> When the blue day-light's in the skies,
> And when the whirlwind's on the hill,
> Or frosty air is keen and still.[13]

Her familiarity to 'every star' and 'every wind' is striking, particularly when we recall that Wordsworth took Martha Ray's name from a London socialite who could not have been more alien to the elements. The first Martha Ray was no literary invention, but a real person, with whom the poet had a number of personal connections. But for him, this first Martha Ray would have had more in common with a very different kind of woman than the destitute Martha of the moor: those city women of impugned virtue, who, according to *The Prelude*, the poet had encountered in London – women who were 'to open shame / Abandoned, and the pride of public vice'.[14]

The first Martha Ray was the kept mistress of John Montagu, the notoriously debauched Earl of Sandwich, First Lord of the Admiralty. We met them both in Chapter Two, in connection with the expeditions to the South Pacific, which had been commissioned by Sandwich in 1771.[15] Ray was a singer, known as 'the Nightingale', who had been Sandwich's consort since 1763. The daughter of a stay-maker from Holywell Street, in London,[16] she was of humble family origins, but her beauty and talent had drawn her to the attention of Sandwich. She had children by him – the exact number is unclear, but in some accounts it is as many as nine – and some representations of Ray even emphasise her maternal virtues.[17] Sandwich was widely unpopular, in particular for his corrupt and ineffectual leadership of the disastrous campaigns against France in 1778 and 1779 in the American War of Independence. As we saw in Chapter Two, through her association with Sandwich, Martha Ray, his known confidante and suspected agent,[18] became the subject of lewd innuendo in political satires, in particular in poems produced in response to the expeditions to the South Pacific. In *Omiah's Farewell* (1776), for instance, she is the 'coelestial Ray', a woman of unconscionable sexual appetites, who provides pleasures for 'Neptune' (Sandwich), as well as for the Tahitian, Omiah, and indeed, by the end of the poem, for the entire British Navy.

There is no child murder in the story of the first Martha Ray. More even than her reputed sexual voraciousness, her fame derived from her own unforeseen and violent death: on 7 April 1779, she was shot dead by a disappointed lover as she left a performance at Covent Garden.[19] Serendipitously, the play she had just seen was Isaac Bickerstaffe's popular comedy of rural manners, *Love in a Village* (first performed in 1763), a tale of romantic intrigues and concealed identities, in which 'bumpkin love' is revealed to be as 'fashionably' and entertainingly 'vicious' as those of society circles. Ray's murderer was the Reverend James Hackman. At the time of the crime he had recently taken religious orders, but previously he had been in the army, and had met Ray when his regiment was stationed near Sandwich's country residence at Hinchingbrooke in 1772. They had fallen in love, and began a passionate affair. But when her feelings faded, and his hopes that she would leave Sandwich to marry him were dashed, Hackman followed her to Covent Garden, with two loaded pistols and one thought on his mind: suicide – the true destiny of a desperate lover. On seeing her, however, he claimed, 'a momentary phrenzy overcame me, and induced me to commit the deed I now deplore', 'to destroy her who was ever dearer to me'.[20]

This crime of passion became a celebrated case – discussed in detail in the daily press, remembered in diaries and memoirs, chatted about in private letters.[21] John Vardill, the author of *The Distracted Lover* (1779), a moralising poem based on the affair, claimed that 'the melancholy incidents which suggested the following poem, are so well known, that a recital of them would be superfluous'.[22] And James Boswell, who attended Hackman's trial, and travelled with him to his execution, commented that Hackman presented a lesson of universal application – a 'solemn... warning of the dreadful effects that the passion of love may produce, [to] all of us who have lively sensations and warm tempers'.[23] The *Case and Memoirs* of both Hackman and Ray were published and reprinted many times, and in the year following the trial, an opportunistic writer and impoverished baronet, Sir Herbert Croft, produced a work that purported to be the correspondence of Ray and Hackman, which enjoyed considerable commercial success.[24] *Love and Madness: A Story Too True* was in effect an epistolary novel that told the tragic story of the decline of a man of feeling, his descent into insanity, and subsequent end. Its focus was Hackman's intended suicide, which gave Croft a pretext for incorporating a long digression on the subject of Chatterton, the prodigious teenage poet and forger, who had killed himself in 1770. Indeed, Croft went so far as to include in *Love and Madness* a number of Chatterton's letters which he had fraudulently obtained from Chatterton's sister – a point that kept his work under scrutiny at least until the turn of the century.[25] Details of the Ray and Hackman case continued to fascinate readers well into the nineteenth century, witnessed in multiple entries in *Notes and Queries* in the 1860s, speculating on, and clarifying points of arcane interest – the date of Hackman's ordination, the occupation of Ray's father, or the place of her grave.

Wordsworth was likely to have known about the Ray and Hackman case through Croft's *Love and Madness*. In 1796, his friends, the poet Robert Southey and the bookseller and publisher, Joseph Cottle, had taken issue with Croft over his devious publication of Chatterton's letters, beginning a campaign that led eventually to their exposing Croft's dirty dealings with members of Chatterton's family in the press.[26] But Wordsworth had a connection with Ray that was even closer to home. At the time at which Wordsworth composed 'The Thorn', he was in the constant company of Martha Ray's small grandson. Martha Ray's son and the boy's father, Basil Montagu, was Wordsworth's friend; the two men are thought to have lodged together in London in 1795, having been introduced by William Godwin.[27]

Basil, the acknowledged son of Ray and Sandwich, was now estranged from his father for having married against his wishes. Basil's wife had since died, leaving him with his young son, also known as Basil. Recognising the difficulties of bringing up a young child in the city – Montagu at this stage was a law student in London – Wordsworth offered to look after and educate the child in return for a fee of £50 a year. Although payment was not always forthcoming from Montagu, William and his sister Dorothy did care for young Basil during the period in which William composed the *Lyrical Ballads*. And it was while walking on Quantock Hill with Dorothy and little Basil one stormy day in March 1798, that Wordsworth noticed the thorn that, by his own account, inspired the poem.[28]

The differences between the first Martha Ray, Montagu's unfortunate mother, and Wordsworth's poetic invention are nevertheless glaring, and why Wordsworth should have chosen to name his woman in 'The Thorn' thus has puzzled literary critics.[29] The first Martha was a society beauty, the second, a poor, destitute peasant; one was from the city, the other from the country; both were involved in love triangles, but while the first Martha was the centre of the triangle, the vied-for love object, the second was herself the cast-off lover, jilted for another woman. The second Martha probably killed her child; the first conspicuously did not. What the two Marthas do have in common, however, is that both were, or were presumed to be, illegitimate mothers; the illicit sex lives of both are unmistakably evident, embodied in their progeny. It is this that provides the link between these two different women. Indeed, Wordsworth's transformation of Martha Ray from the glamorous *femme fatale* whose sexual desire is, in the end, fatal to herself, to the sad, mad Martha, who represents a very different kind of danger, is revealing as an encoding of feelings about illegitimate female sexuality at the turn of the century.

The process by which Wordsworth transformed Martha Ray into the child-killer nonetheless cannot be explained simply. It is likely that a conglomeration of disparate factors converged. One such factor may have been the intriguing inclusion of the Otahetian, Omiah, in accounts of the Ray–Hackman affair, for embedded in this foreign figure are a set of ideas about excessive passion and its unnatural consequence – which turn the love-struck Ray into a potential child-killer.[30] As we saw in Chapter Two, Omiah had been brought back to England as an exotic specimen by Cook's first expedition, and had been a frequent house guest of Sandwich at Hinchingbrooke. In contemporary reports he is frequently presented as the naïve observer of the sexual intrigues there. The reformer Granville Sharp attempted to teach Omiah English language and proper English morals, and recorded Omiah's observations on Sandwich's irregular household:

There was an ink-stand on the table, with several pens in it. He took one pen, and laid it on the table, saying, 'There lies Lord S-' (. . . .) and then he took another pen, and laid it close by the side of the former pen, saying, 'and here lies Miss W[Ray]' . . .' and he then took a third pen, and placing it on the table at a considerable distance from the other two pens, as far as his right arm could extend, and at the same time leaning his head upon his left hand, supported by his elbow on the table, in a pensive posture, and said 'and there lie Lady S-, and cry!'[31]

For Sharp, Omiah is the noble savage, whose innocence allows him, unwittingly, to reveal the corruptions of degenerate aristocratic society. With a complement of sentimental gestures, the primitive man of feeling decries the dissolute morals to which he is witness. For other commentators, however, the innocence and sentimentality of Omiah, the noble savage, were to be treated more sceptically, particularly as the voyages to the South Pacific had revealed goings-on at least as exotic as those of the London aristocrats. As we saw in Chapter Two, according to reports of travellers, including Banks and Cook, life in Otaheite was no perfect idyll; rather, it was a place of promiscuity and vice, epitomised by the customs of the élite society, the Arreoy, whose licentious behaviour notoriously included the disposal of children.[32] At best, the Otahetians were held to mimic the licentiousness of English aristocrats; at worst, they represented new forms of vice to which English libertines could now aspire. In most retellings of the Ray–Hackman affair, therefore, Omiah plays a much more menacing role than in Sharp's representation of him as the naïve truth-teller; he tends to be cast in these as the spy who betrays the lovers to Sandwich, and is a motif of moral depravity.[33] For Croft, in *Love and Madness*, he is the sly voyeur – a degraded version of the gentleman spectator – who suspends his native allegiance to passion to tell tales to Sandwich; he is the 'child of nature' who 'nip[s] in the bud that favourite passion which his Mother Nature planted'. 'What will Oberea [the Otahetian queen] and her coterie say to this, Omiah, when you return from making the tour of the globe?' Croft has Ray say to Hackman. 'What would Rousseau say to it, my H.?'[34]

One of the effects of Omiah's inclusion in Croft's story is to transform Hackman and Ray's environment into an Otahetian world in which passion is all, and virtue nothing, and where obstacles to love – such as children – are annihilated. In this context, Ray's constant outpouring of maternal tenderness, invoking her 'poor, innocent, helpless babes' as the reason for not leaving Sandwich,[35] carries a sinister ambiguity. The first Martha Ray is no literal child-killer for sure, but the associations with Otaheite begin to implant grounds for imagining that her circumstances might make the disposal of her children inevitable. In the midst of hot, unnatural passion, innocent babes will be sacrificed.

The chain of association between the first Martha Ray and her child-murdering namesake is strengthened further by a scientific work by Erasmus Darwin, *Zoonomia: or the Laws of Organic Life* (1794–6), a work that Wordsworth asked Cottle to send him while he was working on 'The Thorn'.[36] In the taxonomy of diseases that constitutes the second part of the work, Darwin describes a condition he calls 'erotomania' or 'sentimental love': it is caused by excessive romantic love, and manifests itself in various kinds of violent, even murderous behaviour. According to Darwin, it is a condition more likely to flourish in society, especially a society influenced by the literary culture of sensibility, than in nature: it is 'described in its excess by romance-writers and poets', he writes, but, on the other hand, is 'not frequently observable in the brute creation, except perhaps', and here he inserts two interesting riders, 'in some married birds, or in the affection of the mother to her offspring'.[37] In this raw, natural state, then, the condition begins to illuminate a surprising connection between the maddening effects of both a kind of romantic love, and maternal love. The connection is pursued more revealingly in his description of the disease in its final stage. Two victims of fatal attacks of erotomania, it transpires, are Hackman and Medea:

> when a lover has previously been much encouraged, and at length meets with neglect or disdain; the maniacal idea is so painful as not to be for a moment relievable by the exertions of reverie, but is instantly followed by furious or melancholy insanity; and suicide, or revenge, have frequently been the consequence. As was lately exemplified in Mr Hackman, who shot Miss Ray in the lobby of the playhouse....
>
> The story of Medea seems to have been contrived by Ovid, who was a good judge of the subject, to represent the savage madness occasioned by ill-requited love. Thus the poet,

> > Earth has no rage like love to hatred turn'd,
> > Nor hell fury like a woman scorn'd.
> >   Dryden[38]

Interesting here is the quick passage from Hackman's 'furious or melancholy insanity' for 'suicide or revenge', which in the event, relieved itself by shooting Martha Ray, to Medea's 'savage madness', the 'fury 'of a 'woman scorn'd' – that turns not against Jason, her erstwhile lover, but against their own children. In Medea's case, her condition as scorned lover merges with that of mother, who in 'brute creation' we already know, is pathologically fond of her offspring. The two conditions for erotomania identified in the natural world conjoin: the 'woman scorn'd' and the mad, over-fond mother.

Darwin's erotomania suggests a neat link between the two Marthas: the first Martha, a victim of Hackman's disorder, the second a fellow-sufferer.

In particular the description of erotomania provides a purportedly clinical rationale for the creation of Wordsworth's character: a version of the sexualised woman as a violent and vengeful woman, but in a context in which that violence will be directed towards children. Martha Ray, 'scorn'd' by Stephen Hill, who 'to another Maid / Had sworn another oath' (lines 124–5), declines into mania:

> Poor Martha! on that woeful day
> A cruel, cruel fire, they say
> Into her bones was sent:
> It dried her body like a cinder
> And almost turn'd her brain to tinder.
>
> (lines 128–32)

The course of the disease described by Darwin determines the victim of her 'fury': like Medea, Martha kills her child, not her inconstant lover, Stephen. Darwin constructs for Wordsworth a particular form of female disorder – the cast-off lover moved by her disappointed passion to child murder.

Wordsworth describes Martha's mania in terms of its bodily effects, as a fire that literally 'dries' her body making it 'like a cinder' and her 'brain' like 'tinder'. In later versions of the poem, this visceral language is toned down and translated into the more familiar, stock terms of mental anguish: he writes in metaphors now of a 'pang' of 'dismay' entering her 'soul', and an unquenchable fire within her 'breast'.[39] But the somatic account in the earlier text shows how Wordsworth presents Martha's condition in pathological terms, so that her situation as an unmarried and abandoned mother becomes, in the end, a clinical condition.

This contextual material begins to show how Wordsworth found the elements for his child murderer in the first Martha Ray. But the new personality and environment that he gives her are striking for their link with local superstition. As critics have pointed out, the idea of superstition is central to the work. However, there has been a tendency simply to pass this off as an aspect of the poem's attention to the individual pathology of the narrator.[40] In this reading, critics follow Wordsworth's own lead in his 1800 note, in which he gives the poem a quasi-scientific purpose of presenting 'superstition' as a psychological condition. He claims that it is an attempt to 'exhibit some of the general laws by which superstition acts upon the mind', and as such is a case history, not unlike those that make up Darwin's medical treatise, *Zoonomia*. Thus he provides an aetiological description for the condition ('indolence', and, more vaguely, 'other predisposing causes'), together with an account of its likely subjects (men 'of slow faculties and deep feelings'). In this light, the events of the poem, including the murder, are the delusionary symptoms of the mind disordered by superstition. But Wordsworth's note has tended to skew interpretations of the poem, for in fact the original text presents an even more troubling degree of ambiguity around Martha Ray and her child. The poem itself locates superstition not in the individual disordered mind, but in the community and even in the landscape. The chain of events – her desertion by Stephen Hill, her likely pregnancy, the presumed murder of the child, its probable burial on the hill of moss – is based not merely on the aberrations of an individual superstitious mind, but on the shared beliefs of the community, the customary knowledge of the place and its past. It roots Martha Ray and her predicament deep in the fabric of rural life, and distinguishes her sharply from her city-based namesake.

There were precedents for Wordsworth to handle the subject in this way: as critics have pointed out, 'The Thorn' reworks a theme that is to be found in both traditional ballads, such as 'The Cruel Mother', but also in contemporary compositions, especially the sensational ballad by the German writer, G. A. Bürger, 'Des Pfarrers Töchter von Taubenheim', translated into English by Charles Taylor as 'The Lass of Fair Wone', and published in the *Monthly Magazine* in May 1796.[41] In all of these works, child murder is presented as the traditional response to unwanted pregnancy in rural communities, an idea that is endorsed by the ballad genre itself, the medium of customary knowledge. Wordsworth's 'The Thorn' reiterates these themes, but more significantly, it dramatises the peculiarly tantalising status of the knowledge of such acts of child murder – presumed to have taken place, but never authenticated. Thus the attempt to bring Martha Ray 'to public justice' by disinterring the body of the child stimulates an uncannily protective response from the landscape:

> ... the beauteous hill of moss
> Before their eyes began to stir;
> And for full fifty yards around,
> The grass it shook upon the ground.
> (lines 236–9)

It is as though Nature itself is implicated in the concealment of Martha Ray's guilt, condoning her probable act in sympathetic identification with her plight. Martha Ray and her dead baby are absorbed into nature: literally buried in the landscape, but also in the community's experience of nature. What is distinctive about this Martha Ray is that she embodies the special status of customary knowledge, and is herself a manifestation of superstition.

The ballad form and content of 'The Thorn' thus naturalise Martha Ray's condition – her unmarried status, the murder of the child, and her madness – as the stuff not merely of the narrator's superstitious mind, but part of the belief and landscape of traditional rural life.[42] The significance of this comes into focus when we recall the first Martha Ray – her urban location, her social mobility, her cosmopolitan connections, her luxury and theatricality, her promiscuity. Wordsworth's co-option of her for 'The Thorn' suggests a deliberate recasting of the figure of the unmarried mother, as a pathetic but traditional and indigenous form of deviancy.

THE FRENCH REVOLUTION AND THE PROBLEM OF WOMEN IN BURKE AND WOLLSTONECRAFT

In 1798, when Wordsworth composed and published 'The Thorn', he did so in the context of a highly contentious discussion of illegitimacy, female sexuality, and child murder that was inspired by the revolution in France. At that time, therefore, the *first* Martha Ray, the London courtesan of the corrupt politician, may have seemed more French than English. Indeed, for Wordsworth – whose early enthusiasms for the Revolution, his travels in France, his mid-decade links with the English Jacobins, especially Godwin, his later turn to the right, and his sympathies with Burke, have been well documented, not least by the poet himself – the encoding of French radicalism through images of promiscuous female sexuality and illegitimacy would have been thoroughly familiar.[43] And as the father of an illegitimate child in France, conceived during the revolutionary period, it is likely that they held special relevance.[44] While critics have already made a case for a biographical reading of 'The Thorn' – mostly reading it as an expression of Wordsworth's guilt for having abandoned his lover, Annette Vallon, and their child, Caroline[45] – read in the context of 1790s gender panic, the poem takes a new and absorbing turn.

Two years before 'The Thorn', Edmund Burke had claimed that infanticide was a quotidian feature of revolutionary society:

With the Jacobins of France, vague intercourse is without reproach; marriage is reduced to the vilest concubinage; children are encouraged to cut the throats of their parents; mothers are taught that tenderness is no part of their character; and to demonstrate their attachment to their party, that they ought to make no scruple to rake with bloody hands in the bowels of those who came from their own.[46]

In this hyper-dramatic climax to the first of his *Letters on a Regicide Peace* (1796), he emphasises the sexual disorder of revolutionary society, where the liberalisation of marriage laws is connected to infanticide and parricide. Such gothic confabulations were anticipated in his earlier *Reflections on the Revolution in France* (1790), a work that had set the terms for subsequent discussion in England of the Revolution. The episode in this that had attracted most attention was his sensational account of the storming of the palace of Versailles on 5 October 1789 by a parade of unruly women. In this scene, the virtue of the royal family, epitomised by the queen, 'almost naked' in her bed chamber, is attacked by a marauding mob, who pierce the queen's bed with 'an hundred strokes of bayonets and poniards', leave the palace 'swimming in blood, polluted by massacre, and strewed with scattered limbs and mutilated carcases', inflict 'promiscuous slaughter', and engage in ritualistic orgies of 'horrid yells, and shrilling screams, and frantic dances, and infamous contumelies, and all the unutterable abominations of the furies of hell, in the abused shape of the vilest of women'.[47]

Throughout the decade, following Burke, the Revolution is repeatedly associated with scenes of sexual excess and violence – usually instigated by women. Gillray's scatological cartoons exaggerate Burke's idiom: in his *Petit souper à la Parisienne, or A Family of Sans-Culottes refreshing after the fatigues of the day* (1792) (Fig. 3), he represents a cannibalistic feast of French revolutionaries: the sans-culottes, shown with bare behinds, defecating on the corpses of the king and queen, unnatural women eating human hearts, demonic children gorging on human entrails, and in the corner, a mother basting her baby, trussed like a chicken, on the fire. The figure of infanticide is common in counter-revolutionary imagery as a motif of social disorder. Indeed, Burke refers to the scene of 5 October at Versailles as 'this great history-piece of the massacre of the innocents', turning the royal family, the clergy, and the noble men, all the victims of mob violence, into the babies slaughtered by Herod, and the whole episode into a biblical story of innocence oppressed by evil. In fact, only a couple of guardsmen were killed and the royal family were conveyed forcibly, but nonetheless safely, to reside in Paris.[48]

For Burke, who in the *Reflections* laid such importance on the idea of inheritance as the very basis of traditional society, the emerging polity in France was profoundly disturbing. 'All their new institutions ... strike at the root of our social nature', he wrote in his *Letters on a Regicide Peace*, but none more so than their laws on marriage. 'Marriage' he claims, is 'the origin of all relations', the means by which the 'Christian Religion' has 'done more towards the peace, happiness, settlement, and civilization of the world,

Figure 3. James Gillray, *Petit souper à la Parisienne, or A Family of Sans-Culottes refreshing after the fatigues of the day* (1792)

than by any other part in this whole scheme of Divine Wisdom'.[49] For the French, however, according to Burke, it was 'no better than a common, civil contract'. Indeed, this had been the substance of a declaration in the National Assembly in September 1791, whereby marriage was taken out of the domain of church law, and established instead as a bond freely entered into by individuals and based on mutual love. The following year, the divorce laws were considerably liberalised, as the National Assembly had come to recognise divorce as a natural consequence of the Declaration of the Rights of Man.[50] Furthermore, there was radical new legislation on inheritance and succession affecting illegitimate children. In November 1793, it was declared that all those 'born out of wedlock between 14 July 1789 and 2 November 1793 should have the same rights of inheritance as legitimate children'.[51]

Burke's *Letters on a Regicide Peace* was one work that Wordsworth is known to have had in his possession in 1798,[52] and it is reasonable to presume that its discussion of the new family laws in France would at least have given him pause. His own illegitimate daughter had been born in Orleans on 15 December 1792 to Wordsworth's young love, the 'zealous Royalist',[53] Annette Vallon. Kenneth Johnstone has pointed out that Wordsworth's daughter was the same age as his young charge, Basil Montagu; and while Basil junior was not illegitimate, his father, Basil senior, was.[54] Indeed, the irregular family of Wordsworth's friend Basil, although a far cry from the radical notion of the family in revolutionary France, may neverthe-less have accrued new significance in the light of Burke's tirade; and the memory of Basil's mother, Martha Ray, the mistress of an aristocratic liber-tine, may have taken on the ghastly complexion of the sexual dissidents of the Revolution. Thus when Wordsworth recast her as the pathetic woman of the moor, static and strikingly inarticulate, we might speculate that he exorcised the traces of this newly dangerous libertine woman.

This chain of associations is strengthened when we remember that one of Burke's constant complaints about French political life was its new theatri-cality. For him, the National Assembly was no more than a stage on which declarations were made by 'certain personated characters', and observed by an audience – a feature that distinguished the French political process from that of the British parliament, with its air of a private debating club.[55] The declaration on the subject of the rights of inheritance, Burke writes,

was bought out in the figure of a prostitute, whom they called by the affected name of "a mother without being a wife". This creature they made to call for a repeal of the incapacities, which in civilised States are put upon bastards.[56]

For Burke, all politicians in the National Assembly were actors, but this spokesperson was doubly condemned for being a woman and an unmarried mother. For Burke, she is no more than a performing prostitute, a prime example of the egregious figure of the 'mother without being a wife'. A woman, unmarried but sexually free, an actress who performs in the political arena, who declaims the script of decisive political change – she is for Burke an icon of revolutionary barbarity, the embodiment of its worst threats. And she recalls the first Martha Ray, the Nightingale – herself a performer, a 'mother without being a wife', and moreover, a woman of renowned political influence through her intimacy with Sandwich.

Although the first Martha Ray and the rakish, aristocratic society in which she mixed were very definitely part of *ancien régime* culture, nev-ertheless counter-revolutionary rhetoric of the late 1790s drew together the debaucheries of *ancien régime* aristocracy – whose degenerative effects were in any case held in part responsible for the Revolution – with the sexual license of revolutionary society itself. Accordingly, Burke transferred the sexual decadence associated with aristocratic rakes, both in France and England, and exemplified by the lives of men such as Sandwich, to Jacobins, sans-culottes, and their sympathisers. There was one important difference, however: now the spotlight fell less on the sexual activities of debauched men, so much as on those more perverse and unnatural acts of women. The late 1790s saw an outpouring of scatological and misogynistic writings that associated women's erotic impulses with the political disorder of revolutionary France, and blamed women for the seepage of revolutionary ideas and behaviour into England. In this context, therefore, Wordsworth's reinvention of Martha Ray might be seen as a subtle and even to a degree sympathetic intervention in a terrain in which women are only vilified as the agents of mayhem.

Writers with a more explicitly conservative political agenda than Wordsworth were far less circumspect. T. J. Mathias, for instance, in his *The Pursuits of Literature: a Satirical Poem* (1797), a lengthy and profusely annotated work, deplored in overblown terms any democratising aspects of British literary culture of the 1790s: 'our peasantry now read the *Rights of Man* on mountains, and moors, and by the wayside; and shepherds make the analogy between their occupations and that of their governors'; and worse, 'our unsexed female writers now instruct, or confuse, us and themselves in the labyrinth of politics, or turn us wild with Gallic frenzy'.[57] It was Mathias that Richard Polwhele addressed in his deeply misogynistic poem, *The Unsex'd Females* (1798). Like Mathias, Polwhele complains of English women's Frenchification, their sexual dissolution, social disruption, and their ambiguity of gender; it is women's 'excessive wantonness', he claims, that leads directly to all kinds of social and political mayhem, including atheism and the destruction of the church.[58]

The charge that the French Revolution had incited English women to sexual profligacy was given certain credence by the fact that it had indeed spurred feminists in England to formulate their own case for equal rights in a spate of feminist writings that appeared in the 1790s. The most famous of these was Mary Wollstonecraft's powerful critique of marriage and sexual double standards, *A Vindication of the Rights of Woman* (1792). In 1798, however, the year after her death, Wollstonecraft herself was revealed to have been that most dangerous persona of the revolution – a 'mother without being a wife' – when a memoir by her husband, William Godwin, gave frank details of her life, including the fact that she had never married Gilbert Imlay, the father of her first child, Fanny.[59]

Rather than seeking to condone or incite vice, however, Wollstonecraft's work, including the *Vindication*, presented a highly principled attack on the sexual morals of men. In the same year that Godwin produced his memoir and in which Wordsworth wrote 'The Thorn', Godwin also brought to publication Wollstonecraft's unfinished novel, *The Wrongs of Woman; or Maria*. This was a scathing critique of the injustices of marriage and the libertinage of men. All the men in the novel are sexually profligate – even Darnford, Maria's accepted lover – and all the women are their victims. Thus her servant, Jemima, herself the illegitimate child of a servant, is raped by her master, and after an abortion, is corrupted by the vices of all the men with whom she has contact; and Maria is incarcerated in a madhouse by Venables, her dissolute husband, whose crimes include an attempt to prostitute her to a friend to pay off a gambling debt, and worse, the abduction and murder of their child. Maria's imprisonment in the asylum literalises the emotional, material, and moral degradation of women by marriage. Maria leaves the asylum, having formed a union on the basis of love with Darnford, but is shunned by society. Darnford is arrested and tried for adultery and seduction, charges for which Maria sends written deposition in his defence. In the course of the trial she claims a divorce from Venables, and denounces marriage on moral grounds: the law of marriage was 'made by the strong to oppress the weak', and had allowed her husband to '[violate] every moral obligation which binds man to man'. The judge, however, unimpressed, opposes her on the basis of English tradition, in a deliberately sub-Burkean vocabulary:

He had always determined to oppose all innovation, and the new-fangled notions which incroached on the good old rules of conduct. We did not want French principles in public or private life – and, if women were allowed to plead their feelings, as an excuse or palliation of infidelity it was opening a flood-gate for immorality.[60]

Nevertheless, his splenetic venting of opinion and prejudice in favour of the 'good old rules of conduct' here pales against the weight of Maria's closely reasoned account of her predicament, and the graphic details of her persecution. *The Wrongs of Woman* exposes not only the injustices of marriage as an institution, but also the embeddedness of these in the fabric of traditional English society. Indeed, the novel can be read as a riposte to Burke and the conservatives' inflammatory rhetoric, showing that the gothic consequences that they claimed for the Revolution are in fact quotidian events of English social life. Maria's incarceration, Jemima's rape and subsequent trials, Venables's debauchery, the abduction and murder of the child, and so on: all of these, she shows, are neither the stuff of revolutionary fervour, nor even gothic fiction, but events apparently sanctioned by English law.

Wollstonecraft's novel counters Burkean sensationalism with a Rousseauian mixture of sentimentality and Enlightenment appeals to reason. As in Rousseau, it is underpinned by a sense of the corrupting influences of civilisation, which it uses as the driving force for reform. In this respect the work is highly reminiscent of the reforming narratives of the 1770s discussed in the previous chapter, to the extent that it draws on the same vocabulary of abstract concepts (e.g., tyranny, enslavement, sacrifice) and dramatises them with similar motifs. The novel also makes powerful use of the figure of child murder. For Burke, child murder is on his list of atrocities committed by the mob, a sign of revolutionary debauchery. But Wollstonecraft, possibly by way of response, draws on the uses of child murder in the complex narratives of civilisation and reform drawn from the literature of the 1770s. Thus on the one hand, she uses child murder to invoke *ancien régime* tyranny, as in the murder held to have been committed by Venables, the dissolute father of Maria's child. On the other hand, in a more covert way, she draws on the notion of a sacrificial child murder that, as we saw in the previous chapter, was at the centre of many of the reform narratives of the late eighteenth century, in particular in anti-slavery literature. Directly recalling the Indian woman on the banks of the Oronooka, cited by William Alexander in his *History of Women*, who wished her own mother had 'kindly stifled [her] at [her] birth', Maria too 'lament[s] that she had given birth to a daughter', given 'the oppressed state of woman'.[61]

More troublingly, in the final fragment of the text, on it having been revealed that her daughter has not in fact been killed by Venables, Maria 'rest[s] the child gently on the bed, *as if afraid of killing it*' [my emphasis].[62] This expression of the containment of violence that is barely admitted reminds us of Raynal's extraordinary account of slave women who 'snatch... their children from the cradle, in order to strangle them in their arms, and sacrifice them with a fury mixed with a spirit of revenge and compassion.' The spirit of the virtuous child murderer emerges tantalisingly in this final fragment, invoking a history of associations between child murder and civic virtue. Her critics, however, are unlikely to have been sensitive to these echoes, and it is likely that the mention of child murder at the end of this unfinished novel would only confirm the author's moral degeneracy, and seal her irredeemable identification with the murderous ends of revolutionary fervour.

At the heart of the novel is a celebration of the virtues of motherhood, combined with an analysis of their fundamental incompatibility with existing marriage laws. Thus for many readers the novel would have provided a certain vindication for unwed mothers. Although strictly speaking

Maria is technically still married to Darnford, and her child legitimate, she nevertheless is identified as a 'mother without being a wife', the dissident single mother. In its representation of the unmarried mother, the novel parallels Wordsworth's 'The Thorn', providing the most positive version yet of Burke's monstrous figure. Unlike in Wordsworth's poem, the unmarried mother is not made mad by her destitution; rather, Wollstonecraft's Maria embraces her condition of destitution rationally as the inevitable result of masculine debauchery and institutional oppression. Thus in contrast to Wordsworth's Martha Ray, Wollstonecraft's Maria is definitely not mad, even though she spends much of the novel falsely imprisoned in a lunatic asylum.

In an early episode in this asylum, Maria encounters a woman who has been driven mad by love. This woman, referred to as the 'lovely maniac', is brought into the next room, and Maria momentarily identifies with her predicament. Maria listens to the 'maniac' sing 'the pathetic ballad of old Robin Gray', and is enraptured by her voice, 'so exquisitely sweet, so passionately wild'. The ballad tells the story of a woman who is compelled to marry a rich old man, instead of her true love, and it mirrors the singer's own predicament: 'she [the 'lovely maniac'] had been married, against her inclination, to a rich old man, extremely jealous . . . and that in consequence of his treatment, or something which hung on her mind, she had, during her first lying-in, lost her senses.' Curiously, this is the very same ballad that Herbert Croft had the first Martha Ray and Hackman refer to throughout their correspondence in *Love and Madness*, as a story that prefigured and framed their own tragedy as told by Croft. But in Maria's prison, the 'lovely warbler' – an epithet that reminds us again of the first Martha Ray, the Nightingale – is truly mad: 'a torrent of unconnected exclamations and questions burst from her, and interrupted by fits of laughter, so horrid, that Maria shut the door, and turning her eyes up to heaven, exclaimed – "Gracious God!"'[63] Maria's initial identification turns to horror as the real nature of the woman's insanity is revealed. Her mania here is no romantic conceit, but the ugly manifestation of an incurably manic state.

The 'lovely maniac' has led us back to both the first Martha Ray, and also to Wordsworth's reinvention of her. Both writers responded to the same cultural determinants and the same awareness of the highly politicised nature of female sexuality. Moreover, in situating Maria in proximity to madness, and in repudiating the maniac, Wollstonecraft implies a knowing resistance to a poetic response to female abandonment typified by Wordsworth's poem. For Wollstonecraft this meant grasping the opportunity to write the script of the virtuous female protagonist of revolutionary society. Wordsworth, on the other hand, whose incorporation of Martha Ray into nature and superstition carefully circumscribes these issues, presents instead a peculiarly impotent sexual dissident.

MALTHUS'S DAME NATURE AND THE MOB

Both Wordsworth and Wollstonecraft present significant reconfigurations of Burke's 'mother without being a wife' in the late 1790s. But they are not the only ones to do so. A third text published in 1798 presents arguably the most influential response to this problem: this was an anonymously authored tract, the *Essay on the Principle of Population*. Laid out in this work was the theory of population that soon became synonymous with its author, whose identity would be revealed as that of the Reverend T. R. Malthus – an Anglican cleric, of unorthodox education and dissenting leanings, who would later be appointed Professor of Political Economy at the East India Company College at Haileybury. His theory was based on two propositions: that population will increase in a geometric series (i.e., 1,2,4,8,16,32 etc.), while food, the means of subsistence, in an arithmetic series (i.e., 1,2,3,4,5 etc.). The outcome, according to Malthus, is that the world's population will inevitably exceed the resources necessary to sustain it; various 'checks' – e.g. famine, disease, war – will emerge which will claw back the population to a sustainable level. The theory held dramatic implications for notions of human progress, morality, and the nature of social relations. It suggested that the improvement of society would always be checked by the limits of natural resources; and that all human relations were potentially hostile, as people were pitted against each other for limited resources. As one contemporary commentator ruefully observed, Malthus's predictions meant that 'if twenty or forty thousand men could not be persuaded every now and then to stand and be shot at, we should be forced to eat one another'.[64] And at the centre of this bleak view of human life was the reproductive woman, whose fecundity was the root of all disasters. Her childbearing potential paradoxically implanted a seed of vice in the plot of human experience, her overabundance being the cause of all natural and unnatural disasters. In the context of 1798, Malthus's work responded directly to the contemporary preoccupation with female sexuality and the dangerous figure of the 'mother without being a wife'. He looked to preventive checks – notably sexual restraint – as a means of staving off the occurrence of collective disasters, but he also inadvertently opened the possibility that the murder of children could be added to the list of such preventive checks, and thus could have a role in the regulation of human society.

The subsequent history of Malthus's essay – its extensive transformations in later editions, its profound impact on the shaping of the poor law in Britain in the first half of the nineteenth century, and its role in the formation of attitudes to and practices of birth control throughout the century – has tended to overshadow the intellectual and cultural origins of the work in the political turmoil of the late 1790s.[65] But Malthus located the first edition of his work very much in the context of his time, intending it to tread a path of moderation between the programmes and aspirations of two extremes: the Burkophilic 'advocate[s] for the present order', on the one hand, and on the other, the perfectibilists, who argued that mankind was capable of improvement, a position represented in the *Essay* most prominently by Wollstonecraft's widower, William Godwin.[66] While Malthus's connection with the Church would have brought him into contact with advocates of the former position, significantly, he also had surprisingly strong social and intellectual links with the latter group. His father, Daniel, had been an enthusiastic follower of Rousseau, and had entertained the philosopher when David Hume brought him to England in 1766. At the time, Robert Malthus was a small baby: John Maynard Keynes, in his biography of Malthus, alludes to the episode whimsically as a visit from two fairy godmothers who 'assigned to the infant with a kiss diverse intellectual gifts', but also, we might observe, implanted in him intellectual roots in a progressive philosophical tradition.[67] In 1782, Robert was sent to the Dissenting Academy at Warrington, where he was the pupil of Gilbert Wakefield, forming life-long friendships with, among others, members of the powerful dissenting family, the Aikins. From Warrington he progressed to Jesus College, Cambridge, which at the time was a centre of republican and latitudinarian thinking. Indeed, while he was a student, his tutor, William Frend, was expelled from the Church of England and the university for his profession of Unitarian beliefs, free thought, and pacifism. Connections he had made at Warrington brought him into contact with the liberal publisher, Joseph Johnson, who published the *Essay on Population*. Johnson's long list of authors included Thomas Paine, author of the politically explosive response to Burke, the *Rights of Man* (1790), William Godwin, whom Johnson introduced to Malthus following the publication of the work, as well as Wollstonecraft, and indeed Wordsworth.[68]

While Malthus did not share all the views of his teachers and friends, he nevertheless was open to their ideas and their projects. Thus the first edition of the *Essay* stands as a work that appears to be *sympathetic* to the political claims of radicalism, but at the same time, certain of the impossibility of their achievement. For Malthus, it is not the state that is the agent of repression, but rather the immovable and unchangeable force of nature. Nature – in the form of the principle of population – thus emerges as the regulatory power and fundamentally conservative force that gives a distinctive new rationale to social conclusions that are in the end essentially Burkean. This is most evident – significantly for our purposes – in his discussion of marriage. 'Let us suppose', he speculates, 'the commerce of the sexes established upon principles of the most perfect freedom. Mr Godwin does not think himself that this freedom would lead to a promiscuous intercourse, and in this I perfectly agree with him.'[69] But were such freedoms permitted, Malthus contests that they would nevertheless have the socially detrimental effect of encouraging large and early families. The result of this would be overpopulation and all its attendant horrors – war, famine, disease, and poverty. The 'institution of marriage', Malthus is able to conclude, would thus be 'the *natural* result' of a community taking into consideration these devastating effects. According to Malthus, Godwin too readily blamed institutions for the problems that were in fact caused by nature; for Malthus on the other hand, institutions, as pernicious as they may be, had developed as a way of managing the conditions of nature. Hence his views on the double standards on sexual morality: 'That a woman should at present be almost driven from society for an offence which men commit nearly with impunity, seems to be undoubtedly a breach of natural justice',[70] he writes, sounding to all intents and purposes like Wollstonecraft. But, he goes on, this stigmatisation of women is a useful effect of the principle of population, teaching nature's lesson that such behaviour is socially destructive and better not repeated. Modesty and shame similarly have their origins in the principle of population: 'What at first might be dictated by state necessity is now supported by female delicacy, and operates with the greatest force on that part of society where . . . there is the least real occasion for it.'[71] Malthus absorbs sexual morality into nature: the 'mother without being a wife', Burke's symptom of French revolutionary chaos, in Malthus's book becomes a disorder of nature, but one for which society must pay the price.

For all its emphasis on restraint and sexual virtue, the *Essay* nonetheless gained the reputation of a licentious work that, according to William Hazlitt, 'rest[ed] on a malicious supposition that all mankind . . . are like so many animals *in season*', and against whose demoralising effects, interestingly, 'young women of liberal education' should be protected.[72] While Malthus had divided nature's role into two distinct functions – on the one hand, nature teems with overabundant life like a prolific mother; on the other hand, it regulates life[73] – his critics failed to observe the distinction between these two functions, holding instead that Malthus made virtues out of vices. For them, Malthus's 'checks to population' doubled as both the symptoms of the moral decay brought about by overpopulation, and also the means of its cure. This apparent double-dealing was held to be most objectionable in relation to sexual practices – the so-called 'unnatural practices', that is, all forms of non-reproductive and non-marital sex – which, it was felt, Malthus encouraged, by attributing to them a role in the regulatory regime of the principle of population. The use of contraception was a case in point: Malthus himself was staunchly opposed to its practice, but many later readers, most influentially neo-Malthusians such as Francis Place, saw the essay as an eloquent rationale for its use. Indeed, Malthus's work drew a critique that saw in it the same errors that conservative writers had found in the Revolution: his emphasis on the regulation of sexuality paradoxically was seen as an incitement to profligacy, and an encouragement to young women to adopt the promiscuous habits of a Wollstonecraft. In a similar vein, Godwin would observe in his 1820 diatribe against Malthus, that 'Mr Malthus trusts to the destruction of infants and young children as the street anchor of our hope to preserve the population of Europe from perishing with hunger',[74] identifying in the work an infanticidal logic that sealed its demoralising intent.

Godwin's analysis in part responded to the rebarbative way in which the social message of Malthusian theory had been underlined in the second edition of the work. In this it was clear that even in its regulatory function, Malthus's nature was a killer. Witness his notorious vignette of nature's feast:

A man who is born into a world already possessed, if he cannot get subsistence from his parents on whom he has a just demand, and if the society do not want his labour, has no claim of *right* to the smallest portion of food, and, in fact, has no business to be where he is. At nature's mighty feast there is no vacant cover for him. She tells him to be gone, and will quickly execute her own orders, if he do not work upon the compassion of some of her guests. If these guests get up and make room for him, other intruders immediately appear demanding the same favour. . . . The guests learn too late their error, in counteracting those strict orders to all intruders, issued by the great mistress of the feast, who, wishing that all her guests should have plenty, and knowing that she could not provide for unlimited numbers, humanely refused to admit fresh comers when her table was already full.[75]

Although Malthus attempted to distance himself from this passage by excising it from all subsequent editions from 1806 onwards, for his critics, including Godwin, it remained the clearest statement of Malthus's intent. According to this, the unemployed and the dispossessed were deemed not the victims but the causes of poverty, with their rude intrusions on nature's bounty, their inveigling supplications, and unreasonable demands for sustenance. The harsh lesson of nature, the 'strict' but 'humane' teacher, was loud and clear: those who cannot work, who have no independent means, must starve. Dame Nature remained the icon of Malthusian cruelty: the matronly assassin of the poor, the weak, and the dispossessed.

The allegorical figure of Dame Nature, a woman who is not a mother, but an instructress or governess, was a version of a figure who was well known at the time from the pedagogical literature, much of which was published very successfully by Malthus's publisher, Joseph Johnson. In these works for children, writers such as Sarah Trimmer, Anna Letitia Barbauld, and Mary Wollstonecraft, presented the character of a female instructor, sometimes a mother, but more often a governess or other female adult – the figure whom Blake alludes to in poems such as 'Nurse's Song' – who teaches her young charges moral lessons by drawing on examples that are found in nature; in these nature emerges as a harsh force that imposes punishments on all who offend against the moral law.[76]

The appearance of a fanciful figure like Dame Nature in the context of the second edition of 1803, however, is particularly striking as Malthus's revisions otherwise made for a much more scholarly production than the first edition. Responding to the charge that the principle of population was merely baseless conjecture, he drew on empirical evidence gleaned from his own travels in Scandinavia and extensive reading of published writings, documented in copious references, to produce a work that attempted to conform to the great natural histories of the Enlightenment, by writers such as Millar, Ferguson, and Robertson, mentioned in Chapter Two. In many cases, his sources were the same as those used by these earlier writers – the works of missionaries and travellers; but he also drew on the Scottish Enlightenment works as authorities in their own right.[77] However, despite the surface resemblance to these Enlightenment histories, Malthus's work told a profoundly different story about human history – a point that is flagged up by the incongruous appearance of Dame Nature. Unlike the Enlightenment thinkers, Malthus's aim was not to show society in a process of improvement from a state of degraded barbarity to its present heady heights of civilisation, but rather to distil from the evidence proof of the universal operations of the principle of population and the eternal necessity for the ministrations of Dame Nature. He did not accentuate the differences between various states of development as Millar and the Scottish Enlightenment writers had done, but rather minimised these, tending to see all societies, at all times, as prone to the same devastating logic of population. His work contained an apocalyptic message about the precarious fabric of civilisation itself – the foreboding sense that any moment it might degenerate into barbarism. But it also implied a strangely enervated temporality, regulated by the rhythms of human reproduction, in which the past would implode into the future, the future into the past: a fairy-tale-like, mythic world, over which Dame Nature would always preside.

Dame Nature's duty of disposal of her surplus charges points to the way in which Malthus's re-conceptualised history has shifted the location of child-killing. No longer the decisive distinction between the past and the present as it had been for Enlightenment writers following Adam Smith, child murder is now lodged as an ever-present possibility, a universally imminent tragedy, an effect of human need. Thus what for earlier writers had been the test case of development, for Malthus is thoroughly incorporated into the logic of human and social necessity. This is clear in the first two volumes of the second edition, in which Malthus presents a compendium of reproductive habits of past and foreign societies. In all the societies in which he notes occurrences of the practices of infanticide – and there are many, including ancient Greek and Roman, Indian, Chinese, and Japanese societies – surprisingly, these are not for him attributes of those societies' difference from civilised states, but rather evidence of the endurance of human needs across time and cultures. Although infanticide is condemned as an 'odious crime', it is nevertheless explained in terms either of economic need (e.g. in China, 'the poverty of the parents is the cause of this crime'), or the desire to maintain social status (in India, 'the fear of sinking from their caste'), or environmental factors (e.g. in 'parts of America... the extreme difficulty of rearing many children in a savage and wandering life, exposed to frequent famines and perpetual wars'). Even 'the preposterous system of Spartan discipline' is accounted for simply as 'a melancholy indication of the misery of the people and the insecurity of the state', again the inevitable outcome of environmental strictures.[78] In the Malthusian worldview, all human life is drawn together, and the distinctive gradations of cultured life that had been structural to the historical writers of the previous generation are abandoned.

The question for Malthus thus becomes not whether children are eliminated, but the way in which they are. In this context, Dame Nature, the official assassin of the undeserving poor, is proffered as a model of a virtuous and economic killer, as a corrective to another, incontinent form of murderer – a mob which was represented as a hysterical woman in a truly Burkean manner, an unnaturally fertile mother, who, with her gargantuan appetite, cannibalises her children:

A mob, which is generally the growth of a redundant population, goaded by resentment for real sufferings, but totally ignorant of the quarter from which they originate, is of all monsters, the most fatal to freedom. It fosters a prevailing tyranny, and engenders one where it was not; and though, in its dreadful fits of resentment, it appears occasionally to devour its unsightly offspring; yet no sooner is the horrid deed committed, than, however unwilling it may be to propagate such a breed, it immediately groans with the pangs of a new birth.[79]

The monstrous mother here is presented as a metonym for the mob, as both a cause and a representation of its horrible disorder. Its slippery representational status intensifies its insidiousness, for this revolting hag is no respecter of boundaries or decorum. Significantly, this emblem and producer of social mayhem is the progenitor in her most dangerous and abject form. It is Malthus's gothic version of the 'mother without being a wife'.

In Malthus's representational scheme, Dame Nature accrues moral authority as the regulator of the incontinent habits of unmarried women that will otherwise lead to the growth of the mob. She is the regulator of populations, and the punisher of the poor. But it is she that will keep the horrifying effects of the mob at bay – the deadly but necessary protector of social order.

Malthus presents a potent and pervasive version of the second of the two female figures identified at the beginning of this chapter – the professional woman, teacher, nurse, guardian, supervisor. We have found this more 'stern' than 'kind' mistress elsewhere – notably in Wordsworth's landscapes, in a ghostly and unformed way as the disciplinary spirit of Nature. In 'The Thorn', for instance, it is this spirit that protects the secrets of Martha Ray from the intrusions of the villagers. But whereas Wordsworth's Nature takes a benign and sympathetic attitude to Martha, the unwed mother, Malthus's Nature occupies a fundamentally antagonistic relation to his version of the 'mother without being a wife' – the mob – to the extent that Dame Nature is a killer too. The guardian of social order, and chilling superintendent of death, Malthus's version of the professional woman will preoccupy writers throughout the following decades, and nowhere more intensely, as we shall see in Chapter Four, than in the furore caused by the Malthusian New Poor Law introduced in 1834.

THE 1803 OFFENCES AGAINST THE PERSON ACT

Before leaving the turn of the nineteenth century, it is necessary to return to the matter of criminal legislation regarding child murder, left hanging at the end of Chapter Two, with the failed attempts in the 1770s to repeal the 1624 statute. With the extraordinary emphasis on the disruptive social and political effects of the 'mother without being a wife' within the writings of 1798 and its aftermath, it is perhaps not surprising that the pressures to find more effective ways of regulating illegitimacy within society would intensify. In this respect, a need to respond to the acknowledged shortcomings of the 1624 statute became increasingly pressing, and in 1803 – the year that Malthus published the edition of his essay with the controversial Dame Nature passage – parliament finally repealed the statute.

The successful repeal was introduced by Lord Chief Justice Ellenborough as a constituent clause in the catch-all Offences Against the Person Act (43 Geo. III c. 58, 1803), as part of a more general restructuring of the legislature following the 1800 Act of Union with Ireland.[80] The new provision for child murder brought a number of changes. First, it ruled that, in cases where there was reasonable proof of live birth, the case should be tried in the same way as any other murder, and would be punishable by death. Second, it made a separate charge of concealment, for which there was a maximum penalty of two years' imprisonment. As Mark Jackson has pointed out, these reforms came about not as the culmination of increasing humanitarian pressure, but rather were shaped by more conservative aims, to make the law more efficient.[81] Ellenborough's guiding principle was the concern that some guilty women were escaping punishment because the law's draconian penalties forced courts to be too sympathetic to their plight. By creating the separate charge of concealment, therefore, Ellenborough created an environment in which aberrant mothers could be more closely regulated, even when they sought to escape the supervision of the law. It is noteworthy, therefore, that the very same act also contained provisions against the procuring of miscarriage in a woman before 'quickening', making abortion a criminal offence for the first time.[82] The impact of the 1803 law was thus to increase the legal regulation of motherhood, and appropriate for the law a supervisory role akin to that Malthus had already assigned to his allegorical figure, Dame Nature.

1803 might be seen, therefore, as the inauguration of the new regime of Dame Nature. And in the 1830s, when Malthusian principles are infused into the very fabric of social relations, she will throw off her feminine amateurism and become a widespread motif of the systematic and alienating power of the state.

CHAPTER 4

'Bright and countless everywhere': the New Poor Law and the politics of prolific reproduction in 1839

THE NEW POOR LAW AND THE CULTURE OF KILLING

The two child murderers that emerge from the Revolution controversy of the 1790s – Martha Ray, the destitute unmarried mother who kills her child in despair, and Dame Nature, the cruel, institutional killer – cast their shadows over British culture throughout the nineteenth century. But they loom most menacingly at the end of the 1830s, especially in radical and plebeian culture.

Open any edition of the Chartist newspaper, the *Northern Star*, for instance, and one is struck by seemingly incessant accounts of infant violation, as child casualties of industrial accidents jockey for space with equally pathetic victims of domestic mishaps: twenty-six children drowned in a coal pit in Silkstone; a roll call of infants killed by tea kettles – Elizabeth Sharpe, Mary Milner, Isaac Hartley.[1] And there are numerous victims of murder. A strong sense emerges that a generalised threat to infant life lies abroad, a fear that all children, like Oliver Twist, the eponymous hero of the 1837 novel, are 'unequally poised between this world and the next'.[2] Their violators are everywhere, encoded in culture both high and low. In August 1838, for instance, the *Northern Star* reports that 'the admirable picture of Medea, by M. Delacroix has been bought... for the museum in Lille'; and there are references to the scandalous case of Maria Monk, whose infamous accounts of rapes and child murders in Canadian convents had titillated a broad reading public since their publication in 1836.[3] But most poignant are the stream of real child murders reported in the press, usually – although not always – committed by poor, unmarried mothers of newborns like Martha Ray, uprooted and deranged by their misfortune.[4] Witness for instance a 'tall woman having on a cloak, [who] was observed to be wandering about the spot' where the corpse of a nameless child was discovered in August 1838, under an arch in Battle Bridge near Bradford[5] – a mysterious female stranger, like a character in a romance or ballad, haunting the newly industrialised landscape.

What is distinctive about the flurry of interest in child murder at this time, however, is that according to the radical press, the greatest threat to infant life was not represented by these poor unwed mothers, but rather by the state itself. The 1834 New Poor Law had introduced new measures for the administration of the poor modelled on Malthusian principles, aimed to cut the cost of poor relief, and to discipline the poor into better habits of self-reliance.[6] Among its highly controversial new provisions was the compulsory incarceration of the poor in workhouses, redesigned to provide minimum levels of subsistence and a measure of discomfort, especially through the separation of married couples and families.[7] It also incorporated new provisions for bastardy, ending the mother's right to petition the father for financial support. With sole responsibility for her illegitimate child, the mother was frequently compelled to enter the workhouse, where the treatment of unmarried mothers was notoriously stringent.[8] While the authors of the 1834 Poor Law Report defended themselves against the objection that the arrangements for unwed mothers 'promote[d] infanticide', their opponents attacked the entire regime as an infanticidal one: the New Poor Law was 'the new starvation law', a 'cannibal invasion of the defenceless hearths and homes of our weaker brethren';[9] it was the repressor of populations, and murderer of babies. Here was the transmogrification of Malthus's Dame Nature into a principle of government. The 'stern mistress' no longer turned the hungry and needy away from the feast; she actively engaged in an assault on society's weakest and most vulnerable charges.

Opposition to the New Poor Law came from many quarters, including from Tories who saw the new legislation as an attack on the forms of patronage and charity that had shaped traditional relations between rich and poor.[10] But the loudest and most troubling protests came from the groundswell of working-class people, those who felt most at threat from the new provisions.[11] Popular opposition to the New Poor Law gathered momentum in 1837, when the Poor Law Commission began to instigate its new policies in the northern industrial regions. Mass demonstrations and riots took place as protestors attempted to obstruct the business of the new boards of guardians, which were designed to play an instrumental role in the law's implementation at a local level, including establishing workhouses in groups of parishes. Prominent among the law's critics were the Chartists, radicals who were increasingly distancing themselves from the Whigs since the Reform Act of 1832 had failed to provide any form of political representation for working people. The Chartists saw the New Poor Law as a further Whig betrayal and sought to use it as a means of harnessing support for their own political ends. Indeed, by 1839 anti-Poor Law protest had become thoroughly enmeshed with the Chartist cause, supplying the northern Chartists with a vocabulary of suffering and violation, and a moral justification for concerted resistance.[12]

In this fraught political context, the spectre of child murder assumed heightened potency. It is noticeable, for instance, that in the radical press, real child-murder cases, reported from the coroner's courts, always elicited political commentary. Thus in 1839, a newborn, strangled by its aunt – a curiously Dame Nature-like figure, a school keeper named Mary Brown – provokes the coroner to exclaim, and the editor of the Newcastle-based Chartist newspaper, the *Northern Liberator*, to concur, that '[t]here is no use in concealing the fact, to this the practice has come, but it is only one of the fruits of the inhuman New Poor Law'.[13] Or the baby found dead beneath the arch at Battle Bridge, is deemed '*another example*, if any were wanting, of the evil-working of the New Poor Law Bill' (my emphasis).[14] A wearying sense of the familiarity of these events always comes through; corpse on corpse is discovered, suggesting a relentless culling of innocent lives. But it is not merely individual acts of child murder that figure in this rhetoric. The deaths of infants are held to be over-determined by the new legislation: workhouses kill children through their harsh, unsanitary conditions; children are not born, because of the New Poor Law's adoption of Malthusian principles of moral restraint and the segregation of husbands and wives in the workhouses; surplus children are transported to the colonies; babies die in shipping accidents when parents emigrate to escape the strictures of the poor law;[15] illegitimate newborns are murdered by their mothers on account of the punitive new bastardy provisions; and, as we shall see, children are killed by their parents for insurance payoffs from burial societies.[16]

Mary Howitt's poem, 'Nature versus Malthus', printed in the radical press in March, 1839, pitches the deathly force of Malthus against the goodness of prolific nature:

> 'Mid the mighty, 'mid the mean,
> Little children may be seen,
> Like the flowers that spring up fair,
> Bright and countless everywhere.[17]

In the context of the infanticidal New Poor Law, natural acts of reproduction are a way of cocking a snook at the authorities. A weaver named Joseph Ashworth who had recently fathered triplets – expanding his family to thirty children – is congratulated in December 1838 in the *Northern Star* under the heading, 'Anti-Malthusianism'.[18] An ideal vision of a swelling, healthy, infant population counters the proliferating infant corpses caused by the New Poor Law, the casualties of this latter-day massacre of the innocents. And as in the depictions of the Biblical episode in the visual iconography of an earlier period,[19] the mass of infant corpses seems to take on the attributes of cherubs, becoming ephemeral and saintly – in Mary Howitt's case, like flower-fairies. Thus etherealised, they seem to undercut the evils of the New Poor Law.

Of course, as we have seen, child murder had been used for polemical ends since the beginning of the eighteenth century. But at the end of the 1830s, it emerges as a topos for political opposition of extraordinary power and varied application, which is used with an intensity that exceeds even that inspired by Jonathan Swift's *A Modest Proposal* in 1729. This is most clearly evident in relation to the so-called 'Marcus' pamphlets and the furore that surrounded them. These scandalous works, which circulated from late 1838, described a government plot to exterminate the third and subsequent children of all poor families. They consciously referred back to Swift's work, repeating his conceit that government policy – in this case, the New Poor Law – was tantamount to child murder, and evoking his idiom of political satire. The pamphlets were extremely controversial, provoking indignation and horror among many of their readers. But what is most intriguing is the variety and style of response they elicited, for while some readers clearly did hold the pamphlets to be in 'grim earnest', as Carlyle claimed them to be in *Chartism* in 1839,[20] other readers colluded with their fictional status in much more knowing ways, engaging with 'Marcus' as political satire, and appropriating his deadly tales to other, subversive ends. The effects of the 'Marcus' pamphlets can be traced across the print culture of the time, as they are taken up by people of diverse political opinions – Chartists of various factions, Owenites, as well as Tories – acting as a conduit of feeling and opinion, and are even constitutive of the very forms in which political resistance took place.

In this chapter, I shall examine the 'Marcus' pamphlets and responses to them alongside another discussion at this time that also focused on the idea of child murder. This was the controversy surrounding burial societies, held by many middle-class writers to be the cause of parental murder of working-class children for monetary gain. Also a response to the New Poor Law, the burial-society controversy should be seen as closely linked to the 'Marcus' affair. Taken together, the two sets of material demonstrate the way in which the figure of child murder had become a highly significant term in political discussion, as a sign open to interpretation, and a tool in a propaganda war.

The mode of these representations of child murder ranges from realism to melodrama to satire, producing a dizzying array of effects, from fear to laughter. One of the distinctive features of this material, however, that pervades all its different manifestations, is that the visceral realities of child murder – its pains and sufferings and injustices – often seem to recede in the midst of an outrageous joke. The figure itself assumes a spectral quality as a term haunted by its forgotten referent. This lends a peculiarly ghostly texture to the representation of society across the writings of political opposition: in 1839, we shall see, the world is supposed to be inhabited by the sinister shadows of murdering mothers, but also by hobgoblins and fairies – the spectres of the infants murdered by the Malthusian machine.

MARCUS'S 'BOOK OF MURDER': SURPLUS POPULATION AND THE CHILD DEATH FACTORY

Rumours of the existence of literature recommending the extinction of children of the working class began to circulate at the end of 1838. On 8 December, the *Northern Liberator* referred to a pamphlet, 'privately circulated at first, but now openly published, recommending the MURDER by wholesale of new-born infants, by a scheme called "Painless Extinction!"' It went on, 'we have the pamphlet in our possession, and shall, if possible give extracts next week; but topics so thicken in that we hardly know where to turn first'. Two weeks later, the paper contained a detailed report of its content.[21] The work in question was *The Essay on Populousness*, 'printed for private circulation'; it had been reprinted in the substantially longer work, *On the Possibility of Limiting Populousness*, authored by the pseudonymous 'Marcus', and printed by John Hill.[22] Both works carried the explicitly neo-Malthusian message: that the root of all current social problems lay in overpopulation. Both claimed that the means of their solution was in the restriction of pauper families to two children per family. And both were taken to be the work of the shadowy 'Marcus'. The second pamphlet adopted the circumlocutory style of political economy: it spoke only of the economic benefits of restricted population, and the environmental factors that in fact did restrict population. However, the first scandalously appended a supposedly scientific plan for achieving this end: 'Marcus's infamous theory of 'painless extinction' – that is, the gassing of new-born children in hospitals constructed specially for the purpose. Drawing on a hotchpotch of contemporary scientific beliefs, about embryological development, excitation of the nervous system, miasmatic poisoning, and adopting the impassive voice of scientific rationality, 'Marcus' outlines his theory: he writes 'before birth, it [the foetus]... was sustained and nourished by the flow of maternal blood and life. But now that supply is cut off...'.[23] Evading direct mention of the fact that after birth, the baby is to be taken into hospital and poisoned by gas, he goes on: 'all vitality sinks by one same cause – want of excitement and of nourishment. No pang is felt, for no sensation is shocked... Instead of growing quickly towards full formation, it decreases; instead of being awakened, it is dulled.' Euphemistic and evasive though it is, the pamphlet outlines a chilling prescription for mass infanticide.

The authenticity and the intent of the pamphlets were never entirely evident.[24] Radical opponents reasoned that they were the work of a philosophical radical, Poor Law Commissioner, or other government agent, but it is not clear that they believed them to be so. Indeed, commentators on the pamphlets tend to drift in and out of an apparent conviction that the pamphlets are an authentic part of government policy, from a much more distanced and knowing participation in the works as satire. The pamphlets' resemblance to Swift's *A Modest Proposal* would have been apparent to a literate readership in the early nineteenth century,[25] and this would have meant that some readers at least would have come to 'Marcus' with the conventions of political satire firmly in mind. The similarity of the name 'Marcus' to Malthus, and the perceived coincidence of their economic and social beliefs encouraged commentators to read 'Marcus' as a monstrous reincarnation of Malthus. Indeed, the theory of painless extinction seemed to some to be a scientific elaboration of Malthus's principle of population, a dramatic extension of the deadly work of Dame Nature.

For a short time between late 1838 and 1840, the name 'Marcus' came to stand for the murderous plot of Malthusian population theory. As the editors of the *Northern Liberator* wrote in an open letter to Lord John Russell, 'MARCUS, MALTHUS, MURDER, THE POOR LAW, AND THE GOVERNMENT, are now all MIXED TOGETHER in the minds of the people, in such a way as hardly to admit of being unmixed again'.[26] 'Marcus' had become a hybrid philosophical-radical-cum-mad-scientist, a parable against the dangers of morally unchecked scientific experimentation, on the lines of Mary Shelley's *Frankenstein* (1815). This

Figure 4. 'Marcus Unveiled', from *Northern Liberator*, 2 March 1839, p. 3

was elaborated in an article in the *Northern Liberator*, entitled 'Marcus Unveiled', a report of a lecture supposedly given by 'Marcus' in an imaginary Hertford College, Cambridge:

On Thursday the 7th of February . . . that celebrated room where the sage Malthus had so often demonstrated to admiring audiences, the deep truths of his profound philosophy was brilliantly lighted up. Additional gas burners had been constructed, so that the hall of sciences shewed . . . one blaze of light.[27]

In this article, possibly authored by the Chartist, Thomas Doubleday,[28] 'Marcus' appears in front of an appreciative audience of Poor Law Commissioners, government ministers, fashionable ladies, and philanthropists, who are covertly named in the article (for instance Lord [Brougham], the Bishop [Blomfield], Miss [Harriet Martineau], and Peter Thimble [Francis Place][29]), and represented in the accompanying illustration (see Fig. 4).[30] 'Marcus' conducts his experiment on a sleeping baby, extinguishing life, to the 'breathless admiration' of the audience: '"Exquisite" whispered Miss [Martinueau], as she watched eagerly the pulses of the beautiful babe – "exquisite". This first light was extinguished!'

'Marcus Unveiled' elaborates on the scientific knowledge that is evidenced in the first of the 'Marcus' pamphlets, wittily underlining some of the targets of the original pamphlet's satire. The emphasis on the 'blaze of light' evokes the use of gas light, newly introduced to the urban streets as part of Poor Law Commissioner Edwin Chadwick's larger project of social and moral hygiene aimed to dissipate the various threats of city life. It suggests here an easy slippage between the use of gas for urban hygiene and human eugenic ends. Carbonic acid, the deadly gas used by 'Marcus', was also associated with urban housing. Chadwick's *Sanitary Report* (1842) is full of accounts of the homes of the urban poor in which carbonic acid is identified as the fatal product of overcrowding.[31] According to Chadwick, overcrowding was the cause of more fatalities than wars. In the *Sanitary Report*, the risks to health posed by poor housing conditions are intensified by the moral dangers of unsegregated sleeping quarters. Miasmatic contagion and unwanted offspring are thus the twin products of slum living.[32] The 'Marcus' satire, however, purposefully transfers blame away from working-class dereliction and moral turpitude, to the state's impoverishment of the poor. In the first pamphlet by 'Marcus', the point is underlined by the satirical imperative that 'the stomach [of the child] be not too full' when the lethal dose of gas is administered.[33] In 'Marcus Unveiled', the joke is extended to attack London decadence, and superciliousness towards the northern working class: carbonic acid is, he declares, 'only known in London as a component part of soda water, ginger pop, bottled ale, treacle beer, imperial, wow-wow and swipes – (hear, hear,) – but in the north is perfectly well known amongst the collieries as "choke damp". The "ignorant colliers"', exclaimed 'Marcus', 'often blunder into it themselves, though the barbarians never have the wit to put their superfluous children into it! (A laugh!)'[34]

A poem that was published in both the *Northern Star* and the *Northern Liberator* announced the spoof lecture. Entitled 'Peter Thimble [Francis Place] to Lord Durham', it provided yet more publicity for the 'Marcus' pamphlets. Treating the event as though it were a reality, it reads:

> .... fortune in our way God sends throws
> A prime philosopher! His name is Marcus
> And he exclaims 'now by the holy poker
> I'll give their surplus progeny choker!'

> In short, my Lord, we find that our salvation
> Rests solely in carbonic acid 'Gas'.
> And to our doctrine to convert the nation
> Is all we now need bring to come to pass:
> To put the matter out of all conjecture,
> 'Marcus', next week, my Lord, intends to lecture![35]

The newspapers' satire invents a fictional world of events that gathers its own momentum. Print produces more print – a textual explosion that eventually encroaches on 'real life'. The radical Tory, G. R. Wythen Baxter, in his compilation of anti-Poor Law writings, *The Book of the Bastiles* [sic] (1841), recorded an anecdote about four pregnant women in a workhouse. 'About the period that "Marcus's" book was talked so much of', the babies of three of four 'unfortunate mothers' died after having been administered medicine in the workhouse. The fourth, however, 'resolutely refused' to take the medicine, and 'both she and her child did well. Does not this fact speak volumes?'[36] The final remark is a chance one – a throwaway cliché of everyday speech – but the idea that a 'fact speaks volumes' nicely draws attention to the slippage between texts and realities that the 'Marcus' hoax exploits.

Immediately following the publication and circulation of the original 'Marcus' pamphlets at the end of 1838, a muted response is registered in the radical and Tory press. But intense outrage is generated by the formidable figure of the Reverend Joseph Raynor Stephens, the radical – at this point, a Chartist – preacher, the 'fire-brand demogague' of Ashton. Stephens's constant references to the pamphlets in his highly politicised sermons and speeches opened a new chapter in the print history of 'Marcus'.[37] Stephens was an outspoken agitator for factory legislation and against the New Poor Law, and it was he who drew the scandalous 'Marcus' even further into the public eye. Stephens was arrested in late December 1838 very controversially for speeches delivered in the previous months, in which he had incited crowds to violence and incendiarism, and in the eight months between his arrest and trial and imprisonment in August 1839, he travelled the country delivering speeches and having them published.[38] In these, he made copious references to the work of 'Marcus' as incontrovertible evidence of the dangerous threat that the government posed for the very existence of the poor. In fact, Stephens had already made powerful use of the idea that the New Poor Law was a killer of children even before the eruption of the 'Marcus' scandal. One speech, for instance, as reported in the *Northern Star* in November 1838, incorporates the following piece of sentimental melodrama:

it had been proved in scores and hundreds of instances, that young women had taken their children and destroyed themselves too in consequence of the operation of that infernal enactment. He had read the other day of one young woman who took her little child, and, with a bandage, fastened it round her own bosom, and plunged herself and her baby into a stream, and as they could not live together, they must die, and trust to god's pity, rather than to man's mercy (great sensation) . . . she must either take herself into the Bastile, and be kept a prisoner all her life, and have the baby taken from her either to be poisoned or strangled, or cut up alive or dead by the damned doctors, or sent abroad to the plantations, – she must do all that, or bind her baby to her broken heart, and together with it plunge into the stream and die. (Tremendous sensation, mingled with horrible groans).[39]

It was not surprising, therefore, that Stephens was one of the first to pick up on the 'Marcus' pamphlets, and publicise their deadly content.

Amid the furore following Stephens's arrest, various radical imprints of the 'Marcus' pamphlets were published, including the *Book of Murder*, published by William Dugdale, the radical publisher and pornographer of Holywell Street, London,[40] and a 'People's Edition', printed in Leeds, and sold through the office of the *Northern Star*. The publishing success of these works must be tied to the controversy surrounding Stephens and his arrest. In the *Northern Star*, for instance, the 'People's Edition' of the *Book of Murder* is advertised week in week out, often alongside advertisements for Stephens's sermons. Stephens and 'Marcus' thus provided mutual publicity for each other – and in fact, after Stephens is imprisoned, in August 1839, the name 'Marcus' gradually slips out of view.

In common with much radical print of the time, the *Book of Murder* is a dialogic text; its many-voiced form makes the authorial intent opaque, and opens the text to a variety of interpretations. Each of its voices is stylistically and typographically marked, and of different and mysterious authorial origins. On the title page, the work is announced as a 'vade mecum' for the commissioners and guardians of the New Poor Law. Selling for three pence, it comprises a cheaply produced edition of the first, privately circulated 'Marcus' pamphlet, together with a 'refutation of the Malthusian doctrine', for 'the edification of the Labourer'. The first section of the *Book of Murder* is an introductory essay, in the authentic voice of the radical, denouncing the New Poor Law on the grounds that it is a Malthusian conspiracy: there are vivid accounts of the sufferings of the poor, of women forced to kill their children, and a legal system that virtually excuses them; and a repetition of Stephens's call to direct action. This has recently been identified as the work of the Owenite, George Mudie.[41] The second and third sections reprint the first of the 'Marcus' pamphlets, and these adopt different voices and styles too: one is in the voice of the political economist, the other that of a popular scientist. The tone of both of them is difficult to gauge, and both open a chasm beneath the more certain terrains of belief and disbelief, of fact and fiction.

The true identity of 'Marcus' was never authoritatively established at the time,[42] and the lack of certainty regarding both authorial designation and intent enabled the pamphlets to circulate like the work of an *agent provocateur*, sending ripples into late 1830s political culture. The pamphlets circulated anonymously, and their political potency accrued in part from this circumstance. The anonymity of 'Marcus' is therefore a significant aspect of the pamphlets' effects. Paradoxically, the secrecy that shrouded them above all seemed to mean that they could not be dismissed as fakes, and, moreover, that various people could be incriminated as their author. Baxter accused Lord Brougham of having written them,[43] and Stephens generated a great deal of publicity by claiming in his speeches that they were the work of one of the three Poor Law Commissioners. This was considered a serious enough charge to provoke letters to the press, from both Edwin Chadwick, the chief Poor Law Commissioner, and his assistant. Stephens penned a long letter of response, denying the accusation of libel, but took the opportunity, in any case, to claim that, if one of the three Poor Law Commissioners had not authored the pamphlets, it must have been Brougham, Place, or Martineau.[44] The correspondence was widely reprinted, and the accusation continued on the title page of *The Book of Murder*: 'Marcus, One of the Three' [Poor Law Commissioners]. Elsewhere, the three commissioners are referred to, with Herodian overtones, as the 'Three Kings of Somerset House', and there are lots of apocalyptic references to three-headed monsters. Like un-fathered or bastard children, the pamphlets brought about all kinds of disorder through their promiscuous reproduction and illegitimate status.

Not surprisingly, perhaps, the accusation of obscenity was never far away. In their open letter to Lord John Russell, the editors of the *Liberator* speculate on the role of a respectable publishing house, Sherwood, Neely, and Piper which had been implicated in the publication of the 'Marcus' pamphlets – a piece of evidence that proves for them that power and influence must be behind 'Marcus':

If it be possible *to speak or write crime*, here it must be spoken and written; or we must dismiss not only law but gospel – make a saint of Herod, and turn the 'murder of the innocents' into a good joke, if not a wise piece of politics. Obscenity, however flagrant, is nothing to this. And therefore, we affirm that the house of Sherwood and Co. would no more have thought of publishing 'Marcus' than they would have thought of publishing the elaborate impurities of John Cleland [author of the pornographic novel, *Fanny Hill*] – *unless* – unless, my Lord, they had been acted upon by motives and strengthened by *guarantees*, of which it is easy to conceive the nature, though difficult to conceive the existence.[45]

Their Malthusian theme connected them to birth-control literature that was circulating around this time, by writers such as Robert Owen, Richard Carlile, and Francis Place. And birth control was associated with sodomy. According to an editorial in an earlier edition of the *Northern Liberator*, 'even sodomy has been covertly defended by its advocates – for a palliation, if not a defence, even of the crime against nature – logically springs from the system of Malthus'.[46] The 'Marcus' pamphlets operated in a context in which pornography, sodomy, and birth-control advice all sparked the same kind of controversy. Reason enough, then, that they should be suppressed by government order in January 1839 – the effect of which was merely to increase their market value, and spread their notoriety.[47]

By early 1839, the infamy of 'Marcus' was so well known that 'Anti-Marcus' had become a name adopted by opponents of the New Poor Law. The correspondence pages of the *Northern Star* printed letters from 'Anti-Marcus', and a long, melodramatic poem by Stephen W. Fullom published in London in 1839, describing the effects of the Poor Law, stands beneath the title, *Poor Law Rhymes: or Anti-Marcus*. There were no direct references to child murder in Fullom's work, but, nevertheless, the poem demonstrated that 'Marcus' had become a by-word for the human degradations brought about by the New Poor Law.

The melodramatic tone of Fullom's poem is typical of much of the writing that exploits the 'Marcus' affair. For instance, G. R. Wythen Baxter, the radical Tory, used the 'Marcus' pamphlets in a highly sentimental account of the demoralisation of the poor brought about by the New Poor Law. In *The Book of the Bastiles* he cited his own open letter to Brougham 'on his creation and advocacy of the demoralizing, starving, poisoning, murdering "painless extinction" New Poor Law' (the allusion to 'painless extinction' is of course a direct reference to 'Marcus'):

gracious heaven! where are thy thunderbolts! by framing an enactment to massacre in cold blood, and that, too, by the most excruciating deaths, *i.e.* by *famine, slow poisons, 'painless extinctions'* (?) and broken hearts, the pauper population of the queendom – an enactment which has paved our streets with the bodies of murdered babes, and choked our rivers with the corrupted remains of their unfortunate mothers![48]

The histrionic style here is the standard fare of radical campaigns of the time. The sentimental appeal to the demoralised domesticity of the 'queendom', and the ironic drawing together of gold and infant corpses (which in this case, 'pave our streets'), recall the terms of the rhetoric against the factory acts, for instance, where similar references are made to notions of respectable domesticity. In a footnote, Baxter adds a direct appeal to the new Queen, calling on her sympathies as a mother to nurture her child-like subjects: 'Queen Victoria, you know...what the pangs of child birth are...I am asking you to become a nursing mother to your people when *you do not suckle your own child*!'[49]

Recent historical and critical work on this period has emphasised the way in which radical rhetoric frequently adopted melodrama as a genre, or 'mode', in which to stage class conflicts.[50] Highly charged emotional scenarios, usually of domestic breakdowns that have been caused by upper-class fecklessness or cruelty, are used as a way of underscoring the political message in the context of a Manichean terrain of good and evil. The references to child murder in New Poor Law opposition can be seen as constituents in such a melodrama: Poor Law Commissioners are turned into evil murderers, and the poor, their defenceless victims. Like the seduction narrative, another common melodramatic plot, whose role in popular opposition has been well documented,[51] the story of child murder exposed the poor as the innocent victims of class exploitation – morally vindicated, if in some cases relieved of agency. Melodrama is used extensively, but by no means exclusively, by radical Tory writers, such as Baxter, who found in the genre a certain kind of nostalgia – what Elaine Hadley characterises as a 'regressive' impulse – which embraced as ideal the social relations of a past, deferential society.[52] Frances Trollope's anti-New Poor Law, child-murder novel, *Jessie Phillips* (1842–3), would fall into this category. In this, Jessie Phillips is punished for killing her illegitimate child, when in fact the real murderer is her seducer, the dastardly son of the squire. The novel thereby dramatises both the injustice, but also, as Trollope puts it, the lack of *chivalry* in the law, harking back to an era of paternalism and deference.

In the aftermath of the 'Marcus' affair, child murder is incorporated into a more complex and diverse array of narratives in which the melodramatic mode combines with other genres and stories, to reflect heterodox political opinion and varied forms of resistance.[53] The Chartist, W. J. Linton, for instance, in *The National*, his journal venture of 1839, takes up the 'Marcus' theme rather differently than Baxter. For him, it elicits a much larger critique of institutions. He wrote under the pseudonym of Gracchus, which linked him to both Roman and French republican radicalism. Gracchus was the egalitarian land-reformer who in 131 BC fruitlessly proposed extensive land distribution, while the French radical Babeuf, who adopted Gracchus as his forename, was organiser of the proto-communist Conspiracy of Equals in Paris in 1795–6. Linton would have been familiar with the Italian Buonarroti's account of the Conspiracy of Equals, that had been published in English translation (by the Chartist, Bronterre O'Brien) in 1836.[54] He uses the 'Marcus' pamphlets as an occasion for attacking the New Poor Law, not for its demoralisation of the poor in itself, but rather for its role in a much larger and more systematic oppression of the people. 'Which is the fouler crime,' he writes,

to destroy an infant; or *to flog a man to death to the sound of martial music, to murder men by thousands on a battle-field, to bind tens of thousands of families to the unresting wheel of misery?* Which is the greater wrong – to deprive a mother of her children; *or to doom those children to a life of agonizing toil, to the horrors of prostitution, and having so disposed of them for the service of the better classes, to separate the parents, to sunder those whom God has joined, and bury them, bowed with their long servitude, and heart-broken, while the breath is yet in them, in divided graves – as a punishment for being crushed by the ruling Evil?*[55]

Linton interweaves an emotional appeal to sentiment, not dissimilar to Baxter's, with a rational discourse in which he weighs the comparative benefits of the death of a child against other social ills. In doing so, he evokes Godwin's critique of Malthus, in which Godwin had claimed, 'I had rather a child should perish at the first hour of existence, than that a man should spend seventy years of life in a state of misery and vice.'[56] For Godwin and Linton, child murder is the lesser evil; in fact, as for Swift in the civic humanist, republican idiom of *A Modest Proposal*, it is a redemptive act in the face of generalised oppression. Linton's affiliation with this tradition is evident throughout *The National*, but especially in his inclusion, in a later edition, of Rousseau's account of the episode from the history of the Roman Republic, in which Brutus condemns to death his own sons for the sake of upholding the law, and the republic. 'Will it be said that Brutus ought to have abdicated the consulship, rather than have condemned his own children? I answer, No!' writes Rousseau/Linton.[57]

   Joseph Raynor Stephens presents a further variant on the child-murder story. In his sentimental descriptions of demoralised domesticity, and his melodramatic dramatisation of the suffering of the poor through the figure of a suicidal and infanticidal woman, his rhetoric also had much in common with Baxter's. However, he then goes on to use the child-murder story as the narrative justification for a call to arms. To give extra weight to his message, he draws on the Old Testament story of the massacre of the innocents in Israel: the affliction of the poor by the government, he claims, is exactly equivalent to that of the Israelites by the Egyptian Pharoahs, who, in a Malthusian way, had legislated that all male children of the Israelites were to be strangled at birth. Moses, who survives abandonment himself, leads the people to freedom following God's words: 'Vengeance is mine, I will repay, saith the Lord.' Stephens goes on: 'Away with the sickly and hypocritical sentimentality of those that affect such horror at the slightest reference to the right to resistance.'[58] For Stephens, the child-murder narrative of this massacre of the innocents, combined with the existence of the 'Marcus' pamphlets, provides biblical and moral underwriting for his exhortation to physical force.

Stephens's rhetoric of vengeance, mediated by the outrage of the 'Marcus' pamphlets, is taken up in the *Northern Liberator*, for the cause of physical force. In an editorial dripping with sarcasm, the 'Marcus' pamphlets are presented as a way of exposing the hypocrisy of the government, and thus providing moral justification for violent revolt:

Oh! how tenderly alive the hypocrites are for the *peace* and order of society! How sensitively alive to the shedding of a single drop of human blood, even though that shedding should be necessary for the establishment of civil rights of the greatest moment to the community at large! What tender innocent doves! No objection, however, to stifle poor little infants; this is scientific and philosophical humanity. No *physical* force! Oh dear no . . .[59]

In the context of the *Northern Liberator*, the 'Marcus' pamphlets take on their most dramatic role. They are not the inspiration of pity for the victims of government oppression, as in the paternalistic rhetoric of the Tory Radicals, nor even the necessary sacrifice that is required to redeem society, as in the abstract discourse of republicanism utilised by Linton. For Stephens, and here in the editorial of the *Northern Liberator*, the child murders of 'Marcus' are used to impel people to insurrection – to resist with physical force the oppressions of the state. Stephens' inflammatory motto, 'For child and for wife, I will war to the knife', was written on banners and chanted enthusiastically by protestors at torchlight meetings. At this moment in January 1839, the 'Marcus' pamphlets are drawn into a tense discussion among radicals about appropriate forms of political action. And they allow Stephens to weigh in on the side of brute force.

The original author's precise intention regarding the pamphlets is impossible to know. What is significant is that these different interpretations emerged in the print culture of the time, generating different forms of resistance, and shaping the styles of political opposition. The 'Marcus' episode illustrates vividly the way in which ideas and motifs circulated within the culture, and were co-opted by different individuals and groups to support widely different political positions: in this case, child murder is incorporated in the rhetoric of people of party and opinion as different as the Tory Radical, Baxter, Chartists of various complexion (Stephens, Doubleday, and the republican, Linton), as well as the Owenite, Mudie. It suggests that there were very fluid channels of communication and exchange of ideas between various groups and factions, and presents a picture of a complex and dynamic culture of political opposition, in which the idea of child murder had come to play a key role.

THE BURIAL SOCIETY CONTROVERSY: CARLYLE, CHADWICK, AND BRYAN PROCTER

The 'Marcus' tale of state-sponsored child murders was not, however, the only account of child murder to receive notoriety at this time. The controversy surrounding burial societies, roughly contemporary with the 'Marcus' affair, also generated sensational tales of infant massacres. Witness, for instance, Bryan Procter's poem, 'The Burial Club, 1839':

> *The Burial Club, 1839*
> Soh! – there's another gone,
> How purple he looks, – but wait!
> We'll tumble him into his coffin;
> And bury the body straight.
>
> No one will see where the poison
> Has trickled and left its trace!
> How curled up he is! I wonder
> How the blue came into his face.
>
> We'll find him a shroud for a shilling;
> We'll cover the limbs up tight:
> Who see him shall swear we are willing
> To do our duty to-night.
>
> Dead! That's a guinea for each:
> No need to spend aught on his meals;
> There's the little one – but she's a-dying;
> And Connor, the boy, – but he steals.

I was once, I confess, chicken-hearted:
His moans made me tremble and shrink:
But I thought of the club and the money,
Grew bolder, and gave him the drink.[60]

This lurid monologue, narrated by an infanticidal parent, describes the business of killing children for a burial fee, or insurance payout. With its chilling mixture of curiosity about the aesthetic effects of poison on a child's body (its colour and shape), and brusque concern for the economic benefits of poisoning, the poem is clearly intended as an indictment of what was considered by many to be a widespread practice among the working class. The poem was published posthumously in 1877, and the date of composition of the poem is unknown, despite the title. But it is likely that the case to which the poem refers is, in fact, one that occurred in the autumn of the following year, 1840. This was the notorious case of an Irish family, the Sandys, which came before the Stockport assizes in October 1842.[61] Robert and Anne Sandys were found guilty of the murder of two of their daughters, and attempting to murder a third, while his brother and sister-in-law, George and Honora Sandys, who lived next door, were indicted for poisoning their daughter. The case caught the public eye precisely because its motive was financial: the Sandys expected to gain £3 8s per child. If Procter did have this case in mind, then the precise dating of the poem in the title is curious: it may imply merely that Procter had a lapse of memory; but, more speculatively, it may suggest a remembered sense on Procter's part, that 1839 was in some way an 'infanticidal' year.

Burial societies were a widespread phenomenon at the time, offering the working class a means of ensuring for themselves and their families a decent burial through subscription to a common fund.[62] Very localised, and often short-lived organisations, based in public houses, schools, or churches, the societies proliferated throughout the century.[63] Like friendly societies and savings banks, burial societies were a form of the mutualist financial organisation very much encouraged under the New Poor Law, as a way of facilitating self-help among the poor. They became, however, the focus of middle-class anxieties about working-class demoralisation and degeneracy. The frequent form in which these anxieties were expressed was through the claim that burial societies encouraged the poor to murder their children for monetary gain – although this was a claim that was disputed by officials.[64]

For literary writers, the burial societies provided a perfect motif with which to illustrate contemporary social malaise. In 1855, the troubled narrator of Tennyson's *Maud* famously refers to 'a Mammonite mother [who] kills her babe for a burial fee'.[65] Earlier, Thomas Carlyle had drawn on the Sandys case for his graphic description of present ills in *Past and Present* (1843). Procter, who was an acquaintance of Carlyle, may well have remembered the case through Carlyle's account of it. 'At Stockport Assizes,' Carlyle writes,

a Mother and a Father are arraigned and found guilty of poisoning three of their children to defraud a 'burial-society' of some £3. 8s. due on the death of each child: they are arraigned, found guilty; and the official authorities, it is whispered, hint that perhaps the case is not solitary, that perhaps you had better not probe farther into that department of things.[66]

In line with many commentators, including Procter, Carlyle emphasises the Irish ethnicity and Catholic religion of the family, calling the crimes a representation of 'depravity, savagery, and degraded Irishism'.[67] And for Carlyle, they are an embodiment of the degraded and demoralised times.

Carlyle, however, hovers between blaming working-class degeneracy and the utilitarian policies of a morally bankrupt government. Indeed, what could express more poignantly the effects of the New Poor Law than the spectacle of working-class people murdering their young for insurance payouts? Here was the culture of greed and selfishness at its most extreme. But for government officials involved in the implementation of the laws, child murders associated with burial societies were the product of working-class depravity itself, a criminal behaviour that the new legislation was designed to punish and cure. Thus, Chadwick, discussing burial societies in his report on 'The Practice of Interment in Towns', in 1843, invokes 'the moral condition of a large proportion of the [working-class] population' when accounting for instances of infanticide for monetary gain.[68] The poor management of burial societies, which had led to the practice of multiple insurances for a single life, and the strong links between burial societies and public houses, according to Chadwick, presented conditions that were ripe for exploitation by unscrupulous parents. For him, the practice could be curtailed by tighter legislation, and in fact, the 1850 Act to Consolidate and Amend the Laws Relating to Friendly Societies (13 & 14 Vic. c. 115) introduced measures to protect children under ten from abuse of insurance by families.[69]

In 'The Practice of Interment in Towns', Chadwick also gives an account of the Sandys case, alongside other cases of child murder and wilful neglect that had been witnessed by collectors from burial societies and other officials. As is typical in such enquiries, the evidence ranged from reports of documented trials, to anecdotes and hearsay: 'a minister in the neighbourhood of Manchester', for instance, is cited as being 'shocked by a common phrase amongst women of the lowest class – "Aye, aye, that child will not live; it is in the burial club"'.[70] Chadwick never doubts the authenticity of these reports: even in 1865 he maintains that murders committed for monetary gain were reasonably widespread,[71] long after most other commentators had accepted that the extent of the practice had been grossly exaggerated. For others, however, the point of concern is precisely the element of gossip and rumour that escalated public fears. In fact, in 1854 a Select Committee on the Friendly Societies Bill (chaired by T. H. S. Sotherton, who had introduced the 1850 amendments), submitted a report that included an examination of whether burial societies really caused child murders, or, instead, the spectre of child murder was a mere chimera, an effect of rumour and scandal.

In the course of the 1854 report many witnesses, including solicitors, coroners, and burial society officials, gave evidence based on prominent cases, such as that of the Sandys. What struck the Committee, however, were the relatively small number of cases recalled, and the even smaller number in which the charged were found guilty. It thus concluded that 'the instances of child murder, where the motive of the criminal has been to obtain money from a burial society are [too] few' to warrant legislation to prevent the crime, and that 'suspicion [has] been almost entirely founded on the few cases brought to trial, exaggerated by the horror with which the idea of a crime so heinous would naturally be regarded.'[72] Significant here is not the minimising of the danger presented by the burial societies to infant life, but rather the Committee's emphasis on the 'exaggerated', or inflationary, effects of reports of child murders. According to this report, there is more talk about child murder than instances of it. The very nature of the crime laid it open to sensation and scandal.

The 'exaggerated' effects of reports of child murder are nicely dramatised by Carlyle in his account of the Sandys murders in *Past and Present*. He records a 'hint' that is 'whispered' by officials at the time of the Sandys crime, that the crime is not an isolated one: 'better not probe farther into that department' he warns.[73] He indicates a suspicion – nothing more; but just to impute this is enough, for the child murders we imagine are more scandalous and more affecting than the ones that are documented.

In this account, then, the real horror of child murder comes to exist in the workings of the imagination, where no facts can be invoked to constrain its extent or its power. It is this very process that the 1854 Report highlights: that talk about child murder creates a false, or at least a falsely inflated, horror. According to the Report, the controversy around burial societies is built on rumour and speculation, suspicions that cannot be substantiated, and whips up anxieties that reason would dampen or dispel. Just like the 'Marcus' pamphlets had done.

THE RUMOUR MACHINE: OVER-PRODUCTION AND OVERPOPULATION IN THE 'BOOK OF MURDER' AND DICKENS, *THE CHIMES*

The figure of child murder in the burial society controversy operates in precisely the way that it did in the 'Marcus' affair. One of the recurrent features in cases of child murder throughout the eighteenth and nineteenth centuries is the difficulty of knowing whether or not a crime has taken place, provoking what I referred to earlier as an epistemological shortfall. But at this stage, this effect seems to be particularly intense. Rumours of widespread infanticide discredit the burial societies, and assure the middle-class commentators of working-class degeneracy; likewise, the rumours inspired and disseminated by 'Marcus' of state-sponsored, industrial-style killings of the babies of the poor discredit the workings of the Poor Law Commission. Indeed, as we have seen, the 'Marcus' scandal provokes a textual explosion that matches the extent of imagined carnage: more and more print, instilling a mass production of child murder, as dead infants multiply before our eyes – dead infants in the workhouse, dead infants in Egypt, dead infants paving the streets with gold, dead infants in the laboratory of 'Marcus'. Indeed, the rhetorical and political potency of the 'Marcus' episode is accrued from this multiplying effect: as the accounts circulate, there are more meetings, more riots, more arrests, more disruption. The impossibility of corroborating his claims, and thus his anonymity, are 'Marcus's most powerful weapons.

In the context of both the 'Marcus' affair and the burial society controversy, child murder performs, in rhetorical terms, as a figure whose meanings are constantly inflating: born out of hearsay and rumour, it over-produces effects from a cause that is barely verifiable. The economy of representation that this implies is striking for in a curious way it resembles the very economic system that the figure critiques. Child murder consistently focuses attention on the faults and contradictions of an economic system that is seen to be all-consuming and autonomous: the 'Juggernaut of capital', as Marx would later put it, which obliterates the labourer, his life and labour, his wife and his child.[74] In each of the writers examined here, however, the critique is different. For Carlyle, the problem lies in the dissolution of a distinction between the economic and the human – a distinction that for Carlyle has become almost sacred. Thus, for him the child murders provoked by burial societies are the symptoms of a profane society that has mistaken the limits of the market, and ascribed monetary value to human life itself. For Chadwick, on the other hand, who has no qualms about reckoning human lives in monetary terms, child murder comes to highlight anxieties about the inflationary tendencies of the market, and about market transparency. For him, parents kill children, not because their lives are insured, but because, without proper regulation, they may be over-insured, and their value grossly inflated. Child murder thus becomes the dangerous symptom of an autonomous and unregulated market, which ascribes value in a reckless and inflationary way. For both Carlyle and Chadwick, however, child murder draws attention to the autonomy of the market that undermines both individual agency and the certainties of human value.

The 'Marcus' affair uses the child-murder figure to present a more sustained and differently-conceived critique than Chadwick or Carlyle. It emphasises the notion that the market has produced what it terms, in Malthusian language, a 'surplus population': the scheme of 'Marcus', to murder the children of the poor, is a dramatisation of a theory that holds that a proportion of the population exceeds economic purpose, and thereby turns what had been the source of wealth – labour – into its parasite. According to Fergus O'Connor, in his editorial in the *Northern Star* in March 1838, entitled 'The Cause of all our Problems Answered, Over-Production and Over-Population', with its new reliance on mechanised labour, and immersion in world markets, capital has turned labourers into pariahs, a 'squalid race of living skeletons marching in sad procession... from the den of misery to the loathsome factory... to the dungeon of the remorseless Devil King'. 'It is as if the order of nature were reversed', he writes; 'the scale of population should be made subservient to the commercial speculation of the capitalist, the wants of the lords of the soil, and to the financial necessities of a money-mongering government.'[75] An inverse relationship between population and production has been established, so that capital can only expand at the expense of population, money increase as people die. And like 'the squalid race of living skeletons', the mass of murdered infants invoked by the 'Marcus' affair is another representation of the products of this system. They are ghostly and disembodied, dehumanised products of the 'money-mongering' system. The murdered infants of 'Marcus' are the waste products of the new economic system: hollow and meaningless, they constitute a ghostly almost-presence in the new world order.

In the 'Marcus' pamphlets, there is a long description of a burial ground for murdered babies, an 'infants' paradise', which 'every parturient female will be considered as enlarging or embellishing'.[76] His detailed accounts of the disposal of the dead are a joke at the expense of public health officials, such as Chadwick, who were preoccupied with the hygiene of death; but they also raise the intriguing idea that the dead babies have an embodied form of afterlife. For J. R. Stephens, this will be no 'infants' paradise', but a 'garden of ghosts':

the bodies of the little innocents [. . . are consigned] to the paradise of infants, called up by the genius of the 'New Poor Law' whose magic wand has swept away the paradise of Eden, and left us in its stead the garden of the ghosts of our little ones scientifically slaughtered by the high priests of Moloch, the blood-thirsty monster, whom they would impiously install in the holy seat of the eternal.[77]

In Stephens's account, as in that of 'Marcus', there is a suggestion that the murdered infants stand for the surplus population of the poor, starved and made ghostly by the New Poor Law, and occupying the same demi-world as the ranks of skeletons invoked by O'Connor. In these writings, the pseudo-ghosts and skeletons have a supernatural power, haunting the world in their aggrieved half-life.

There is a strong gothic streak in these representations of a surplus population. The fashion for the gothic, which infused both élite and popular culture throughout the nineteenth century, had derived from traditional folk beliefs in a supernatural world, inhabited by fairies and goblins, and a host of other forms of unworldly beings; and had, in turn, fuelled the development of a scholarly interest in folklore. Through the collection and documentation of folk stories from different parts of the world, but especially from the Celtic fringes of Britain, a new breed of scholar set out to preserve the beliefs of traditional societies at a time that was perceived to be one of rapid demographic and economic change.[78] One of the unwitting effects of this was to popularise in literary form the residual folk beliefs of immigrant groups, especially the Irish, who now formed part of a new industrial working class – more often than not, as 'surplus population'.

Within folk beliefs, there is much to link dead children with fairies: Katherine Briggs notes that the most commonly held understanding of the origin of fairies at this time was that they were the souls of the dead, often children, especially un-baptised or still-born children;[79] and the belief in fairy changelings, as documented in such works of folklore as Thomas Crofton Croker's *Fairy Legends and Traditions of the South of Ireland* (1828) and Thomas Keightley's *The Fairy Mythology* (1833)[80] – that is, the exchange of new-born human babies with ugly, fairy children – further intensified this identification. Against this background, then, we might see that Stephens's suggestion that dead children have a supernatural afterlife makes them seem something like fairies.

Alongside the folklorists' documentation of fairy belief, a fashion for fairy painting was developing, through which visual conventions for fairy appearance took shape.[81] These often emphasised the childishness of fairies, mainly through their diminutive size, which was usually conveyed through their multitudinousness: in visual representations fairies typically appear in vast crowds, suggesting that there are populations of fairies – populations of diminutive beings, like children, or even dead children. As in Mary Howitt's 1839 poem, 'Nature versus Malthus', cited at the beginning of this chapter, a fairy population of children inhabiting the 'woodland dells' and 'mountain glens'[82] can be interpreted as the surplus population of Malthusian population theory, imaginatively transformed into fairies.

By 1839, the growing interest in folklore beliefs in literary culture thus provided an arena in which it was possible to use the figure of the fairy as a way of memorialising the surplus population of the poor that has been imagined obliterated by 'Marcus's murder machine.[83] This structure of sensibility can be seen clearly in Dickens's *The Chimes: A Goblin Story*. Published in 1844, and illustrated by, among others, the renowned fairy painters, Daniel Maclise and Richard Doyle, it was inspired by the tragic case of Mary Furley, a destitute sempstress who had attempted suicide with her baby so as to avoid the workhouse;[84] Mary was saved, but her baby drowned, and she was subsequently tried and found guilty of child murder. For many commentators at the time, the cruel irony of the Mary Furley case represented the worst of the government's abuses of the poor. In *The Chimes*, a fate like that of Mary Furley is proposed as the likely destiny of Meg, the daughter of the central character, Trotty Veck; at a crucial point in the story, Trotty is shown a vision of Meg, destitute and desperate like Furley, on the point of drowning herself and her child. The vision is presented as a way of educating him in the errors of Malthusian thinking: only through this vision is Trotty able to see that his daughter's destruction of herself and her baby is an act of love rather than of negligence, and that the value of human love by far exceeds that of money, against the teachings of the various Poor Law officials who have indoctrinated him in Malthusianisms. The significant point is that the vision is shown to him by a host of goblins, which

Figure 5. Meg takes her baby to the river. Engraving after John Leech.
'Third Quarter', From *The Chimes*

inhabit the belfry of the chimes, their multitudinous presence mocking the
Malthusian discourse of surplus population. In Richard Doyle's illustration
of this episode, Trotty is surrounded by a crowd of chiding goblins; the same
that surround Meg in a later illustration, as she takes her baby to the river,
but now in less menacing, more sympathetic, imploring mode, as though
they mean to take it to safety themselves (see Fig. 5). The goblins in fact

do not appear in the written text until Trotty's encounter with them in the belfry, but their presence is evident in the illustrations right from the beginning, and it is these that emphasise the fairy theme in the story. The opening illustrations by Maclise draw on the conventions of fairy painting – crowds of floating, diaphanous creatures, and small goblins entwined in the calligraphy – and place the work securely in the genre of the fairy tale.

As Michael Slater has noted, *The Chimes* marks a stage in the development of Dickens's novelistic method, as 'his first overt entry as a novelist into the political arena'.[85] On its publication, the story was praised in the *Northern Star* for the manner in which it 'champion[ed]...the poor.'[86] In this light, it is striking that it adopts the motifs and conventions of fairy tales to the extent that it does. Nevertheless, it seems that its supernatural effects were felt to be its most dangerous weapon. In the following year, an anonymously authored 'counterblast' was published, entitled *Old Jolliffe: Not a Goblin Story*.[87] *Old Jolliffe* recast the story of *The Chimes*, making the characters happy with their lot and grateful for the beneficence of the workhouse. Most significantly, it was '*Not* a Goblin Story', erasing all traces of a menacing supernatural world. For this writer, at least, there is no way of co-opting goblins: to make the story anodyne, the goblins must be expurgated, as though the goblins were the stuff of the over-heated imaginings of political radicals.

When Dickens wrote in defence of fairies in 1853 that 'In a utilitarian age...it is a matter of grave importance that Fairy tales should be respected',[88] it is likely that he had in mind something more complex and particular than merely a liberal defence of the imagination. *The Chimes* suggests that there was a strong political dimension to his view. In this connection it is also worth remembering that the term 'hobgoblin' was sometimes used to refer to radicals and socialists. In March 1839, for instance, the Owenite paper, *New Moral World*, records a remark at a meeting in Coalbrooke, in which socialists are compared to 'a host of hobgoblins, who came to frighten the people, and in time would disappear.' And we may recall that the first English translation of the Marx and Engel's *Manifesto of the Communist Party*, published in the *Red Republican* in 1850, spoke of 'a frightful hobgoblin [that] stalks throughout Europe', rather than the 'spectre' that famously opens the now standard translation.[89] This sense that the world is haunted, I suggest, is an attribute of the texture of ghostliness or abstraction that has been introduced by the capitalist system, and especially by Malthus's theory of population. As Marx will observe in the *Grundrisse*, 'Malthusian man, abstracted from historically determined man, exists only in his brain'[90], meaning that to live in a world organised on the basis of mistaken statistical principles is to live in an artificial world of abstractions, distanced from the real conditions of one's existence.

This is an insight that in fragmentary and diverse ways is implicit in oppositional literature around 1839, and one to which the child-murder figure contributes poignantly. This particularly intense and fluid use of child murder as a figure of implied economic critique fades in later decades, even though the concern about child murder as a *social* problem increases, reaching a peak in the 1850s and 1860s. But the varied meanings of child murder at this particular moment of social change and resistance remain embedded in the figure, and erupt again in the powerful representations of violent deaths of infants that appear in the later part of the century.

CHAPTER 5

'A nation of infanticides': child murder and the national forgetting in Adam Bede

Or l'essence d'une nation est que tous les individus aient beaucoup de choses en commun, et aussi que tous aient oublié bien de choses.
Ernest Renan, 'Qu'est-ce qu'une nation?' [1882][1]

Our dead are never dead to us until we have forgotten them.
George Eliot, *Adam Bede* [1859][2]

THE EPIDEMIC OF CHILD MURDER IN 1850S AND 1860S BRITAIN

In the late 1850s and 1860s, Britain was stricken by an apparent epidemic of child murder.[3] In 1866, the Reverend Henry Humble conveyed the sense of panic in the air, with his lurid scenes of grotesque acts happening on a daily basis. The surface of everyday life had been disrupted by the obtrusion of surprise and horror. In London, he writes,

bundles are left lying about the streets, which people will not touch, lest the too familiar object – a dead body – should be revealed, perchance with a pitch plaster over its mouth, or a woman's garter around its throat. Thus, too, the metropolitan canal boats are impeded, as they are tracked along by the number of drowned infants with which they come in contact, and the land is becoming defiled by the blood of her innocents. We are told by Dr Lankester that there are 12,000 women in London to whom the crime of child murder may be attributed. In other words, that one in every thirty women (I presume between fifteen and forty-five) is a murderess.[4]

A ruined city, clogged with the corpses of innocents and stained by their blood, inhabited by a swelling population of murdering mothers: the official statistics of Dr Lankester, coroner for Middlesex, imparted an extraordinary truth – that among the women that one passed on the streets of the capital every day, no fewer than 12,000 had killed their children.[5] For at least a decade, public and professional concern about the extent of child murder had been mounting, and now Lankester gave statistical substance to the worst fears. The cherished notion of *laissez-faire* seemed impeded by the obstructions caused by bodies – not the etherealised goblin bodies of Chartist imaginings discussed in the previous chapter, but the all too substantial corpses of unwanted babies. The entire capital was in danger of coming to a standstill, the centre of commerce choked, its thoroughfares obstructed by the detritus of unwanted babies.

It is as though the infant corpses threatened the very mobility and speed of modern life. Four years earlier, a doctor named William Burke Ryan had described a similar scene in almost the same, gothic terms. Ryan's landscape of infanticide has a more pastoral feel than Humble's – his scenes of discovery are always in retreat from urban places: in bedrooms, on evening walks, on journeys to the suburbs. But his emphasis on the blockage of transportation networks prefigures Humble's. 'In the quiet of the bedroom', he writes,

we raise the box lid, and the skeletons are there. In the calm evening walk we see in the distance the suspicious-looking bundle, and the mangled infant is within. By the canal side, or in the water, we find the child. In the solitude of the wood, we are horrified by the ghastly sight; and if we take ourselves to the rapid rail in order to escape the pollution, we find at our journey's end that the mouldering remains of a murdered innocent have been our travelling companion, and that the odour from that unsuspected parcel too truly indicates what may be found inside.[6]

Canals, roads, trains: the modern metropolis was haunted by child murder, the traces of its primeval, torpid past. The murdered infant was the 'too familiar object', as Humble had it, when the civilised and modern were not familiar enough.

Graphic descriptions such as these infused the national press throughout the decade. According to the new sensational newspaper, the *Pall Mall Gazette*, Britain had come to be known by (of all people) the French, as a 'nation of infanticides'. It was now a 'terrible epoch of national life': infanticide was 'the great social evil of our day', 'a national institution'.[7] What is striking in all these accounts is the way in which the problem is always construed as a sign of a *national* disorder, just as its elimination would be a cause of patriotic pride. The very geography and temporality of the modern British nation were at stake; its networks of communication, its hygiene, its moral stature, all were threatened by the persistence and primordial stagnancy of child murder. It was a disease of modern life for sure; and its cure something for which, according to Ryan, 'no surer sign of patriotism need be sought'.[8]

It was medical men, like Ryan, who took up the challenge to rid the nation of this pest.[9] Child murder was now cast as a socio-medical problem that could be cured by medical treatment and legislative regulation, rather than by political or social change as it had been conceived in the radical rhetoric of the late 1830s and 1840s. Rather, the epidemic would respond to the ministrations of modern, medical professionals, as had the cholera epidemics of 1832 and 1849. It was not a problem for 'quacks', with their 'homeopathic delusion';[10] or for women. Indeed, women were a large part of the problem. The discussion, especially in the medical press, revolved around the forms of labour that were deemed inappropriate in a new professional world. The issues were strikingly gendered. One particular target was the wet nurse, a degraded worker, whose fallen status (wet nurses were often represented as unmarried mothers) threatened the nation's offspring with her insanitary habits and dangerous morals.[11] Moreover, the scandals that broke concerning baby farms around this time highlighted another group of female workers – the so-called baby farmers. Baby farms were, in effect, cheap child care – nurseries to which, for a fee, lower-class women entrusted the care of their infants. A number of high profile cases, however, drew public attention to levels of neglect in such establishments that seemed tantamount to murder. The sensational case of Margaret Waters and Sarah Ellis, who ran a baby farm in Brixton, led to the constitution of the Select Committee on Infant Life Protection (1870) and eventually to legislation regulating child care, the Infant Life Protection Act (1872).[12] Women workers emerged from these discussions in a particularly sinister light, as mid-century incarnations of Malthus's prototypical professional woman, Dame Nature: wet nurses, baby farmers, and even the careless lower-class women who abandoned their own children to their care, all became killers in a massacre of the innocents that endangered the very basis of civilised society.

In contrast, for professional men, infanticide was an issue around which to consolidate their identity and prestige. For instance, Thomas Wakley, Lankester's predecessor as coroner for Middlesex, and one of the first medical practitioners to hold the office, begun to focus attention on the question of infanticide in the 1850s.[13] A Radical member of parliament for Finsbury between 1835 and 1852, as well as the founding editor of the *Lancet* from 1823 until his death in 1861, Wakley was an important spokesperson for coroners at a transitional moment in their development as a professional group. Opposition to coroners came both from lawyers, who were reluctant to relinquish ground to the scientific opinion of medical men, but also from the public in general, which harboured deeply rooted prejudices

against forensic techniques, popularly associated with murdering and god-
less, Burke-and-Hare body-snatchers.[14] For Wakley, who had made a special study of infant suffocation, it was the typically complex cases of infant
mortality that presented the most compelling evidence of the need for
both more extensive use of inquests, and the inclusion of medical opinion
in trials. According to Wakley, all manner of violent crimes went undetected 'under the dark shadow of the term "still-born"', and he proposed
a number of measures for exposing them, including the registration of
stillborns, which enhanced the role of the coroner in the administration
of justice.[15] When Edwin Lankester took over Wakley's mantle as coroner
of Middlesex in 1862, an appointment that was hotly contested by the
lawyers, he persisted in Wakley's campaign to reduce infant mortality.
Carrying out many more inquests than had ever been performed before,
Lankester produced evidence of child murders taking place at an alarming
rate, and published his findings in his many articles and papers, complete
with statistics of the kind cited by Henry Humble.

Lankester's figures, however, were a statistical 'mirage', summoned up to
boost the professional status of coroners in their competition with lawyers.[16]
Studies have suggested that Lankester and the coroners inflated the extent
to which child murder was occurring, and that, moreover, newspapers
conspired in exaggerating the problem, thus whipping up moral panic on
an unprecedented scale. This makes the epidemic a strangely ephemeral
affair, a phantom of public opinion, rather than a case of mass murder.
The new modern professionals seemed to have conjured the very barbaric
practices that their success was predicated upon eliminating.

The child-murder epidemic coincided with two instances of the act in
pivotal texts by major literary figures of the period – George Eliot and
Matthew Arnold – demonstrating that the interest in infanticide extended
well beyond coroners and newspapers. The first of these, and the example
with which this chapter is chiefly concerned, was in *Adam Bede*, George
Eliot's first full-length novel. Written between 1857 and 1858, and published
the following year, this novel marked the blossoming of George Eliot's career as Britain's foremost realist novelist, whose work would have a powerful
influence on the shape and style of the English novel for many generations.[17]
Five years after the publication of *Adam Bede*, Matthew Arnold incorporated a fleeting reference to 'a shocking child murder' by 'a girl named
Wragg' at a critical point in his essay, 'The Function of Criticism at the
Present Time' (1864). This child murder had a crucial role in Arnold's conception of 'disinterested criticism', and lay at the heart of his project to
renew English culture, redeeming it from its alleged decline. In different

ways, both texts can be seen to be participating in a wider project of this era to build a distinctively literary national culture. And in both these defining texts, child murder occurs like a founding sacrifice, opening the way to a national cultural renaissance.

The relationship between the social manifestations of the child-murder epidemic and these literary instances is usually rendered as a causal one: that is to say, in their depictions of child murder, George Eliot and Arnold are thought to be reflecting the preoccupations of their time.[18] But this is to diminish the role of their work in shaping those very preoccupations. If we consider the epidemic to be a cultural phenomenon rather than solely a social experience, then we can see that they are involved in the phenomenon in a much more active way. These literary texts provide us with different insights into the questions raised by the epidemic: why does child murder become a subject of such intense preoccupation at this juncture? And why in the late 1850s and early 1860s should child murder be so wrapped up with notions of Britishness or Englishness? To address these questions I turn to the child murders that George Eliot finds etched in the literary landscape of Britain.

MEMORY AND THE NATION

The most famous child murder of nineteenth-century English literature is that which takes place in George Eliot's *Adam Bede* (1859). The novel follows the familiar infanticide plot – inter-class seduction, female destitution, murdered child. Hetty Sorrel, a beautiful milkmaid, is seduced and abandoned by the squire's grandson, Arthur Donnithorne. Finding herself pregnant, but now engaged to another man, Adam Bede, she goes in desperate search of Arthur; unable to find him, she wanders the countryside in a daze, contemplating suicide. After she has given birth, she buries the infant in a woodpile where it soon dies. Fatally, she returns to the scene of the crime because she is haunted by her memory of the baby, but is discovered there and arrested. Tried for murder, found guilty, and condemned to death, Hetty finally repents, and seeks God's forgiveness through the ministry of her cousin, Dinah Morris, a Methodist preacher. In a melodramatic twist, Arthur obtains a pardon for her, and charging on horseback to the gallows where Hetty awaits her death, his eyes 'glazed by madness', he announces that her sentence has been commuted to transportation. Hetty's expulsion allows Adam to realise the true worth of Dinah, whom he eventually marries. In the final scene, set exactly eight years from the beginning of the novel, we visit Adam and Dinah, their children, and Adam's brother

Seth, awaiting the return of Arthur Donnithorne to the village, Hayslope, from an army posting abroad. Disgraced but forgiven, Arthur, who is now a sick man, will be reabsorbed into the community.

Typically for George Eliot, social change is understood in a Burkean way, as though it is achieved through a process of gradual evolution, rather than by violent or catastrophic revolution. Thus Adam's social rise, from employed artisan to self-employed, property-owning, small business man, and Arthur's eventual re-incorporation into the community, are presented as changes that are as inevitable as the passing of the seasons. The final scene presents a vision of a new English society in which authority has come to lie with the emerging middle class, the vestiges of the old order absorbed naturally into the contours of the new.[19]

But not everyone can be incorporated: especially not Hetty, the child murderer. As Eve Kosofsky Sedgwick points out, the new society has a sexual economy that excludes certain kinds of femininity.[20] The process of social transformation entails that female sexuality be disciplined; but while the sensual and rhapsodic preacher, Dinah, can be contained within the role of wife and mother, the pleasure-seeking Hetty cannot. In this reading, Hetty's child murder is an attribute of her dissident sexuality, the most extreme manifestation of a wild, transgressive desire that threatens the stability of the emerging bourgeois society.

The symbolic significance of the child murder, however, extends beyond this, for the entire narrative of social progress is underpinned by the traditional associations between child murder and barbarity on the one hand, and child loving and civilisation on the other. As Adam Smith famously noted in his *Theory of Moral Sentiments*, only those deriving from 'savage nations' would kill a child. Through the ejection of Hetty, the new society of George Eliot's modern England accrues the veneer of child-loving civilisation and enlightenment rationality. Moreover, her destination – the savage environment of the colonial peripheries, the place best suited to her infanticidal nature – helps to demarcate the boundaries of the new society, organising its imaginary territory.[21] The child murder in *Adam Bede* is thus crucial to the novel's attempt to define and locate the new society, as civilised and child-loving, inhabited by healthy, reproductive families, rather than the wild child-killers who are expelled beyond its borders. But it is also the event around which the new society bonds, and in that sense is something like a founding sacrifice. Indeed, as a contribution to the literature of child murder, *Adam Bede* is striking for its utilisation of two opposing child-murder narratives: child murder is at once the marker of cultural alterity; but also the redemptive sacrifice.

The success of *Adam Bede*, and the rapid succession of the equally admired *The Mill on the Floss* (1860) and *Silas Marner* (1861), allowed George Eliot quickly to establish a reputation for herself as the novelist of an influential narrative about the development and character of modern England, its gradual emergence from traditional, rural communities.[22] Her plots were set in the past, and their environmental and social details always meticulously researched, usually from printed sources such as newspapers and magazines from the appropriate era, and books of history and natural history.[23] Moreover the chronologies were carefully crafted according to clock and calendrical time – obsessively so in *Adam Bede*, where the events of different characters in the various locations of the novel are coordinated against a backdrop of the relentless passing hours, days, and months.[24] This is the 'homogeneous, empty time' of the nation – a concept Benedict Anderson borrows from Walter Benjamin, to describe the 'transverse, cross-time' temporality of the modern nation, for which the genre of the novel (along with the daily press) provided 'the technical means for re-presenting'.[25] According to Anderson, '[t]he idea of a sociological organism moving calendrically through homogeneous, empty time is a precise analogue of the idea of the nation, which also is conceived as a solid community moving steadily down (or up) history.' In George Eliot's novels, this 'empty time' exists in a dimly remembered past – the events of *Adam Bede* begin in 1799, not within her own living memory for sure, but within that of her parents' generation; and in the landscape of her childhood – the heartland of England, the rural midlands on the cusp of industrialisation.

For contemporary readers, George Eliot was the novelist of a common memory, an archivist of a national past. Memory is an important theme across her oeuvre, but while in the later novels, especially *Daniel Deronda* (1876), she explores the somatic effects of involuntary and individual memory, in the early works, like *Adam Bede* and *The Mill on the Floss*, the concern is with the memory of communities, and its function in knitting together societies. Leslie Stephen, in his obituary of her in 1880, commented appreciatively on her depiction of the 'quiet English country life,' 'its last traces … vanishing so rapidly amidst the changes of modern revolution that its picture could hardly be drawn again'.[26] In a process of metonymic substitution, the past of rural England stands for the past of the nation, just as her own personal memory comes to double as a national memory: in a review of *Adam Bede*, in *Bentley's Quarterly Review*, Anne Mozley slipped easily from the third person (denoting Eliot/the narrator) to the first person plural (we), when she commented on the nostalgic framing of the narrative, the way in which the narrator 'looked back upon [scenes] with an almost passionate tenderness, as though the senses ached for the genial old home', presenting 'spots to which habit has so closely allied us that we see ourselves reflected in them'.[27] The last phrases invoke a Wordsworthian vocabulary: the 'spot of time', with which according to the poet, 'our minds / Are nourished and invisibly repaired'.[28] In Mozley's account, we 'see ourselves reflected' in these 'spots', and these in turn reflect George Eliot's sense of her own literary heritage, and draw her into a particular national literary tradition. For this narrator of the nation, the common, customary memories of a place and a past interweave with the imaginings of a national literature. Indeed, in *Adam Bede*, the child murder theme itself helps to consolidate these literary connections. George Eliot's account of Hetty's child murder refers back insistently to Wordsworth's 'The Thorn' – a poem first published in the *Lyrical Ballads* in 1798, the year before that in which the action of the novel begins. Arthur's receipt of a copy of the volume near the beginning of the novel – a work he judges to be 'twaddling stuff' (p. 65) – is thus both topical and thematically significant. The novel is strewn with reference to thorns, from Adam's mother's insistence that her husband, Thias, should be buried beneath the white thorn, to the rendition at the harvest supper towards the end of the novel of 'My Love's a Rose without a Thorn' (p. 570). Furthermore the entire novel draws heavily on Scott's *The Heart of Midlothian*, which also had paid tribute to 'The Thorn'.[29] Through the child-murder association, therefore, George Eliot's quintessentially *central* English location merges with the geographically disparate and peripheral regions of Wordsworth's 'The Thorn' (Alfoxden in the South West) and Scott's *The Heart of Midlothian* (Scotland and the Borders). This composite literary landscape – a landscape scored through with shards of infant corpses – becomes home for the imagined community of Britain.

George Eliot's narrative of the nation in *Adam Bede*, therefore, is an interweaving of places, texts, and recollections, a confabulation of memories and desires, rather than an entity defined by 'race... language... religion... [or] the course of rivers... [or] the direction taken by mountain chains'.[30] Although race, language, religion, and territory are important terms in the definition of the nation in the novel, they are nevertheless superimposed on an identity that is fundamentally made out of memories.[31] The quotation is taken from Ernest Renan, the French analyst of nationalism broadly contemporary with George Eliot. His influential 1882 lecture 'Qu'est-ce qu'une nation?' presents a version of nationhood that is surprisingly close to George Eliot's. Like George Eliot in the early novels, he emphasises the construction of a cultural memory as the basis of national identity. Renan developed this version of the nation against the German tradition of nationalist thought, developed by Herder, which emphasised the determinations of race, language, or territory. For Renan, the nation belonged to the more shadowy realm of memory and desire: the nation, he claims, is 'the common possession of a rich legacy of memories... [and] the will to continue to value one's undivided inheritance'.[32] Although George Eliot's intellectual roots were strongly in the German tradition, nevertheless, in the early novels she produces a version of the nation like Renan's.[33] For her, the nation's memory is drawn largely from literature – imaginative literature like 'The Thorn' and *The Heart of Midlothian*, but also the other printed sources that she researched; it is projected onto a landscape and onto the bodies of the local people, which only then come to embody the remembered national past.

Renan, however, wrote in France during the Third Republic – a very different context to George Eliot's 1850s Britain. For Renan, the national project was to construct an expanded democratic political culture out of a republican tradition whose roots were in the Terror. A national memory needed to be constructed in order to 'forget' the Terror and the King's death; the symbolic significance of the latter was deeply embedded in French national consciousness, as the event which founded the Republic – as Robespierre pronounced in 1792, '[The King] must die because the Republic lives'.[34] Renan thus writes of the necessity of forgetting the violent deeds that 'are at the origin of all political formations', and the 'historical error' that is required for consolidation of national belonging.[35] In many ways, the lecture can be read as an extended apologia for the compulsion to forget, where forgetting itself becomes a contrived rather than an involuntary process: he uses the formulation 'doit avoir oublié' to invoke the process by which events 'must have been forgotten' in order that the nation might be constituted.[36] Symptomatically, perhaps, the Terror is not mentioned in the lecture, as though it really has been forgotten – although this is unlikely, as the monarchical opposition to the Third Republic referred to it endlessly: the violent deeds that Renan writes about as the foundations of the nation are located in a much more distant past – the massacre of Saint Bartholemew in 1572, or the massacres in the Midi in the thirteenth century – than the relatively recent First Republic. Nevertheless, the lecture is haunted by an involuntary memory of the Terror that remains the unspoken reference point for Renan's theorisation.

In contrast to the violent past of the French Republic, monarchical Britain prided itself on the absence of revolution in its own national history – despite the fact that, of course, they too had executed a king. For Edmund Burke, whose *Reflections on the Revolution in France* (1790)

portrayed the national history as a seamless, organic growth, the very contrast between the convulsions of the French national past and the smooth-
ness of the British was a point from which British identity was to be drawn.
However, this Burkean sense of the British past, very much perpetuated
by George Eliot in her fiction, entailed concerted amnesias of its own: the
wilful forgetting of periods of popular discontent and violent uprising, conflicts between the constituents of the Union, and – in the late 1850s, when
Adam Bede was written and published – rebellions in India, that drew into
question the very nature of Britain's authority as a colonising nation. Traces
of this vexed past and present, I will suggest, are in fact embedded in the
figure of child murder; so that for George Eliot in 1859, the murdered child
comes to be a repository of a national forgotten in much the way that the
murdered king would be for Renan in 1882. In *Adam Bede*, child murder is
a figure in which the less than consensual national past has been buried –
a burial that duplicates Hetty's attempt to evade the consequences of her
past by burying the baby. The project, as we shall see, turns out to be
as vexed as Renan's attempt to forget the king; and is pursued as am-
bivalently as Hetty's disposal of her child. Hetty leaves the child in the
woodpile so that someone might find it and 'save it from dying'; but finding it gone, she is 'struck like a stone, with fear' (p. 454). In telling a tale
of the national past, I will suggest, the novel, too, returns to the scene
of burial, hoping that the events it has buried might have been forgotten; but at the same time filled with dread that they will return to be its
undoing.

The novel's relationship to child murder is a rich and complicated one.
Child murder by burial here is an allegorical enactment of the process of
nation-making by forgetting. As an allegory, it screens us from the material
that it tries to forget; but paradoxically, the screen also acts as a trigger to
memories of precisely the material that is repressed. The child murder in
the novel is thus an aid to forgetting in the construction of the national
past; but, paradoxically and uncomfortably, operates as an *aide mémoire*
too.

REMEMBERING 1803 AND 1839

What forgotten memories lie buried in the figure of child murder in *Adam
Bede*? George Eliot herself gives us some clues. On 30 November 1858, two
weeks after completing the manuscript, she entered a piece in her journal
entitled 'The History of Adam Bede', in which she gave an account of the
genesis of the novel.[37] 'The History' is a revealing document, because it

recalls the historical resonances of the act of child murder that are buried in the novel.

George Eliot claims that the 'germ' of the novel was an anecdote that had been told to her by her aunt, the Methodist preacher, Elizabeth Evans, in 1839 – a year familiar to readers of this book. At the time, George Eliot was still Mary Ann Evans, eighteen years old, and living in her family home in Warwickshire. The anecdote concerned a young woman who had been found guilty of killing her child and was awaiting execution in a Nottingham gaol; Elizabeth Evans had visited the woman in prison, and ministered to her, until the convict confessed, and sought redemption.[38] Its bearing on *Adam Bede* is very clear: it prefigures the scene towards the end of the novel – intended by George Eliot as its climax – in which Dinah, also a Methodist preacher, elicits a confession from Hetty. Literary historians have traced the story to a case of child murder concerning a woman called Mary Voce, whose trial took place in 1802. The case achieved local notoriety, and was recorded in the broadsheet literature published in Nottingham at the time.[39] The story, George Eliot tells us, 'affected her deeply', but she 'never mentioned it through all the intervening years, till something prompted me to tell it to George [Lewes] in December 1856, when I had begun to write the "Scenes of Clerical Life" '.[40]

According to this account, the 'germ' or source of the novel was an anecdote from experience – 'an anecdote from her aunt's own experience'; but it is also an anecdote from her own experience of hearing the aunt tell the tale, and indeed of her subsequent retelling of it to George. Wrapped up in this account is a series of moments, all carefully dated: 1856, when she told George about it, 1839, when her aunt told her, and 1802, when Mary Voce was condemned and redeemed by Elizabeth Evans. Interestingly, all three of these dates mark episodes of frenetic activity in the discursive history of child murder – moments at which the meanings of child murder are highly fraught and politically charged – and with which George Eliot's personal history happens to intersect.

The dramatic action of George Eliot's novels usually takes place in a society on the brink of change – a change that is often marked by a shift in legislation.[41] Hetty's trial takes place in the spring of 1800 – two years before that of Mary Voce.[42] Both Hetty and Mary are tried before the repeal of the notorious 1624 Act to Prevent the Murthering and Destroying of Infant Bastards in 1803. In *Adam Bede*, the point of transition is thus the new child-murder legislation, introduced in 1803 in Lord Chief Justice Ellenborough's catch-all Offences against the Person Act (43 Geo. III c. 58, 1803), an act that brought an end to what we might think of as an infanticidal *ancien régime*. As we have seen,[43] the reform was driven less by sympathy for unwed mothers and illegitimate children, than by a desire for administrative efficiency, to make the law effective in regard to a crime in the treatment of which it had long been regarded as ineffectual. It gave courts a new measure of regulatory control over women and their reproductive functions in a context in which women's unlicensed sexual expression had come to assume deep associations with forms of political disruption.

1800 was itself also a year of major legislative change of another sort which impacted on the history of infanticide. The Act of Union with Ireland that year extended the parameters of British nationhood, and the reach of national legislation. The 1803 Offences against the Person Act was in fact part of the process of legislative rationalisation and political restructuring that followed the Act of Union. The new act replaced not only the 1624 statute, but also a parallel Irish statute (1 Anne. c. 4, Irish statutes, 1707), and aimed to provide consistency in the treatment of dissident mothers across the newly 'united' England and Ireland. It thus participated in the new regime of colonial regulation: drawing together a miscellany of a wide variety of violent crimes – 'malicious shooting, and attempting to discharge loaded Fire-Arms, stabbing, cutting, wounding, poisoning, and the malicious using of Means to procure the Miscarriage of Women; and also the malicious setting Fire to Buildings', as well as the repeal of the murder of infant bastard statutes. Not only did it subject the Irish to a centralised, English legal system, but also, in its individual clauses, it targeted specific acts of Irish criminal and insurrectionary violence. The 1803 legislation on infanticide was thus part of a battery of measures aimed at making the Irish fit for British nationhood. The inclusion of cases of incendiarism, and the special provision made by Ellenborough to correct an anomaly in the Irish law that permitted the burning of one's own house, is instructive. At the time of the Act's construction, the Irish nationalist Robert Emmet led a campaign of buying buildings and burning them as a tactic in a rebellion that was finally suppressed by the British in 1803 with the execution of Emmet and twenty-one of his compatriots.[44]

The turn of the century context, which George Eliot highlights through her aunt's story, draws attention to the broader significance of child murder in the novel – the way in which it enables the text to broach issues of modernisation and nationhood. As Ireland is embedded within the texture of the infanticide legislation of 1803, it also leaves its traces in the novel. When the pregnant Hetty went to look for Arthur in February 1800, he had been posted with his regiment, the invented Loamshire Militia, to Ireland, where martial law had been established in 1798.[45] It is likely that he would have returned to Ireland after the trial, and possibly stayed at least until 1803, and perhaps was involved in the suppression of Emmet's Rebellion. When he returns to Hayslope at the end of the novel, in 1807, it is unclear where he has been, only that he returns with a fever, perhaps indicating a tropical posting. As a member of the British army in this period he could have been in many other places – possibly the West Indies – policing the colonies, or annexing new ones. This period marks an important stage in the development of the British Empire, in which military campaigns eliminated other colonising powers, facilitating free trade. Arthur's absence from Hayslope in the latter parts of the novel is a reminder of Britain's expanding domain, and the military effort that was required for the sustenance of the colonial regime.

If the turn of the eighteenth century marks a moment in which notions of child murder and nationhood were imbricated with personal memory and novelistic emplotment, the same can be said of 1839. This is the second year referred to in the journal entry, the year in which George Eliot first heard the story that was to be the 'germ' of the novel, but it was also very much an infanticidal year.[46] As we saw in Chapter Four, 1839 was the time that the protests against the New Poor Law were at their height, when violent demonstrations took place across the country, and indeed, the time of the first large-scale Chartist rallies; and newspapers were overflowing with accounts of child murders, which were often drawn into intensely political debates. Against this background, in the spring of 1839, Elizabeth Evans visited the brother's family from her home in Wirksworth, near Nottingham, where she lived and had worked in a lace factory. This was an industrialised area, quite different from the rural Warwickshire home of her niece. Elizabeth Evans had also been a Methodist minister until female ministry was outlawed in 1803, and for a short period, the aunt and her husband joined a breakaway sect so that she could continue preaching.[47] In 1839, when it 'occurred to' her to tell her niece the story of Mary Voce, another Methodist minister was attracting a great deal of publicity – the Reverend Joseph Raynor Stephens, the firebrand demagogue of Ashton, the anti-Poor Law protestor, who at the time was awaiting trial. As we saw in Chapter Four, in the period between his arrest in December 1838 and his trial in the summer of 1839, Stephens toured the country giving politically explosive sermons about the New Poor Law, with his inflammatory references to the plots of 'Marcus' to murder the children of the working class. George Eliot implies that the aunt's recollection in 1839 of the events of more than thirty years ago, came on quite spontaneously: 'We were sitting together one afternoon during her visit to me at Griffe', she writes, 'when it occurred to her to tell me how she had visited a condemned criminal...'[48] Yet the events of the day may well have acted as a prompt to that spontaneity.

The case of Mary Voce provides an instructive corrective to the politically controversial narratives like those of Joseph Raynor Stephens, in which child murder was purported to be a consequence of state oppression, and which in 1839 had provoked a series of violent uprisings. Mary Voce had been convicted for poisoning her six-week-old daughter with arsenic in 1802. Unlike Hetty Sorrel, Voce was a married woman, but, very definitely, a promiscuous one. She had had lots of affairs, cohabited with other men, and killed her daughter when her husband castigated her for her infidelities and left her. The broadsheets tell different versions of the story. According to one, she killed the child in a Medea-like fury, to revenge her husband; but in another, she says she did it for expediency, because without her husband, she was poor, and needed to work.[49] Nevertheless, all of them emphasise Voce's culpability and promiscuity, in a way that contrasts strikingly with the politically and emotionally powerful stories that were being peddled by the radicals and Chartist sympathisers, and seems instead to hark back to the tenor of earlier, turn-of-the-century discussions of child murder, which highlighted the relationship between child murder and women's sexual disorder. Unlike the desperate acts of women driven to sacrifice their own children, Mary Voce's child murder is a vicious and immoral deed from which she herself must be redeemed. In the context of 1839, Mary Voce redefines child murder as an individual crime of licentiousness, rather than a political act of sacrifice.

It is impossible to say whether George Eliot remembered the political climate of 1839 when, nearly twenty years later in the midst of another episode in the history of child murder, she recalled her aunt's visit. We do know from her journal, however, that during the time she was writing *Adam Bede* she read from Dickens's *Christmas Books* – possibly even his anti-New Poor Law child-murder story, *The Chimes* – and we can speculate that Dickens's vehement attacks on the injustices of Malthusian and utilitarian social policies prompted her to reflect on the events of 1839.[50] Moreover, the issues raised in 1839, especially regarding political representation of the working class, were still live ones; George Eliot saw the political dilemmas of her own time as a response to the unresolved problems of the Reform Act of 1832, the burgeoning resentment of the working class which found expression in the Chartist movement and associated forms of popular re-sistance, including that against the New Poor Law.[51] Of course Hetty is not Mary Voce, no more than she is the noble Meg in *The Chimes*; but her promiscuity, although in milder mode than Voce's, is encoded in the novel, as she circulates too freely among men, and thinks too much of sensual pleasures. In a muted way, Hetty too corrects the tales of the desperate, destitute women who killed their children to save them from the work-house, or the 'Marcus' stories of mass state infanticide, tales that inspired an episode of civil insurrection.

There is no direct reference to 1839 in *Adam Bede*. Of course, the turn-of-the-century setting of the novel precludes this. But the memory buried deep in George Eliot's journal entry reminds us not only of the troubled context of that moment, but also of George Eliot's need to forget it. In the context of the Burkean narrative of gradual development and growth, the protests of 1839, like the rebellions in Ireland against the 1800 Union, are events that, in Renan's formulation, *have had to be forgotten*: the repression necessary for the perpetuation of the nation.

INDIAN INFANTICIDE AND THE 1857 UPRISING

The historical resonance of child murder is further intensified by the third date mentioned in George Eliot's journal: December 1856, the date of her retelling the story to George Lewes and the last stage in her retrieval of the anecdote. Critics have usually understood the child-murder theme in the novel to be a topical reflection of the British infanticide epidemic, and it is certainly the case that there was no shortage of cases in the daily press in December 1856 or in the intervening months before George Eliot began work on the novel for real, in October 1857.[52] However, there are other ways in which infanticide would have resonated at this time. As we have seen, throughout the later eighteenth and nineteenth centuries, infanti-cide was a practice associated with foreigners; discussions of infanticide, from Malthus onwards, invariably relayed lists of suspects from Sparta and Solon, China and Otaheite. But by the mid-1850s, infanticide had come to be associated with one particular foreign nation: India – Britain's largest and most valuable colony.[53] The widespread practice of female infanticide in regions of India, along with other indigenous social features, such as the practice of widow burning (*sati*), and the bands of itinerant bandits (*thagi*), were for the British proof of Indian barbarity, and all were targets of British colonial humanitarian reforms.[54] Discussions of British infan-ticide often contained comparisons with India seeing the new epidemic as an 'Indianising' of British society. For instance, Henry Humble, cited at the beginning of the chapter, saw the problem in Britain to be one of 'caste' as though the existence of infant corpses automatically shifted the social structure of Britain into an oriental one. Disraeli's comment in his

1845 novel, *Sybil*, that 'Infanticide is practised as extensively and as legally in England as on the banks of the Ganges',[55] had already encapsulated the odd mixture of repudiation and identification that would characterise these comparisons as the worries about child murder in Britain rose in pitch over the next decades. In 1857, however, India's role in Britain's imagination as a child-murdering nation was dramatically transformed: in the context of the revolt in northern India which began in 1857 and lasted until the end of the following year, Indians changed from being the killers of their own children, to the dangerous assassins of British babies. By 1857, therefore, child murder had become an over-determined sign of oriental danger.

Knowledge of the practice of female infanticide, collated by colonial administrators, had been gradually trickling into Britain since its first documentation in 1789 by a colonial official at Benares, Jonathan Duncan.[56] In 1823, parliament ordered a compilation of correspondence regarding 'Hindoo Infanticide', which resulted in the publication in 1824 of an extensive record of official reports, surveys, and communications between administrators and local élites, as well as passages from Hindu scriptures and other indigenous literature, all considered to be of relevance to the practice of female infanticide and colonial efforts to suppress it. More compilations were published in the parliamentary papers of 1828 and 1843, providing a stock of material that was disseminated further through reviews, essays, and books.[57] But a swathe of publications in the 1850s had brought its practices to public attention in a more insistent way than ever before.[58] There is no question that George Eliot would have encountered essays on the subject, published as they were alongside her work, and George Henry Lewes's, in volumes of *Blackwood's*.[59]

The accounts of Indian infanticide that are to be found in the publications of the 1850s are a repetitive outpouring of the same stories, anecdotes, and analysis, much of which had been culled from the Parliamentary Papers, and the element of rumour and hearsay that characterises this knowledge recalls the ways in which details of child murder circulated in other instances, especially the 'Marcus' affair in 1839 discussed in Chapter Four. In this case, Indian society is represented in characteristically orientalist terms: overly sensual, riven by divisions of caste, its people driven by petty pride and vanity, its men brutal and despotic, an ancient society participating in its own decline. While attention is paid to different kinds of practices in the various regions of India, in the end all seem to merge into one under a hazy cloud of exotic names, as infanticide comes to operate as a generalised sign of Indian degeneracy. Emphasis is laid on the Rajputs of North Western areas, a high caste warrior group who for various reasons had lost their wealth, but sought to maintain their social status.[60] Aristocratic and strongly patriarchal, their faded glamour and violent sensuality played to British fantasies of oriental life. R. H. Patterson's vignette of Rajput infanticide, included in an article on 'Our Indian Empire' published in *Blackwood's* in 1856, was typical of much of the writing on the topic in the almost pornographic idiom it assumed: 'When a messenger from the zezana announced to him the birth of a daughter', he writes, 'the Rajpoot chief would coolly roll up between his fingers a tiny opium ball, to be conveyed to the mother who thereupon rubbed on her nipple the sleepy poison, and the babe drank in death with its mother's milk.'[61] The Rajput's cool authority, the sensuality of his fingers, the enclosed female society of the zezana, the soporific opium, the mother's softly tampered breast – all elements are choreographed with a controlled reserve that mirrors that of the Rajput himself, intensifying the erotic charge.

As is typical of such orientalist literature, the accounts present an accumulation of diverging rationales, layers of analysis superimposing moral, scientific, and aesthetic explanations over each other, and creating a spectre of intransigent racial and cultural difference. Running throughout the material is an anthropological analysis of the practice in terms of Rajput marriage customs: daughters must marry according to the principles of exogamy, that is, outside the caste, but into a family of equal or higher standing; the determining causes of female infanticide were thus the cost of marriage, added to the lack of suitable husbands, and the 'shame' of spinsterhood. Any kind of moral or cultural relativism implicit in such a materialist analysis, however, is usually checked by a heavy overlaying of expressions of Indian degeneracy: thus according to J. W. Kaye, in *The Administration of the East India Company*, it is 'the unchastity of the female that is the proximate cause of the crime'; or, for John Wilson, it 'originates in [the Rajput's] execrable pride and selfishness'.[62] Or indeed, it is checked by descriptions of the Indians' own flimsy belief systems that are rooted only in 'obscure fables' (Kaye), the oriental tales that were popular in Britain at the time.[63] 'In England', writes Kaye, 'infanticide is peculiar to the lower orders; in India it is peculiar to the higher. In England it is the activity of degradation; in India the activity of pride.'[64] In India it is a crime caused by no more than vanity, the phantasm of an ancient caste system; a reason that recedes into nothing, its oriental evanescence in sharp contrast with the brute realism of English infanticide provoked by poverty and degradation.

Indian infanticide thus exposed the distinctively barbaric characteristics of native society to British eyes. Blind adherence to vanity and tradition had produced a culture that was curiously detached from the material concerns of the society: Indian infanticide was deemed to be a direct consequence of this state of deracination and superficiality, a symptom of native false consciousness. In contrast, it reflected back to Britons the superiority of their own culture – in which customs were rooted in material conditions, and where even infanticide was an honest reflection of a material reality. Indian infanticide also presented ample opportunities for British colonials to demonstrate their own civility. The literature on female infanticide contains accounts of the diverse measures put in place in various regions and at different times to outlaw the practice. There is nothing that amounts to a single campaign; rather, a series of forays, each of them turning colonial administrators into heroic champions of Indian infant life. In the period leading up to the Rebellion, the tactics were underpinned by the utilitarian philosophy that dominated the East India Company administration, combining schemes of regulation and surveillance, rather than those of coercion.[65] Sumptuary measures were introduced – the establishment of an infanticide fund, for instance, which used fines inflicted on communities in which the practice continued, to provide grants to defray marriage costs for surviving girls. The accounts of female infanticide in British publications overflowed with charts of statistics, the result of an obsessive counting of bodies, by gender and mortality. Censuses, inquests, the compulsory registration of births, marriages and deaths, constituted a project of surveillance that made Indians among the most scrutinised people in the world, and, in the British cultural imaginary, India something akin to Bentham's panopticon.

In addition, heavy emphasis was laid on education – especially an English literary education – as a means of eradicating the practice.[66] As John Cave Browne wrote in *Indian Infanticide*, 'the infusion of English ideas and English modes of thought will greatly tend to expand the native mind'.[67] Thus schools were set up in villages, with texts such as Adam Smith's *Theory of Moral Sentiments*, with its expressions on the savagery of child murder, high on the curriculum.[68] The word was spread in native tongues too: a prize essay on female infanticide to be written in English and translated into Gujarati was instituted,[69] and specially commissioned stories and poems by native writers on the evils of infanticide were published. An agent at Sehore reported that he had commissioned 'one of the most intelligent and most respected Brahmins', to compose in Hindu verse 'the strongest condemnation of the crime', which he duly disseminated; as well as a tale

THE DESTRUCTION AND PRESERVATION OF INFANTS IN INDIA, pp. 32, 35, 61.

Figure 6. 'The Destruction and Preservation of Infants in India', Frontispiece,
James Pegg, *The Infanticide's Cry to Britain*

written by an Indian author, Ram Bhao, 'relating an exceedingly barbarous instance of the crime'.[70] 'It has often struck me', he goes on, expanding his generic range, 'that any pictorial representation, exhibiting the actual perpetration of the crime with all its horrors, or one emblematically exhibiting the British government in India using its influence in the cause of humanity would... serve to keep men's hearts alive to the feelings of our better nature.' An illustration in the Reverend James Pegg's *The Infanticide's Cry to Britain*, 'The Destruction and Preservation of Infants in India' (see Fig. 6), may have served such a purpose, as it portrays the contrast between the furtive dealings of native people abandoning infants, and a group of British soldiers welcoming an orderly procession of child-nurturing natives.

Such interventions were compromised, and perhaps even shaped, by the complicated relationship that existed between British and native people. The forms of control over native customs were limited by the fact that vast areas of India, including many of the regions in which infanticide had been documented, had not yet been annexed. Britain's trade interests depended on the collaboration of local elites, and administrators were sharply aware of the need to flatter rather than to criticise. Indeed, the people with whom they dealt often included the high-caste Rajputs who practised female infanticide. Thus the preference for modes of diplomacy, the gradual changing of public opinion through education, and the circulation of poems and pictures, was motivated as much by expedience as it was by an ideological commitment to the virtues of persuasion over physical force or formal leg-islative enactment. But the question of the extent to which the British could and should intervene in native customs lay at the heart of debates about colonial government. By no means all agreed with the liberal conviction that the British role in India should include humanitarian reforms; many conservatives, on the contrary, felt that their presence was necessary only to facilitate and develop trade, and they distrusted the liberal campaigns as a complication of commercial relations.

These differences of opinion came sharply into focus in the spring of 1857 at the outbreak of the Indian Rebellion, an insurrection that rapidly spread across India, and lasted until the following year.[71] Conservatives blamed liberals for having caused the rebellion by breeding malcontent among native people through meddling with local customs – the first episode of the revolt had been sparked by the sepoys' protest against the pork and beef fat that greased their cartridges – and it is worth remembering that Rajputs from areas in which the British had attempted to suppress female infanticide made up a large percentage of the sepoys whose disaffection had fuelled the rebellion. The significance of what came in Britain to be known as the Indian Mutiny cannot be underestimated: a subaltern rebellion on an unprecedented scale, suppressed by the British army with excessive force.[72] It changed the nature of colonial rule in India, and drew the whole question of Britain's role as a colonial nation into public debate. Indeed, following the uprising, India became part of the British Empire for the first time – like Ireland – and it is striking that in both cases the colonial relation is framed by the spectre of child murder.

It was against this backdrop that George Eliot wrote *Adam Bede*. During the period, she pursued a characteristically serious interest in the issues by reading Harriet Martineau's *History of British India* (1857) and essays by Macaulay on Clive and Hastings.[73] But accounts of the revolt of a more populist and sensational nature saturated British culture: regular reports were printed in the daily press telling of the latest attacks, and the mutiny became a favourite topic of popular fiction.[74] Such accounts emphasised the violence committed against British families – not only against soldiers, but women and children too. As Jenny Sharpe has pointed out, they often drew on biblical and classical narratives of atrocities – including the mas-sacre of the innocents[75] – utilising a conventional vocabulary of suffering, which included copious references to infant death and violation. Take, for example, Charles Ball's description of an incident at Allahabad in his serial publication, *The History of the Indian Mutiny* (1858):

Infants were actually torn from their mothers' arms, and their little limbs chopped off with bulwars yet reeking with their father's blood; while the shrieking mother was forcibly compelled to hear the cries of her tortured child, and to behold through scolding tears of agony, the death writhings of the slaughtered innocent.[76]

This graphic account of the infants' dismemberment, framed by the mothers' agony, recalls Rousseau's depiction of pity in the *Second Discourse*, discussed in Chapter Two. What is most remarkable about these popular narratives of the Mutiny is not the inclusion of child murders, nor even the gruesome detail with which they are portrayed. Rather it is the way in which the references to child murder mark a transformation in the popular representation of Indians: no longer the killers of their own young, an ancient people involved in a mysterious and melancholy process of self-annihilation, Indians had been transformed into the menacing assassins of British babies.

Between December 1856, when George Eliot told George Henry Lewes the anecdote of Mary Voce, and October 1857, when she started to write the novel, child murder had been thrown into public consciousness, as a confusing sign of both subaltern barbarity and rebellion. It now occupied a complex position in the representation of colonial authority. Infanticidal customs made India both a site of civilising endeavour for the British, and also a place of absolute alterity, justifying the more coercive measures that were put in place after this violent episode. Moreover, Britain's own sense of nationhood in the late 1850s and 1860s was formed in part through the internalisation of the varied fantasies of India as a child-murdering nation, creating an identity fissured by both desire and loathing. The fact that at this very moment, Britain was thought to be entering its own child-murder epidemic could perhaps be seen as a symptom of this. The lurking fear that Britain was a 'nation of infanticides' – a phrase that recalled the expression to be found in the pages of the *Parliamentary Papers* on 'Hindoo Infanticide', that India was a 'race of infanticides' – points to the ambivalence that is absorbed into the idea of Britishness at this time.[77] The murdered infant had returned to Britain across the intricate networks of colonial desire.

The emergence of the phantasmatic epidemic of child murder in Britain at this moment – the moment that is also that of George Eliot's *Adam Bede* – is thus very striking. For at the very point at which India presented a challenge to British colonial authority, the traditional manifestation of Indian barbarity, child murder, turned against its civilising force, Britain, too, found itself plagued by a proliferation of child murders that made it seem

as barbaric as unruly India. Infanticide seems like a terrible Indian epidemic infecting British shores. In this it resembled cholera, a scourge that
had also originated in the Indian subcontinent, so it was no wonder that
medical men saw infanticide as another chance to promote their own interests. Despite the tenor of much of the literature on female infanticide
in India, the child-murder outbreak in Britain in the late 1850s and 1860s
shared many characteristics with its occurrence in India. In Britain, as in
India, the phenomenon was not new in itself, but one that was newly
detected in the secret interstices of society, and by the same techniques of
surveillance that had been used in colonial India. Wakley's reference to the
untold violent crimes that went undetected 'under the dark shadow of the
term "still-born"' is interesting because it makes stillbirth seem something
like a place – like the zezana, perhaps, the all-female communities that
shielded Indian women from the prying eyes of foreigners, and which was
one of the main obstacles to colonial supervision.[78] The techniques of de-
tection and regulation adopted by the medical professionals in Britain were
those that had been used in India – censuses, registrations of births and
deaths, more use of inquests, a relentless counting of the people. Moreover,
the *Lancet* called for the better education of mothers, and the dissemination of literature that would encourage women to improve maternal care,
echoing the colonial emphasis on education as the most effective means of
civilisation.[79] The effect of these disciplinary measures was to make Britons
seem like colonial subjects: in the newly modernised professional nation,
the 'people' were paradoxically like subalterns.

The coroners' endeavours against infanticide must be seen alongside a series of other socio-medical, public health campaigns of the mid nineteenth
century all of which set out to 'civilise' the poor, usually in inner-city areas.
The insanitary environment of the urban poor was often construed in terms
of a racial difference, and reformers saw themselves as intrepid explorers
broaching the 'dark continent' of urban poverty.[80] The tumultuous events
of the Indian rebellion thus gave a spur to the social regulatory aspect of
such campaigns, because they dramatically illustrated the cost of native
insubordination in the dark interiors of the nation. As Humble and Ryan's
phantasmagoric cityscapes graphically evinced, the child-murder epidemic
made Britain not only disordered and barbaric, but also *stolid*, like India,
by blocking up its conduits of trade and communication. As we have seen,
the nation's modernity, staked on its regime of regulation and surveillance, had created the barbarism it sought to exclude. It was as though
the modern nation had summoned a ghostly foreign double to its very
heart.

BURYING THE BABY: REALISM AND REPRESSION
IN *ADAM BEDE*

These complex connotations of child murder at the end of the 1850s thus triggered the associations that the act had attained in the earlier histor-ical moments around 1803 and 1839. The choice of child murder as the theme for George Eliot's 1859 novel, *Adam Bede*, thus seems intensely sig-nificant. Child murder is indeed a social-realist detail – something that was quite likely to have happened in turn-of-the-century rural communities like Hayslope, and which in the 1859 context was very topical. But it is also a highly charged oriental event, an over-determined sign of a barbarous threat, and one, moreover, that bears memories of the other instances in which national boundaries and national authority had been brought un-der critical review. These associations and memories lie deeply buried in the novel, only to be reconstructed by following the faint traces that re-main in the text. Within *Adam Bede*, I suggest, child murder functions as in the Renanian construction, as the bearer of memories that have to be forgotten for the perpetuation of the nation. The nature of compulsory forgetting, however, means that in a covert way the text is preoccupied with the very processes of forgetting. Hence the novel's dominant motif – burial – specifically child murder-by-burial.[81] Paradoxically, the figure of forgetting is also the bearer of those memories that must be forgotten, so that to forget means also to remember.

Even before she had begun to conceive *Adam Bede*, child murder was a theme that concerned George Eliot, and one, moreover, that had a distinctly oriental flavour. In 1848 the young author – then Mary Ann Evans – wrote a letter to her friend, Sara Hennell, in which she mythologised her own genesis as the narrow escape from infanticide at the hands of a drunken Dame Nature and her Indian helper, the Vishnu Sprite. The method of murder envisaged here is smothering – like the death suffered by Hetty's buried-alive child. The little oriental tale provides a curious frame in which she performed her own self-fashionings at this early stage in her literary development.

Mother Nature – who by the bye is an old lady with some bad habits of her own – like other great dames does her work by deputy and gets both credit and discredit that don't properly belong to her. The vulgar may not know it, but she in fact leaves the creation of her plants her animals and her homunculi to a whole herd of sprites and genii some of whom make but laughing work of it. Now over a quarter of a century ago there was a very young sprite who forsooth having turned out some respectable toads and a few indifferent lemurs and marmosets must fain try his hand at a human article and one 22d of November he presented to Dame Nature at her evening levee a rough though unmistakeable sketch of a human baby. The Old Mother had been rollicking all the autumn in the vintage and wanted no less than a winter's sleep to sober her. Being rather cross-grained in her cups she was in no humour to make the best of a bad business so she said, What have we here? in such a snappish tone, flourishing a bunch of nettles of the while, that the poor little Prometheus of a sprite began to look very snubbed. 'A pretty piece of work I should have to patch up this thing into a human soul and body that would hang together! Here,' she called to one of her Vishnu-sprites, 'smother it at once to save further harm.'

But on the pleadings of the other sprites, who promise to bring companions for the poor 'sketch' – 'many gentle maidens and high-browed, brave men ... to be friends to this poor brattling' – Dame Nature agrees to spare her. 'The poor sketch of a soul was found by the dark eyed maiden and those other bright and good mortals and they pitied and helped it, so that at last it grew to think and to love.'[82]

The cultural indicators here are confusing: a parody of the icon of Malthusian virtuous restraint, Dame Nature is as drunk as an Irish woman, and resembles the insanitary midwives and baby farmers of popular representation; while her fairy assistants combine Celtic sprites with an oriental executioner, Vishnu, an expert in the Indian arts of infant extinction. Mary Ann escapes extermination on the intercession of other sprites who offer to provide a sympathetic community for her. Providing 'love to soothe and grave warning to reclaim', they embed her within a Wordsworthian regime of love and admonition, fostering for her a cocoon of Englishness to shield her from the murderous attacks of drunken and parodic Dame Nature and her oriental aide.

This strange little tale prefigures the concerns that will shape George Eliot's early fiction, especially *Adam Bede*. Its passage from exotic oriental and implicitly Celtic licence to a version of English moral virtue, a Wordsworthian sympathetic community, mirrors her determined literary respectability, and the restraint her realism exerts on the imagination, in pursuit of the documentation of social realities. It thus rehearses a transformation from the folk tale and the oriental tale – dangerous worlds where infant lives are threatened by the whims of powerful rajahs or Vishnu sprites – to the solid certainties of English social life that will dominate her work. Critics have noted the stringent defence against other more popular genres, especially romance and melodrama, which George Eliot mounts in her fiction.[83] This is particularly evident in *Adam Bede*, so much of which teeters on the edge of popular melodrama.[84] But it is important to note that in her fiction, George Eliot also aimed to distinguish her work from the genres of the folk tale and the oriental tale. The latter is of particular importance, for it is this which many commentators of the time used to encapsulate the true state of native Indian barbarity. For instance, the *Parliamentary Papers on Hindoo Infanticide* note a contrast between fantastical oriental 'tales of infancy' that are told in India to explain the practice of female infanticide, and the deathly realities – the 'grave history of a transaction involving the fate of a numerous portion of the human race' – that they conceal. The contrast is suggested even more sharply by George Trevor in an article published in *Blackwood's* in September 1857, the edition that also included instalments of both George Eliot's 'Janet's Repentance' and Lewes's 'Sea-Side Studies'.[85] In this, Trevor accounted for Indian savagery in terms of the cultural deracination epitomised by the oriental tale, which he explains in terms of the culture's adhesion to tradition at the expense of a connection to the land, or territory. Because of this, he claims that India could never achieve the status of a nation: Indians, he asserts, have 'nothing national within them', making India the perfect location for a colonial regime.

George Eliot's realism, with its preoccupation with material details as the basis for social explanations of human behaviour as opposed to the mythic and whimsical explanations provided by oriental tales, and its determination to root the dramas of human life in the land, conjoining an adherence to tradition with a sense of national territory, becomes a distinctive project of nation building, and a robust defence against the encroachment of oriental nationlessness and colonial subjection. Her style must be seen as a determined repression of both. *Adam Bede's* opening sentence, an initial flourish of orientalism – 'With a single drop of ink for a mirror, the Egyptian sorcerer undertakes to reveal to any chance comer far-reaching visions of the past' (p. 49) – is quickly smothered under a heap of details of English rural life. But it nevertheless serves to alert us to the oriental associations of the very English child murder that will dominate the work.

There is something peculiarly symptomatic about this opening sentence in the way in which it draws attention to the very things that the novel wishes to repudiate. The same might also be said of the novel's insistence on the idea of burial. As the central motif of the novel, instances of burial always operate symptomatically, to remind us of the material that they aim to forget. The most significant burial in the novel is Hetty's child murder-by-burial, but this is prefigured in the early chapters by the burial of Adam's father, Thias. Even before Thias dies, Adam builds a coffin not for, but on behalf of his father. This odd event is psychologically charged: in the process of building the coffin, Adam unconsciously wills his father's death. And as if to underline the fulfilment of a parricidal wish, Adam and Seth discover their father's corpse while they are carrying the empty coffin. In the context of a novel preoccupied with forms of authority that are appropriate to the modern nation, this symbolic challenge to traditional order seems at once inevitable, but also worryingly disruptive and a defiance of the relations of deference that George Eliot prefers. The novel, however, dwells on neither Thias's death, nor on Adam's Oedipal wish for it; indeed they are, in a sense, buried underneath the more dramatic and significant (in terms of the narrative) murder of Hetty's child, which is a repetition, in many respects, of the prior death: both are experienced with degrees of ambivalence; both corpses are found abandoned in the countryside; and the final burial of Thias, underneath a white thorn, prefigures the child's death through its traditional associations with illegitimacy, and its recollection of Wordsworth's 'The Thorn'. Pushed into the background, and overwritten by the murder of the child, the symbolic death of the father is thus rendered natural and inevitable, as the novel turns historical processes – in this case, the rise of the new bourgeois order represented by Adam's social and economic rise – into natural cycles.

The idea of burial is also evoked, in a more metaphorical sense, in George Eliot's realist aesthetic. Central to this, I argue, is a kind of emotional restraint – the overlaying or containment, or burial – of spontaneous feeling. Of all her fiction, *Adam Bede* contains the fullest and most direct account of her realist principles. In chapter 17, 'In which the story pauses a little', she describes her practice in distinctively Wordsworthian terms, as an attempt to create 'sympathy' in her readers for their 'everyday fellow man', the 'vulgar citizen[s]' (p. 179), or, elsewhere 'common coarse people' (p. 178). But by her own account, sympathy is an emotion that is saved only for situations in which a more uncritical love is impossible; it is love felt *despite* some flaw: as in the 'fibre of sympathy connecting me with that vulgar citizen who weighs out my sugar in a vilely assorted cravat and waistcoat', or when 'my heart should swell with loving admiration at some trait of gentle goodness in the faulty people who sit at the same hearth as me' (p. 179). While the references to the 'vulgarity' and 'faultiness' of the people are meant in part to reflect ironically on the narrator, nevertheless, in comparison with the emotional excesses and spontaneity represented in and provoked by melodrama, sympathy implies a much more measured emotional economy, one that is slightly condescending and always reserved: it is love felt when one's spontaneous repulsion is restrained or held back.

George Eliot's commitment to this kind of emotional restraint in her account of realism, however, seems forced and in the end, disingenuous;

it is perhaps a repression, or burial, of a narrative preference for the less respectable modes of melodrama and romance. Thus she writes that sympathy is to be achieved by representing the flaws of common people, and not idealising them, like inferior novelists, who would present them in a picturesque or sentimental cast. She mentions the 'squat figures, ill-shapen nostrils, and dingy complexions' (p. 177) of the rural poor as the characteristics to be represented, and, developing a comparison with Dutch paintings, claims that a novel should depict people engaged in repetitive and mundane domestic and agricultural tasks – scraping carrots, or digging the ground. One of the effects of this is to give a strong sense of the immobility of the people; but one that, paradoxically, makes them seem like a backdrop to the main actors of the drama.[86] In fact, in *Adam Bede*, the interest in the novel lies not in the depiction of repetitive, unexceptional activities of the generality of the people – the men in the carpenters' workshop, for instance, or the servants at the Chase, or the labourers at Hall Farm; rather the real drama lies with Hetty, Arthur, Dinah, and Adam, all distinguished by their beauty, and, in some cases, their moral nobility, and the exceptional and sensational events in their lives which describe and inspire emotions of a much more vivid kind. Despite the avowed attention to the drab details of daily life through which sympathy is to be summoned, the narrative energy is generated instead by events such as inter-class seduction, illegitimate pregnancy and, of course, child murder-by-burial. In this case, it is as though the murder-by-burial *stands in for* the projected emotional repressions of the stated claims for realism.

This notion of emotional restraint or burial is, nevertheless, central to other aspects of the novel too. The central characters, Adam and Dinah, are schooled in this kind of emotional restraint over the course of the novel. Dinah's too passionate Methodism is subdued into the more acceptable fabric of domestic relations in her marriage to Adam, and Adam's severity to his father and indulgence towards Hetty (he repeatedly regrets that he has been 'too hard' on his father and 'too soft' on Hetty) finds measured expression in his more reasonable love for Dinah. Adam's 'blending', however, is prefigured in the narrative in his racial characteristics, as a mixture of Saxon and Celt, mentioned in the opening chapter and repeated throughout. Adam is presented as the autochthonous Briton – a man of the soil, a true native – but his racial identity locates him more specifically as the representative of post-Union Britain, inclusive of the different constituents of the newly united Kingdom. In this casting then, emotional restraint is identified as authentically British, when British is understood as a stage in the political construction of the nation presented under the guise of racial authenticity.

Throughout the novel, the idea of emotional restraint is frequently expressed in terms of a racial narrative, but one that is surprisingly muddled. Like the central characters, the villagers also undergo an emotional education, but from a primitive state that is coded as much more exotically foreign. In their initial representation at Dinah's open air preaching, they are presented in a way that makes them seem strange and surprisingly foreign: they appear as a people of different and strange religious groups or sects (Methodists), and prone to bizarre, instinctual behaviour and mystic rhapsodies – like Indians, or even the popish Irish. Bess Crange's response to Dinah's rhapsodic sermon – sobbing loudly, and thrusting her gaudy earrings on the ground – becomes an example of the unrestrained, mystical, and peculiarly exotic behaviour of the local people – especially as inculcated by Methodism. Bess's gypsy earrings are another hint of an Indian origin – since gypsies were held at the time to have originated from India. Bess's outburst is reported to Dr Irvine, the Anglican minister, as proof of the degenerate influence of Methodism on the English rural poor. The sense of the foreignness of the preaching scene is conveyed in particular by the way in which it is presented through the impressions of an anonymous traveller, who turns out to be a magistrate. Riding through the countryside on horseback, observing the customs of the people, the magistrate resembles a colonial administrator. He has no significance in the plot at all, except that his legislative and condescending gaze, recording the strange behaviour of the native people, provides a colonial frame of reference for the story.[87]

Given the context of the novel's production, during the period in which the British press focused on the Indian rebellion, the associations made in the text between the villagers and Indians are potent, and are intensified by the novel's child-murder theme. Significantly, however, by the end of the novel, the idea of English primitiveness has transformed from this early articulation, as a form of mystical, and racially inflected, oriental, religious experience, to a very different idea of inherited, indigenous, and secularised folk culture. The progress of the novel is one of the Anglicisation of primitive rural people from an Indian-like foreignness, a process that requires them to acquire an English past. Their oriental associations at the beginning of the novel are superscribed, buried beneath a vision of an English culture that is projected over them. This is evident in the harvest supper at the end of the novel – the final appearance in the novel of the village people.

After a feast of English roast beef and plum pudding, they begin the 'great ceremony of the evening' – the harvest song, or 'rhapsody', a term which recalls Dinah's rhapsodic religious experience. However, by this stage, the rhapsody has become a constituent of indigenous English folk culture. Addressing the question of the origin of the rhapsody, the narrator offers a newly rationalised idea of the primitive:

As to the origin of this song – whether it came in its actual state from the brain of a single rhapsodist, or was gradually perfected by a school or succession of rhapsodists, I am ignorant. There is a stamp of unity, of individual genius, upon it, which inclines me to the former hypothesis, though I am not blind to the consideration that this unity may rather have arisen from the consensus of many minds which was a condition of primitive thought, foreign to our modern consciousness. (p. 519)

The choice is now between 'a consensus of minds', and 'individual genius'. Eliminated is the wild passion of religious ecstasy. This sense of regulation, even within the term 'primitive', is striking. This new version of folk culture provides a way of memorialising a 'primitive' culture within a modern society to which it is 'foreign' – the term rings incongruously here in this discussion of supposedly native culture – and allows for the knitting together of notions, conceived of here as incompatible, of consensus and individualism within this final view of national culture. The memorial function of folk singing is similar to that envisaged by George Eliot for the novel as a genre: a recollection of a past that can be bound together with an experience of a modern present.

The idea of folk culture, the remembered past of the community, is thus superimposed onto the villagers, covering over their former foreignness. The structure of nation formation is similar to that proposed by Renan – a nation made up of shared memories of a folkish past, in this case, in the somewhat vague form of remembered techniques of performance, which are projected onto the village people at this late stage in the novel, as a version of their shared inheritance. Although the novel makes allusions to race (Adam's Saxon-Celt origins), place (rural locations), and language (a mild form of dialect spoken by the central characters) – the identifying features of the nation that Renan refutes – in the end these are all subjugated to the overarching emphasis placed on cultural memory. These memories are ascribed to the people at the end of the novel, who have become in the process remarkably disjunct from their early manifestations as rhapsodic Methodists. Memory is offered here as a detachable and inscribable thing, having no determinate link to race, location, or language. It is also presented as something that is itself repressive, and which buries former identifications and modes of society.

Significantly, therefore, the folk-singing leads seamlessly to a discussion among the local people of the present political state of the nation. The reference is to the temporary peace with France, struck in 1802, which serves to remind us of the historical time of the novel. This is a comic moment in the novel: the people's views are expressed in dialect, and based on prejudice and custom rather than knowledge of events (newspapers are criticised by the locals as giving false information – 'you see no more into this thing nor you can see into the middle of a potato' (p. 566)), and are corrected by Adam's condescending voice, telling them that the French are not 'such poor sticks' (p. 567). Nevertheless, following the long account of folk culture, this melange of received belief and ill-informed opinion – that 'the war's a fine thing for the country, an' how'll you keep up prices wi'out it?', and, on the other hand, Mr Craig, the gardener's opinion that 'furriners like them can do half th'harm them ministers do with their bad government[.] If King George 'ud turn 'em all away and govern by himself, he'd see everything is righted' – presents a vision of a sturdy, traditional British nation, subject only to the gradual and consensual changes which will be brought about by the insights derived from education and experience.

This is the vision of the nation that the novel endorses. And it achieves it, like Renan, through the compulsory forgetting of moments of violent opposition and challenge to national authority. In *Adam Bede*, the things that must be forgotten are encrypted in the murder of Hetty's baby. We have occasion to remember this at the very end of the novel. As Dinah, Adam, and Seth anticipate the return to Hayslope of Arthur, Adam tells them of a remark lately made to him by Arthur, which in fact was the recollection of a comment made to him by Adam at the time of the murder. Referring to the wrong perpetrated by Hetty in killing her child, he says that 'there's a sort of wrong that can never be made up for'. A reported account of a reported speech, its strangeness is marked in the text by the fact that it is enclosed by three sets of speech marks. As memories of a shared past draw together Arthur, Adam, and Dinah, they also define the new community by remembering that Hetty herself will never be assimilated, destined as she is for eternal abjection. In so far as the new community is presented as an allegory of the nation, this is a moment of nation-building through memory. Remembering Hetty, therefore, is a matter, rather, of remembering to forget her. Her child murder achieves the symbolic function of the founding sacrifice of the nation, which must be forgotten in order for the nation to exist.

MATTHEW ARNOLD: CULTURE AND CHILD MURDER

In *Adam Bede*, Hetty's child murder-by-burial encrypts various challenges to British authority, reminding us to forget them: the result is a powerful vision of Britain as a consensual and organic community. In this fulfilment of the Renanian construction, however, the events that are to be eliminated from memory are thus summoned to the very heart of the nation. This deeply ambivalent gesture repeats that identified at the beginning of this chapter, in the context of the supposed epidemic of child murder. Here, as we saw, the newly professionalising class of doctors and coroners, led by Wakley and Lankester, located a barbarism active at the centre of the nation – witnessed in the thousands of murdered children reported in the press – that required the medical expertise of professional medical men for a cure. In both cases, it is the unwed, murdering mother who occupies this position as the primitive core of the modernising nation. As we shall see in the next chapter, this core will often be marked as racially different, and new legislation for the protection of the child, introduced in the next decades, will serve to make motherhood deviant for a whole group of working-class, predominantly Irish women.

Five years after the appearance of *Adam Bede*, Matthew Arnold published his musings on Wragg, the child murderer, in his essay, 'The Function of Criticism at the Present Time'. He cites verbatim a newspaper report of 'A shocking child murder':

A girl named Wragg left the workhouse there on Saturday morning with her young illegitimate child. The child was soon afterwards found dead on Mapperly Hills, having been strangled.[88]

In the context of the essay, the appearance of Wragg serves to throw into relief the ludicrously chauvinistic statements of politicians from across the political spectrum, who had celebrated the 'unrivalled happiness' of the English, named the 'best [breed] in the whole world'; for Arnold such statements are representative of the present state of English culture, degraded by philistinism with its 'practical' and overly partisan newspaper and periodical press. Wragg punctures this puffed up sense of national perfection with an image of demoralisation that reflects both on English institutions, and, more generally, the morals of the people. Wragg is thus the absolute embodiment of a degraded national culture, but also the means of its redemption. It is therefore significant that Wragg is located, not on the periphery, but rather at the very heart of England. Her crime takes place in Nottingham, the geographical centre; and her name is the butt of Arnold's jokes, not for its foreignness, but rather for its very Englishness ('has any one reflected what a touch of grossness in our race...is shown by the natural growth amongst of such hideous names'). As Hetty in *Adam Bede*, Wragg is the primitive core of Englishness, the strangeness at the heart of the nation that we must 'remember to forget'.[89]

Indeed, Wragg's crime is committed at the very same spot as Hetty's and Mary Voce's, suggesting that Arnold has in mind a literary landscape also. There are echoes of Martha Ray here: Arnold 'stumbles' on Wragg in a newspaper, much as the narrator of Wordsworth's 'The Thorn' had stumbled on Martha Ray on the moor. But Wragg's is an altered landscape, newly industrialised, and no longer embalmed in the rural gloss of George Eliot's literary provinces, or Wordsworth's poetic regions. The location of the discovery is thus a composite space drawing together these geographical places and textual inscriptions: newspaper print is superimposed over this dirty, industrial landscape, which in turn, lies over the literary and rural landscapes of Eliot and Wordsworth.

This process of overlaying or metaphorical burial is similar to that detected in George Eliot's work, but here it is reversed. Whereas George Eliot's text buried allusions to things that could not be incorporated in the body politic, the burial in Arnold's case is a negative process of repression carried out by a philistine modernity, and against which English culture requires defence. Wragg allows this defence: through the allusions to former texts and conditions that she contains, she enables, not the restoration of the conditions of a former age, but the recollection of their difference from the present. For Arnold, Wragg is a creature that embodies contrasts: 'there is profit for the spirit in such contrasts as this; criticism serves the cause of perfection by establishing them'. Paradoxically, therefore, Wragg thus becomes a kind of cultural critic herself, opening up a field of memory and critique. It therefore seems significant that Wragg does not bury her child like Hetty, but strangles it, and leaves the corpse on the surface of the English landscape.

This is where Arnold departs from George Eliot's version of child murder, in which forgetting happens once – represented in the once-and-for-all banishment of Hetty. Arnold implies a different temporality, in which remembering and forgetting are endlessly repeated, in an eternal present suspended in an engulfing memory of the past. This different temporality is reflected in Wragg too, as she is both the product of industrial modernity and a throwback to ancient times: Arnold's comic contention that 'by the Illissus there was no Wragg, poor thing!', draws to mind that there were indeed child murderers in ancient Greece, as Arnold well knew.[90] As the embodiment of contrasts, Wragg oscillates between the gloom of industrial England and the Arcadian delights of ancient Greece.

Arnold will develop his theory further in his longer work, *Culture and Anarchy*, written over a period of two years, between 1867 and 1869, and in it, as we shall see in the next chapter, the figure of the child murderer, Wragg, persists as a haunting presence shaping the work of Culture. Unlike Hetty, Wragg has not been banished to the periphery of the nation, but will remain, 'in custody', at the centre of English Culture. Likewise, as Arnold later sees, the phantom that modernity finds at its heart cannot be eliminated, but in fact has a new resilience in the late decades of the century, returning to the centre in manifestations of social unrest. In this context, Wragg, the child murderer, returns but now as a solution to the problem of which she was once the symptom.

CHAPTER 6

Wragg's daughters: child murder towards the fin de siècle

Might women not exterminate children altogether if they pleased?
Mona Caird, *The Morality of Marriage* (1897)[1]

NEW WOMEN

The regime of the infanticidal outsider discussed in the previous chapter began to loosen its hold on British culture in the last decades of the century. Matthew Arnold had hinted at this with his figure of Wragg, the parodic representative of the nation, whose very English name mocked the preening chauvinism of English politicians. His vision suggested that rather than a marginal interloper who could be ejected from the body politic, the spectre of the child murderer loomed at the very heart of the nation, her rude presence undermining the values of the establishment.

In the late decades of the century, examples of infanticidal women proliferated in public debates in Britain. The 'infanticide epidemic' of the late 1850s and 1860s, discussed above, had provoked the creation of various philanthropic societies for the care of children, such as the Infant Life Protection Society (1870), and the National Society for the Prevention of Cruelty to Children (1889).[2] These had mounted successful campaigns for the introduction of laws to enable a much higher degree of policing of working-class families than ever before. The registration of births and deaths, the regulation of child care through the establishment of a register of nurses, and the Prevention of Cruelty Act of 1889, the so-called 'Children's Charter', which for the first time made it possible to convict parents for cruelty to their own children – all were measures set in place to protect children from dangerous parents.[3]

From the 1860s to the end of the century, anxieties about a new kind of child murderer had come into focus: what if the child murderer was not an outsider, and could not be exiled to the peripheries of empire like Hetty? What if instead she lodged in the bourgeois home, threatening the lives of innocent babies, and subverting cherished notions of domestic order and social harmony? Significantly it was not only feckless mothers – the poor and often unmarried women who were the main target of the new legislation for the protection of children – that were associated with acts of infanticide. Some middle-class women, those who by the 1890s would be called the 'New Women', were also cast in the role of child murderer. These women were associated with promoting social legislation aimed at broadening female independence. Many had themselves been involved in campaigning on such issues as divorce, married women's property, the custody of children, the education of girls, rights for women to pursue careers in the professions, and latterly, votes for women – causes that would impact on the nature of the traditional family.[4] Moreover, the participation of a wide cross-section of women in the national campaign, led by Josephine Butler, against the Contagious Diseases Acts – legislation introduced in the 1860s to regulate prostitution – highlighted a growing female involvement in matters concerning sexuality, also evidenced in the growing use of contraception.[5] The campaign against the Contagious Diseases Acts saw large numbers of women eschewing their traditional roles as wives and mothers, attending public meetings, engaging in direct action during parliamentary elections, and openly discussing men's double sexual standards. This visible politicisation of women across different classes turned them into a powerful force.

Given the currency that child murder had acquired in popular and élite culture since the early eighteenth century, it was predictable that a charge of child murder would be levelled against such women. It is more surprising, however, that it was an accusation that some happily accepted – metaphorically at least. The role of child murderer would be inhabited by many New Women, including Mona Caird, whose somewhat flippant remarks – that women might 'exterminate children altogether if they pleased' – are cited at the beginning of this chapter.

Caird's talk of the extinction of a whole group of people is a reminder of the extent to which the idiom of social thinking in the second half of the century had been shaped by Darwinian science. Charles Darwin's *The Origin of Species* (1859) was a highly technical work of evolutionary biology, but its social and philosophical ramifications ensured it notoriety within Victorian society and culture. Although Darwin himself was reluctant to derive a fully-fledged social philosophy from his findings, the impact of his work spread from the evolution of species to broader issues of societal organisation, helped by the emergence of new strains of sociology, anthropology, criminology, and psychology, disciplines that were themselves strongly

imprinted with Darwinian motifs. The scientific application of evolutionary explanations to society itself – social Darwinism, broadly conceived –
provided the backdrop against which the new discussions of child murder were played out. In a sense, this was appropriate, since evolutionary
discourses themselves drew on the existing lexicon of infanticide through
which to formulate and express their theories. As before, acts of infanticide
were identified as the pastime of primitives; but they were also held to be
an adaptive mechanism, a force for change in the onward march of evolutionary progress. In Darwin's evolution, barbarism and modernity had
moved into a new conjunction.

The fascination with evolutionary progress that consumed thinkers in
the second half of the nineteenth century thus fuelled a corollary concern,
that, rather than surging forward to higher forms of species development,
people might slip down the evolutionary ladder to wallow in more primitive
forms of being. In the late nineteenth century, a theory of pathological
hereditary decline – or degeneration – taken from the medical and biological
sciences, where it had particular purchase in the treatment of insanity and
criminality, provided a compelling explanation for a more general social
malaise.[6] The evidence presented by urban centres was seen by many as the
spectacle of a civilisation in decline. Overcrowding, endemic poverty and
unemployment, epidemic disease, crime – all suggested that the aetiology
of individual deviance could be projected onto an entire society.[7] Thus
theories of degeneration combined with a still prevailing Malthusianism to
provide a common framework for late Victorian social thinking. Darwin
was heavily influenced by Malthus's *Essay on Population*, and his thesis that
animal species evolved by virtue of their capacity to adapt to environmental
conditions could be – and was – read as a Malthusian parable.[8] The spectre
of Malthus's Dame Nature throwing away the unwanted babies of the poor
cast her shadow over much social Darwinist thinking, an apprehension
given shocking representation by the grimly Malthusian multiple child
murder and suicide staged in Thomas Hardy's *Jude the Obscure* (1896).
Moreover, as I shall suggest, Malthus's other child murderer – the prolific
and licentious mother who eats her own young, his allegorical figure of the
unruly mob – is also evident in the frequent accounts of the overcrowded
slums of Britain's cities, the natural habitation of the degenerate working-
class mothers whose prolific and sickly offspring die from neglect and ill
health.

An important consequence of the integration of degeneration theory
into social Darwinism over the last decades of the nineteenth century was
the familiarisation and naturalisation of racial theory. World history, viewed

through the increasingly aggressive lens of the 'new imperialism', seemed to highlight an evolutionary battle for survival, in which the establishment of a hierarchy of races legitimised imperial expansionism. Moreover, the application of the racial hierarchy internally within Britain suggested that certain groupings should be discouraged from breeding. Classically invoked under this heading were the Jews, though also on some lists were the degenerate working classes, themselves constituted of different racial groups – especially the Irish and, by the end of the century, Jewish immigrants from Eastern Europe. Hopes focused on the emergence of a Darwinian reproductive technology of 'eugenics' – a term coined by Darwin's nephew, Francis Galton, in 1883. Eugenics offered a ready solution to the social problems of the age, and was adopted widely by a diverse range of writers, including feminists and New Women writers. For some women, eugenics provided a way of raising the stakes of motherhood, giving them an important role in the future development of the species. As Anna Davin has written, such thinking was harnessed by those who wished to encourage the propagation of a strong, healthy breed of children to assist in imperial efforts at the end of the century, and to correct the effects of the prolific breeding on the part of the poor and infirm.[9] The Angel in the House was transmogrified into a murderer – the eugenic handmaiden of social Darwinism.

It is in eugenics that the idea of child murder as a sacrifice, which had been in circulation at least since the beginning of the eighteenth century, finds its most literal and disturbing exposition. In previous examples, the sacrificial child murder, the infanticide for the greater good of society, had operated primarily as a metaphor or a figure of speech. Brutus, who allowed his sons to die for the good of the Republic, the slave woman who killed her child to save it from the life of degradation, the poor woman who drowned herself and her baby to avoid the workhouse following the 1834 New Poor Law – in all these examples, the child murder is presented as though it were an act of redemption within a highly rhetorical polemic of amelioration and reform. But in the late decades of the nineteenth century, in a culture infused with eugenic thinking, the rhetoric of sacrifice transformed into social policy and turned metaphor into disturbing reality.

These are themes that characteristically can be followed in a wide variety of apparently separate, but in fact interlocking, venues: in the work of Darwin and Galton, but also in anthropology, social criticism, Matthew Arnold's cultural theory, in birth-control propaganda, and in the work of feminist and New Women writers and their critics. Evolutionary debates infuse all these writings, and with them the haunting protagonists of earlier infanticide debates. Thus Malthus's murdering women, Dame Nature and the unruly mob, will reappear in many different guises, as will Medea, the archetypal murdering mother, the passionate and vengeful outsider, whose tragedy holds new resonance for women.

One of the most troubling aspects of evolutionary science for nineteenth-century readers was the idea of the necessary death, especially of newborns. In Charles Darwin's controversial view, graphically depicted in *The Origin of Species*, Nature is a battlefield for survival, in which 'every single organic being... may be said to be striving to the utmost to increase its numbers', but in which death was the occupational hazard of life. Darwin saw in operation in the animal and vegetable world a yet more extreme version of Malthus's principle of population:[10] here, some species of animals, lacking the tempering effects of 'prudential restraint from marriage' and the 'artificial increase in food' through agriculture, overproduced offspring precisely to counter the vulnerability of their own species to external threats. This was an even more sinister vision of teeming life than that portrayed by Malthus, for now the surplus population had a special function of its own – to die. 'If many eggs or young are destroyed', he wrote with dismal logic, 'many must be produced, or the species will become extinct.'[11] Under natural selection – the evolutionary process that Darwin isolates by which each species adapts and struggles for existence – individual lives are sacrificed for the survival of the species.

In this process the mother becomes nature's agent, choosing which of her offspring will survive. Thus Darwin gives the example of a queen bee – a creature that throughout the previous century had figured in allegorical representations of human society[12] – as the example *par excellence* of a dramatic definition of the maternal role that was strikingly at odds with Victorian ideals of motherhood. 'It may be hard', he avers,

but we ought to admire the savage instinctive hatred of the queen-bee, which urges her instantly to destroy the young queens her daughters as soon as born, or to perish herself in the combat; for undoubtedly this is for the good of the community... maternal love or maternal hatred though the latter fortunately is most rare, is all the same to the inexorable principle of natural selection.[13]

Darwin ascribes to infanticide a progressive function in the development of the species. With the example of the queen bee, he imagines a new and shocking style of maternal behaviour: anthropomorphised, the bee becomes the heroine of progress, sacrificing her children for evolution's cause. For all her brutality, and her seeming unnaturalness, there is something poignant about the queen bee: her tragedy is to be the victim of instinct. She kills her daughters for the 'good of the community'. The element of sacrifice here refers back to the various sacrificial infanticides that we have encountered, that figured as signs of republican virtue: like the Abbé Raynal's slave mother, the queen bee is a mother who kills her children for a greater good than her own, and attains a certain nobility through doing so. She also resembles Malthus's Dame Nature discussed in Chapter Three. Like Dame Nature, the queen bee is a cool regulator of populations.[14] But unlike Dame Nature, the queen bee is a mother, and this changes her murders into sacrifices, and evokes a yet more chilling world in which the distinctions between maternal love and hatred are obliterated. No wonder that, for many, Darwin's vision meant the crumbling of the moral foundations of society.

The idea that infanticide might assume a similarly adaptive role in the development of human societies was one that also had considerable purchase in the later decades of the nineteenth century among evolutionary anthropologists. This can be seen in the work of the ethnographic writer, John F. McLennan, whose work was widely read, even prompting Darwin into scholarly debate. In a review article entitled 'Hill Tribes of India' (1863), McLennan had discussed practices of infanticide and polyandry in India, and followed others in claiming that these were aberrations rather than a stage in the evolution of society, and moreover, that they provided an effective means of differentiating Indian society from the child-nurturing British.[15] But when he came to write his most influential work, *Primitive Marriage*, published two years later in 1865 – drawing heavily on material from the earlier article – he developed a complex theory of the development of civil society based on a new assumption that female infanticide was a universal custom within primitive societies, which preceded marriage and all notions of family inheritance. In a work that shows signs of the influence of Darwinian science, infanticide was now redefined as a universal, and, most importantly, an adaptive process in the evolution of society.[16] Infanticide was no longer for McLennan the stigmata of bastardy, but rather it sustained close and complex relations with the institution of marriage.[17]

As noted above, marriage was a topical and highly controversial subject at this time, and the subject of extensive political debate. A lawyer by profession, McLennan had already written on the subject in an article on 'Marriage and Divorce – the Law of England and Scotland' in the *North British Review* in 1861. But *Primitive Marriage* was a work of ethnology that was concerned with the origins of the institution rather than its current legal constitution. Following a trend among intellectuals of his day that can be traced back to the Scottish Enlightenment, he adopted the comparative method, and used accounts of primitive societies in his contemporary world as evidence of the ways in which his own society had evolved.[18] The picture as he surveyed it showed that female infanticide was 'common among savages everywhere', and a crucial stage in the development of the family. Female infanticide, he argued, 'rendered women scarce, [and] led at once to polyandry within the tribe, and the capturing of women from without'.[19] From these brutal beginnings slowly evolved the idea of ties through blood – initially through the mother, and later through the father too. McLennan's account not only offered a historical and comparative perspective on a social institution perceived by most to be natural, but it also assumed that the systematic practice of female infanticide was, paradoxically, the primary mechanism in the evolution of civil society, the necessary stage in the development of human progress.

Critics would find the implications of McLennan's theory to be deeply troubling, for in a departure from other analysts of legal institutions, he had used the ethnographic evidence provided by Indian society to launch a trenchant attack on the traditional, patriarchal family. Ironically, McLennan's work had been inspired in part by Henry Maine's *Ancient Law* (1861). Maine, whose lectures McLennan had attended when a law student in Edinburgh, used the evidence of ancient Indo-European law to deduce the universality of marriage as a patriarchal institution.[20] McLennan, on the contrary, was persuaded not only that marriage was the product of a much longer process of evolution than Maine assumed, preceded by a period of sexual promiscuity and polyandry, but also that, in their initial form, families were built around mothers, and that fathers were a relatively late addition to the social structure. Moreover, McLennan's work emphasised that marriage in its earliest manifestation was a brutal process of abduction and rape, the symbolism of which, he argued, still permeated modern marriage ceremonies. It was this latter point that captured the imagination of his reviewers, whose somewhat bemused accounts of the work were full of references to McLennan's bizarre interpretations of seemingly harmless customs of modern marriages, such as carrying the bride over the threshold and throwing the boot at the bride.[21] The scientific press responded more seriously, taking issue with

McLennan on various aspects of his argument, although none argued against his assumption that infanticide was a universal practice, or disagreed with his claim that it had an adaptive role in the evolution of human society.[22]

For some readers, McLennan's work held radical potential, especially in relation to contemporary marriage legislation.[23] In her highly controversial discussions of marriage and the family in the 1880s and 1890s, Mona Caird would name McLennan as one of her authorities, alongside other anthropologists who also worked on the prehistory of the family.[24] For her, these writers had demonstrated that in its origins, the family was a matriarchal organisation, and that its modern patriarchal state was an attenuation of a temporary stage in its development. She wrote in the *Morality of Marriage* that 'the greatest evils of modern society had their origin, thousands of years ago, in the dominant abuse of patriarchal life: the custom of woman purchase', and that 'this system still persists in the present form of marriage and its traditions, and that these traditions are holding back the race from its best development'. Drawing on the language of evolution, and using the analogy of plant life, she argued that the patriarchal family should be allowed to die like an old tree, and give way to a social organisation whose form was as yet unknown. This was a 'young plant' that had been trained to 'bring forth that flower which, for many generations, can bloom only in the imagination of a small minority'.[25] The 'flower' refers to a vision of a society in which women's roles would be detached from their traditional function as mothers. Caird's analogies drawn from nature are highly specific: rather than a nature that ties women to their biological roles and traditional social functions, she invokes the nature that is implicit in the science of evolution – a forward-looking force that drives change and is the spur for future development. This enables her to pitch tradition as a retrograde force against the progressive and *natural* development of the race. The emancipation of women is thus in Caird's terms an imperative of human evolution.[26]

The adaptive power, she claims, 'appears to be invariable among organic beings: it is indeed the condition of their survival'. 'Were it not for the existence of this adaptive power, the sufferings of many people – the Jews for example – must have ended in their extermination.'[27] Her work is shot through with similar references to the possible extinction of various groups – men, women, Jews: hence her passing remarks on women's extermination of children. Infanticide assumes a significant role within a context in which human progress is imagined as a struggle for survival in a violent and hostile environment; and, as an act that displays woman's abnegation of the maternal role, it becomes a powerful emancipatory gesture. Caird's references to the Jews are significant, because women's campaigns for independence were played out alongside other liberation movements of the time, including the emergent Zionist movement, and anti-imperialist Home Rule movements, notably in Ireland and India. Paradoxically, however, the feminists' relationships to these other organisations were highly complex and ambiguous, since their arguments often drew force from social Darwinist and imperialist thinking, and rather than finding points of identification with racially differentiated groups, were as likely to emphasise their difference.[28]

Against this backdrop, the mythological child murderer, Medea, appears as an important icon of both female potency and women's oppression. In the second half of the nineteenth century, there is a growing fascination among women writers with Medea, as a figure through which to explore both their exclusion from patriarchal power and their means of redress. And in the context of social Darwinist thinking, her racial difference – as a Colchian among Corinthians – will take on a new significance.

THE NEW MEDEAS: AUGUSTA WEBSTER, GEORGE ELIOT, AND AMY LEVY

A revival of interest in the Medea myth, witnessed by a resurgence of theatrical renditions, dates from about 1845 and is linked to the contemporary debates about marriage reform. Edith Hall records that from this time, performances of *Medea* on the London stage incorporated references to parliamentary debates on the subject, 'inaugurat[ing] a tradition of popular entertainments based on the Medea myth, which lasted throughout the period of legislation around women's position in marriage and divorce'.[29] The tragedy of an abandoned, infanticidal woman raised highly topical issues of male infidelity, child custody, and maternal rights and duties. Stage versions of the Medea myth by male writers played throughout the period with tremendous success, and attracted leading actors and actresses. In most cases, however, Medea's acts were tempered so as to conform to conventional notions of maternal decorum, and the deaths of the children were either avoided altogether, or represented as virtuous acts of maternal duty.

In the late 1860s, however, Medea started to become a theme for women writers. In these literary versions – albeit not designed for stage performance – Medea is represented unambiguously as the killer of her children, yet as one whose deeds are sometimes socially advantageous. It is,

I suggest, the new ways in which child murder had figured in evolutionary discourse, as the heroic act of the queen bee, or the primal mechanism for social adaptation, that allowed Medea to be reinterpreted as not merely a victim of patriarchal oppression, but also a champion of women's emancipation. Medea becomes a force of social progress. But she is also a tragic figure, because, like the queen bee, her act makes her a casualty of evolutionary progress, an anachronism, unfit for the world as it exists. In literary renditions by women writers, Medea emerges as a complex character through which to explore women's position in a society from which they seem fated always to be estranged. In the late nineteenth century, she is the archetypal figure of female alienation and disenfranchisement.

Witness, for instance, Augusta Webster's dramatic monologue, 'Medea in Athens' (1870).[30] Webster was a campaigner for women's rights: an associate of Francis Power Cobbe and John Stuart Mill from the 1860s, she wrote and lectured widely on women's emancipation, especially on the themes of education and female suffrage.[31] In her 'Medea in Athens' – a soliloquy spoken by Medea on the death of Jason – she presents a striking exposition of a woman's rage at marital betrayal. An accomplished scholar of Greek literature, Webster had already published a full translation of Euripides' *Medea* in 1868, and the poem, 'Medea in Athens' builds on this as an exploration of Medea's motivations. In the poem, Medea's violent passion is rendered in unexpurgated terms: her hatred for Jason is as impassioned as her love for him had been, and the murder of the children is presented as an act of will on her part. In relation to conventional norms of feminine behaviour, this display of extreme anger is highly provocative. Webster's Medea, however, owes much to evolutionary discourse of the time: she is the mistress of evolution, whose triumph is to have made Jason's line extinct, and like Darwin's queen bee, the tragic heroine of species-instinct.

Jason's betrayal of Medea is represented as the sign of his weakness, his failure of judgement: he 'schemed amiss', was a 'dolt', and becomes 'a laughing stock to foes!'[32] In evolutionary terms, he seems less well adapted to the world than the stronger, more passionate, and more intelligent Medea. It is therefore significant that he dies in the sea, his watery grave evoking the ancient and extinct species of marine life that fascinated evolutionary biologists.[33] Given Jason's evolutionary shortfall, the death of his two sons is something of an inevitability. Jason mourns them in terms of his own extinction: 'My house is perished with me: ruined, ruined!' he moans, and he repeatedly refers to them as his lost hope of perpetuity in the world. Medea considers their deaths to be necessary for the same reasons. She claims:

> If they had lived, sometimes thou hadst had hope:
> for thou wouldst still have said "I have two sons",
> and dreamed perchance they'd bring thee use at last
> and build thy greatness higher: but now, now,
> thou hast died shamed and childless, none to keep
> thy name and memory fresh upon the earth
> none to make boast of thee "My father did it."[34]

Alive, the children reflect back and enhance Jason's worldly status; dead they obliterate his memory. The poem is transfixed by ideas of memory and forgetting to the extent that being remembered by others represents one's worldly instantiation (being 'fresh upon the earth'). Killing the children therefore means that Jason cannot be remembered by them, only by Medea; and she, as a consequence, by him. The two are thus tied together in the morbid interdependence of mutual memorialisation.

Medea's infanticides thus seem to be acts of compulsion: acts of 'savage instinctive hatred', like those of the queen bee, in Darwin's account. It is worth noticing, too, that Webster's Medea inhabits a similar emotional world to that described by Darwin, in which love and hatred are 'all the same to the inexorable principle of natural selection'. In Medea's case it is sexual rather than maternal love and hatred that operate in this way. The intensity of Medea's hatred for Jason turns it into a kind of love. Love and hatred are both forces that bind them together: they were 'near by hate last and once by so strong love', and she requires Jason 'Ever to think of me – / with love, with hate, what care I? hate is love.' Thus when he dies, his death paradoxically inaugurates her own; forgotten by Jason, she no longer has a place in the world. In fact the poem begins and ends with a description of the way in which the world has been made strange to her by Jason's death, as though she somehow no longer belongs in it. She describes an emotional numbness, a lack of feeling, which seems like death in comparison with the intensity felt for Jason when alive. His death is announced by a 'stranger' in the first line of the poem – 'Dead is he? Yes, our stranger guest said dead' – (the formulation – an allusion to the Greek idea of the 'stranger', someone unknown to whom hospitality is given – is nevertheless odd here: the guest is stranger than whom?). And the word 'strange' is repeated to encapsulate Medea's response to the news. The death is 'mere strange', she says; but 'this most strange of all / that I care nothing'. And later, 'It were so strange a world / with him not in it.' When Medea claims at the end of the poem, that 'I have forgotten thee',[35] she evokes a sense of emptiness that is far from triumphant. Jason's death has cast her out of the world, estranged her from the very environment in which she paradoxically had proved herself to be fitter for survival.

George Eliot, another woman writer with strong classical interests, also explores the Medea myth in two of her later novels, namely *Felix Holt* (1865) and *Daniel Deronda* (1876). As noted above, George Eliot had already recognised the symbolic complexity of child murder in *Adam Bede*,[36] but in these later works, the act of child murder is perceived differently. It is now associated with women's anger in a way that brings it closer to the shocking acts of Webster's Medea than those of the pathetic Hetty.[37] Mrs Transome, for instance, in *Felix Holt*, is a Medea-like figure; her rage with the world rumbles portentously throughout the narrative.[38] She is the cast-off mistress of the lawyer, Jermyn, whom the narrative identifies as a Jason-figure: he is the 'fortunate Jason', who 'as we know from Euripedes, piously thanked the goddess, and saw clearly that he was not at all obliged to Medea'.[39] Mrs Transome's associations with Medea are also made apparent through her infanticidal urges; from the beginning of the novel we know of her 'desire that her first, rickety, ugly, imbecile child should die, and leave room for her darling, of whom she could be proud'.[40] The very patent evolutionary trajectory here prefigures that in Webster's poem: Mrs Transome, as Medea, is a mistress of evolution, a Dame Nature figure, who attempts to control the future generations.[41] But in the end, she will lose out in the evolutionary struggle. She and her brood of degenerate types – her aristocratic and cretinised husband and her mixed-race grandchild,[42] who roam around her house like dogs – are destined only for extinction, and will be usurped by new and stronger forms of social life, represented both by the unctuous Jermyn, but also, more positively, by the eponymous Felix Holt and his new wife, Esther Lyon – the couple being a sturdily adaptive amalgam of different classes and physical and intellectual strengths.

In *Daniel Deronda*, the Medea story has a firmer presence as a myth that reflects more directly on the central themes of the novel – illegitimacy and social exclusion. The most direct references to Medea are made in relation to Lydia Glasher, like Mrs Transome, a spurned mistress. She, too, is cast as Medea. This is evident in the observations of other characters ('It's a sort of Medea and Creusa business', observes one of the minor characters. 'Grandcourt is a new kind of Jason . . . I think I hear Ristori [the actress] now, saying "Jasone! Jasone!"'). It is also apparent in the plot: Lydia Glasher's dramatic gift of diamonds to Gwendolen on her wedding night bears the significance of the poisoned dress sent to Creusa by Medea. The novel explores both Glasher's situation as an abandoned mistress, but also

Gwendolen's, the legitimate wife's, participation in Glasher's abandonment; the guilt felt so keenly by Gwendolen ties the two together, so that in the end they seem to merge. Mrs Glasher's condition of being outcast, becomes for Gwendolen the condition of all women: Glasher inspires in her a 'sort of terror: it was as if some ghastly vision had come to her in a dream and said, "I am a woman's life" '.[43]

'A woman destitute of acknowledged social dignity', Lydia Glasher's situation as outcast, moreover, mirrors that of other outsiders who are incorporated in the novel, and it is this that draws the various narrative strands together. The condition of the woman is compared with that of the Jew – the archetypal migrant, and victim of religious intolerance. The two social positions of estrangement run along side each other throughout the novel, but while the resolution of the novel finds Daniel, the Jew, married and on the way to a new homeland, the woman, Gwendolen remains alienated from society, as homeless and uprooted at the end of the novel as she was at the beginning. Indeed, in the final passionate interview between Gwendolen and Daniel, in which he reveals his intention to marry Mirah, and leave for the 'East', he is shown to betray Gwendolen for what becomes at this point a marriage of political expedience (like Jason's), that will further his ambition to 'restore a political existence to my people, making them a nation again, giving them a national centre, such as the English have...'. At this moment, therefore, Daniel is cast as a kind of Jason figure; and Gwendolen, the 'victim of his happiness', occupies the Medea role, the cast-off mistress. The references to the Medea story at this stage are deeply sublated, but also transformed: like Lydia Glasher, the first Medea, Gwendolen sends a wedding gift, but this one 'more precious than gold and gems', a letter, expressing her desire, rather than for revenge, to 'make others glad that they were born'.[44] Gwendolen's philanthropic aspirations, however, remain somewhat inchoate, and we leave the novel with a sense of her continuing estrangement from the world that contrasts strongly with Daniel's rehabilitation. There is a sense in which the woman and the Jew have exchanged identities: the woman will wander, like a Jew, while the Jew will be planted in a new homeland, settled in a new domestic setting like a wife.

In *Daniel Deronda*, George Eliot uses the figure of Medea through which to associate women's righteous anger with the world with their situation as outsiders, the disenfranchised of society, analogous with the Jews. Amy Levy, the Jewish poet, in her 1881 'Medea: A Fragment in Dramatic Form, after Euripedes', also makes this connection, but in a far more discomforting way. She too explores ideas of racial difference, but whereas in *Daniel*

Deronda the situation of the Jew was presented as an analogue to that of the woman, in Levy's case racial difference re-inscribes feminine difference, doubling the alienation of the woman.[45] In this version of Medea, besides which Webster's and George Eliot's accounts of female rage and violence pale – Levy has Medea's children kill Kreon and his daughter Glauce on Medea's instructions, and then, when they return to her for comfort, she stabs them, saying 'I will not have ye, for I love ye not!'[46] – Levy makes Medea's position as an 'alien' the cause, rather than in Webster, the effect, of her anger. Thus while Webster's Medea is estranged from the world by Jason's death, Levy's Medea is from the beginning 'alien'. She repeats this word 'alien' as insistently as Webster repeats the word 'strange'. Her condition as 'alien' is marked by her racial and national difference: there are constant references to the 'cold' and 'straight-backed' Corinthians, compared with her warmth and darkness, her Colchian blood that is 'redder' than theirs. It is also indicated by her lack of maternal feeling: Nikias, an observer, recounts how he once saw her with her child:

> She held
> Her lips to his and looked into his eyes,
> Not gladly, as a mother with her child,
> But stirred by some strange passion; then the boy
> Cried out with terror, and Medea wept.

Her unnatural relationship to the child – 'stirred by some strange passion' – is as puzzling to observers as it is distressing to the child. When she stabs her children later on, we are told that 'all her face grew alien'; but her alienness has been assured since the beginning. This is the point of Levy's version of the story: that Medea is an outsider from the beginning, and her acts of vengeance are a response to this, rather than, as for Webster, deeds that turn her into an outsider. She is perceived as a pollutant throughout the poem (Jason calls that no man will 'pollute our hands / With her accursed body'),[47] not only after she has killed the children. Her alien status is redefined by Levy as an existential state of womanhood, and one that is made more emphatic by her racial difference.

In the final lines of Levy's poem, Medea is pictured alone 'groping' in the 'deep, dense heart of the night'. She says she has 'fought with the Fates / And I am vanquished utterly'. Of these 'Fates', she writes:

> One climbs the tree and grasps
> A handful of dead leaves; another walks,
> Heedless, beneath the branches, and the fruit
> Falls mellow at his feet.[48]

Levy's Medea is relinquished to a primeval environment of rotting veg-
etation, inhabited by simian creatures. A bleak vision indeed: here is no
progressive evolution, only degeneration.

DEGENERATION AND THE ATAVISTIC CHILD MURDER IN *THE DESCENT OF MAN* AND *CULTURE AND ANARCHY*

The evolutionary theme that is evident in Levy's poem evokes a very different trajectory from that implicit in other contemporary women writers.
According to Mona Caird, for instance, women had a positive role in the future development of the species. As the poet, Emily Pfeiffer, wrote, women
were a 'force that should sublime the race': they were 'pilgrims of progress',
whose 'finer touch / ... helps the future to control'.[49] Against this, Levy
suggested rather that women were destined to slither in the primeval slime
of a degenerate patriarchal society. And while Caird had appropriated the
idea of the sacrificial child murder as women's weapon in the struggle for
evolutionary adaptation, Levy, on the other hand, saw child murder as the
product of a barbarous and atavistic society. In the case of her Medea, it
was an act forced upon her by a degenerate and backward-looking society.

Curiously, it has similar connotations in Charles Darwin's later work,
The Descent of Man and Selection in Relation to Sex (1871) – a work in
which he appeared to temper some of the social implications of his earlier
work. Citing McLennan's *Primitive Marriage* as his source, he discusses the
ubiquity of infanticide among 'savages', explaining it in Malthusian terms
as a response to restricted resources. But unlike McLennan, and against
the thrust of his own account of the infanticidal practices of the tragic
queen bee in *The Origin of Species*, Darwin is now less convinced of the
adaptive function of infanticide. In this later work, infanticide has become
an impediment to development and an enervating factor against the onward
force of evolution.

In societies where infanticide is practised, he claims, 'the struggle for
existence will be in so far less severe', thus creating a kind of torpor that in
many accounts was the overriding characteristic of savage society. Infanticide, according to this, will actively impede the 'power of sexual selection',
as cross-breeding between tribes as a consequence of the shortage of women,
will, he claims, make all people 'uniform in character'. It is one of several
customs that 'prevail with savages which would greatly interfere with, or
completely stop, the action of sexual selection'. In contrast to savage society, Darwin looks to an even earlier stage of evolution, the primordial stage
'when man had only doubtfully attained the rank of manhood', which he

paints in idyllic terms as a time at which there was a clearly differentiated sexual economy, and life was organised by a natural morality driven
by 'instinctive passions', rather than 'foresight or reason'. At this stage, he
writes with a certain longing, man 'would not then have been so utterly
licentious as many savages now are; and each male would have jealously
guarded his wife or wives. *He would not then have practised infanticide*; nor
valued his wives merely as useful slaves; nor have been betrothed to them
during infancy.'[50] Darwin's preference for this early stage of evolutionary
development is clear: as he states at the end of the work,

for my own part I would as soon be descended from that heroic little monkey,
who braved his dreaded enemy in order to save the life of his keeper; or from that
old baboon, who, descending from the mountains, carried away in triumph his
young comrade from a crowd of astonished dogs – as from a savage who delights
to torture his enemies, offers up bloody sacrifices, practises infanticide without
remorse, treats his wives like slaves, knows no decency, and is haunted by the
grossest superstitions.[51]

Infanticide persists in the list of attributes of savagery, a human invention
that divides the savage from the 'heroic little monkey' or the 'old baboon',
and becomes the eternal marker of a barbaric past that still pervades the
primitive peoples of the world. Darwin thus transfers the attributes of
the Noble Savage to the monkey, shifting the eye of moral approbation
from primitive peoples to the more benign animal world. In the process,
infanticide has been redefined: no longer the noble sacrifice for 'the good
of the community', it is now the mark of primitive man, and the cause of
both moral and evolutionary torpor.

   In sharp contrast to the queen bee who sacrifices her young for the future
good of the species, a second child murderer emerges from the evolutionary narrative: the licentious savage, careless, amoral, and uncivilised. The
queen bee and the savage shadow Malthus's two child murderers: the first
resembles Malthus's Dame Nature; the second is like the unruly mob, represented allegorically as the feckless mother who eats her own children. In
social criticism of the period, heavily inflected by the discourses of both
social Darwinism and Malthusian economics, the two figures are frequently
in evidence. As I have shown, they have been apparent in writings about
society and the poor since Malthus published his *Essay on Population*. But
in the new context of the late nineteenth century, the two child murderers are presented as though they are in direct competition with each
other, engaged in a life-and-death struggle of their own. The struggle between the two child murderers, which is staged in a wide range of locations,

comes to stand for a battle of the Future against the degenerative pull of the
Past.

The domain of the barbaric child-killer was, of course, not restricted to
evolution's distant past, for contemporaries were quick to perceive the signs
of atavism in British society. As the middle-class philanthropists who pen-
etrated Britain's urban slums would reveal, in the physically and morally
derelict environment of the cities, infant life was held cheaply. Children
were dying: the lives of the nation's young were threatened by malnutrition,
disease, and most worryingly, violence from neglectful and violent parents.
Urban slums were a breeding ground for the weak and degenerate, and
whoever managed to survive was destined only to replicate the patterns
of degeneration, to perpetrate the deadly process of human deterioration.
Embedded in this account of urban degeneration was a version of Malthus's
allegorical figure of the unruly mob – the prolific mother who destroyed
her offspring as quickly as she produced them. It was no coincidence that
in the imaginations of middle-class social commentators, the inhabitants
of these slums also constituted the crowds of alienated people whose insurrectionary behaviour made them a political force to be reckoned with.[52]
And the solution to problems presented by the mob at this stage was often a
Malthusian one: the regulation of population, or the rule of Dame Nature.

Staged in a wide range of writings in the late nineteenth century, therefore, is a struggle between two infanticidal regimes: the regime of Dame
Nature, versus that of the mob, the degenerate, too prolific, and unruly
poor. A version is to be found at work in Matthew Arnold's *Culture and
Anarchy* (1868), a work that in fact slightly predates Darwin's *Descent of
Man*. *Culture and Anarchy* is Arnold's particular response to the problems
of urban degeneration and social and political instability experienced at this
time, and exemplified for him by the recent riots in Hyde Park, and acts of
Fenian terrorism. Like many, he presents an implicitly Malthusian analysis,
focusing on the crowd as both the symptom and cause of the decline.

Arnold's distaste for the crowd as both a mechanism of political dissent
and a source of social degeneration is evident throughout *Culture and
Anarchy*. He deplores the 'multitudinous processions in the streets of our
crowded town, multitudinous meetings in their public places and parks',
that bring the 'risk of tumult and disorder'. And it is as a defence against the
incipient anarchy of the crowd that he develops his highly particular view of
the State: an ideal community that transcends class and is constituted as the
amalgam of our 'best selves'. This is a formation of ambiguous singularity,
an aggregate of individual and disembodied selves, and is directly opposed
to the collective mass of bodies in the crowd. The 'best self' is a conception

of the ideal self, differentiated from our everyday, embodied selves, and is achieved through the critical and reflective functions of Culture – or 'the study of perfection', the 'endeavour to come at reason and the will of God by means of reading, observing and thinking'.[53] The work of culture is a prophylactic against the crowd, and is closely related to the function of criticism as adumbrated in his earlier essay, 'The Function of Criticism'. However 'gross' they may be, there are shades of Wragg here, the grim suppresser of the poor. Indeed, *Culture and Anarchy* is a work haunted by the memory of Wragg – the anti-heroine of his earlier 'Function of Criticism'. But in the later work, Wragg's child-murdering functions are split into two, so that she is remembered both as the barbaric or atavistic child murderer – in Malthusian terms, the mob – and as the prophylactic Dame Nature, thinning the crowd for the good of the nation. Wragg is both Anarchy *and* Culture.

The Malthusian logic in Arnold's thinking is made clear in the latter part of *Culture and Anarchy*, when he tackles the difficult question of embodied selves – selves, like Wragg's, imbued with appetites and desires that disrupt the order of an ideal society. Relating the morbid conditions of slum life in London's East End, he writes:

I remember, only the other day, a good man looking with me upon a multitude of children who were gathered before us in one of the most miserable regions of London, – children eaten up with disease, half-sized, half-fed, half-clothed, neglected by their parents, without health, without home, without hope, – said to me: 'The one thing really needful is to teach these little ones to succour one another, if only with a cup of cold water; but now, from one end of the country to the other, one hears nothing but the cry for knowledge, knowledge, knowledge!' And yet surely, so long as these children are there in these festering masses, without health, without home, without hope, and so long as their multitude is perpetually swelling, charged with misery they must still be for themselves, charged with misery they must still be for us, whether they help one another with a cup of cold water or no; and the knowledge how to prevent their accumulating is necessary, even to give their moral life and growth a fair chance![54]

With their ill-nourished bodies, the pauper children seem to be on the point of extinction, murdered through squalid housing and parental ne-glect. While these casualties of urban overcrowding at first receive his com-passionate attention, his tone changes when he refers to them as a 'multitude [. . .] perpetually swelling': no longer individual, suffering bodies, they are now a collective mass, an eternally pregnant body that recalls Malthus's demon mob – figured as the unmarried mother who destroys her young, but continually replenishes them. The amelioration of suffering can be achieved, Arnold suggests, not through popular education, the shibboleth of liberal policies for social improvement – the call for 'knowledge, knowledge, knowledge'; nor through the inculcation of Christian virtues – as the 'good' but misled man thinks. Rather, it will be achieved through the dissemination of a different kind of 'knowledge': prophylactic knowledge – how to stop the multiplication of the poor; in Arnold's statistical terms, 'the prevention of accumulation', or the regulatory work of a Malthusian Dame Nature.

Arnold is as vague about the details of this knowledge as he is ambivalent about the value of the pauper children, and one must assume that he has in mind late marriage as a preferred form of birth control. However, in the text there is also an implicit alignment between culture and contraception, as though the 'study of perfection' will serve a contraceptive function, and help to prevent the accumulation of bodies, and regulate the expansion of population – turning culture itself into something like Malthus's Dame Nature figure. Embedded in his logic is the struggle between Dame Nature and the Mob: here it is the social conditions of urban living that perform the work of the atavistic child murder; and Culture or contraception that will beat it by controlling population in the way of Dame Nature.

ANNIE BESANT AND THE TRIUMPH OF THE QUEEN BEE

Paradoxically, it was the radical and secularist, Charles Bradlaugh, whom Arnold names throughout *Culture and Anarchy* as the arch-enemy of civilisation, who, less than ten years later, would answer this very call for contraceptive knowledge. Yet Bradlaugh's intervention was in every way antithetical to Arnold's views. Bradlaugh had set up the Malthusian League in the early 1860s, the aim of which was to eliminate poverty through the dissemination of birth-control advice to working people.[55] In 1877, with his collaborator Annie Besant, Bradlaugh was tried for obscene libel. They used their trial to publicise their cause further, and their intervention is seen to have marked a watershed in the reproductive practices of British families and the beginning of a fall in the birth rate.[56] Significant, however, is the fact that in defending themselves and disseminating their message, Besant and Bradlaugh invoked the very same narrative as that identified in Arnold's work: the story of the atavistic child murder which will be stamped out by the modernising spirit of Culture.

The offending text published by Bradlaugh and Besant was not a new work. Charles Knowlton's *The Fruits of Philosophy* had first been published in the 1830s, and remained in print ever since. Previously it had been published by the freethinker, James Watson, circulating only among a small group of cognoscenti – like-minded radicals such as Bradlaugh. In 1877, however, Bradlaugh and Besant produced a cheap edition of this work, which they aimed to make available to a much broader public. The initial provocation for their action was a perceived assault on the freedom of the press. James Watson's widow had recently sold the plates of Knowlton's *Fruits* to another freethinker, Bradlaugh's comrade, Charles Watts, who had allowed a Bristol bookseller named Cook to produce an illustrated edition. When Cook was arrested on an obscenity charge, Watts, the publisher, was charged too. Unbeknown to Watts, Cook already had a criminal record for selling pornography, and when Watts saw the edition, he decided that he must plead guilty to the charge. Bradlaugh, however, was outraged: fired with righteous indignation, Bradlaugh declared that Knowlton's work was 'defensible', and that he and Besant intended to 'deny the right of anyone to interfere with the full and free discussion of social questions affecting the happiness of the nation'.[57] That the purpose of Bradlaugh and Besant's publishing venture was to challenge the authorities is clear: as soon as it was printed, they rushed around London, delivering copies to the police with notice of where and when they intended to sell it. And as anticipated, they were arrested.

The ensuing trial attracted huge publicity. Sales of the pamphlet and other birth-control material rocketed, and lectures by Besant on the benefits of contraception drew massive crowds. Membership of Bradlaugh's Malthusian League mushroomed – by 1879 it had over twelve hundred members – and metamorphosed from a small clique of radicals into a popular movement.[58] At the end of the trial, Bradlaugh and Besant were found guilty; but, on appeal, the case was later dismissed on a technicality. They published the proceedings of the case week by week in Bradlaugh's paper, the *National Reformer*,[59] and Besant used her testimony as the basis for a further pamphlet, *The Law of Population* (1878), offering more up-to-date contraceptive advice. The trial was reported assiduously in the press and accounts reflected a spectrum of opinion; but whether newspapers expressed approval or disapproval, all were equally avid in their coverage of the case.[60]

Given that Knowlton's work was forty years old at the time of its reprinting, and as both Bradlaugh and Besant admitted, the advice it contained already dated, it is paradoxical that both based their defence on the claim that its dissemination was a necessary stage in the modernisation of the nation. In their testimony, they consciously situated the work in the context of contemporary science and technology, making frequent reference to Darwin and Galton, for instance, and quoting at length from works such as *The Descent of Man*;[61] in classic social Darwinist mode, they argued that medical science had lessened the checks on population, allowing the weak and infirm to survive where otherwise they would have died, so that, they claimed, it was incumbent on science to redress the imbalance it had created. Birth control was thus presented as the scientific solution to a scientific problem. 'Nature, left to herself, balances herself', asserted Besant; 'but if we interfere with nature by curing the sickly whom she is killing, and preserving the life which she has doomed, it becomes necessary to substitute scientific for natural checks'.[62] Much of Bradlaugh's testimony is concerned with claiming status for the work as specialised medical knowledge, so as to distance it from works of pornography. To this end he drew comparisons with Acton's recently published treatise on venereal disease – another work that trod the fine line between science and obscenity. And he compared birth control with forms of new technology – the telegraph, for instance. Bradlaugh and Besant, however, were not concerned with the production of scientific knowledge as such; their interest was rather in disseminating and applying that knowledge. Hence the aptness of the comparison with the telegraph: 'the telegraph', Bradlaugh explained,

is an admirable means of communicating from one country to another: but suppose you took a labourer or his wife into the operating room and showed them the apparatus for working the electric machine; they could not comprehend it, to them it would be useless; you must give them the information which would enable them to turn it to account.[63]

Bradlaugh and Besant's intervention performed the work of instruction they allude to here, and was thus a form of communication that, by association, was as modern as the telegraph. They constructed themselves as the champions of science and technology, hi-tech teachers and disseminators.

In contrast to these descriptions of the civilising impact of technology, their testimony was strewn with accounts of the degenerate poor, dying in urban squalor. With reference to the new scientific criminology of Lombroso, Besant accounted for the emergence of atavistic types in the city:

the unhealthy children who are born of drunken and dissolute parents, amidst such awful associations, growing up feeble, blood-poisoned, and only half human in many ways. It has often been remarked that when you get to the lowest grade of the criminal class you observe a kind of marked type. This is because the lives of their parents have so unhumanized then, that the children born of such parents are literally a lower race than those of parents whose happier circumstances have raised them above that condition.[64]

In these conditions, the spectre of child murder looms large. Besant narrated the affecting story of 'a child found dead in Brownlow Street' – the

location all the more poignant, given that Brownlow had been a prominent philanthropist in the recent history of Coram's foundling hospital.
The cause of death: his bedclothes.

On inquiry it was learnt that the mother, a widow, and six children slept in one
bed in a small room. The death of the child was attributed to the bedclothes. In
such an atmosphere as a room so occupied must have, the vital power necessarily
becomes weak, and to kill is easy.[65]

The social conditions weaken the moral will, making murder 'easy'. Indeed,
the very fabric of the environment seemed to kill children. Thousands of
children are 'literally slaughtered' by their poor living conditions: want of
clothes, food, and care, baby farming, overlying (16,000 women are guilty
of overlaying their children, Besant informs us), and the hereditary effects
of syphilis.[66] The conditions of urban poverty are truly degenerative.

Urban degeneration, we learn, threatens to turn England into Ireland,
the epitome of a backward society, and a nation known to the English since
Swift's *A Modest Proposal*, for its child-murdering tendencies. Besant cites
Professor Fawcett, the liberal MP and professor of political economy, who
had noted 'the terrible misfortunes brought upon [Ireland] by an undue
increase in population'.[67] According to Fawcett, a lethal combination of
the Catholic Church, which encouraged early marriage, and the notoriously incontinent habits of the Irish people, conspired to create the social
depravity that culminated in the famine. The Irish famine, Besant claims,
was only ended by emigration from Ireland, and ironically the consequent
overcrowding of English cities: 'what is there to prevent that happening in
England which has happened in Ireland', she warns, 'if we go on ignoring
with Irish recklessness questions like that for which I am pleading to-day?'.[68]
The technological innovation of birth control, therefore, promised to in-
oculate England against the degenerative infection of Ireland.

Bradlaugh and Besant's insistence on their civilising project is carefully
constructed to counter their critics who were equally assured of the degenerative tendencies of birth control. Resistance to birth control as a spur to
vice and promiscuity was deeply rooted. The fact that Francis Place, the
Malthusian author of birth-control tracts, was the target of much of the
satire generated by the 'Marcus' scandal in 1839 discussed in Chapter Four
suggests the disrepute in which birth controllers were held even among
working-class radicals. Even feminists such as Josephine Butler, whose successful campaign against the Contagious Diseases Acts was supported by
Besant and Bradlaugh, were opposed to the use of birth control on the
grounds that it encouraged prostitution and worsened women's position in
marriage.[69] Criticism of birth control was typically articulated in the form

of the charge of baby murder. Angus McLaren cites a letter from a female correspondent in Drysdale's *Political Economist and Journal of Social Science* in January 1857, saying of her opponents: 'their argument is "it is murder". Once remove this false notion and the way will be a little clearer.'[70] During the trial, similar accusations were made about Besant and Bradlaugh: Besant refers to a newspaper editor who had 'charged [her] with child murder, and referred to [her] as an advocate of promiscuous intercourse'.[71] Hence their emphasis on the work of birth control as the protector of infant life, and its importance as a civilising force.

Besant, however, was also alert to the more positive rhetorical possibilities of the charge, and embraced the role of child murderer – but not as the atavistic child murderer; rather she saw herself as the sacrificial and progressive child murderer, and harnessed the evolutionary connotations of infanticide as an adaptive force and mechanism of progress. Thus she refers to both Darwin's *Origin of Species* and Malthus's *Essay on Population*, and describes the natural checks in the population growth, from the animal and vegetable kingdoms, to 'savage nations', and specifically, the mother in the 'ruder tribes of America' who murders her surplus offspring as soon as they are born to save them from inevitable death.[72] This is her role model – the virtuous child-killer, the queen bee of evolution.

In fact Besant's identification with the sacrificial mother was, ironically, enhanced by her unfortunate loss of her own daughter, Mabel, in a custody battle following the trial. She was already separated from her husband, an Anglican cleric, but following the trial, the husband used her newfound notoriety to petition for custody of their child. Annie defended herself using the provisions for infant custody, the new Infant Custody Act, 1873 (36 Vic. c. 12),[73] that for the first time favoured mothers. Significantly, even the women who had fought for this legal reform held Besant in such suspicion that they did not support her.[74] For her advocates, however, the loss of Mabel was yet further evidence of Annie's courage, and it sealed her position as the sacrificial heroine of the secularist cause.[75]

CHILD MURDER AND THE NEW WOMAN IN *ALAN'S WIFE*
AND *JUDE THE OBSCURE*

The struggle between the two kinds of child-killing that is staged in such different locations as Matthew Arnold's analysis of culture and Besant and Bradlaugh's polemic for contraception underpins much social thinking in this period. In essence, it provides a compelling narrative for the logic of eugenics – the idea of selective breeding. With its legacy of meanings and allusions accrued over its long history, child murder embeds eugenics within a cultural tradition of representations of national virtue: ideas of sacrifice, of progress, and modernity. The narrative – in which the virtuous child-killer suppresses the barbarous and atavistic child-killer – thus has extraordinary potency, especially in the 1890s when the panic about degeneration was at its most intense. It is appropriated in particular by the New Women, who in many cases saw themselves as agents of eugenic progress.[76] Indeed, the New Women highlight the peculiar contradictions implicit in the discourses on degeneracy. For while the New Women often pictured themselves as warriors against degenerative decline, others perceived them to be symptoms of that very decline.[77]

In *Alan's Wife*, a play by New Women playwrights, the Anglo-American partnership Florence Bell and Elizabeth Robbins, based on a short story by the Scandinavian writer Elin Ameen, a mother commits the eugenic murder of a crippled child.[78] *Alan's Wife* is perhaps the clearest presentation of the struggle between the infanticidal forces of atavism and progress. First performed in London in 1893, the play naturally caused something of a stir for its treatment of a eugenic theme and its frank representation of a murdering mother.[79] Moreover, the play presents the killing as an act of bravery in the context of tragedy. As one critic wrote, linking the play to debates about euthanasia,

Are there not... cases of hopeless mania or incurable disease – cancer, say, or rapid consumption – in which it would be 'a mercy' to put sufferers out of their misery at once?... To my thinking the great tragic value of the theme lies in the fact that we can do neither [kill nor preserve] with a whole heart... *Alan's Wife* belongs to a... tragic category not yet recognised by official criticism – we may call it the tragedy of Fatality.[80]

As a drama of impossible choice, this 'tragedy of Fatality' thus offers a heroic role for the woman, implicitly turning Medea into Agamemnon.

To do this, the protagonist, Jean, draws on the familiar lexicon of child murder through which not merely to justify her act, but also to elevate it. In a monologue leading up to the murder, she imagines a conversation between herself and her child, now grown to an adult, in which he chastises her for not having killed him at birth:

Oh, I seem to see you in some far-off time, your face distorted like your body, but with bitterness and loathing, saying 'Mother, how *could* you be so cruel as to let me live and suffer? You could have eased my pain; you could have saved me this long martyrdom; when I was little and lay in your arms. Why didn't you save me. You were a coward – a coward!'[81]

The scene establishes the woman's heroism by invoking the motif of maternal sacrifice. The imagined reproach of the son repeats the Indian woman's lament on the banks of the Oronooka, reported by Gumilla and cited in William Alexander's *History of Women* a hundred years before. It also recalls the words of the slave mother, in Raynal's account, who kills her child to save it from a life of misery.[82] In its earlier instantiations, however, the motif emphasises the victimisation of the woman, often capitalising on the identification between the mother and child, which is usually a daughter. In this case, however, there is no such identification between mother and child – the baby is a boy, and while she kills him to save his suffering, theirs is not a shared affliction. Moreover, the act becomes associated specifically with her emancipation, rather than his: it is her 'one act of courage' through which she reaches a state of transcendence, even a kind of self-fulfilment. This is an Ibsenesque moment in the play, as contemporary critics were quick to notice, when Jean becomes transfigured in a way similar to Nora in *A Doll's House* (1879). In the end, Jean receives the death sentence, but she goes willingly to death, assuming herself the mantle of the child's projected martyrdom, as she goes to join the child and her dead husband 'up yonder' in a closing vision of ethereal domesticity. Indeed, mother and child are one in death – and so the identification that is presumed in earlier versions of the motif, but denied in this one, is in a sense achieved by the end of the play.

The use of the motif of infanticide as a means of female emancipation is at its most raw in *Alan's Wife*, where, in the bare and un-elaborate idiom of Naturalism, it is presented as social reality. Elsewhere, however, the motif is wrapped in mythological coverings that muffle its more shocking implications – the story of Medea, for instance, or the rich seam of mythic infanticides mined by Mona Caird, in which to present her social vision of the future. Caird uses different versions of mythic child-killers to evoke both, as she puts it, the 'parrot-like iteration' of custom, and a eugenic vision of the future. 'When sacrifices of children were made to Moloch', she writes,

it was necessary that the parents should offer them willingly, otherwise the gift was of no avail. 'The parents stopped the cries of their children by fondling and kissing them, for the victim ought not to weep, and the sound of the complaint was drowned in the din of flutes and kettledrums. Mothers, according to Plutarch, stood by without tears or sobs; if they wept or sobbed, they lost the honour of the sacrifice, and their children were sacrificed notwithstanding.' ['Pheonicia', George Rawlinson] Such is the power of tradition![83]

The silent and highly ritualistic sacrifices of these ancient mothers are contrasted with the child murders of modern women, the 'retaliatory massacres of infants'[84] – part Herod, part Medea – that Caird envisages as a revenge on patriarchal authority. In this instance, the atavistic murder is the sign of the blind following of tradition, the enslavement to patriarchal authority that is the mark of primitive society, while the second is presented as an act of will – and of vengeance.

These are issues that are explored in a highly critical way in Thomas Hardy's late novel, *Jude the Obscure* (1896) – his astonishing critique of the infusion of the Malthusian paradigm in contemporary culture and society. The brilliance of Hardy's analysis – that encompasses both the social stranglehold of cultural élites, as well as the problems of marriage, sexuality, and gender roles that many considered the root cause of individual oppression – lies in his realisation that the strategy for change that was most readily available to his contemporaries, namely one underpinned by the discourse of eugenics, relies on the very same Malthusian logic that keeps the social hierarchies in place. Hence the centrality of child murder to this novel in its shocking climax, the suicide of Jude's eldest son, known as Old Father Time, and his murder by hanging of his two siblings. In Hardy's version, the two kinds of child-killing – the atavistic and barbarous, and the sacrificial and progressive – merge into one, and are no longer distinguished from each other. Hardy's bleak and uncompromising vision of British society depicts an intransigent world in which the old system of privilege is absolutely unbending, and the efforts to change it marred by the inadequacies of those who seek change – like Sue and Jude.

Much of the novel is devoted to an examination of the phenomenon of the New Woman, through the character of Sue Brideshead.[85] Hardy's judgement on her is harsh. While sympathetic to her predicament, the novel nevertheless reveals the New Woman to be only semi-enlightened and egotistical – 'half wiser than my fellow-women? And not entirely wiser!' in Sue Brideshead's self-assessment. Her rival, Arabella, on the other hand, is worse: voluptuous, earthy, manipulative, and selfish. The two women are pitched against each other as competitors for Jude's affections: Arabella, sensual and conniving; and Sue, refined, politically and socially progressive, emotionally wrought, hysterical, and repressive. In a certain way, the two conform to Malthus's two child-murdering figures: the promiscuous mother, or the mob, who eats her own children (here of course Arabella doesn't literally eat her child, but she abandons Old Father Time to Jude in order to pursue her own capacious appetites); and Sue is the repressive Dame

Nature, who coaches the children in Malthusian logic – that they 'would be better out o' the world than in it', 'because they are too menny'.[86] In this context, the violent deaths of Old Father Time and his half-siblings are over-determined. They are atavistic child murders – the degenerate act of the offspring of Arabella, the primordial type; but they are also examples of the progressive child murder – sacrifices for the future of the coming race, the eugenic acts of the offspring of the New Woman. For Hardy, these two types of child murder are not posited in evolutionary competition with each other as in the other texts we have examined. Rather, the two child murders merge into one, so that neither sustains its meanings. This is a profoundly nihilistic gesture that evacuates the motif of child murder of all the manifest meanings that it has accreted over the history of its usages.

Sue's unsteadiness in relation to her progressive principles – her repeated returns to Philpot, her legal husband – is presented in the text as a symptom of the fundamentally contradictory rhetoric she adopts. In this, figures of a progressive future slip all too easily into those of an atavistic degeneration – primarily through the unstable motif of child murder. Thus when rational-ising the deaths of the children to Philpot, she does so in the language of the New Woman: 'My children – are dead – and it is right that they should be! I am glad – almost. They were sin-begotten. They were sacrificed to teach me how to live! – their death was the first stage of my purification. That's why they have not died in vain!'[87] Sue suggests that their deaths have an evolutionary purpose, but like Alan's wife, Jean, in Bell and Robbins's play, Sue appropriates this purpose for her own self-renewal: it is the 'first stage in [her] purification', for which they 'have not died in vain'. The language here underlines the egotism of the sacrifice. However, the comparison with *Alan's Wife* stops here, for in this case, her 'purification' means the repres-sion of her real desires, the end of her courageous attempts to flout custom: in Mona Caird's words, her 'purification' has become instead the sacrifice of children in the 'parrot-like iteration' of tradition. The vision at the end of the novel is of a bleak, degenerate civilisation, incapable of renewal or transformation. All Sue's children are dead, including the baby she was bearing at the time of the murders. Jude dies of disease and a broken spirit. Sue is imprisoned in a conventional and loveless marriage to Philpot, and Arabella lurches on in a life of drunkenness and casual sex. The forces of progress merge into those of regress.

In *Jude the Obscure*, the figure of child murder is relieved of all its mean-ings historically accrued. Neither a metaphor for a progressive nor a degen-erate future, the child murder now comes to figure as the end of meaning itself – the apocalyptic arrival of a new, nihilistic zeitgeist, in which cultural

signs are stripped of their meanings and values, a time of which Old Father
Time is identified as a representative. Jude reports that:

The doctor says there are such boys springing up amongst us – boys of a sort
unknown in the last generation – the outcome of new views of life. They seem
to see all its terrors before they are old enough to have staying power to resist
them. He says it is the beginning of the coming universal wish not to live. He's an
advanced man, the doctor: but he can give not consolation to – [88]

This is a world without consolation, and without meaning: and child murder has now come to figure the end of meaning itself.

Hardy's *Jude the Obscure*, like Old Father Time, delivers a very new view
of child murder – one that is no longer valued for its historically assimilated
meanings, but rather for its challenge to meaning itself. Undoubtedly, earlier
writers had found a similar fascination with child murder – Blake, for
instance, in his perplexing proverb of the Devil: 'sooner murder an infant in
the cradle than nurse an unacted desire'. But at this particular moment, on
the brink of the twentieth century, in the new context of eugenic thinking,
it is the abysmal meaninglessness of child murder that brings to a close the
long history of child-murder rhetoric of the previous two centuries.

CHAPTER 7

English babies and Irish changelings

In this final chapter, I wish to focus on a theme in the infanticide debates that has tended to lie submerged beneath the surface, only sporadically raising its profile – namely Ireland. In April 1891, Annie Besant who had already transformed herself once before, from vicar's wife to secularist campaigner, underwent another conversion. Under the influence of the occultist, Madame Blavatsky, Besant, the former advocate of contraception, converted to theosophy; she withdrew from circulation her work, *The Law of Population*, and declared self-control rather than birth control to be the best method of restraining population. In 1893, she made her first visit to India, where she would settle two years later and would become an important player in the Indian Home Rule movement, so beginning a new phase in this long and in many respects remarkable career.

In writing her autobiography in 1893 – retrospectively this would be a premature self-evocation for she lived until 1933 – she styles herself as the heroine of anti-imperial struggle. The loss of her daughter Mabel in the custody battle following the obscenity trial is a key episode, which both overshadows her involvement in a cause now abandoned, and creates for her the role of the sacrificial mother, with all its manifest associations – the bearer of republican virtue like Brutus; the emancipatory, infanticidal slave mother; and the agent of evolutionary progress, Darwin's queen bee.[1] It is thus significant that Besant should locate her own roots not in London, the imperial city of her birth and education, but rather in the land of her ancestors, the wild – and traditionally infanticidal – Ireland.[2]

At the dawn of her participation in the Indian Home Rule movement, Besant claims a national heritage in another site of anti-imperial struggle, and, of course, according to British representations, alongside India, another home of the barbarous child-killer. Given the whiff of hibernophobia that infiltrates her earlier work on contraception, where, in line with contemporary social commentators, she sniffs out the Irish immigrants in English cities as the cause of the sufferings brought on by overpopulation, her freshly declared embrace of this altogether more picturesque Ireland is especially revealing. This is the Ireland of musical tongues, of garrulous and friendly peasants, decaying families, and 'hot Irish blood'; she even accounts for her newfound belief in theosophy in terms of her 'Keltic' roots – her 'faculty for seeing visions and dreaming dreams'. But it is also the Ireland that is struggling for national independence: in her autobiography, she sets the moment of her radicalisation at the time of the Fenian disturbance in Chester in 1867.[3] All these elements combine, so that in her *Autobiography*, Besant will overlay her portrait of the degenerate Irish child-killer – the inhabitant of English slums, the pollutant of English domesticity, the promiscuous mother of the mob – with her own profile as the progressive, sacrificial mother of national independence. She is Mother Ireland – later she will become Mother India – who has relinquished her child in the struggle against empire.

Besant's self-mythologisation is useful for plotting a new shift in the uses of child murder at the end of the nineteenth century. One of the concerns of this book has been to trace the transformation of child murder from a motif for expressing responses to commercial modernity in the early eighteenth century, to, by the middle of the next century, a carrier of highly complex ideas about British national identity. In George Eliot's novel, *Adam Bede*, for instance, it is the trigger for remembering the history and territory of the British nation – and for forgetting its border conflicts. But in Hardy's late novel, *Jude the Obscure*, the motif of child murder implodes: evacuated of meaning, it is instead merely a statement of nihilism. It is as though British national identity, which gloried in its civilising impulse, its role as the agent of progress that could take order and enlightenment to near- and far-flung regions of untamed habitation, had dissolved under the strain of a too modern, newly degenerate culture. In the middle of the century, the child-murdering customs of exotic peoples acted as a foil against which to measure Britain's civilisation. Yet at the end of the century, these foreign habits turned instead into a mirror, reflecting back a horrible image of Britain's supposedly civilised self. The dark continents were now projected onto the inner heart of the metropolis, which had been found to be seething with degenerate life.

Around this time, as Besant's autobiography suggests, the motif of child murder was taken up by Irish writers as a way of refiguring Ireland's relationship to the metropolitan centre. As I have shown, the idea that the Irish were child-killers had been in place in British colonial representations since before Jonathan Swift in his subversive way both satirised and popularised those very associations in his *A Modest Proposal*. Moreover the inclusion of child murder in the efforts to regularise the legislature of the two nations following the 1800 Act of Union further indicated the importance of child murder as a recurrent sign of native unruliness for the colonising British. This continued to be evident in the persistent representation of Irish immigrants as atavistic child murderers in the degenerate cities of mainland Britain. But in the last years of the nineteenth century, in the context of the Irish struggle for Home Rule, Ireland's associations with child murder were dramatically transformed. In the 1890s, Irish writers replaced images of Ireland as the dissipated nation killing its children through careless disregard, poverty, or primitive conditions, with the motif of virtuous child sacrifice, as a way of inscribing Ireland's incipient modernity as the emergent independent nation. If, in the mid nineteenth century, child murder provided a set of discourses through which a writer like George Eliot could negotiate ideas of British national belonging, in the 1890s, the very same discourses provided the basis for Irish writers to articulate a divergent notion of Irish national independence.[4]

The motif of child sacrifice already had an important place in Irish republican tradition. The allegorical figure of Mother Ireland, sacrificing her sons in the struggle for national independence, increased in potency in the later part of the nineteenth century partly through the growing cult of Mariology among Irish Catholics.[5] The figure, moreover, held particular resonance in a society haunted by recent memories of famine, and traumatised by the repeated experience of emigration. The lament of the mother who lost her children through starvation or migration was a frequent component of Irish literary expression, and one that has particular significance in the idiom of Irish republicanism. The sacrificial mother shares many characteristics with other versions of the sacrificial child murderer that I have identified in the English radical and reformist traditions – the figure of Brutus, the hero of virtuous restraint who placed the good of the republic over personal ties, and the slave mother who killed her children to save them from a life of oppression. In the Irish version, however, the children are invariably boys, not girls (as in the case of the slave woman); and the children are patriots, not traitors (as in the case of Brutus' sons). Moreover the sacrifice is committed not to save the child from a terrible life, as in the slave woman's sacrifice, but rather to save the nation – which is the allegorical extension of the mother herself. In a curious way, it seems to be a double discourse of both maternal martyrdom and maternal salvation. By the end of the century, the figure is highly politicised, and has become a central conduit for the expression of nationalist feeling. Take, for instance, Padraic Pearse's quasi-liturgical 'The Mother', a *stabat mater* for Ireland:

I do not grudge them: Lord I do not grudge
My two strong sons that I have seen go out
To break their strength and die, they and a few,
In bloody protest for a glorious thing,
They shall be spoken of among their people,
The generations shall remember them,
And call them blessed.[6]

A more complicated rendering appears in the Anglo-Irish writer, Emily Lawless's elegiac poem that takes up the theme of emigration, 'After Aughrim', from her collection, *With the Wild Geese* (1902). In this work that commemorates an earlier episode of migration in Irish history – the exile to the continent following the battles of the Boyne in 1690, and Aughrim in 1691, which had violently confirmed England's political hegemony over Ireland – Mother Ireland is represented as a sacrificial mother who presides over a race of patriot sons. But Lawless's presentation of the mother is much more critical that Pearse's, turning her into a maternal tyrant, tossing her patriot sons into the sea.

She said, 'They gave me of their best
They lived, they gave their lives for me
I tossed them to the howling waste
And flung them to the foaming sea.'

[...]

She said, 'Not mine, not mine that fame:
Far over sea, far over land,
Cast forth like rubbish from my shores,
They won it yonder, sword in hand.'

She said, 'God knows they owe me nought,
I tossed them to the foaming sea,
I tossed them to the howling waste,
Yet still their love comes home to me.'[7]

The image is a complex one that superscribes the terms of Darwinian science over the figure of Irish patriotism, suggesting that the sacrificial Mother Ireland is an agent of evolutionary progress carrying out a necessary process in a stage in the history of the nation. But the depiction of her sons as refuse – 'tossed into the waste' and 'cast forth like rubbish from my shores' – jars with the unconditional love that is returned to the mother, and the tone of the mother's voice fluctuates uncomfortably between tragic stoicism and wilful neglect.

The Irish appropriation of figures of child sacrifice in this period must be seen in part as a response to – often a direct repudiation of – the figure of the Irish barbaric child-killer that was rife in British colonial discourses. In the late nineteenth century, against the backdrop of the struggle for Irish Home Rule, and within the explanatory terms of urban degeneration, the Irish are shown repeatedly to be not only killers of their own babies, as Swift had shown in his *A Modest Proposal*, but murderers of English children too in the overcrowded slums of British cities. Commentators have observed the way in which English social commentary at this time – of the kind written by Henry Fawcett and commented on by Besant and Bradlaugh in their trial testimony[8] – conceptualises Irish immigrants as a source of infection, contaminating both the social and moral health of England.[9] In the more whimsical terms inspired by Celtic fairy tales and folkloric traditions, Irish immigrants were also seen as a population of changelings, the wizened and ugly babies left by the fairies in the place of healthy English children.

Throughout the nineteenth century, Irish immigrants had been represented as a supernatural and ghostly population, haunting England's cities and usurping resources from trueborn English men. For instance, the Irish were widely known for their preternatural ability to survive on meagre food, if any at all, giving them a ghostly transparency – in *London Labour and London Poor*, Henry Mayhew notes the immigrant Irish rural worker's ability to undercut even the Jews, because they were simply, in his words, 'more starving', able to 'live harder'.[10] The Irish habit of undercutting English workers in the labour market was a frequent complaint of the English working class. When, in the context of the agitation against the New Poor Law, English radicals represented the unemployed and the poor – in economic terms, the 'surplus population' – as a band of fairies made ghostly through starvation, they drew on these associations between Irish migrants among the working class, and belief in fairies.[11] The interest in Irish folklore, even in its more picturesque forms, became increasingly significant in the second half of the nineteenth century in helping to cement the racial distinction between the rational and modern Anglo-Saxon English and the romantic and superstitious Celtic fringe.[12] This apprehension of Irish racial characteristics converged with a belief in social Darwinist notions of the competition between 'species' and struggle for survival, to create a context in which stories of fairy changelings provided a ready narrative for dramatising the more immediate threat of the Irish: the Irish in Britain were an invading population, surreptitiously abducting the birthright of healthy English babies with their prodigious broods of sickly infants that will, in any case, wither and die.

The belief in changelings, however, has further significance here. For in recording Irish folk stories and superstitions, it was often the belief in changelings that was taken to be a signature of Ireland's dislocation from modern, civilised life. Take for example, Thomas Crofton Croker, who, in the second volume of his *Fairy Legends* (1828), included a newspaper account of a trial for child murder of an old woman, Ann Roche, in Tralee in July 1826: a small boy in the woman's care, Michael Leahy, had been drowned; the boy 'could neither stand, walk, or speak – *it was thought to be fairy struck*'. When examined, the woman said that her intention had been not 'to kill the child, but to cure it – to put the fairy out of it', and she was found not guilty.[13] In a similar vein, in *Irish Popular Superstitions* (1852), W. R. Wilde records the story of a Kerry man who had 'roasted his child to death, under the impression that it was a fairy'. 'He was not brought to trial', Wilde notes, 'as the crown prosecutor mercifully looked upon him as insane.'[14] In both these cases belief in changelings not merely assures an English readership of the sinister whimsy of the Irish, but more importantly, it seems to remove the Irish from the reach of the law.

In fairy tales, this attribute is a quaint feature of Irish daily life. But in the context of governance and the administration of a subordinate people it had more disturbing implications. In the politically turbulent context of the 1890s, the connotations of folkloric belief, such as that in changelings, became much more worrying. A *cause célèbre* of 1895, the controversial case of Bridget Cleary, a Tipperary woman who was burnt to death by members of her family in the belief that she was a fairy changeling, drew public attention to the unruly customs of the native Irish. The likely involvement of the woman's father in the case, moreover, turned this into an instance of infanticide of a kind, showing that the barbaric Irish had once more reverted to type. As Angela Bourke's recent study has shown, the case was taken up at the time by Unionists as a sign that the Irish were unfit for home rule.[15] Exactly contemporaneous with the trial in London of Oscar Wilde for committing acts of 'gross indecency', the case provided more incontrovertible evidence of Irish degeneracy. Both cases displayed the degraded domestic habits of the indigenous Irish that proved the necessity of colonial rule.

The meanings of this unruliness had, however, changed in the new context of the *fin de siècle*. For now indigenous Irish beliefs began to make Ireland seem no less ungovernable. Not now because it was an atavistic and uncivilised culture, but rather, I suggest, because it was strangely modern. The connection is perhaps most apparent in a short essay on 'Changelings' by the writer Andrew Lang in the *Illustrated London News* – a piece that was a direct comment on the Bridget Cleary case. Lang gives a functionalist explanation for the belief in changelings: it is a rational response to weak or sick children.[16] In Lang's terms, the belief in changelings is not a primitive superstition but a eugenic device – a way of disposing of the weak and infirm – and, in the context of the 1890s, the most modern solution to the social problems of the age. Moreover, he also sees belief in changelings as a psychological disorder – 'hysteria, epilepsy or what not'. It is as though the Irish peasant were an overwrought bourgeois housewife – or perhaps a New Woman.[17]

Lang's essay replicates the move that is sketched out in Max Nordau's *Degeneration* (1893, English trans. 1895).[18] Whereas the criminologist Lombroso, to whom Nordau famously dedicated his work, had located the phenomenon of degeneration in the primitive societies of Sicily (Italy's Ireland), Nordau held that modern societies were equally degenerate in that the remnants of the primitive past returned, newly charged, to become the characteristics of the modern, urban, metropolitan world. According to Nordau, the degeneracy of modern societies was paradoxically the product of too much civilisation, rather than too little. In Lang's account, similarly, changeling belief is transformed from being the identifying feature of prim- itive, uncivilised barbaric culture into that of an advanced society, as the Celtic fairy world begins to accrue the characteristics of the modern world: a world where reproduction is eugenically controlled, and the inhabitants are nervous, hysterical types – indeed fairies, even Wildean fairies. Angela Bourke points out the wealth of associations that the term fairy begins to hold in the 1890s.[19] For the first time in print, the term fairy refers to homosexuals. Bourke also cites a short letter from Lady Gregory published in the *Spectator* in 1895, in which she makes a connection between New Women and fairies, on the basis that both are 'cross' and 'clever'.[20] Thomas Hardy surely had this association in mind when he repeatedly cast his New Woman, Sue Brideshead as 'a sort of fay, or sprite – not a woman'.[21] Else- where socialists and radicals are described as fairies.[22] All of them are now interpreted as the degenerate types of modern life.

The fairy changeling will steal your baby and probably kill it. To rid your family of the changeling, you must drown it, burn it, destroy it. En- visaged here is a veritable carnage of infants. But consider how different these wilful acts of destruction are to the typical Malthusian vision of child killing through sexual incontinence and neglect that had dominated the social discourse on the Irish problem in Britain. What is interesting here is not merely the persistence of the child-murder motif but its radical transformation into a disconcerting emblem of Ireland's aspiration to independence and ensuing modernity.

The Irish New Woman writer, George Egerton, explores this complex and intensely topical motif in challenging ways and it is to her work that I now turn. When Egerton's two collections of short stories, *Keynotes* and *Discords*, broke onto the literary scene in 1892 and 1893 respectively, they were hailed by critics as representatives of a new kind of fiction, and a new kind of femininity.[23] Sexually explicit and formally experimental, the stories found new narratives in which to represent female passion – narratives which drew on the figure of child murder in complicated ways. The conservative critic Hugh Stutfield grudgingly praised her as the 'ablest of our women writers of the neurotic school', but nevertheless found her work 'simply dismal and disgusting'. He grouped *Discords* with *Jude the Obscure*, as 'excessively morbid': 'to read them one would think that the only fleeting moment of happiness the authors enjoy is when they can invent some new thrill or shudder'.[24] For the New Woman writer, Laura Marholm Hansson, however, in her book *Modern Women*, translated into English in 1896, it is precisely these qualities that make Egerton a distinctively modern woman – she is part of a 'new race of women, more resigned, more hopeless, and more sensitive than the former ones'.[25] The word 'race' is repeated over and over again, and each time encodes both Egerton's Irishness and her femininity, in a way that recalls Amy Levy's similar association between racial and sexual difference in her Medea poem discussed above.[26] It is Egerton's Irishness, as well as her femininity, that make her instinctive, overwrought, excitable: in Hansson's terms it is this that gives her 'highly developed nerves'. There is a clear racial and gender economy at work, whereby women and Ireland are opposed to men and England – 'the heavy Englishman ... and the untameable woman who is prevented by race instinct from loving where she ought to'.[27]

The story that Hansson refers to at this point in her discussion is George Egerton's 'Virgin Soil' in *Discords*, in which a very young woman marries a libertine man, and returns to her maternal home later in the story, to chastise her mother. As the title suggests, the young woman is implicitly identified with the virgin soil of a newly colonised country; and marriage by extension with that process of colonisation. When the woman recriminates her mother for making her marry the man, she uses a formulation that should by now be familiar: she says 'Why didn't you strangle me as a baby? It would have been kinder; my life has been hell, mother.'[28] Here is the lament of the Indian woman on the banks of the Oronooka recorded by Father Gumilla, cited by William Alexander in 1777. By using these words, Egerton locates the woman's lament in the tradition of critiques that associate the oppression of women with primitive cultures, and finds marriage, like Mary Wollstonecraft had done a hundred years before, a state of barbaric enslavement.

George Egerton was the pseudonym of Mary Chavelita Dunne, born in Australia to an Irish father and Welsh mother, travelling to New Zealand and Chile, before the family returned to Ireland, where she was educated. Her father, John Y. Dunne was involved in the Home Rule movement, and in her correspondence, Egerton records her own intense attachment to Ireland.[29] Nevertheless, she travelled extensively, like a modern woman, to New York, London, Germany, and Scandinavia, before the beginning of her publishing career – composing both *Keynotes* and *Discords* while living in West Cork.[30] This sense of itinerancy is reflected in the stories, which shift from London to Paris to Dublin to Christiana to New York.[31] Often, one is not quite sure where one is as the identifying spatial features are rarely national ones. But in her account of the genesis of the stories in a piece she wrote some years later, their Irish origin is emphasised, for it is to the enchanted, 'fairy' landscape of West Cork that she attributes the inspiration for the stories: 'we were living in a long, white-washed, thatched cottage, on a slope above the station', she writes; 'down in a field to the left a Fairy Fort – I used to sit on the stile in the dusk and listen to the music coming from it'.[32] Here is an idea of Irishness in which the extremes of the primitive and the modern meet and mingle – a distinctive mixture of a fairy landscape, and the insignia of modernity, in the railways, and later references to emigration to South Africa. It is this that will be condensed into the instinctive passions of her modern women protagonists.

But if the women bear the traces of the Irish landscape, they are also conceptualised as colonised territory in another sense. In the same piece, Egerton suggests that women's lives are like 'plots' in a field of narratives which have been colonised by male writers: 'There was only one small plot left for her [the woman writer] to tell: the *terra incognita* of herself, as she knew herself to be, not as man liked to imagine her.'[33] Playing with the double meanings of the word 'plot', she argues that writing about the life of a woman is tantamount to a process of decolonisation.

In 1890s Ireland, the discourse of national decolonisation or Home Rule shadows George Egerton's conceptualisation of women's emancipation. The most powerful story in *Discords* is 'Wedlock', which, as the title suggests, is an excoriating critique of marriage, represented here as a torpid state of degeneration – or deadlock. As elsewhere in Egerton's work, there are obvious analogies throughout between marriage and colonisation. In this story, the protagonist, a woman, has an illegitimate child, who is looked after by her sister while she is in service. So that she can bring up her own child, she marries a widower who promises her that her daughter will be adopted into their new family. He reneges on his promise; rather than being united with her own child, she has to keep house for him, and his three children. In disappointment she takes to drink, while he to violence. When her own daughter dies without her knowledge – concealed from her by her husband – she murders his children in revenge. This multiple child murder is an adaptation of the various child murders we have encountered in this book. It is presented, on the one hand, as the New Woman's act of self-fulfilment, like that of Jean in *Alan's Wife*, but also as a perverse twist to the motif of maternal – perhaps Irish – sacrifice.

The world described in the story is a degenerate world of 'jerry-built' gentility, inhabited by all kinds of degenerate, modern types – cripples, drunks, spooky children, and a New Woman writer. The central character is trapped in this world, in her hereditary drunkenness and her terrible marriage. Throughout the story the woman is being watched – first by some builders, then by the New Woman writer who is her lodger, by the stepchildren, and by the women at her daughter's funeral.[34] There is an illicit feel to these spectators. They spy on her, twitching curtains, glimpsing through windows, listening from behind closed doors, and all cast judgement on her. The narrative itself is a composite of these different viewpoints, as the woman is caught in the gazes of others, subjected to their various assessments. This emphasis on her surveillance draws analogies with a colonial regime, to the extent that we are invited to read the woman as a colonised nation – like Ireland – and her child murder as a symbolic bid for emancipation.

In the final passage the tone changes in a striking way. The woman is now alone, watched only by the 'tearful moon'. And the colour changes, from monochrome to dazzling colour:

Upstairs in a back room in the silent house a pale strip of moonlight flickers over a dark streak on the floor that trickles slowly from the pool at the bedside out under the door, making a second ghastly pool on the top step of the stairs – a thick sorghum red, blackening as it thickens with a sickly serous border. Downstairs the woman sits in a chair with her arms hanging down. Her hands are crimson as if she has dipped them in dye. A string of blue beads lies on her lap, and she is fast asleep; and she smiles as she sleeps, for Susie is playing in a meadow, a great meadow crimson with poppies, and her blue eyes smile with glee, and her golden curls are poppy-crowned and her little white feet twinkle as they dance, and her pinked-out grave frock flutters, and her tiny waxen hands scatter poppies, blood-red poppies, in handfuls over three open graves.[35]

The calmness of the woman, smiling in her sleep, is foreboding because the red colour that now swims over the scene is literally the blood of the children she has just murdered. It is an extraordinarily disturbing moment. Her extreme violence is represented as not only a rational act, but also one that is deeply satisfying for the woman – it brings her first moment of peace in the entire story. It is also one that is heavily imbued with religious significance. The scene itself is presented in strikingly painterly terms – like a baroque rendering of a religious scene. The blood is like dye, and the scene is given the colours and textures of an oil painting – the light and dark of chiaroscuro, the red, blue, and gold colours, the 'sorghum' red blood 'blackening', bordered with 'serous' white, as though it were a cloak. The iconography, moreover, recalls that of the *Pietà*. In this case, however, the woman encompasses both mother (the child's beads on her lap like the Virgin's rosary beads), *and* son (*her* arms 'hanging down' like Christ's), and the three graves remind us of the three crucifixes on the Hill of Golgotha. But here, all the associations of child sacrifice from the Christian tradition are suddenly transposed into a different register – that of revenge. Maternal martyrdom is covered over by an act of retribution, as Mary becomes Medea. The story redefines the woman's sacrifice of her own child as an act of murder by her oppressor; and her murder of his children as an act of revenge. This is a bleak but triumphant moment, and it can be read, allegorically, as the triumph of Mother Ireland, vengefully murdering the offspring of her oppressor.

George Egerton adapts the motif of child murder in a way that draws on, but also strikingly repudiates, the long tradition of meanings of child murder that I have traced during the course of this book, and provides a fitting place to end this study. Of course, child murder does not slip out of representation after this, any more than it was absent before Swift and Mandeville drew it into their accounts of commercial society at the beginning of the eighteenth century. But it is the case that during the twentieth century, significant changes in the context from which figures of infanticide had derived their meanings make child murder operate as an idea within culture in different ways. The more widespread use of technologies for the control of fertility in the twentieth century, especially contraception, led to a decrease in the numbers of infanticides like Jane Cornforth's, recorded at the beginning of this study.[36] Child murder was no longer the banal, everyday kind of event that it was for the spectators of Cornforth's crime. Moreover, the widespread acceptance of theories of eugenics at the beginning of the twentieth century shifted the idea of sacrificial child murder for progressivist reasons – the kind of child murder represented by Malthus's

Dame Nature, or Darwin's queen bee – into a new, and disturbingly literal register that dulled some of its symbolic potential. Indeed, as I have argued, its uses as a motif that recorded *both* primitive barbarism *and* alternatively a civilising force, became more difficult to sustain in the cultural context dominated by theories of degeneration that increasingly failed to mark a distinction between the two.

The map of meanings of child murder in the twentieth and twenty-first century will look very different from that of my period. I would speculate that one important landmark for any study of child murder in this later period might be Freud's 1919 essay, 'A Child is Being Beaten',[37] for, while it invokes the very same triangle of spectator, child, and violator established in the late eighteenth century, as a structure through which to imagine forms of masculine subjectivity, it nevertheless changes the emphasis in a crucial way. Freud's new insight is that the child might also be the spectator of his own violation, and that the fantasy of child beating is a sado-masochistic one. While earlier versions of child murder that I have studied certainly generated sympathy for the child-victim, this was usually mediated through the mother. When the victim's point of view is presented, it is invariably through the voice of an adult who *wishes* that she had been killed at birth, to escape from a life of constraint or oppression. Freud's essay alters this wish for violation completely. Not only does the child now take pleasure in his violation, but also the fantasy of being violated is understood as a phase in the development of adult sexuality.[38] This formulation gives a new centrality to the child, bringing it into focus as the subject, rather than as the object, of these concerns. It also suggests a different relationship between child and adult, and by extension, a collapse of the absolute distinction between primitive (or childish) and civilised (or adult) peoples, a distinction on which most anthropological thinking of the earlier period depended. It is perhaps the different notion of temporality implicit in Freud's work that is crucial in displacing the strongly progressive narratives of child murder that dominated the earlier period.

Nonetheless, it would be a mistake to suggest that the meanings accreted since the beginning of the eighteenth century suddenly disappear in the new context of the twentieth century. Evidence suggests, on the contrary, that they linger on, emerging sometimes very strikingly. They are very apparent, for example, in the continuing debates around abortion, in which the pro-life strategy is to give the foetus personality and to dramatise its suffering – as, for instance, in the film, *The Silent Cry*[39] – making abortion an act of murder of a sentient human child by a barbaric and uncivilised society. On the other side of the debate, while the pro-abortion lobby usually adopts a discourse of rights, nevertheless their language is infused with the sense that abortion is a force of progress, in much the same terms that Annie Besant had used at the end of the nineteenth century in her arguments for the use of contraception.

Furthermore, recent debates about abortion and contraception often have a national aspect to them. This is particularly apparent in Ireland, where all discussions about reproductive customs continue even now to be framed by strong ideas of national and religious identity, which are hardened by the vexed relation to Britain, and a memory of a colonial heritage in which ideas of Irish child-murdering were so deeply laid, and latterly, as I have argued in this chapter, heavily contested. For instance, the mysterious and highly controversial case of the Kerry Babies, two murdered infants discovered in Kerry in April 1984 around the time of the abortion referendum in Ireland, provided a context in which different parties could argue on the one hand that Ireland was an inherently civilised society which, in contrast to other European countries, disallowed abortion and kept child murderers at bay; and on the other hand, a barbaric nation that failed to modernise its reproductive habits, and harboured child murderers.[40] Reproductive habits are still invoked as a measure of the relative progress of different nations, and are frequently used to mark the resistance of Third-World nations to the forces of modernisation. In such contexts, the figure of child murder operates as a 'lieu de mémoire', through which notions of national difference and identity are remembered and re-inscribed.[41]

In this study, I have traced the meanings of child murder across the eighteenth and nineteenth centuries, and followed the disquieting presence of the murdered child as an idea and as a trope as it shifts around a complex network of beliefs and desires. Child murder emerges as an important term in debates about modernity, progress, commerce, and nationhood, and about men, and women, and children. That we continue to be traumatised by such crimes is evident in the daily news. But it is equally clear that we should be alert to the larger cultural meanings of such acts, and the legacies they may hold.

Appendix

ON THE IDENTITY OF 'MARCUS'

The potency of the 'Marcus' pamphlets accrued from their anonymity, and the true identity of the author remains a mystery. Nevertheless, there are various clues which suggest possible designations. John Knott notes that the *Manchester Guardian*, 20 February 1839, suggests that the pamphlets may have been translations from the French.[1] The allusion is possibly to François-Noël ('Gracchus') Babeuf, the protocommunist, who authored a work entitled *Système de dépopulation... de Carrier* (1795), exposing a purported plot on behalf of Robespierre's Committee of Public Safety to depopulate the Vendée.[2] There is, however, no evidence that Babeuf authored a work such as the 'Essay on Painless Extinction'.

The interest in 'Marcus' shown by the *Northern Liberator*, the Newcastle-based radical newspaper, is more intense than that of any other contemporary publications. It is worth speculating that 'Marcus' may have been the invention of one or other of the group working on the *Liberator*, possibly Thomas Doubleday. Doubleday founded the *Liberator*, in collaboration with Robert Blakey, who was its first publisher, and Auguste Beaumont.[3] Later it was published by Arthur James Cobbett, who also published Stephens's sermons. Doubleday and Stephens often spoke at the same meetings. The articles authored by Doubleday in the months preceding the emergence of 'Marcus' in December 1838 display the same satirical tone as the 'Marcus' pamphlets: like the 'Marcus' pamphlets, they focus the critique of the New Poor Law through a discussion of Malthus as a violent criminal; place a heavy emphasis on contemporary scientific practise; and refer back to Swift. Doubleday's enthusiasm for Swift is most evident in both his *Political Tale of the Tub*, and also in a series entitled 'Neglected Biographies', reprinted as *Northern Lights* (1839), an anthology of writings from the *Northern Liberator*. 'Neglected Biographies' are ironically hagiographic biographies of characters such as Esther Hibner, who was hanged for starving children in the workhouse in 1829, 'Sawney Bean', the notorious Scottish cannibal, and Margaret Tinkler, a midwife-murderer. The essays are laden with heavily ironic references to Malthus, alongside others to Swift. For instance, in relation to the murders of 'Sawney Bean', he writes: 'Here, in the wilds of Galloway, were not only discovered the leading doctrines of the Malthusian philosophy – but even that more refined portion of it which the celebrated *Dean Swift* was thought first to have proposed to the world, was here *actually in practice!*' Doubleday was also the author of an anti-Malthusian work on population, entitled *The True Law of Population* (London, 1842), which proposes that nutrition and fertility are inversely related to each other. As well as being involved in publishing radical newspapers, Doubleday also contributed to mainstream, middle-class journals, *Blackwood's* and *Tait's*, and the outline of *The True Law of Population* is laid out in an article addressed to Lord Brougham and Vaux, published in *Blackwood's* in March 1837. His range of social contacts would have given him access to respectable booksellers such as Sherwood and Neely, associated with the second 'Marcus' pamphlet.

Gregory Claeys has recently attributed the authorship of *The Book of Murder* to the Owenite, George Mudie.[4] Mudie's *Alarm Bell*, of which two issues are extant, includes a long article entitled, 'To the Rich and Influential Classes of the British People' which incorporates extensive references to 'Marcus', reading him as an extension of Malthus. Interestingly, Mudie adopts a very striking medical language of healing and disease in this article, which develops the scientific idiom of the 'Marcus' satire. I am grateful to Gregory Claeys for showing me copies of the *Alarm Bell*. If Mudie is the real 'Marcus', then the *Liberator's* exploitation of the pamphlets would seem to be merely opportunistic.

Notes

INTRODUCTION: PLOTS AND PROTAGONISTS

1. *OBSP* (May 1774), case no. 386, pp. 206–8; *London Chronicle* (23 May 1774), p. 490; *Lloyds Evening Post and British Chronicle* (hereafter *Lloyds*) (20 May–23 May 1774), pp. 485, 487.
2. For trials of eighteenth-century child murder cases, see Mark Jackson, *Newborn Child Murder: Women, Illegitimacy and the Courts in Eighteenth-Century England* (Manchester, 1996). See also J. M. Beattie, *Crime and the Courts in England, 1660–1800* (Oxford, 1986), pp. 117–23.
3. *Lloyds* (23 May 1774), p. 491. Public processions such as these from Newgate to Tyburn ended in 1783, when executions were held in the confines of Newgate. See Peter Linebaugh, *The London Hanged: Crime and Civil Society in the Eighteenth Century* (1991), p. 363.
4. *OBSP* (1774), p. 206.
5. Ibid., p. 207.
6. The insanity plea was not instigated until the nineteenth century. See Roger Smith, *Trial By Medicine: Insanity and Responsibility in Victorian Trials* (Edinburgh, 1981), pp. 143–50. Yet an embryonic form of such a plea – that a woman was 'out of her senses' – is increasingly evident in the seventeenth and eighteenth centuries. See Jackson, *New-Born Child Murder*, pp. 120–3, and Dana Rabin, 'Bodies of Evidence, States of Mind', in Mark Jackson (ed.), *Infanticide: Historical Perspectives on Child Murder and Concealment, 1550–2000* (Aldershot, 2002), pp. 73–92. Rabin discusses the Cornforth case in n. 38, p. 84. See also Joel Eigen, 'Intentionality and Insanity: What the Eighteenth-Century Juror Heard', in William Bynum, Roy Porter, and Michael Shepherd (eds.), *The Anatomy of Madness: Essays in the History of Psychiatry* (1985), pp. 34–51.
7. *Lloyds* (20 May 1774), p. 485.
8. Historical accounts of child murder usually divide between those that deal with the periods before and after the 1803 repeal of the 1624 Statute. On the eighteenth century, the fullest is Jackson's excellent *New-Born Child Murder*, but see also Peter C. Hoffer and N. E. H. Hull, *Murdering Mothers: Infanticide in England and New England 1558–1803* (New York, 1981); Beattie, *Crime and the Courts*; R. W. Malcolmson, 'Infanticide in the Eighteenth Century', in J. S. Cockburn (ed.), *Crime in England, 1550–1800* (1977), pp. 187–207; and

Marilyn Francus, 'Monstrous Mothers, Monstrous Societies: Infanticide and
the Rule of Law in Restoration and Eighteenth-Century England', *Eighteenth-
Century Life*, 21 (1997), pp. 133–56. Book-length studies of child murder in the
nineteenth century include Margaret L. Arnot, 'Gender in Focus: Infanticide in
England, 1840–1880' (Ph.D. thesis, University of Essex, 1994) and Lionel Rose,
The Massacre of the Innocents: Infanticide in Great Britain, 1800–1939 (1986).
See also George K. Behlmer, 'Deadly Motherhood: Infanticide and Medical
Opinion in Mid-Victorian England', *Journal of the History of Medicine*, 34
(1979), pp. 403–27; A. R. Higginbotham, '"Sin of the Age": Infanticide and
Illegitimacy in Victorian London', in K. O. Garrigan (ed.), *Victorian Scandals:
Representations of Gender and Class* (Athens, OH, 1992), pp. 257–88; Roger
Sauer, 'Infanticide and Abortion in Nineteenth-Century Britain', *Population
Studies*, 32 (1978), pp. 81–93; and essays in Jackson (ed.), *Infanticide*.

9. On the relationship of the 1624 statute to the Poor Law, see Jackson, *New-Born
   Child Murder*, p. 31. See also Peter Laslett, 'Introduction: Comparing Illegitimacy Over Time and Between Cultures', in Peter Laslett, Karla Oosterveen,
   and Richard M. Smith (eds.), *Bastardy and its Comparative History* (1980),
   pp. 1–65.

10. According to Jackson, 'around two or three cases were brought before the grand
    and trial juries every year until the end of the century' in the Northern Circuit
    assize courts of Yorkshire, Northumberland, Cumberland, and Westmorland
    (*New-Born Child Murder*, pp. 6, 16–23). Yet the full extent of child murder in
    the period is impossible to gauge. See Malcolmson, 'Infanticide', p. 191; Beattie,
    Crime and the Courts, pp. 117–23; Hoffer and Hull, *Murdering Mothers*, ch. 3.
    In the nineteenth century, the situation is no less unclear. For discussion of
    unreliable statistical evidence, see Ch. 5.

11. On servants and child murder, see Amy Masciola, '"The Unfortunate
    Maid Exemplified": Elizabeth Canning and Representations of Infanticide
    in Eighteenth-Century England', in Jackson (ed.), *Infanticide*, pp. 52–72.

12. But see Jackson's study, which reveals the limitations of positivist approaches
    to the history of child murder, and focuses instead on the ways in which
    the processes of law and medicine participated in generating the mysteries
    surrounding the crime. *New-Born Child Murder*, pp. 8–16.

13. On the interpretation of the statute, see Jackson, ibid., pp. 140–51; Beattie,
    Crime and the Courts; and Leon Radzinowicz, *History of English Criminal Law
    and its Administration from 1750* (4 vols., 1948), vol. 1. There were other crimes
    at this time where the emergent presumption of innocence was reversed, e.g.
    coining.

14. This point has been made by various historians, classically Radzinowicz. But cf.
    Jackson, *New-Born Child Murder*, ch. 6. The assumption of innocence was an
    emergent principle of law in the eighteenth century. On this and developments
    in standards of proof, see Barbara J. Shapiro, *'Beyond Reasonable Doubt' and
    'Probable Cause': Historical Perspectives on the Anglo-American Law of Evidence*
    (Berkeley, CA, 1991).

15. Jackson, *New-Born Child Murder*, p. 3.

16. Angus McLaren, *Reproductive Rituals: the Perception of Fertility in England from the Sixteenth Century to the Nineteenth Century* (1984), p. 131; Malcolmson, 'Infanticide', in Cockburn (ed.), *Crime in England*, p. 197; and Beattie, *Crime and the Courts*, p. 120.

17. On 1803, see Jackson, *New-Born Child Murder*, pp. 168–76; Radzinowicz, *History of English Criminal Law*, vol. I, p. 436; Hoffer and Hull, *Murdering Mothers*; and see Ch. 4.

18. On the application of the law in the nineteenth century, see Arnot, 'Gender in Focus', and Rose, *Massacre*.

19. See Beattie, who argues that the most significant factor in the decline in convictions for child murder was 'the change in attitude towards the unmarried mother', signalled by the rise of charitable institutions – e.g., Coram's foundling hospital, lying-in hospitals – directed towards the care of mothers and illegitimate children; and Hoffer and Hull, *Murdering Mothers*, p. 81, who point to 'literary and documentary evidence' which suggests a culture more interested in sentimental aspects of mothering. On the rise of the sentimental family, see below, n. 24.

20. On the prevalence of gossip and hearsay in cases of child murder, see Laura Gowing, 'Secret Births and Infanticide in Seventeenth-Century England', *Past and Present*, 156 (August 1997), pp. 87–115; Jackson, *New-Born Child Murder*, esp. ch. 2; and Regina Schulte, *The Village in Court: Arson, Infanticide, and Poaching in the Court Records of Upper Bavaria 1848–1910*, trans. Barrie Selman (Cambridge, 1994).

21. On David, see Thomas E. Crow, *Painters and Public Life in Eighteenth-Century Paris* (New Haven, 1985), pp. 247–54. For a related discussion of the gendering of republican virtue, see Joan B. Landes, *Women and the Public Sphere in the Age of the French Revolution* (Ithaca, 1988), pp. 152–68.

22. There are, of course, other mythological and biblical child murderers and potential murderers: notably Abraham, whose sacrifice of his son, Isaac, is in the end pre-empted by God, and whose dilemma presents the central philosophical problem for Kierkegaard in *Fear and Trembling* (1843); Adam's first wife, the disobedient Lilith, who in Hebrew myth kills uncircumcised boys and girls before the age of twenty days, sometimes including her own, and appears in vampiric form in late nineteenth-century gothic stories, such as George MacDonald's *Lilith* (1895); and in the classical tradition, Chronos and Saturn, who eat their own children, as represented, for example, in Goya's 'Saturn devouring one of his own children', *c.* 1820–23.

23. Jackson's point (*New-Born Child Murder*, pp. 6–7), that in the eighteenth century, the word 'infanticide' had not yet acquired its specific, twentieth-century legal meanings, and was used indiscriminately to refer to the violent deaths of people of a wide range of ages, is instructive. It suggests a high degree of flexibility in the conceptualization of such acts, and that correspondences were perceived to exist between, say, a father's murder of an adult son, a mother's abandonment of an illegitimate newborn, and, indeed, a government's neglect of its people. It should also be remembered that the term 'infant' is similarly

indeterminate, used in different contexts to refer to individuals from newborns, to minors, that is anyone under twenty-one.

24. Histories that have emphasised the sentimental bonds that characterise the family from the early modern period have followed Philippe Ariès, and his discussion of the 'obsessive love' of children that 'dominates society from the eighteenth century on'. See Philippe Ariès, *Centuries of Childhood* (Harmondsworth, 1973), p. 397. See also Lawrence Stone, *The Family, Sex and Marriage in England 1500–1800* (1977); J. H. Plumb's 'The New World of Children', in Neil McKendrick, John Brewer, and J. H. Plumb, *The Birth of a Consumer Society: The Commercialisation of Eighteenth-Century England* (1982), pp. 286–315; and on the Romantic idea of the child, Peter Coveney, *Poor Monkey: The Child in Literature* (1957). Other historians have disputed the strength of these claims, especially the implication that pre-modern societies neglected their children. See, for example, Linda A. Pollock, *Forgotten Children: Parent–Child Relations from 1500 to 1900* (Cambridge, 1983), and on the love of children in ancient and medieval societies, John Boswell, *The Kindness of Strangers* (1988). The debate is, in a sense, superseded by Carolyn Steedman's *Strange Dislocations: Childhood and the Idea of Human Interiority, 1780–1930* (1995), which makes a compelling argument for the significance of the idea of childhood in the emergence of modern notions of subjectivity. On representations of working-class children against the backdrop of middle-class ideals, see Hugh Cunningham, *The Children of the Poor: Representations of Childhood since the Seventeenth Century* (Oxford, 1991). Cf. Viviana A. Rotman Zelizer, *Pricing the Priceless Child: the Changing Social Value of Children* (1985; Princeton, NJ, 1994), who locates a 'profound transformation in economic and sentimental value of children' at the turn of the twentieth century.
25. Lloyd de Mause (ed.), *The History of Childhood* (New York, 1974). For a critique, see Carolyn Steedman, *Childhood, Culture and Class in Britain: Margaret Macmillan, 1860–1931* (1990), pp. 63–4.
26. E.g. Rose, *Massacre*.
27. On child murder as a bearer of meanings across the *longue durée*, see my 'Child Murder in George Eliot's *Adam Bede*: Embedded Histories and Fictional Representation', *Nineteenth-Century Literature*, 56: 2 (2001), pp. 228–59.
28. J. Laplanche and J. B. Pontalis, *The Language of Psychoanalysis*, trans. Donald Nicholson-Smith (1973), pp. 111–14.
29. See my 'Infanticide and the Nation: the Case of Caroline Beale', in *New Formations*, 32 (1997), pp. 11–21.
30. Pierre Nora, 'Between Memory and History: Les Lieux de Mémoire', trans. Marc Roudebush, *Representations*, 26 (1989), pp. 7–25.
31. See Michel Foucault, 'Nietzsche, Genealogy, History', in *Language, Counter-Memory, Practice*, ed. D. Bouchard, trans. Bouchard and S. Simon (Ithaca, NY, 1977); and Friedrich Nietzsche, *The Genealogy of Morals*, trans. Douglas Smith (Oxford, 1996).
32. See Catherine Gallagher, 'Counter-history and the Anecdote', in Gallagher and Stephen Greenblatt (eds.), *Practising New Historicism* (Chicago, 2000), pp. 49–74.

33. Ibid., pp. 51–2.
34. Robert Darnton, *The Great Cat Massacre and Other Essays in French Cultural History* (Harmondsworth, 1984). The methodology I employ differs substantially from Darnton's historical-anthropological approach, which highlights contextual over textual explication.

I CHILD MURDER AND COMMERCIAL SOCIETY IN THE EARLY EIGHTEENTH CENTURY

1. Cf. 'A Child is Being Beaten: A Contribution to the Study of the Origin of Sexual Perversions' (1919), *Standard Edition of the Complete Psychological Works of Sigmund Freud* (24 vols., 1953–74), vol. XVII, pp. 177–204, and see below, Ch. 2, n. 7, and Ch. 7.
2. Bernard Mandeville, 'Essay on Charity and Charity Schools', in *FB*, vol. I, pp. 253–322, 255. All further page references will be given parenthetically in text by volume and page number.
3. *MP*, pp. 109–18, 111. Subsequent references will be given parenthetically in the main body of the text.
4. On eighteenth-century consumerism see McKendrick, Brewer, and Plumb, *Birth of a Consumer Society*; John Brewer and Roy Porter (eds.), *Consumption and the World of Goods* (1993), pp. 19–39; Ann Bermingham and John Brewer (eds.), *The Consumption of Culture 1600–1800: Image, Object, Text* (London and New York, 1995); Elizabeth Kowaleski-Wallace, *Consuming Subjects: Women, Shopping and Business in the Eighteenth Century* (New York, 1997). On contemporary debates about luxury, see Christopher J. Berry, *The Idea of Luxury: a Conceptual and Historical Investigation*, (Cambridge, 1994), esp. pp. 126–77; and Maxine Berg and Helen Clifford (eds.), *Consumers and Luxury: Consumer Culture in Europe 1650–1850* (Manchester, 1999). See also P. G. M. Dickson, *The Financial Revolution in England: a Study in the Development of Public Credit* (1967). On the historiography of consumerism, see Jean-Christophe Agnew, 'Coming up for Air: Consumer Culture in Historical Perspective', in Brewer and Porter (eds.), *Consumption*, pp. 19–39.
5. Agnew, *Worlds Apart: the Market and the Theatre in Anglo-American Thought, 1550–1750* (Cambridge, 1986), ch. 4.
6. Roy Porter, 'Consumption: Disease of the Consumer Society?', in Brewer and Porter (eds.), *Consumption*, pp. 58–84; and Porter, 'Diseases of Civilization', in W. F. Bynum and Roy Porter (eds.), *Companion Encyclopaedia of the History of Medicine* (2 vols., 1993), vol. I, pp. 585–600.
7. John Dennis, 'An Essay upon Publick Spirit' [1711], cited in McKendrick *et al.*, *Birth of a Consumer Society*, p. 19.
8. But cf. Bermingham, 'Introduction' to *The Consumption of Culture*, ed. Bermingham and Brewer, pp. 1–22, esp. 9–14, on the limits of emulation as an explanatory model for the growth of consumption in the eighteenth century.
9. Swift, *Prose Works*, ed. Herbert Davis (14 vols., Oxford, 1951) vol. VII, p. 95, cited in McKendrick et al., *Birth of a Consumer Society*, p. 19.

10. Charlotte Sussman, *Consuming Anxieties: Consumer Protest, Gender and British Slavery, 1713–1833* (Stanford, CA, 2000), ch. 2.
11. On biblical sources see Andrew Carpenter, 'Two Possible Sources for Swift's "A Modest Proposal"' in *Irish Booklore*, 2 (1992), pp. 147–8; on classical sources, James William Johnson, 'Tertullian and A Modest Proposal', *Modern Language Notes*, 73 (1958), p. 561; and Donald C. Baker, 'Tertullian and Swift's "A Modest Proposal"', *Classical Quarterly*, 52 (1957), 219–20; on Irish sources, see George Wittkowsky, 'Swift's Modest Proposal: The Biography of an Early Georgian Pamphlet', *Journal of the History of Ideas*, 4 (1943), pp. 75–109; and Bryan Colebourne, '"We flea the People and seel their Skins": A Source for a Modest Proposal?', in *The Scriblerian and the Kit Cats*, 15: 2 (1983), pp. 132–3; on romance sources, see Paul N. Hartle, 'A New Source for Swift's "Modest Proposal"', *Swift Studies*, 7 (1992), pp. 97–100; Tiffany Potter, 'A Colonial Source for Cannibalistic Breeding in Swift's "A Modest Proposal"', *Notes and Queries*, 244, n.s. 46: 3 (1999), pp. 347–8.
12. Irvin Ehrenpreis, *Swift: the Man, his Works and the Age* (3 vols., 1962–83), vol. III, p. 629.
13. Cf. Oliver W. Ferguson, *Jonathan Swift and Ireland* (Urbana, IL, 1962), p. 171.
14. Joseph McMinn, 'A Weary Patriot: Swift and the Formation of Anglo-Irish Identity', *Eighteenth-Century Ireland*, 2 (1987), pp. 103–13. See also L. M. Cullen, *An Economic History of Ireland Since 1660* (1978), pp. 34–49; Ferguson, *Swift and Ireland*, pp. 171–5; R. F. Foster, *Modern Ireland 1600–1988* (1988), pp. 180–3; Clayton D. Lein, 'Jonathan Swift and the Population of Ireland', *Eighteenth-Century Studies* 8 (1974–5), pp. 431–53; Eoin Brady, 'The Petty Concerns of Jonathan Swift: William Petty, Jonathan Swift and the Rational Ideal' (MA Dissertation, University College Cork, 1995).
15. On the flexibility of Swift's political idiom, see J. G. A. Pocock, *The Machiavellian Moment: Florentine Political Thought and the Atlantic Republican Tradition* (Princeton, NJ, 1975), p. 446.
16. There were periods of famine caused by crop failures in 1708–10, 1718–21, and 1726–30. Lein, 'Swift and the Population of Ireland', p. 443.
17. See Swift, *A Short View of the State of Ireland* (1727–8), in *Prose Works*, vol. XII, pp. 5–12. Cf. Sussman, *Consuming Anxieties*, pp. 70–80, for the ways in which English colonial policy turned the Irish into worse than livestock.
18. Cited in Ehrenpreis, *Swift*, vol. III, p. 628.
19. See [David Binden], *A Scheme for Supplying Industrial Men with Money...* (Dublin, 1729); Sir John Browne, *A Collection of Tracts Concerning the Present Size of Ireland* (1729); Louis A. Landa, 'A Modest Proposal and Populousness', *Modern Philology*, 40 (November 1942), pp. 161–70; Lein, 'Swift and Population'; Ferguson, *Swift and Ireland*, esp. Appendix B. For Petty, see *The Political Anatomy of Ireland* (1672; repr. Shannon, 1970).
20. Fynes Moryson, *Itinerary* (1617), cited in Claude Rawson, '"Indians" and Irish: Montaigne, Swift and the Cannibal Question', *Modern Language Quarterly*, 53: 3 (September 1992), pp. 299–364. See also Rawson, *God, Gulliver, and Genocide:*

Barbarism and the European Imagination, 1492–1945 (Oxford, 2001), pp. 79–91; and Wittkowsky, 'Swift's Modest Proposal', pp. 92–3; Rawson observes that 'old women are the greediest cannibals' ('"Indians" and Irish', p. 304). On English representations of the Irish as barbarians and cannibals, see Joep Leerssen, *Mere Irish and Fíor-Ghael: Studies in the Idea of Irish Nationality, its Development and Literary Expression prior to the Nineteenth Century* (1986; Cork, 1996), esp. ch. 2. On cannibals, see also Frank Lestringant, *Cannibals: the Discovery and Representation of the Cannibal from Columbus to Jules Verne*, trans. by Rosemary Morris (Berkeley, CA, 1997), esp. p. 181. On cannibalism in fairy tales, see Marina Warner, 'Fi Fie Fo Fum: The Child in the Jaws of the Story', in Francis Barker *et al.* (eds.), *Cannibalism and the Colonial World* (Cambridge, 1998), pp. 158–82.

21. *Intelligencer*, 18 (November 1728). Cited in Rawson, *God, Gulliver, and Genocide*, pp.70–2.

22. See, e.g., Rawson, '"Indians" and Irish', p. 345, and *Order from Confusion Springs: Studies in Eighteenth-Century Literature from Swift to Cowper* (1985), p. 130.

23. Salmanaazor, or Psalmanazar, achieved celebrity as an exotic specimen, in a similar way to the South Pacific islander, Omai, later in the century (see below, Ch. 3). Salmanaazor, however, was a fake – a French man in disguise. It is reasonable to assume that Swift was familiar with the hoax. According to Ben Downing, in the years following Salmanaazor's discovery, '"Formosan" was a winking byword for "fraudulent"', and sport for satirists. See Downing, 'Psalmanazar the Amazing,' *Yale Review*, 90: 3 (2002), pp. 46–80, esp. p. 65. See also Robert Adams Day, 'Psalmanazar's "Formosa" and the British Reader (including Samuel Johnson)', in G. S. Rousseau and Roy Porter (eds.), *Exoticism in the Enlightenment* (Manchester, 1990), pp. 197–221. In later eighteenth-century writings, the island of Formosa figures repeatedly as a representative location of savage behaviour. See, for example, Adam Ferguson, *An Essay on the History of Civil Society* (1767) (Cambridge, 1995), pp. 134–5; and John Millar, *Observations Concerning the Distinction of Ranks in Society* (1771), p. 30.

24. Pocock, *Machiavellian Moment*; E. G. Hundert, *Enlightenment's Fable: Bernard Mandeville and the Discovery of Society* (Cambridge, 1994), pp. 8–12.

25. Pocock, *Machiavellian Moment*, p. 447.

26. M. M. Goldsmith, 'Liberty, Luxury and the Pursuit of Happiness', in A. Pagden (ed.), *Languages of Politics in Early Modern Europe* (Cambridge, 1987), pp. 225–52; Elizabeth Rawson, *The Spartan Tradition in European Thought* (1969; Oxford, 1991), ch. 13.

27. On the place of Brutus in the development of a republican tradition in eighteenth-century Britain and France, see Ian Donaldson, *The Rapes of Lucretia: a Myth and its Transformations* (Oxford, 1972), esp. ch. 6. On Swift's admiration of Brutus, see ibid., pp. 112–13.

28. Walter Benjamin, 'Theses on the Philosophy of History', in *Illuminations*, ed. Hannah Arendt, trans. Harry Zohn (1970), pp. 255–66, 258.

29. There are, in fact, few direct references to Mandeville in Swift's work, although the two writers were immersed in the same spheres in early eighteenth-century London. On the political culture that connected the two, see M. M. Goldsmith, *Private Vices, Public Benefits: Bernard Mandeville's Social and Political Thought* (Cambridge, 1985), esp. ch. 1, and 'Liberty, Luxury', in Pagden (ed.), *Languages of Politics*, pp. 237–41.
30. Goldsmith, 'Liberty, Luxury', in Pagden (ed.), *Languages of Politics*, p. 248.
31. On Mandeville's primitive man, see Paolo Rossi, *The Dark Abyss of Time: the History of the Earth and the History of Nations from Hooke to Vico*, trans. Lydia G. Cochrane (Chicago, 1984), pp. 230–5. On Mandeville and Rousseau, see Malcolm Jack, 'One State of Nature: Mandeville and Rousseau', *Journal of the History of Ideas*, 39 (1978), pp. 119–24.
32. On the history of the text of the *Fable*, see Kaye in *FB*, vol. 1, pp. xxxiii–xxxvii.
33. Philip Harth, 'Introduction', *Fable of the Bees* (1989), p. 10. On the hybrid genre of the work, and its precursors, see Ben Rogers, 'In Praise of Vanity: The Augustinian Analysis of the Benefits of Vice from Port-Royal to Mandeville,' (D.Phil. thesis, University of Oxford, 1994), esp. ch. 7.
34. See Kaye, *FB*, vol. II, pp. 418–53; W. A. Speck, 'Bernard Mandeville and the Middlesex Grand Jury', *Eighteenth-Century Studies*, 11 (1978), pp. 362–74.
35. Speck, 'Mandeville and the Middlesex Grand Jury'. On Mandeville's politics, see H. T. Dickinson, 'The Politics of Bernard Mandeville', in I. Primer, ed., *Mandeville Studies* (The Hague, 1975), pp. 80–97. Mandeville's views were particularly offensive to members of the influential Societies for the Reformation of Manners. See T. C. Curtis and W. A. Speck, 'The Societies for the Reformation of Manners: A Case Study in the Theory and Practice of Moral Reform', *Literature and History* 3 (1976), pp. 45–63. On Mandeville and civic humanism, see Hundert, *Enlightenment's Fable*, pp. 8–15, and Goldsmith, 'Liberty, Luxury', in Pagden (ed.), *Languages of Politics*, p. 239. Hundert points out that Mandeville's views on the poor were not a cause of concern for moral philosophers such as Hutcheson, Butler, Hume, Rousseau or Adam Smith. Hundert, *Enlightenment's Fable*, p. 193.
36. By the 1830s, Mandeville is already a forgotten figure. See Kaye in *FB*, vol. II, pp. 443 and 446.
37. Dario Castiglione, 'Excess, Frugality and the Spirit of Capitalism: Readings of Mandeville on Commercial Society', in J. Melling and J. Barry (eds.), *Culture in History: Production, Consumption and Value in Historical Perspectives* (Exeter, 1992), pp. 155–79, 161.
38. Hundert, *Enlightenment's Fable*, pp. 219–36; Louis Dumont, *From Mandeville to Marx: the Genesis and Triumph of Economic Ideology* (Chicago, 1977), pp. 63–81.
39. Georg Simmel, *The Philosophy of Money*, 2nd edn, trans. Tom Bottomore and David Frisby (1990); Hundert, *Enlightenment's Fable*, pp. 246–7.
40. Mandeville, *A Modest Defence of Public Stews (1724): Augustan Reprint Society Publication No. 162* (Los Angeles, CA, 1973). On echoes between this and Swift's *A Modest Proposal*, see Hundert, *Enlightenment's Fable*, p. 121.

41. Mandeville, *Modest Defence of Public Stews*, p. 50. On the extent of the problem in urban centres, Trumbach cites Saunders Welch, writing in 1758, who claims that there were 3000 prostitutes active in London. On responses to the problem of prostitution, see W. A. Speck, 'The Harlot's Progress in Eighteenth-Century England', *British Journal of Eighteenth-Century Studies*, 3 (1980), 127–39; Randolph Trumbach, 'Modern Prostitution and Gender in Fanny Hill', in G. S. Rousseau and Roy Porter (eds.), *Sexual Underworlds of the Enlightenment* (Manchester, 1987), pp. 69–85; Vivien Jones, 'Scandalous Femininity: Prostitution and Eighteenth-Century Narrative', in Dario Castiglione and Lesley Sharp (eds.), *Shifting the Boundaries: Transformation of the Language of Public and Private in the Eighteenth Century* (Exeter, 1995), pp. 54–70, and 'Placing Jemima: Women Writers of the 1790s and Eighteenth-Century Prostitution Narratives', in *Women's Writing* 4: 2 (1997), 201–20. On prostitution, see also Kowaleski-Wallace, *Consuming Subjects*, pp. 139–42.

42. Defoe, *Some Considerations upon Street Walkers with a Proposal for Lessening the Present Number of Them* (1726), p. 4. On the differences between Defoe and Mandeville, see Jones, 'Scandalous Femininity'. As Jones demonstrates, Defoe casts the prostitute in a sentimental or humanitarian narrative, which, I suggest, Mandeville parodies.

43. Hundert, *Enlightenment's Fable*, p. 216.

44. Mandeville, *Public Stews*, pp. 64–5.

45. On Mandeville's role in uniting Christian and mercantile views, see Donna T. Andrew, *Philanthropy and Police: London Charity in the Eighteenth Century* (Princeton, NJ, 1989), pp. 32–41.

46. See, e.g., Thomas Man, *The Benefit of Procreation. Together with some few Hints toward the Better Support of Whores and Bastards* (1739), p. 9.

47. Others linked prostitution directly with a depletion of population that had already occurred. Defoe, for instance, identified a cycle of demoralisation in which the 'dislike of old Wives' caused men to seduce other women, and contribute to the 'Rabble of Harlots which infect our Publick ways'. He called for sumptuary laws to encourage reproduction in marriage, and regulations against marriage to women beyond child-bearing age, so as to guard against the effects of the loss 'to the world of the Produce of one Man'. See *Street Walkers*, pp. 7 and 8.

48. Andrew, *Philanthropy and Police*, pp. 54–7.

49. Jenny Bourne Taylor, '"Received, a Blank Child": John Brownlow, Charles Dickens, and the London Foundling Hospital – Archives and Fictions', *Nineteenth-Century Literature*, 56: 3 (2001), pp. 293–363; Jenny Uglow, *Hogarth: a Life and a World* (1997), pp. 429–34; Toni Bowers, *The Politics of Motherhood: British Writing and Culture 1680–1769* (Cambridge, 1996), pp. 4–15; Ruth K. McClure, *Coram's Children: the London Foundling Hospital in the Eighteenth Century* (New Haven, CT, 1981).

50. Ronald Paulson, *Hogarth: His Life, Art, and Times* (2 vol., New Haven, CT, 1971), vol. II, pp. 102–3; Uglow, *Hogarth*, pp. 493–500.

51. 43 Geo. III c. 58m, 1803. See below, Ch. 3, pp. 95–6.

52. On the emergence of the new culture of surveillance, see Michel Foucault, *Discipline and Punish*, trans. Alan Sheridan (Harmondsworth, 1977), esp. pp. 195–228; and Michael Ignatieff, *A Just Measure of Pain: the Penitentiary and the Industrial Revolution* (1978; Harmondsworth, 1989).
53. Shapiro, *"Beyond Reasonable Doubt"*, p. 167.
54. See Jackson, *New-Born Child Murder*, esp. ch. 7, Hoffer and Hull, *Murdering Mothers*, pp. 65–91; Francus, 'Monstrous Mothers, Monstrous Societies'; Rabin, 'Bodies of Evidence, States of Mind'.
55. Alexander Welsh, *Strong Representations: Narrative and Circumstantial Evidence in England* (Baltimore, ML, 1992), ch. 1.
56. Shapiro, *"Beyond Reasonable Doubt"*, p. 288. The category was required only 'as long as a sharp distinction was drawn between findings of fact, based on eyewitness testimony and findings based on inference from reported circumstances'. Gilbert's treatise begins with a summary of Locke's *Essay Concerning Human Understanding* (1690).
57. William Paley, *Principles of Moral Philosophy* (2nd edn., 1786), p. 355. Cited in Shapiro, *"Beyond Reasonable Doubt"*, p. 219. See also Welsh, *Strong Representations*, p. 16.
58. See, e.g., Samuel Farr, *Elements of Medical Jurisprudence* (1787; 3rd edn, 1815).
59. Jackson, *New-Born Child Murder*, ch. 4.
60. Hunter, 'On the Uncertainty of Signs of Murder, in the case of bastard children', reprinted in William Cummin, *The Proofs of Infanticide Considered* (1834). On the use of Hunter in courts, see Jackson, *New-Born Child Murder*, pp. 118–23. Cf. Thomas Laqueur, 'Bodies, Details and the Humanitarian Narrative', in Lynn Hunt (ed.), *The New Cultural History* (Berkeley, CA, 1989), pp. 176–204. And see below, Ch. 2, n. 4.
61. Hunter, 'Uncertainty of Signs', in Cummin, *The Proofs of Infanticide*, p. 5.
62. Smith, *Theory of Moral Sentiments*, p. 219.
63. See above, 'Introduction'.
64. Defoe, *Moll Flanders*, pp. 173–4. On motherhood in Defoe, see Bowers, *Politics of Motherhood*, pp. 98–123; and Felicity A. Nussbaum, *Torrid Zones: Maternity, Sexuality, and Empire in Eighteenth-Century English Narratives* (Baltimore, ML, 1995), ch. 1.
65. See Andrew Ashfield and Peter De Bolla (eds.), *The Sublime: a Reader in British Eighteenth-Century Aesthetic Theory* (Cambridge, 1996).
66. The reference here is to Thomas De Quincey's 'On Murder considered as one of the Fine Arts' (1827, 1839, and 1854) a series of essays which opens with a protracted joke about the ethics of Kantian aesthetics, including the observation that the best murder would be of an innocent baby with a spotless soul. The final essay includes accounts of real murders, in which prime place is given to John Williams, the murderer whose victims included a small baby. On the aesthetics of violence, see Joel Black, *The Aesthetics of Murder: A Study in Romantic Literature and Contemporary Culture* (Baltimore, ML, 1991), and my 'Do or Die: Problems of Agency and Gender in the Aesthetics of Murder', *Genders*, 5 (1989), pp. 119–34.

2 'A SQUEEZE IN THE NECK FOR BASTARDS': THE UNCIVILISED
SPECTACLE OF CHILD-KILLING IN THE
1770S AND 1780S

1. Rousseau, *A Discourse on Inequality*, trans. Maurice Cranston (1984), p. 100.
2. See Marina Warner, *Alone of all her Sex: the Myth and Cult of the Virgin Mary* (1976). On the forms of desire and consolation framed by the Stabat Mater, see Julia Kristeva, *Tales of Love*, trans. Leon S. Roudiez (New York, 1987).
3. *FB*, vol. I, pp. 255–6.
4. Cf. Laqueur, 'Bodies, Details and the Humanitarian Narrative'. Laqueur analyses the production of a 'humanitarian narrative' in a nexus of eighteenth-century texts, locating a repeated pattern in which the reader is required to identify with the spectator of human suffering, who, in turn, identifies with the body of the suffering object. My examination of accounts of child murder is informed by Laqueur's work, especially his analysis of William Hunter's 'On the Uncertainty of Signs of Murder'. However, exploration specifically of child-murder narratives reveals the ease with which the humanitarian narrative shifts into other narratives that encompass different kinds of emotion. I suggest that the humanitarian response is one possibility in a grammar of emotional response, and is much less stable than Laqueur's work implies.
5. On the historical context of the flowering of reform in this period, see Paul Langford, *A Polite and Commercial People: England 1727–1783* (Oxford, 1989); and Linda Colley, *Britons: Forging the Nation 1707–1837* (New Haven, CT, 1992). See also Thomas L. Haskell, 'Capitalism and the Origins of Humanitarian Sensibility', *American Historical Review*, 90 (1985), pp. 339–61, 547–66. On the culture of sensibility, see Markman Ellis, *The Politics of Sensibility: Race, Gender and Commerce in the Sentimental Novel* (Cambridge, 1996), ch. I; G. J. Barker-Benfield, *The Culture of Sensibility: Sex and Society in Eighteenth-Century Britain* (Chicago, 1992); and John Mullan, *Sentiment and Sociability: the Language of Feeling in the Eighteenth Century* (Oxford, 1988). On sympathy, see David Marshall, *The Surprising Effects of Sympathy: Marivaux, Diderot, Rousseau and Mary Shelley* (Chicago, 1988). On philanthropic movements see Andrew, *Philanthropy and Police*; and David Owen, *English Philanthropy, 1660–1960* (Cambridge, MA, 1965); on penal reform, Radzinowicz, *History of English Criminal Law*, vol. I; and V. A. C. Gattrell, *The Hanging Tree: Execution and the English People* (Oxford, 1994).
6. The difficulty of differentiating between different kinds of response – for instance, the insistent collapse of boundaries between pleasure and pain – was central to many of the aesthetic discussions of the period, as witnessed in the discourse on the sublime.
7. The shifting identifications that are generated by Rousseau's scene of infant suffering appear to prefigure those generated by the Freudian fantasy of a child being beaten. Cf. John Forrester, *Language and the Origins of Psychoanalysis* (1980), pp. 131–65. Forrester's analysis demonstrates the way in which the fantasy operates as though it is a sentence, as subject positions can change in the way of

a grammar. This is suggestive for a reading of this eighteenth-century material, in which subject positions are also highly flexible, but in a format that has different constraints than Freud's. See below, Ch. 7.

8. On Rousseau's anthropology, see Terry Jay Ellingson, *The Myth of the Noble Savage* (Berkeley, CA, 2001), pp. 80–95; and Ronald L. Meek, *Social Science and the Ignoble Savage* (Cambridge, 1976), pp. 76–91.

9. Rousseau, *Discourse on Inequality*, p. 100.

10. Smith, *Theory of Moral Sentiments*, pp. 209–10.

11. Adam Smith, 'Letter to the *Edinburgh Review*', in *Essays on Philosophical Subjects*, ed. W. P. J. Wightman and J. C. Bryce (Oxford, 1980), pp. 242–54, 250–1.

12. The most systematic account of this is in his lectures in Glasgow in 1762–3, and later in *The Wealth of Nations*. See P. J. Marshall and Glyndwr Williams, *The Great Map of Mankind: Perceptions of New Worlds in the Age of Enlightenment* (Cambridge, MA, 1982), pp. 146–7; Donald Winch, *Riches and Poverty: an Intellectual History of Political Economy in Britain, 1750–1834* (Cambridge, 1996); Dorinda Outram, *The Enlightenment* (Cambridge, 1995), pp. 108–9; and Michael Ignatieff and Istvan Hont (eds.), *Wealth and Virtue: the Shaping of Political Economy in the Scottish Enlightenment* (Cambridge, 1983).

13. On travel literature, see Marshall and Williams, *Great Map*, pp. 45–63. See also 'Introduction', in Nigel Leask, *Curiosity and the Aesthetics of Travel Writing 1770–1840; From an Antique Land* (Oxford, 2002); Mary Louise Pratt, *Imperial Eyes: Travel Writing and Transculturation* (1992); and Charles L. Batten Jr., *Pleasurable Instruction: Form and Convention in Eighteenth-Century Literature* (Berkeley, CA, 1978). On the importance of Cook's voyages as a turning point in conceptions of historical time and primitivism, see Kathleen Wilson's 'Pacific Modernity: Theatre, Englishness and the Arts of Discovery, 1760–1800', in Colin Jones and Dror Wahrman (eds.), *The Age of Cultural Revolutions: Britain and France, 1750–1820* (Berkeley, CA, 2002), pp. 62–93.

14. The uneven development of societies across the globe was explained in terms of differences in climate. Each of the four stages of society was determined by local factors including climate and environment. Thus while, in theory, all people were considered to be of the same origin – an idea made popular by Montesquieu in *The Spirit of the Laws* (1748), widely read across Europe in the second half of the century – and all societies therefore capable of progressing through the four stages, nevertheless, the extreme climatic conditions of some regions would arrest progress. Thus the people of the so-called 'torrid zones' were destined to remain as primitives. On this see Nussbaum, *Torrid Zones*, esp. pp. 7–14.

15. Edmund Burke, *Correspondence* (10 vols., Cambridge, 1958–78, 1961) ed. Thomas W. Copeland, vol. III, pp. 350–1, cited as epigraph to Marshall and Williams, *Great Map*.

16. David Spadafora, *The Idea of Progress in Eighteenth-Century Britain* (New Haven, CT, 1990).

17. Hume, 'On the Populousness of Ancient Nations', in *Philosophical Works*, ed. Thomas Hill Green and Thomas Hodge Grose (4 vols., Aalen, 1964), vol. III, pp. 381–443, 408 n. The comparative age of different societies was a point of dispute in the eighteenth century. While Hume held that European civilisations were young in comparison with the ancient and decaying civilisations of the East, others, notably the Italian philosopher Vico, held 'primitives' to be young, like children in relation to the mature civilisations of the West.

18. Hume, 'Populousness', p. 396

19. The source of Hume's knowledge about China was the Jesuit *Lettres édifiantes et curieuses* published between 1702 and 1773. Various English translations were produced in 1707–9, 1714, 1743, and 1762, the latter two edited by John Lockman. Hume is more likely to have read the French versions. See Marshall and Williams, *Great Map*, pp. 80–7. Reports of Chinese infanticide were confirmed by other European travellers later in the century. See John Meares, *Voyages made in the years 1788 and 1789 from China to the North West Coast of America* (1790); and Sir George Staunton, *An Authentic Account of the Earl of Macartney's Embassy from the King of Great Britain to the Emperor of China* (2 vols., 1797). Both are cited in the second edition of Malthus's *Essay on Population* (1803). See T. R. Malthus, *An Essay on the Principle of Population*, 2 vols., ed. Patricia James (Cambridge, 1989), vol. I, pp. 124–30.

20. Hume disagrees with the champions of the foundling hospital, who, as we saw in the previous chapter, argued on the basis of population too. See above, p. 29.

21. Radzinowicz, *History of English Criminal Law*, vol. I, pp. 3–4.

22. *The Parliamentary History of England* (1765–71), vol. XVI, col. 1125.

23. On Meredith's and other attempts to repeal the law in the 1770s, see Jackson, *New-Born Child Murder*, pp. 158–68; Radzinowicz, *History of English Criminal Law*, vol. I, pp. 430–6.

24. *Parliamentary History* (1771–4), vol. XVII, col. 452–3. In the report, individual voices are not designated, so it is impossible to say which of the four is speaking.

25. On the presumption of innocence as a principle of law that comes into force in the eighteenth century, see above, pp. 30–31. They are also objecting to the bastardy laws which forced women to murder. Illegitimate children were, in effect, squeezed between two sets of legislation. See Jackson, *New-Born Child Murder*, pp. 30–2.

26. Lockhart in *Parliamentary History*, vol. XVII, col. 699.

27. See Ch. 3.

28. John Byron's travels in Patagonia are held to be the inspiration for his grandson, Lord Byron's *Don Juan* (1819).

29. Byron, *The Narrative of the Honorable John Byron* (1768). See Neil Rennie, *Far-Fetched Facts: the Literature of Travel and the Idea of the South Seas* (Oxford, 1995), pp. 83–4. A mark of the public interest inspired by Byron's 1765 voyage is the fact that an anonymous narrative of this journey was published in 1767,

and translated into most European languages. See Marshall and Williams, *Great Map*, p. 264. See *Byron's Journal of his Circumnavigation 1764–66*, ed. Robert E. Gallagher (Cambridge, 1964). See also Andrew Sharp, *The Discovery of the Pacific Islands* (Oxford, 1960).

30. See Richard Altick, *The Shows of London* (Cambridge, MA, 1978), pp. 34–49; Bernard Smith, *European Vision and the South Pacific* (2nd edn, New Haven, CT, 1985), pp. 104–7.

31. Byron, *Narrative*, 'Preface', p. iii.

32. Ibid., pp. 148–9.

33. Stone, *The Family, Sex and Marriage*; Jay Fliegelman, *Prodigals and Pilgrims: the American Revolution Against Patriarchal Authority* (Cambridge, 1982), pp. 2–25.

34. Fliegelman, ibid., p. 33 and passim. See also Lynn Hunt, *The Family Romance of the French Revolution* (1992) for the way in which similar family dramas are played out in the context of the French Revolution.

35. Ferguson, *An Essay on the History of Civil Society*, p. 135. See also Millar, *Origin*, ch. 2: 'Of the jurisdiction and authority of father over his children'.

36. Smith, *Theory of Moral Sentiments* p. 210.

37. Images of the killing of children, particularly by fathers, are used recurrently in this literature to represent the law at its most tyrannical or most corrupt. Sometimes they mark a point of decline in a civilisation, a moment at which moral indigence sets in, and society falls into degeneracy. Thus Edward Gibbon draws attention to the 'exclusive, absolute and perpetual dominion of the father over his children' which he claims, was 'peculiar to the Roman jurisprudence', a 'power of life or death' over a child that could be exercised at will with little or no public censure. This, according to Gibbon, runs counter to the 'law of nature', which 'instructs most animals to cherish and educate their infant progeny'. The persistence of infanticide is a 'stubborn' obstacle to the realisation of full civilisation, which 'not even the lessons of jurisprudence and christianity' could 'eradicate'. *Decline and Fall of the Roman Empire* (6 vols., 1788), vol. IV, pp. 370–4.

38. Millar, *Origin*, p. 176. See Robin Blackburn, *Overthrow of Colonial Slavery 1776–1848* (1988), pp. 52–3, on the situation of the work in the context of contemporary humanitarianism: it 'radiated confidence in the emergent bourgeois order while seeking to identify and remedy its weaknesses and inconsistencies'.

39. Millar, *Origin*, p. 234. The work concludes with a long critique of slavery.

40. Millar, *Origin*, p. 103; Smith, *Theory of Moral Sentiments*, p. 142.

41. Smith, *Theory of Moral Sentiments*, p. 202.

42. Ibid., p. 192. See pp. 6–7.

43. Smith, *Theory of Moral Sentiments*, p. 219.

44. For example, in Henry Fielding's *The History of Tom Jones* (1749).

45. Edith Hall, 'Medea and British Legislation Before the First World War', *Greece and Rome*, 2nd series 46: 1 (April 1999), pp. 42–77, 48.

46. Glover's *Medea* was not originally intended for performance, but it was staged (as a benefit for the actress Mrs Yates, who took the lead role) in Covent Garden on 17 March 1767, with subsequent performances in 1768 and 1771, and transferred to Drury Lane for performances in 1775 and 1776. Richard Glover, *Medea* (1761). See George Winchester Stone (ed.), *The London Stage 1660–1800 Part 4* (3 vols., Carbondale, IL, 1962).

47. Charles Beecher Hogan (ed.), *The London Stage 1660–1800 Part 5* (3 vols., Carbondale, IL, 1968); Hall, 'Medea', p. 49. Mrs Crouch, the actress, recalls a performance of Colman's ballet in her memoirs: 'the evening's entertainment concluded with the grand ballet of Medea and Jason, most ludicrously burlesqued.' 'The manager had the greatest cause to be satisfied with the success of his whim, which attracted immense crowds every night; even their majesties went to enjoy the laugh with their subjects.' M. J. Young, *Memoirs of Mrs Crouch...* (2 vols., London, 1806), vol. I, p. 118.

48. Vestris had worked for Noverre, but now the two put on rival productions, and squabbled over who had produced the first version. See Ivor Guest, *Ballet of the Enlightenment: the Establishment of the Ballet d'Action in France, 1770–1793* (1996), pp. 44–8, 76–82, 148–9; Lincoln Kirstein, *Movement and Metaphor: Four Centuries of Ballet* (New York, 1970), pp. 122–3.

49. Joseph Uriot, *Lettres Wurtembourgeoises...* (Freiburg, 1766). Letter VI, Stuttgart, 12 July 1766. Cited in Deryck Lynham, *The Chevalier Noverre, Father of Modern Ballet* (1950), p. 59.

50. See Charles Edwin Noverre, *The Life and Works of the Chevalier Noverre* (1882), pp. 9–14. Noverre was in fact Swiss. George Winchester Stone Jr and George M. Kahrl, in *David Garrick: A Critical Biography* (Carbondale, IL, 1979) cite from *The Dancers Damned*, a contemporary pamphlet: 'These sixty dancers are come over with a design to undermine our constitution... Swiss, what the devil do we know of Swiss! A Swiss is a foreigner, and all foreigners are Frenchmen; and so damn you all.' (p. 136).

51. See Noverre, *Life and Works*, pp. 32–5. One French commentator objected to the scene, not for its violence but its absurdity: 'Je n'aime point à voir les enfants de Jason, / Egorgés en dansant par leur mère qui danse, / Sous des coups mesurés expirer en cadence' (I don't want to see Jason's children murdered while they're dancing by their dancing mother, beaten to death and dying in time to the music). M. J. Chénier, 'Essai sur les arts', in *Oeuvres Complètes* (8 vols., Paris, 1829), vol. VII, p. 201. Cf. Kirstein, *Movement and Metaphor*, p. 123.

52. Guest, *Ballet of the Enlightenment*, pp. 44–50.

53. Colman, *Preludio*, 2 August 1781, Larpent MS 565, p. 1.

54. The publication of a four-volume digest of the relevant sections of Blackstone's *Commentaries* two years before Alexander's work appeared suggests that it should be seen in the context of concerted interest in the legal status of women. See *The Laws Respecting Women*, (1777). Sylvia Tomaselli, in 'The Enlightenment Debate on Women', in *History Workshop*, 20 (1985), pp. 101–24,

points out that Millar is in line with other European Enlightenment thinkers in the way in which he considers the status of women to be indicative of the level of civilisation. See also Nussbaum, *Torrid Zones*, pp. 11–12.

55. William Alexander, *The History of Women*... (2 vols., 1779), vol. I, pp. 174–5.
56. See above, pp. 21–2.
57. Alexander, *History of Women*, vol. I, p. 175 n.
58. According to Blackburn, fifty-five editions in five languages were published over the thirty years following its first publication in 1770. *Overthrow of Colonial Slavery*, p. 53. See also Anatole Feugère, *Bibliographie critique de l'Abbé Raynal* (Angoulême, 1922).
59. Blackburn, *Overthrow of Colonial Slavery*, pp. 53–4.
60. Alexander, *History of Women*, vol. I, p. 175 n. Cited from [Abbé Raynal], *A Philosophical and Political History of the... East and West Indies*, trans. J. Justamond (4 vols., Edinburgh, 1776), vol. III, bk. II, pp. 137–8.
61. Alexander, *History of Women*, vol. I, p. 175 n.
62. Ibid., p. 137.
63. I am grateful to Peter Kitson for this point.
64. Helen Maria Williams, 'A Poem on the Bill Lately Passed for Regulating the Slave Trade' (1788) lines 21–22, 25–30, in Andrew Ashfield (ed.), *Romantic Women Poets, 1788–1848* (2 vols., Manchester, 1998), vol. II, pp. 12–19.
65. Thomas Clarkson, *The History of the Rise, Progress, and Accomplishment of the Abolition of the African Slave Trade by the British Parliament* (2 vols., 1808) vol. I, p. 11.
66. Cf. George Colman, the Younger's variation on this in his abolition play, *Inkle and Yarico* (first staged 1787) in which the slave woman, Yariko, is described as 'a smiling babe; which to the ruffian that would murder it, stretching its little naked, helpless arms, pleads, speechless its own cause'. Frank Felsenstein (ed.), *English Trader, Indian Maid: Representing Race, Gender and Slavery in the New World: An Inkle and Yarico Reader* (Baltimore, ML, 1999), p. 217.
67. On women in the anti-slavery movement, see Clare Midgley, *Women Against Slavery: the British Campaigns, 1780–1870* (1992), esp. pp. 9–40. See also Kate Davies, 'A Moral Purchase: Femininity, Commerce and Abolition, 1788–1792', in Elizabeth Eger *et al.* (eds.), *Women, Writing and the Public Sphere, 1700–1830* (Cambridge, 2001), pp. 133–62; Moira Ferguson, *Subject to Others: British Women Writers and Colonial Slavery, 1670–1834* (New York, 1992), Harriet Guest, *Small Change: Women, Learning, Patriotism, 1750–1820* (Chicago, 2000); and Anne K. Mellor, *Mothers of the Nation: Women's Political Writing in England 1780–1830* (Bloomington, IN, 2000).
68. Barbauld, 'Epistle to William Wilberforce, Esq., on the Rejection of the Bill for Abolishing the Slave Trade', (1791), line 104, in Ashfield (ed.), *Women Romantic Poets*, vol. I, pp. 43–6.
69. More, 'Slavery', ll. 95–8, in Ashfield (ed.), *Women Romantic Poets*, vol. I, pp. 21–7.

70. Yearsley, 'A Poem on the Inhumanity of the Slave Trade', line 307, in Ashfield (ed.), *Women Romantic Poets*, vol. 1, pp. 21–7.
71. Cf. Donna Landry's discussion of Yearsley's radical interrogation of the maternal role, in *The Muses of Resistance: Labouring-Class Women's Poetry in Britain, 1739–1796* (Cambridge, 1990), ch. 4 and esp. pp. 260–7.
72. On Barrett Browning, see Dorothy Mermin, *Elizabeth Barrett Browning: the Origins of a New Poetry* (Chicago, 1989).
73. Capel Lofft, *Eudosia: or, a Poem on the Universe* (1781), line 372, p. 216 n.
74. For the complex story of the death of Cook, and the mythologisation of it, see Rod Edmond, *Representing the South Pacific: Colonial Discourse from Cook to Gauguin* (Cambridge, 1997), pp. 23–62. For the contemporary debate in anthropology and postcolonial studies, see Marshall Sahlins, *How 'Natives' Think: about Captain Cook, for example* (Chicago, 1995); and Gananath Obeyesekere, *The Apotheosis of Captain Cook: European Mythmaking in the Pacific* (Princeton and Hawaii, 1992).
75. Helen Maria Williams, *The Morai: an Ode*, in Andrew Kippis, *A Narrative of the Voyages Round the World performed by Capt. James Cook...*, (2 vols., 1788), vol. 1, pp. 520–7, 526, 527.
76. Anna Seward, *Elegy on Captain Cook...*, 3rd edn (1781), p. 14 n.
77. 'We know from truth itself that the death of Herod was for a similar offence... Besides, though a stick or stone may be worshipped blameless, a baptised man may not. He knows what he does, and by suffering such honours to be paid him, mars the guilt of sacrifice.' See William Cowper, *The Works*, ed. Rev. T. S. Grimshaw (Boston, 1854), pp. 201–3. Cited by Obeyesekere, *Apotheosis*, p. 126. See also Edmond, *Representing the South Pacific*, p. 28.
78. Rennie, *Far-Fetched Facts*, pp. 109–21.
79. Hawkesworth, *An Account of the Voyages* (3 vols., 1773), vol. II, p. 208. Hawkesworth's source is *The Journals of Captain Cook on his Voyages of Discovery*, ed. J. C. Beaglehole (4 vols., 1968–74), vol. 1, pp. 127–8, and Banks, *The Endeavour Journal, 1768–1771*, ed. J. C. Beaglehole (2 vols., Sydney, 1962), vol. 1, pp. 351–2. According to Beaglehole, Banks's account of the *Arioi*, a group who performed religious rituals with dance and drama, is generally accurate. The infanticides were 'an aid to... celibacy, so advantageous to public performers... and a measure of population control'. Banks, *Endeavour Journal*, p. 352. On Hawkesworth's representations of native promiscuity, see Smith, *European Vision*, pp. 34–51.
80. Kippis, *Narrative*, vol. 1, pp. 181–2.
81. John Lawrence Abbott, *John Hawkesworth: Eighteenth-Century Man of Letters*, (Madison, WI, 1982); *DNB* for Hawkesworth; Rennie, *Far-Fetched Facts*, pp. 94–5.
82. Marshall and Williams, *Great Map*, pp. 55–7.
83. Hawkesworth, *Voyages*, 'Preface', vol. 1, pp. iv–v. For details of Hawkesworth's revisions, see Rennie, *Far-Fetched Facts*, pp. 95–103, and Jonathan Lamb,

'Circumstances Surrounding the Death of John Hawkesworth', *Eighteenth-Century Life*, 18: 3 (1994), pp. 97–113.

84. See Rennie, *Far-Fetched Facts*, pp. 95–6, *DNB* for Hawkesworth, citing James Prior, *Life of Malone* (1860), p. 441.

85. Hawkesworth, *Voyages*, vol. ii, pp. 208–9. Hawkesworth follows his source material fairly closely here. See Banks, *Journal*, vol. i, p. 352. '[the Arreoy is] a title as disgraceful among these people as it ought to be honourable in every good and well govern'd society'. Hawkesworth's main revision is to transpose Banks's vocabulary of rational government into one of sentiment.

86. On maternal ideals and travel literature, see Brigid Orr, '"Stifling Pity in a Parent's Breast": Infanticide and Savagery in Late Eighteenth-Century Travel Writing', in Steve Clark (ed.), *Travel Writing and Empire: Postcolonial Theory in Transit* (1999), pp. 131–46.

87. Banks, *Journal*, vol. i, p. 351.

88. Ibid.

89. Hawkesworth, *Voyages*, vol. ii, p. 209.

90. Ibid., p. 207. On Hawkesworth's modes of spectating, see Jonathan Lamb, *Preserving the Self in the South Seas, 1680–1840* (Chicago, 2001), pp. 76–113.

91. Randolph Trumbach, 'Erotic Fantasy and Male Libertinism in Enlightenment England', in Lynn Hunt (ed.), *The Invention of Pornography: Obscenity and the Origins of Modernity, 1500–1800* (New York, 1996), pp. 253–282.

92. *Otaheite: A Poem* (1774), pp. 12–13, 15–16.

93. For the adultery case, see Lawrence Stone, *Road to Divorce: England 1530–1987* (Oxford, 1990), pp. 214, 224. The case involved the testimony of the butler, who had spied on the lady through a hole in the bedroom door. As such, it provides a clear instance of the slippery line between pornography and surveillance. There are no obvious references to this in the poem, which is about an illegitimate child of a mother whose identity is uncertain. See *DNB* entry for Richard Grosvenor, 1st Earl Grosvenor (1731–1802). Cf. Rennie, *Far-Fetched Facts*, p. 104.

94. [John Courtenay], *A Poetical Epistle...* (1775), lines 278, 288–92.

95. On the folkloric significance of the thorn, see below, p. 79.

96. [William Preston], *Seventeen Hundred and Seventy-Seven* (1777), p. 21.

97. Altick, *Shows of London*, p. 48.

98. On Omiah's London life, see Rennie, *Far-Fetched Facts*, pp. 124–40. See also Michael Alexander's unreliable *Omai, 'Noble Savage'* (1977), and Thomas Blake Clark, *Omai: First Polynesian Ambassador to England* (San Francisco, 1940). On Reynold's portrait of Omai, see Smith, *European Vision*, pp. 80–1.

99. [John Scott], *An Epistle from Oberea, Queen of Otaheite to Joseph Banks esq...*, 3rd edn (1774), which was followed by *A Second Letter* (1775). See also the unascribed *An Epistle from Mr Banks, Voyager, Monster-Hunter, and Amoroso to Oberea Queen of Otaheite...* (1774); and *An Historic Epistle, from Omiah to the Queen of Otaheite, ...* (1775), all on the theme of corruption.

100. *Omiah's Farewell* (1776), p. 7 n.
101. I discuss the Ray and Hackman episode further in the next chapter.

3 1798/1803: MARTHA RAY, THE MOB AND MALTHUS'S
MISTRESS OF THE FEAST

1. William Blake, *The Complete Poetry and Prose*, ed. David V. Erdman (Berkeley, CA, 1982), p. 38. For the proverb as an incitement to murder, see, for instance, Hazard Adams, 'Blake and the Post-Modern', in *William Blake*, ed. Alvin H. Rosenfeld (1969), pp. 12–13, cited by Gary Taylor in 'Blake's Proverb 67', *Explicator*, 32: 2 (October 1973), p. 8. On reading its irony, see David Simpson, *Irony and Authority in Romantic Poetry* (1979), pp. 84–5. Malcolm Bradbury famously dramatises the potential (mis)-readings of the proverb in *The History Man* (1975; 2000) as either a 'seducer's charter' or an injunction to 'kill desires (rather) than nourish ones you can never satisfy' (p. 153). On the context of 1790s London, see esp. John Mee, *Dangerous Enthusiasm: William Blake and the Culture of Radicalism in the 1790s* (Oxford, 1992), esp. pp. 50–8.
2. Colley, *Britons*. See also Gerald Newman, *The Rise of English Nationalism: a Cultural History, 1740–1830* (New York, 1987).
3. Diana Donald, *The Age of Caricature: Satirical Prints in the Reign of George III* (New Haven, CT, 1996), p. 79–81; and Michael Duffy, *The Englishman and the Foreigner* (Cambridge, 1986), pp. 31–9.
4. James F. Traer, *Marriage and the Family in Eighteenth-Century France* (Ithaca, NY, 1980).
5. 'First Letter on a Regicide Peace', in *The Writings and Speeches of Edmund Burke*, vol. IX, ed. R. B. McDowell (Oxford, 1991), pp. 187–264, 243.
6. Phillips in Robin Hamlyn and Michael Phillips (eds.), *William Blake* (2000), pp. 144–5; Blake, *Poetry and Prose*, p. 19.
7. Lyrical Ballads *and Other Poems, 1797–1800*, ed. James Butler and Karen Green (Ithaca, NY, 1992), p. 350. All citations from 'The Thorn' will be from this edition.
8. Beaumont gave the painting to Wordsworth, who comments in 1843 that 'the sky in this picture is nobly done... The only fault... is the female figure, which is too old and decrepit for one likely to frequent an eminence on such a call.' Cited in *Poetical Works*, ed. Ernest de Selincourt, (5 vols, 2nd edn, Oxford, 1952), vol. II, p. 511.
9. On the crises of 1798, see essays by Michael Duffy and Roger Wells in Mark Philp (ed.), *The French Revolution and British Popular Politics* (Cambridge, 1991), pp. 118–45, and 188–226, and Peter Jimack, 'England and France in 1798; the Enlightenment, the Revolution and the Romantics', in Richard Cronin (ed.), *1798: the Year of the Lyrical Ballads* (1998), pp. 151–69. On the Irish context, see Marianne Elliott, *Partners in Revolution: the United Irishmen and France* (New Haven, CT, 1982), pp. 163–240.

10. Mary Jacobus, 'Malthus, Matricide and the Marquis de Sade', in *First Things: the Maternal Imaginary in Literature, Art and Psychoanalysis* (New York, 1995), pp. 83–104.

11. Wordsworth's most direct statements against political economy in general and Malthusian theory in particular date from the 1830s, in the context of poor law reform, but from the late 1790s, his sympathies were with Coleridge and Southey, and their concerted campaign of hostility against Malthus's *Principle of Population.* See Donald Winch, *Riches and Poverty: an Intellectual History of Political Economy in Britain, 1750–1834* (Cambridge, 1996), ch. 11, esp. pp. 318–20. Despite this, there is a compelling case for reading Wordsworth in a Malthusian framework. See Frances Ferguson, 'Malthus, Godwin, Wordsworth, and the Spirit of Solitude', in *Solitude and the Sublime* (New York, 1992), pp. 114–28. On continuities between Romanticism and Malthus, see also Gregory Dart, '"Strangling the Infant Hercules": Malthus and the Population Controversy', *Rousseau, Robespierre, and English Romanticism* (Cambridge, 1999), pp. 139–62; and Clifford Siskin, 'Great Sex and Great Decades', *The Historicity of Romantic Discourse* (Oxford, 1988), pp. 164–78.

12. *The Fourteen Book Prelude*, ed. W. J. B. Owen (Ithaca, NY, 1985), bk. 1, p. 302.

13. 'The Thorn', lines 69–74. My discussion of the sources draws on Karen Swann, '"Martha's Name," or The Scandal of "The Thorn"', in Yopie Prins and Maeera Shreiber (eds.), *Dwelling in Possibility: Women Poets and Critics on Poetry* (Ithaca, NY, 1997), pp. 60–79; Mary Jacobus, *Tradition and Experiment in the Lyrical Ballads* (Oxford, 1976), pp. 240–50; and James H. Averill, 'Wordsworth and "Natural Science": the Poetry of 1798', *Journal of English and Germanic Philology*, 77: 2 (April 1978), pp. 232–46.

14. *The Prelude*, bk. 7, lines 386–7.

15. Sandwich was known as 'Jemmy Twitcher', the name of a character from Gay's *Beggar's Opera* (1728), after his denunciation of former associate and now political opponent John Wilkes, in the House of Lords in 1763. Wilkes had been Sandwich's friend and co-member of Sir Francis Dashwood's club, the 'Monks of Medmenham', a society of rakes. Sandwich impeached Wilkes by reading out an obscene poem, thought to have been authored by Wilkes, 'An Essay on Women'. The episode is recounted in the entry in the *DNB* entry for John Montagu, 4th Earl of Sandwich, in which it is remarked that 'No public man of the last (18th) century was the mark of such bitter, such violent invective'. On Sandwich's sexual notoriety, see *Notes and Queries*, 4th series, 3 (1869), pp. 488, 489. See also Louis Clark Jones, *The Clubs of the Georgian Rakes* (New York, 1942), pp. 90–2 passim.; and George Martelli, *Jemmy Twitcher: a Life of the Fourth Earl of Sandwich, 1718–1792* (1962), esp. pp. 51–66. Martelli finds Sandwich a man's man, or a 'club man' (p. 43). Colley argues that Sandwich's aristocratic debauchery becomes less acceptable as the century proceeds and modes of domestic decency become dominant. See Colley, *Britons*, p. 189.

16. On Holywell Street, see Ch. 4, n. 44.
17. See John Doran, *Saints and Sinners* (2 vols., 1868), vol. I, p. 139, and *Notes and Queries* 3rd series, 4 (1869), p. 447. On her maternal virtues, Martelli (*Jemmy Twitcher*, p. 177) cites the following, published on her death: '... A fond and tender mother too, / Instructor of the young, / A friend to every one she knew / Her heart went with her tongue.'
18. In 1773, the *Evening Post* published details of a case, supposedly of common notoriety, of a commissionership on the navy board, offered to a Captain Luttrell by Ray for a payment of £2000. Sandwich sued for libel, and won. See *DNB* for Montagu.
19. The Ray–Hackman case is well documented in contemporary sources. See *Morning Chronicle*, for 9, 17, 20 April 1779, and *Morning Post* for same dates; *Gentleman's Magazine*, 94 (1779), pp. 210, 212, 213; *Case and Memoirs of the late Rev. James Hackman* (1779); *Case and Memoirs of Miss Martha Ray* (1779); *Celebrated Trials* (1825), vol. V, pp. 1–43. The most prominent retelling of the story is Sir Herbert Croft's sentimental novel, *Love and Madness: a Story Too True* (1780). See also *DNB* for James Hackman; Frank Brady, *James Boswell: the Late Years* (1984), p. 186; Swann, '"Martha's Name"'; and Martelli, *Jemmy Twitcher*, pp. 165–77. On Hackman, see Doran, *Saints and Sinners*, vol. I, pp. 139–41.
20. *Gentleman's Magazine*, 94 (1779), p. 213.
21. See, for instance, n. 19 above, and *Notes and Queries*, 4th series, 3 (1869), p. 339.
22. 'Advertisement', Vardill, *The Distracted Lover* (1779).
23. Boswell in *St James Chronicle*, 17 April 1779. Cited in *Notes and Queries* 3rd series, 4 (1863), pp. 232–3.
24. On Croft see Brian Goldberg, 'Romantic Professionalism in 1800: Robert Southey, Herbert Croft, and the Letters and Legacy of Thomas Chatterton', in *ELH*, 63 (1996), pp. 681–706.
25. On the Chatterton letters and the feud that ensued, see Joseph Cottle, *Reminiscences of Coleridge and Southey* (1847), p. 145; Goldberg, 'Romantic Professionalism in 1800'; and Nick Groom, '"With certain grand Cottelisms": Southey and Cottle and the Making of Chatterton's *Works*' (unpublished paper).
26. Cottle, *Reminiscences*, pp. 144–5 n.
27. Nick Roe, *Wordsworth and Coleridge: the Radical Years*, (Oxford, 1988), p. 190; Kenneth Johnstone, *The Hidden Wordsworth* (New York, 1997), pp. 449–50, 475–6. Basil Montagu went on to have a distinguished career as a lawyer, and as a penal reformer. See Gattrell, *Hanging Tree*, pp. 396–403.
28. Mary Moorman, *William Wordsworth: a Biography. The Early Years, 1770–1803* (Oxford, 1957), pp. 261–9. See also Johnstone, *The Hidden Wordsworth*, pp. 449–50. Young Basil is the 'boy of five years old' in Wordsworth's 'Anecdote for Fathers' in *Poetical Works* (1798). Mark L. Reed cites evidence from Dorothy's journal supporting young Basil's role in the composition of 'The Thorn'. See Dorothy Wordsworth's *Journals*, 2 vols., ed. Ernest de Selincourt (1959), vol. I, p. 13, cited in Reed, *Wordsworth: the Chronology of the Early Years*,

1770–1799 (Cambridge, MA, 1967), p. 227. See also Johnstone, *Hidden Wordsworth*, p. 605.

29. See, for example, de Selincourt (ed.), *Poetical Works*, vol. II, p. 514 'It is strange that Wordsworth should have given his heroine the name of Basil Montagu's mother'; or R. L. Brett and A. R. Jones, (eds.), *Lyrical Ballads* (1963), p. 286n.: 'It is completely inexplicable why Wordsworth should have chosen the name of his friend's unfortunate mother to be the heroine of the poem'; or Stephen Parrish, '"The Thorn": Wordsworth's Dramatic Monologue', in *ELH*, 24 (1957), pp. 53–64, 160: '(In naming Martha Ray thus) Wordsworth may have been obeying a law of association, even one of the "laws by which supersitition acts upon the mind"'; for other biographical readings, see W. J. B. Owen, '"The Thorn" and the Poet's Intention', in *Wordsworth Circle*, 8 (1977), pp. 5–8, and Johnstone, *The Hidden Wordsworth*, p. 449; for a psychoanalytic reading, see Karen Swann.

30. On Omiah's involvement, see Alexander, *Omai, 'Noble Savage'*. Croft emphasises Omiah's racial otherness, associating him with Othello and Zanga. See *Love and Madness*, p. 27. The two epigraphs to the work are from *Othello* and *Oronooko*.

31. Prince Hoare, *Memoirs of Granville Sharp Esq.*, 2nd edn (2 vols., 1828), vol. I, p. 227.

32. See above, pp. 61–6.

33. *Case and Memoirs of Hackman*, pp. 2–3; *Case and Memoirs of Ray*, p. 28; Croft, *Love and Madness*, pp. 6, 18, 40.

34. Croft, *Love and Madness*, p. 6.

35. Ibid., p. 19.

36. See *The Letters of William and Dorothy Wordsworth: the Early Years, 1787–1805*, ed. Ernest de Selincourt (Oxford, 1967), p. 199, cited in Averill, 'Wordsworth and "Natural Science"', p. 238. As Averill ('Wordsworth and Natural Science') and others have pointed out, 'Harry Gill and Goody Blake' is based on a case study by Darwin which appears in the same section in *Zoonomia* as the references to Hackman.

37. Darwin, *Zoonomia; or the Laws of Organic Life* (2 vols., 1794–96), vol. II, p. 363.

38. Ibid., p. 365.

39. In the 1815 edition, the lines are revised as: 'A pang of pitiless dismay / Into her soul was sent; / A Fire was kindled in her breast, / Which might not burn itself to rest.'

40. Much of the critical discussion of this poem has revolved around the uncertainty as to whether the murder really happened, or is a phantom of the narrator's mind. See for instance, Geoffrey Hartman, *Wordsworth's Poetry, 1787–1814* (New Haven, CT, 1964), pp. 141–7; Stephen Parrish, *The Art of the Lyrical Ballads* (Cambridge, MA, 1973), pp. 98–106; David Simpson, *Wordsworth and the Figurings of the Real* (1982), pp. 20–1; Paul D. Sheets, '"'Tis Three Feet Long and Two Feet Wide": Wordsworth's "Thorn" and the Politics of Bathos', in *Wordsworth Circle*, 22: 2 (1991), pp. 92–100, who all argue for a reading of

the poem as a psychological study, in which it is not necessary to assume 'the objective existence of Martha Ray' (Sheets, '"Tis Three Feet Long', p. 98). But cf. Jacobus, *Tradition and Experiment*, p. 248, who argues that Wordsworth's narrative reflects the 'interplay' between the psychology of the 'hypothetical sea-captain', and the 'elusive nature of Martha's suffering'.

41. It is likely that Wordsworth knew at least two versions of 'The Cruel Mother': one published in David Herd's *Ancient and Modern Scottish Songs* (1769) and an alternative version in Johnson's *Scots Musical Museum* (Edinburgh, 1787–1803). See *Lyrical Ballads*, p. 352. Both are reprinted in Francis James Child, *The English and Scottish Popular Ballads* (5 vols., 1882; repr. New York, 1957) along with eleven other variants. See Child, *English and Scottish Popular Ballads*, vol. I, pp. 218–28. The edition of the *Monthly Magazine* containing Taylor's 'Lass of Fair Wone' was in a consignment of books sent to Wordsworth by James Losh in 1796, and Duncan Wu offers March–April, 1797 as a likely reading date. See Wu, *Wordsworth's Reading, 1770–1799* (Cambridge, 1993), p. 20. On Wordsworth's experimentation with the ballad genre, see Jacobus, *Tradition and Experiment*, p. 74. See also Anne Janowitz, *Lyric and Labour in the Romantic Tradition* (Cambridge, 1998), ch. 2.

42. On ballads, customary knowledge and child murder in Scotland, see Deborah H. Symonds, *Weep Not for Me: Women, Ballads, and Infanticide in Early Modern Scotland* (Pennsylvania, PA, 1997).

43. See e.g. James Chandler, *Wordsworth's Second Nature* (Chicago, 1984), in which a shift from Rousseau to Burke is tracked in Wordsworth's works of the 1790s.

44. George McLean Harper, *Wordsworth's French Daughter. The Story of her Birth, with Certificates of her Baptism and Marriage* (Princeton, NJ, 1921).

45. For instance, Johnstone, *The Hidden Wordsworth*, pp. 572, 585–6. Also Owen, '"The Thorn" and the Poet's Intention'.

46. Burke, 'First Letter', in *Writings and Speeches*, p. 245.

47. *Reflections on the Revolution in France*, vol. VIII of *Writings and Speeches of Edmund Burke*, ed. L. G. Mitchell (Oxford, 1989), pp. 54–293, pp. 121–2.

48. Ibid., p. 123.

49. Burke, 'First Letter', in *Writings and Speeches*, p. 243.

50. Traer, *Marriage and the Family*; Roderick Phillips, *Putting Asunder: a History of Divorce in Western Society* (Cambridge, 1988).

51. *Procès-verbal de l'Assemblée des Communes et de l'Assemblée Nationale,...* (75 vols., Paris, 1789–96) XIII, p. 76 and XXIV, p. 277, cited by McDowell in Burke, 'First Letter', in *Writings and Speeches*, p. 244, n. 1. Cf. John Robison, *Proofs of a Conspiracy...* , 4th edn (1798), pp. 437–8: 'By a decree of the Convention (6 June 1794), it is declared, that there is nothing criminal in the promiscuous commerce of sexes.' He cites the Senators: 'It is to prevent her from murdering the fruit of unlawful love, by removing her shame, and by relieving her from the fear of want'...'the Republic wants citizens,...[children are] the property of the nation, and must not be lost'. Robison comments: 'The woman all the while is considered only as the she-animal, the breeder of Sans Culottes.'

52. See Chandler, *Wordsworth's Second Nature*, p. 88; and Wu, *Wordsworth's Reading*, pp. 22–3.

53. Dorothy's description of Annette Vallon, cited by Harper in *Wordsworth's French Daughter*, p. 9.

54. Johnstone, *The Hidden Wordsworth*, p. 449.

55. Burke's perception of the theatricality of revolutionary politics in France was bound up in complex debates about theatricality and the politics of represen- tation, in which Burke, too, was accused of theatricality. See James T. Boulton, *The Language of Politics in the Age of Wilkes and Burke* (1963), pp. 142–8, David Karr, 'Thoughts that Flash Like Lightening: Thomas Holcroft, Radical Theatre and the Production of Meaning in 1790s London', *Journal of British Studies*, 40: 3 (July 2001), pp. 324–56; and Gillian Russell, 'Burke's Dagger: Theatricality, Politics and Print Culture', *British Journal for Eighteenth-Century Studies*, 20: 1 (1997), pp. 1–16. See also Russell, *The Theatres of War: Performance, Politics, and Society, 1793–1815* (Cambridge, 1993), pp. 23–4 and 85–6.

56. Burke, 'First Letter', in *Writings and Speeches*, p. 243.

57. T. J. Mathias, *The Pursuits of Literature . . .* (6th edn, 1798), p. 194. The second citation is used by Polwhele as the epigram to *The Unsex'd Females . . .* (1798; New York, 1974).

58. Polwhele, *The Unsex'd Females*, p. 22n. Polwhele makes extensive reference to Spartan women, whose athleticism and promiscuity encouraged by Lycurgus turn them into concubines for 'the good of the community'. Throughout he draws heavily on Robison's *Proofs of a Conspiracy*.

59. William Godwin, *Memoirs of the Author of A Vindication of the Rights of Woman* (1798).

60. Mary Wollstonecraft, *The Wrongs of Woman; or, Maria*, in *Works*, ed. Janet Todd and Marilyn Butler (1989), pp. 75–184. On Wollstonecraft's represen- tation of divorce legislation, see Elaine Jordan, 'Criminal Conversation: on Mary Wollstonecraft's *The Wrongs of Woman*', *Women's Writing*, 4: 2 (1997), pp. 221–34.

61. Wollstonecraft, *The Wrongs of Woman*, p. 120.

62. Ibid., p. 184.

63. Ibid., p. 95. In the ballad, as it is recorded in Herd's *Ancient and Modern Scottish Songs*, vol. II, pp. 196–7, the woman does not go mad, and Robin Gray is kind not cruel. Moreover, Herd includes it in his section of 'Comic Ballads'. By contrast, Wollstonecraft's and Croft's uses of the ballad are in tragic mode.

64. Anna Letitia Barbauld, 'Dialogue in the Shades' (n.d.), in *Works* (2 vols., 1825), vol. I, p. 348.

65. For textual revisions, see the two-volume Malthus, *An Essay on the Principle of Population*, ed. Patricia James (Cambridge, 1989). All references to the 1803 edition will be to this, by date, volume, and page number. References to the 1798 edition will be to *An Essay on the Principle of Population*, ed. by Anthony Flew (1970) by date and page number. The fullest account of the intellectual origins of the *Essay* is Winch, *Riches and Poverty*, pt. 3, but see also Dart, '"Strangling the Infant Hercules"'; and Marilyn Butler, 'Revolving in Deep

Time: The French Revolution in Narrative', in Keith Hanley and Ray Selden (eds.), *Revolution and English Romanticism: Politics and Rhetoric* (Brighton, 1990), pp. 1–22.

66. Malthus, 1798, p. 68. See Winch, *Riches and Poverty*, p. 253.

67. John Maynard Keynes, *Essays in Biography* (1933; new edn, 1951), p. 84.

68. Patricia James, *"Population" Malthus* (Cambridge, 1979), pp. 19–21. On links with the Aikins, see Betsy Rodgers, *Georgian Chronicle: Mrs Barbauld and her Family* (1958), pp. 50, 188–9. On Johnson, see Gerald P. Tyson, *Joseph Johnson: A Liberal Publisher* (Iowa, 1979). Johnson had strong links with the Warrington circle, and acted as its London publisher. His list included Darwin's *Zoonomia*, and works by Wordsworth, although not the *Lyrical Ballads*, for which Coleridge had signed with Cottle.

69. Malthus, 1798, p. 135.

70. Ibid., p. 142.

71. Ibid., p. 142.

72. Hazlitt, *Reply to the Essay on Population* in *Complete Works*, vol. 1, p. 236.

73. On the regulatory function of nature, see Christopher Hamlin, *Public Health and Social Justice in the Age of Chadwick: Britain, 1800–1854* (Cambridge, 1998), pp. 25–7.

74. William Godwin, *Enquiry Concerning Population* (1820), p. 320.

75. Malthus, 1803, vol. II, pp. 127–8.

76. See Alan Richardson, *Literature, Education and Romanticism: Reading as Social Practice, 1780–1832* (Cambridge, 1994).

77. The most cited work in the 1803 edition is the 24-volume Jesuit *Lettres édifiantes*, followed by Cook's *Voyages*, and Robertson's *History of America*. See Edward Gray, 'Preface' to Jesus College Cambridge, *The Malthus Library Catalogue* (New York, 1983), p. XVI.

78. Malthus, 1803, vol. I, pp. 129, 118, 135, and 58–9.

79. Ibid., vol. II, p. 123.

80. This in turn was part of Ellenborough's larger aim of restructuring the law following the Union with Ireland in 1800. See Ch. 5, pp. 134–5.

81. Jackson, *New-Born Child Murder*, pp. 168–76.

82. On early nineteenth-century abortion law, see McLaren, *Reproductive Rituals*, ch. 5.

4 'BRIGHT AND COUNTLESS EVERYWHERE': THE NEW
POOR LAW AND THE POLITICS OF PROLIFIC
REPRODUCTION IN 1839

1. *NS* (14 July 1838), p. 1; (26 May 1838), p. 5; (21 July 1838), p. 4. Industrial accidents, often involving children, formed a focal point for activists in the factory movement. On this see, Robert Gray, *The Factory Question and Industrial England, 1830–1860* (Cambridge, 1996); also Jane Humphries, 'Protective Legislation, the Capitalist State, and Working-Class Men: the Case of the 1842 Mines Regulation Act', *Feminist Review*, 7 (1981), pp. 1–34; Jill Liddington, 'Gender,

Authority and Mining in an Industrial Landscape: Anne Lister, 1791–1840',
History Workshop Journal, 42 (1996), pp. 59–86. There is considerable overlap
between the factory campaigns and agitation against the New Poor Law. The
most prominent leaders and spokespeople contributed to both campaigns: for
instance, John Fielden, Joseph Raynor Stephens, and Richard Oastler. Nevertheless, there is a distinctive character to anti-Poor Law rhetoric, which derives
from its focus on the deaths of newborns, rather than on child labourers, as
in the factory campaigns. The use of the violated child trope in the factory
campaigns lies outside the scope of this chapter.

2. Charles Dickens, *Oliver Twist*, published serially between 1837 and 1839, p. 1.
Infant mortality rates were high at this time: a quarter of all deaths were of
babies under one year old. In 1839, 151 of every 1000 liveborn babies died under
the age of one year. See B. R. Mitchell and Phyllis Deane, *Abstract of British
Historical Statistics* (Cambridge, 1962), p. 36. On the natural deaths of children
see Pat Jalland, *Death in the Victorian Family* (Oxford, 1996), pp. 96–142; and
Lawrence Lerner, *Angels and Absences: Child Deaths in the Nineteenth Century*
(Nashville, 1997). Neither Jalland nor Lerner discusses violent deaths of infants.
For a social history of child murder in the Victorian period, see Rose, *Massacre*.

3. *NS* (18 August 1838), p. 3; report of the trial of Rev. M. Aug. Gathercole for
libel, *NS* (21 July 1838), p. 6. Gathercole was tried for libelling a Catholic
religious order. The *Northern Star* reprints the offending article, *A Romish Fox
Unkennelled*. It begins, 'Fellow Britons! Only think! Maria Monk in England.
"Yes, Maria Monk in England"', and proceeds to describe scenes of rape and
child murder in the heart of the English countryside. *Awful Disclosures of Maria
Monk* was first published in London in 1836.

4. In September 1838, for instance, there is a 'supposed child murder' case reported
in Dublin, in which the 'sister of a highly respectable gentleman' is held in
custody. *NS* (1 September 1838), p. 3. This is the first of a run of child-murder
cases reported that month. On 8 September 1838, two infanticide cases are
reported; 15 September, five children and their mother found killed by poison;
29 September, Mary Evans, 'a very young girl' killed her baby after leaving the
workhouse. September is no exception: the death toll is similar in other months.

5. *NS* (4 August 1838), p. 5.

6. Raymond Cowherd, *Political Economists and the English Poor Laws* (Athens, OH,
1977), pp. 251–69; Ann Digby, 'Malthus and the Reform of the English Poor
Law', in Michael Turner (ed.), *Malthus and his Time* (1986), pp. 157–69; Felix
Driver, *Power and Pauperism: The Workhouse System, 1834–1884* (Cambridge,
1993); Ursula R. Q. Henriques, *Before the Welfare State: Social Administration
in Early Industrial Britain* (1979), pp. 39–65; and Lynn Lees, *The Solidarities of
Strangers: the English Poor Laws and the People, 1700–1948* (Cambridge, 1998),
pp. 115–52.

7. On the principle of 'less eligibility', i.e. the notion that the material conditions
of the workhouse should be worse than those enjoyed by the poorest workers
outside, see Lucia Zedner, *Women, Crime, and Custody in Victorian England*
(Oxford, 1991), pp. 114–15.

8. Jutta Schwarzkopf, *Women in the Chartist Movement* (Basingstoke, 1991), p. 31.
9. *Report from His Majesty's Commissioners for Inquiring into the Administration and Practical Operation of the Poor Laws* (1834), p. 198. *NS* (19 Jan 1839), p. 3. So sensitive was the government to the charge that the New Poor Law caused infanticide, that it ordered a statistical survey of child-murder cases since 1832, concluding, however, that no evidence existed to support the alleged increase. See *Report from the Select Committee to Inquire into the Administration of the Relief of the Poor* (3 vols., 1837–8), vol. II, report 34.
10. Peter Mandler, *Aristocratic Government in the Age of Reform: Whigs and Liberals, 1830–1852* (Oxford, 1990), pp. 131–41.
11. M. E. Rose, 'The Anti-Poor Law Agitation', in J. T. Ward (ed.), *Popular Movements, c. 1830–1850* (1970), pp. 78–94; Nicholas C. Edsall, *The Anti-Poor Law Movement, 1834–44* (Manchester, 1971), especially pp. 167–86; John Knott, *Popular Opposition to the 1834 New Poor Law* (1986); Anna Clark, *The Struggle for the Breeches: Gender and the Making of the British Working Class* (Berkeley and Los Angeles, 1995), pp. 179–96; and I. J. Prothero, *Artisans and Politics in Early Nineteenth-Century London: John Gast and his Times* (1987).
12. James A. Epstein, *Radical Expression: Political Language, Ritual and Symbol in England, 1790–1850* (Oxford, 1994), p. 12.
13. *NS* (13 April 1839), p. 2; *NL* (6 April 1839), p. 4.
14. *NS* (4 August 1838), p. 5.
15. See P. B. Templeton, 'To the "Dear Little Dead"', a poem on the death of three babies and their mother, crossing to Canada, in *NS* (19 Jan. 1839), p. 7.
16. See pp. 112–16.
17. The poem was printed in both the *Northern Liberator* and the *Northern Star*. See *NL* (13 April 1839), p. 4; *NS* (20 April 1839), p. 7.
18. 'Anti-Malthusianism' *NS* (1 December 1838), p. 5.
19. See Marina Warner, *No Go the Bogeyman: Scaring, Lulling and Making Mock* (1998), pp. 208–17; and Laura Jacobus, 'Motherhood and Massacre: The Massacre of the Innocents in Late-Medieval Art and Drama', in Mark Levene and Penny Roberts (eds.), *The Massacre in History* (New York and Oxford, 1998), pp. 39–54.
20. Thomas Carlyle, *Chartism*, in *Critical and Miscellaneous Essays: IV*, in *Works*, vol. XXIX, pp. 118–204, 202.
21. *NL* (8 December 1838), p. 3, (22 December 1838) p. 3. This is the first notice of 'Marcus' in the press that I have seen. The following month, the *Northern Star* (12 January 1839), p. 4, refers to an earlier notice of the pamphlets, 'so long ago as November 24th, by a London daily paper', although I have not been able to track this down. The fullest account of their publication and circulation is given by Knott, *Popular Opposition*, pp. 237–43.
22. *An Essay on Populousness*, printed for private circulation (n.d.); 'Marcus', *On the Possiblity of Limiting Populousness* (1838).
23. 'Marcus', *An Essay on Populousness*, p. 18.
24. Recent assessments of the pamphlets differ in this respect. Gertrude Himmelfarb takes 'Marcus' to be 'a fanatical Malthusian' (see *The Idea of Poverty* [1984],

pp. 125–6). Ruth Richardson, in *Death, Dissection and the Destitute* (1989), p. 268, holds that they were 'by no means a spoof on Swiftean lines' but '[were] taken with deadly seriousness'. See also Elaine Hadley, *Melodramatic Tactics: Theatrical Dissent in the English Market Place, 1800–1885* (Stanford, CA, 1995), p. 253: n. 101, 'the opposition found it more productive to read them literally rather than ironically' even though they were 'probably a satire, perhaps a hoax'. Anna Clark (*Struggle for the Breeches*, p. 190) admits in passing that they may have been the work of a satirist or *agent provocateur*. But cf. Knott, who writes that what was significant 'was not that people believed it to be true but that they were able to conceive of such a possibility'. *Popular Opposition*, p. 242. See also Hamlin, *Public Health and Social Justice*, pp. 33–5. For the relationship of the 'Marcus' pamphlets to contemporary anxieties about dissection, see Richardson, *Death, Dissection and the Destitute*; and Hamlin, *Public Health and Social Justice*, on their intersection with concerns about public health.

25. On Chartist readers of Swift, see Jonathan Rose, *The Intellectual Life of the British Working Classes* (New Haven, CT, 2001), pp. 35–8. For the influence of Swift on radical satire in the early decades of the century, see Marcus Wood, *Radical Satire and Print Culture, 1790–1822* (Oxford, 1994), p. 36.

26. *NL* (26 January 1839), p. 3.

27. *NL* (2 March 1839), p. 3.

28. Doubleday was one of the editors and main contributors to the *Northern Liberator*; his novel, *Political Pilgrim's Progress*, was serialised in the preceding numbers of the paper. Of middle-class origins, he had been active in the reform movement in 1832, and subsequently took up the Chartist cause. See Holyoake's entry on Doubleday in *DNB*, and Ian Haywood, 'Introduction' to Doubleday's 'The Political Pilgrim's Progress', in *Chartist Fiction* (1999), pp. 1–16.

29. Francis Place, under the nickname, 'Peter Thimble', the radical, is the target of much of the satire in the 'Marcus' material. He is marked out not only for his controversial views on contraception, but more importantly for his affiliations with the Philosophical Radicals. See Clark, *Struggle for the Breeches*, p. 189.

30. The illustration is also included in a single-volume reprint of Doubleday's *The Political Tale of the Tub* (Newcastle-upon-Tyne, 1840).

31. The *NL* (8 December 1838), p. 2 (reprinted in *Northern Lights* no. 38, unpaginated) included a joke related to this in an article entitled 'Suppressed Papers of the British Association Left in Newcastle upon Tyne in August Last', incorporating an account of the Right Honourable Lord Howick's paper, a 'Proposal to accustom the poorer classes to live on air': 'This is a very curious paper, and shews the great chemical as well as politico-economical love of his lordship.' The emphasis on clean air picks up on the central interest in sanitation and miasma held by the Poor Law Commissioners. See Hamlin, *Public Health and Social Justice*, esp. ch. 4.

32. Mary Poovey, *Making A Social Body: British Cultural Formation, 1830–1864* (Chicago, 1995).

33. 'Marcus', *An Essay on Populousness*, p. 25.

34. *NL* (2 March 1839), p. 3. Carbonic acid was also associated with mining accidents. On this see, e.g., *The Times* (29 October 1838), p. 6, where, with linguistic playfulness similar to that of the 'Marcus' scandal, an accident is reported in which a man, appropriately named *Goodchild* died of carbonic gas poisoning, after a man named *Slaughter* failed to save him.

35. *NS* (23 February 1839), p. 7; *NL* (16 February 1839), p. 3.

36. Baxter, *The Book of the Bastiles; or, the History of the Working of the New Poor Law* (1841), p. 134.

37. George Jacob Holyoake, *The Life of J. R. Stephens* (1881); Michael S. Edwards, *Purge This Realm: a Life of J. R. Stephens* (1994); Eileen Yeo, 'Christianity in Chartist Struggle 1838–1842', *Past and Present*, 91 (May 1981), pp. 47–73.

38. Harold Underwood Faulkner, *Chartism and the Churches: a Study in Democracy* (New York, 1916), pp. 94–5; R. G. Gammage, *History of the Chartist Movement 1837–1854* (Newcastle, 1894), pp. 55–9. At his trial, Stephens conducted his own defence; his speeches in this context are highly politicised, with copious references to 'Marcus.' See *Reports of State Trials*, n.s., vol. III, 1831–40, ed. John MacDonell (1888–98), pp. 1125–6.

39. *NS* (17 November 1838), p. 6. On Stephens's rhetorical style, see Patrick Joyce, *Visions of the People: Industrial England and the Question of Class 1848–1914* (Cambridge, 1991), pp. 33–4, and as a preacher, see Yeo, 'Christianity'. On the reporting of speeches in the press, see Kevin Gilmartin, *Print Politics: the Press and Radical Opposition in Early Nineteenth-Century England* (Cambridge, 1996), ch. 2.

40. 'Marcus', *The Book of Murder* is reprinted in Gregory Claeys (ed.), *The Chartist Movement in Britain 1838–1850* (6 vols., 2001), vol. I, pp. 383–437. Holywell Street had long associations with both radical and pornographic presses. Dugdale was known for both. On Dugdale, see Iain McCalman, *Radical Underworld: Prophets, Revolutionaries, and Pornographers in London, 1795–1840* (Oxford, 1988), ch. 10; and on Holywell Street, see Lynda Nead, 'Mapping the Self: Gender, Space and Modernity in Mid-Victorian London', in Roy Porter (ed.), *Rewriting the Self: Histories from the Renaissance to the Present* (1997), pp. 167–85. Holywell Street was also the place where Martha Ray's family lived. See above, p. 73.

41. See Claeys, *The Chartist Movement*. Mudie was the editor of *The Alarm Bell*, which is referred to in the introductory essay of *The Book of Murder*. Beatrice Webb (in *English Poor Law History, Part II, vol. I* (1963), p. 163, cited in Knott, *Popular Opposition*, p. 245, n. 31) records that Francis Place thought Mudie to be the author of the preface. For Mudie, see Gregory Claeys, *Machinery, Money and the Millennium: from Moral Economy to Socialism, 1815–60* (Cambridge, 1987), pp. 67–89, esp. p. 72.

42. It is still a matter for debate. For possible designations, see Appendix.

43. 'The Height of Political Ingratitude', Baxter, *Book of the Bastiles*, pp. 76–7.
44. Letters from Chadwick and Gedge, *The Times* (10 January 1839), p. 6; letter from Stephens, *The Times* (17 January 1839), p. 3. See Knott, *Popular Opposition*, pp. 238–9.
45. *NL* (26 January 1839), p. 3. According to Knott, the Liverpool Chartist, James Whittle, obtained a copy of the pamphlet at the shop of Sherwood and Company in early January, 1839. See Knott, *Popular Opposition*, p. 240.
46. *NL* (22 December 1838), p. 3: The article goes on to name Richard Carlile, author of *Every Woman's Book, or What is Love?* (1828), and Robert Dale Owen, also an advocate of birth control, as propagators of 'disgusting and silly notions'. On working-class sexual morality in the context of Poor Law agitation, see Clark, *Struggle for the Breeches*, pp. 179–96. See also Michael Mason, *The Making of Victorian Sexual Attitudes* (Oxford, 1994), ch. 3.
47. According to an advert printed in *NS* (9 February 1839), p. 1, the price of the pamphlets rose from two shillings to two guineas after suppression. See also *Book of the Bastiles*, p. 77 n.: 'but now one is not to be procured under … £5; as it has been suppressed'. On the suppression of the pamphlets, see Knott, *Popular Opposition*, p. 241.
48. Baxter, *Book of the Bastiles*, p. 79.
49. Ibid., n. The precise date of Baxter's letter to Brougham is not clear in *Book of the Bastiles*, but is likely to be early 1839, when the 'Marcus' furore was at its height. The note appended in the book, cited here, must have been added later – Victoria's first child was not born until November 1840 – although Poor Law protestors, especially women, did address petitions to the queen before this. See Clark, *Struggle for the Breeches*, p. 191. The invocation of the queen appears to have been widespread in the rhetoric of opposition. Even Mudie calls on the queen's womanhood – drawing on a confusing mixture of her 'virgin' innocence, and maternal love: 'May Her Majesty, in accordance with the universal character of her sex, purge from her councils the influence of principles and doctrines calculated to make woman's milk curdle in her breasts, and to fire the veins of every man possessing the ordinary characteristics of his species.' 'To the Rich and Influential Classes of the British People', *The Alarm Bell*, no. 1 (1839 (?)), p. 12.
50. Peter Brooks, *The Melodramatic Imagination: Balzac, Henry James, Melodrama and the Mode of Excess* (1976; New Haven, CT, 1995), esp. ch. 1; Patrick Joyce, *Democratic Subjects: the Self and the Social in Nineteenth-Century England* (Cambridge, 1994), pp. 176–80, ff.; Carolyn Steedman, 'A Weekend with Elektra', *Literature and History*, 6 (1997), pp. 17–42. See also Martha Vicinus, '"Helpless and Unfriended": Nineteenth-Century Melodrama', *NLH*, 8: 1 (1981), pp. 127–44. The term 'melodramatic mode' is taken from Hadley, *Melodramatic Tactics*.
51. Anna Clark, 'The Politics of Seduction in English Popular Culture, 1748–1848', in Jean Radford (ed.), *The Progress of Romance: the Politics of Popular Fiction* (1986), pp. 47–70.

52. Hadley is right to point out that melodrama tends to look back to a past society of ideal social relations. However, her sense that it is therefore 'profoundly reactionary' (p. 11), mistakes the politically potent 'golden age' of utopian narratives in radical discourse for a literal 'harkening back to a deferential society'. She also overplays the role of Tory Radicals in Poor Law agitation; while Tory Radicals did indeed supply leaders and spokespeople for the movement, such as Oastler and Stephens, it does not follow that the people adopted the politics of deference, nor that opposition was dominated by middle-class interests. See Felix Driver, 'Tory Radicalism? Ideology, Strategy and Locality in Popular Politics during the 1830s', in *Northern History*, 27 (1991), pp. 120–38, for the strategic relations between classes in Poor Law agitation; and Dorothy Thompson, 'Women and Nineteenth-Century Radical Politics' in Juliet Mitchell and Anne Oakley (eds.), *The Rights and Wrongs of Women* (1976), pp. 121–37, for women's participation at grass roots level. Especially in the 1838/39 period, the crossovers between Chartist and anti-Poor Law causes were so strong that it suggests much more fluid and provisional relations between political causes and narratives and rhetoric. On 'golden age' narratives in radical discourse, see Joyce, *Democratic Subjects*, pp. 178, 190–2. See also James A. Epstein, 'Some Organisational and Cultural Aspects of the Chartist Movement in Nottingham', in Epstein and Dorothy Thompson (eds.), *The Chartist Experience: Studies in Working-Class Radicalism and Culture, 1830–60* (1982), pp. 221–68; and Steedman, 'A Weekend', p. 24.
53. In fact, melodrama had been a mixed genre from its inception, and the modes of interpretation that it elicited were always varied. See Jacky Bratton, 'The Contending Discourses of Melodrama', in *Melodrama: Stage, Picture, Screen*, ed. Jacky Bratton *et al.* (1994), pp. 38–49; and Simon Shepherd and Peter Womack, *English Drama: a Cultural History* (Oxford, 1996), p. 194.
54. F. B. Smith, *Radical Artisan: William James Linton 1812–97* (Manchester, 1973).
55. 'Noxious Gasometers', *The National: a Library for the People* (1839), p. 102.
56. William Godwin, *Thoughts Occasioned by the Perusal of Dr Parr's Spital Sermon* (1801), in *Political and Philosophical Writings* (1993), vol. II, p. 199. A similar point is made by the socialist physician, Charles Hall, in *The Effects of Civilisation on the People of the European State* (1803; repr. 1850), p. 9 n.: 'The Chinese who suffer the exposition of their children, and even appoint men to destroy them, seem to act more humanely than the Europeans, who cause the long, languishing sufferings of children.' The evocation of Godwin locates Linton in a tradition of republicanism, which he embraced throughout his life. On Linton in the context of late Chartism and Mazzinian republicanism (to which he converted in 1841), see Margot Finn, *After Chartism: Class and Nation in English Radical Politics, 1848–1874* (Cambridge, 1993), pp. 107–18; and Janowitz, *Lyric and Labour*, ch. 7.
57. *The National* (1839), p. 340. See above, p. 22.
58. J. R. Stephens, *The Political Preacher: an Appeal from the Pulpit on Behalf of the Poor* (1839), pp. 34 passim.

59. *NL* (19 January 1839), p. 2.
60. Bryan Waller Procter, 'The Burial Club, 1839', in *An Autobiographical Fragment and Biographical Notes* (1877), pp. 226–7. Procter (1787–1874), by profession a lawyer, had a relatively successful literary career under the pseudonym, Barry Cornwall. According to the *DNB*, his literary ambitions were more or less abandoned on his marriage in 1824. His wife, Miss Skepper, was the daughter of Basil Montagu (senior)'s third wife, making him the step-brother-in-law of little Basil who accompanied Wordsworth in the period in which he composed his infanticide poem, 'The Thorn'. See above, Ch. 3.
61. *The Times* (23 October 1840), p. 7; *NS* (31 October 1840), pp. 3 and 8. There is copious reference to it in the evidence given to the Select Committee on the Friendly Societies Bill of 1854. See, for example, the testimony of Mr J. Dunstan, constable of Chester Castle, from para. 441, and Mr H. Coppock, a solicitor at Stockport, and the attorney prosecuting the Sandys, from para. 489. *Report from the Select Committee on Friendly Societies Bill* (1854). See also Judith Knelman, *Twisting in the Wind: the Murderess and the English Press* (Toronto, 1998), pp. 124–5.
62. P. H. J. H. Gosden, *Self-Help: Voluntary Associations in the Nineteenth Century* (1973), ch. 5; Richardson, *Death, Dissection, and the Destitute*, pp. 275–6; Rose, *Massacre*, pp. 136–40.
63. Edwin Chadwick, 'An Essay on the Means of Insurance against Casualties of Sickness, Decrepitude and Mortality', *Westminster Review*, 18 (April, 1828), cited in Gosden, *Self-Help*, p. 69.
64. Gosden, *Self-Help*, p. 130.
65. Alfred Tennyson, 'Maud', line 45, in *Poems of Tennyson* (Oxford, 1913).
66. Carlyle, *Past and Present* (1843) in *Works* (30 vols., 1896–99), vol. x, p. 3. Cf. Carlyle's letter to the poor law reformer, Thomas Chalmers, 11 October 1841: 'Did you observe the late trial at Stockport, in Cheshire, of a human father and human mother, for poisoning three of their children to gain successively some £3 8s. from a Burial Society for each of them?' *Collected Letters of Thomas and Jane Welsh Carlyle* (Edinburgh, 1987), vol. XIII, p. 275.
67. Carlyle, *Past and Present*, p. 11. Procter encodes Irishness through speech ('Soh') and through the name of the boy, 'Connor', which appears to be Procter's invention. The names, and sex, of the children vary elsewhere too: Elizabeth, Mary Ann (or Marianne) and Catharine in the newspapers; Tom, Jack and Will, in *Past and Present*.
68. Edwin Chadwick, *Report on the Practice of Interment in Towns* (1843), p. 64, para. 61.
69. Gosden, *Self-Help*, p. 130.
70. Chadwick, *Report on the Practice of Interment in Towns*, p. 64, para. 62.
71. Chadwick, 'Address to the Social Science Association at Sheffield', 1865, cited in Gosden, *Self-Help*, p. 130.
72. *Report from the Select Committee on Friendly Societies Bill*, pp. iv–v.
73. Carlyle, *Past and Present*, p. 3. See, too, Carlyle's letter to Chalmers: 'A barrister of my acquaintance [...] informs me positively that the official people durst

not go farther into this business; that this case was by no means a solitary one there; that, on the whole, they thought it good to close up the matter swiftly […] and investigate it no deeper.' *Collected Letters*, vol. XIII, p. 275.

74. Karl Marx, *Capital: a Critique of Political Economy* (3 vols., 1867; Harmondsworth, 1976–81), vol. I, p. 798.

75. O'Connor, 'The Source of All Our Evils, "Over-Population" and "Over-Production" answered', *NS* (31 March 1838), p. 3.

76. 'Marcus', *The Book of Murder*, p. 42. In the euphemisms of public health officials, 'Marcus' calls this graveyard 'a repository for the privileged remains of these infants unadmitted into life'.

77. Stephens, *Political Preacher*, p. 19.

78. On folklore and the invention of popular culture at the beginning of the nineteenth century, see Peter Burke, *Popular Culture in Early Modern Europe* (1978), ch. 1; and Joep Leerssen, *Remembrance and Imagination: Patterns in the Historical and Literary Representation of Ireland in the Nineteenth Century* (Cork, 1996), pp. 157–223.

79. Katherine Briggs, *The Fairies of English Tradition and Literature* (1967; repr. 1989), pp. 141–50.

80. See esp. Thomas Crofton Croker, *Fairy Legends and Tradition of the South of Ireland* (3 vols., 1828), vol. II, p. vi, for an account of child murder associated with fairies. See also Walter Scott's influential 'The Fairies of Popular Superstition', in *Letters on Demonology and Witchcraft* (1830), an expanded version of 'The Minstrelsy of the Scottish Boarders' (1802).

81. Jane Martineau (ed.), *Victorian Fairy Painting*, exhibition catalogue (1997); Alison Packer *et al.*, *Fairies in Legend and the Arts* (1980).

82. Mary Howitt, 'Nature vs. Malthus', lines 4 and 15.

83. Cf. Nicola Bown's discussion of fairies as a fantasy response to the alienating effects of industrialisation in 'Small Enchantments: the Meanings of the Fairy in Victorian Culture' (D.Phil. thesis, University of Sussex, 1997), ch. 3, esp. pp. 93–114, and *Fairies in Nineteenth-Century Art and Literature* (Cambridge, 2001), pp. 82–97.

84. Michael Slater, 'Dickens's Tract for the Times', *Dickens 1970*, ed. Michael Slater (1970), pp. 99–123, esp. pp. 102–4. See also Slater's introduction and notes to the Penguin edition of *The Chimes*, in *The Christmas Books*, vol. I (1971). On the supernatural in *The Chimes*, see Harry Stone, *Dickens and the Invisible World: Fairy Tale, Fantasy, and Novel-Making* (1979), pp. 126–30, 135. On Maclise and Doyle as fairy painters, see Martineau (ed.), *Victorian Fairy Painting*, pp. 88–92, 126–34. Daniel Maclise had also illustrated Croker's *Fairy Legends*.

85. Slater, 'Dickens's Tract for the Times', p. 102.

86. *NS* (21 December 1844), p. 3.

87. [Mrs Mackarness], *Old Jolliffe: Not a Goblin Story, by The Spirit of a Little Bell awakened by 'The Chimes'* (1845). Slater, 'Introduction' to *The Chimes*, pp. 140–1.

88. Dickens, 'Frauds on the Fairies', *Household Words*, 1 October 1853.

89. *New Moral World*, 2 March 1839, p. 301; Marx and Engels, 'Manifesto of the German Communist Party' (1848), trans. Helen Macfarlane in *The Red Republican*, 1, 21 (9 November 1850), p. 161.
90. Karl Marx, *Grundrisse* (1857–8) p. 277.

5 'A NATION OF INFANTICIDES': CHILD MURDER AND
THE NATIONAL FORGETTING IN *ADAM BEDE*

1. 'Yet the essence of a nation is that all individuals have many things in common, and also that they have forgotten many things.' Ernest Renan, *Oeuvres Complètes* (10 vols., Paris, 1947), vol. 1, pp. 887–906, 892, trans. by Martin Thom as 'What is a Nation?', in Homi Bhabha (ed.), *Nation and Narration* (1990; 1999), pp. 8–22, p. 11.
2. *Adam Bede*, ed. Valentine Cunningham (Oxford, 1996), p. 103. Subsequent references will be included parenthetically in the main body of the text.
3. Behlmer, 'Deadly Motherhood'. See also Sauer, 'Infanticide and Abortion in Nineteenth-Century Britain', pp. 81–93, 85–90; and Rose, *Massacre*.
4. Henry Humble, 'Infanticide, Its Cause and Cure', *The Church and the World: Essays on Questions of the Day*, ed. Rev. Orby Shipley (1866), pp. 51–69, 57.
5. On Lankester's baroque statistical methods, see Behlmer, 'Deadly Motherhood', pp. 424–5. These scenes of the ruins in the city coincide with the incorporation of ruins in the visual imagery of the present in London in the 1860s, as the city underwent a process of rebuilding. See Lynda Nead, *Victorian Babylon* (London and New Haven, CT, 2000), esp. pp. 212–15.
6. William Burke Ryan, *Infanticide: Its Law, Prevalence, Prevention and History* (1862), pp. 45–6.
7. Cf. Behlmer, 'Deadly Motherhood', p. 406. *Pall Mall Gazette* (30 April 1866), p. 9; 'Infanticide', *Saturday Review*, 20 (1865), pp. 161–2; 'Child Murder – Obstetric Morality', *Dublin Review*, 45 (1858), pp. 54–106, 54; *Morning Star* (23 June 1863). All cited in Behlmer, 'Deadly Motherhood', pp. 404–6. Infanticide was a favoured subject of the sensational New Journalism, developed by W. T. Stead in the *Pall Mall Gazette*. Stead aimed to 'rouse the nation' with stories provoking 'pity and horror'. On this, see Judith R. Walkowitz, *City of Dreadful Delight* (1994), esp. pp. 84–5.
8. Ryan, *Infanticide*, p. 46.
9. Ryan's work was recognised in 1856 by the London Medical Society with the award of the Fothergillian Gold Medal Society for his essay, 'On Infanticide in its Medico-Legal Relations'.
10. Ryan, *Infanticide*, pp. 169–70. Ryan associated quacks with abortionists (see p. 131). On the troubled relationship between medical professionals and abortion, see McLaren, *Reproductive Rituals*, ch. 5.
11. Jill L. Matus, *Unstable Bodies: Victorian Representations of Sexuality and Maternity* (Manchester, 1995), pp. 157–67.
12. Margaret Arnot, 'Infant Death, Child Care and the State: the Baby-Farming Scandal and the First Infant Life Protection Legislation of 1872', *Continuity and Change*, 9: 2 (1994), pp. 271–311. The issues of baby farming and wet nursing

are examined in relation to the plight of the heroine of George Moore's tender novel, *Esther Waters* (1894).

13. See Behlmer, 'Deadly Motherhood', pp. 409–10. On Wakley, see Ian Burney, *Bodies of Evidence* (Baltimore, ML, 1999), pp. 12, 16–20, 55–6, and 80–1.

14. On the Anatomy Act, see Richardson, *Death, Dissection and the Destitute*. For a striking representation of prejudices against new medical techniques, and associated professional disputes in an earlier period (1832), see George Eliot's *Middlemarch* (1871–2).

15. *Lancet* (27 January 1855), p. 103; (22 October 1859), pp. 415–6.

16. Behlmer, 'Deadly Motherhood', p. 423. See also Christine L. Krueger, 'Literary Defences and Medical Prosecutions: Representing Infanticide in Nineteenth-Century Britain', *Victorian Studies*, 40: 2 (Winter 1997), pp. 271–94, esp. p. 282ff.; and Higginbotham, '"Sin of the Age"'.

17. See, for instance, F. R. Leavis, *The Great Tradition* (1947; repr. 1973); and, from a different perspective, Raymond Williams, *The Country and the City* (1976), esp. p. 170.

18. See, for instance, Higginbotham, '"Sin of the Age"', p. 322 and Rosemary Gould, 'The History of an Unnatural Act: Infanticide and *Adam Bede*', *Victorian Literature and Culture*, 25 (1997), pp. 263–77.

19. On the ideological commitments of the novel, see Terry Eagleton, *Criticism and Ideology: a Study in Marxist Form* (1975; repr. 1992), pp. 112–14.

20. Eve Kosofsky Sedgwick, *Between Men: English Literature and Male Homosexual Desire* (New York, 1985), pp. 137–45. See also Margaret Homans, 'Dinah's Blush, Maggie's Arm: Class, Gender and Sexuality in George Eliot's Early Novels', *Victorian Studies*, 36: 2 (1993), pp. 155–78; and, for a reading that explores these themes in relation to the wet-nursing controversy, see Matus, *Unstable Bodies*, pp. 167–79.

21. The transportation of female convicts was introduced in the decade preceding the composition of *Adam Bede*. See Zedner, *Women, Crime, and Custody*, pp. 171–7. On the transportation of women to Australia, see L. L. Robinson, *The Convict Settlers of Australia* (Melbourne, 1965), ch. 4.

22. See my 'Early Novels', in G. Levine (ed.), *Cambridge Companion to George Eliot* (Cambridge, 2001), pp. 38–56.

23. George Eliot, *A Writer's Notebook 1854–1879, and Uncollected Writings* ed. Joseph Wiesenfarth (Charlottesville, VA, 1984), pp. xxi–xxiii, and 23–36.

24. John Sutherland reconstructs the time schedule of the novel in *Was Heathcliff a Murderer?* (Oxford, 1996).

25. Benedict Anderson, *Imagined Communities*, (1983; rev. edn 1991), pp. 22–32, 26; Benjamin, 'Theses on the Philosophy of History', *Illuminations*, p. 265.

26. [Leslie Stephen], obituary notice for George Eliot in *Cornhill Magazine*, 17 (February 1881), pp. 152–68. Reprinted in David Carroll (ed.), *George Eliot: the Critical Heritage* (1971), pp. 464–84, citation at pp. 468–9.

27. [Anne Mozley], unsigned review in *Bentley's Quarterly Review* (July 1859), i., pp. 433–56. Reprinted in Carroll, *Critical Heritage*, pp. 86–103, citations at pp. 89 and 91.

28. Wordsworth, *The Prelude* (1815), bk. 12, lines 214–15.

29. On intertextual relations, see Jay Clayton, 'The Alphabet of Suffering: Effie Deans, Tess Durbeyfield, Martha Ray and Hetty Sorrel', in Clayton and Eric Rothstein (eds.), *Influence and Intertextuality in Literary History* (Madison, WI, 1991), pp. 37–60. On Eliot's admiration of Scott, see Diane Elam, *Romancing the Postmodern* (1992), pp. 102–40.

30. 'L'homme n'est esclave ni de sa race, ni de sa langue, ni de sa religion, ni du cours des fleuves, ni de la direction de chaînes de montagnes', Renan, 'Qu'est-ce qu'une nation?', in *Oeuvres*, vol. I, p. 905; Thom, 'What is a Nation?', p. 20.

31. See pp. 150–2.

32. 'La possession en commun d'un riche legs de souvenirs... [et] la volonté de continuer à faire valoir l'héritage qu'on a reçu indivis', Renan, 'Qu'est-ce qu'une nation?', in *Oeuvres*, vol. I, pp. 903–4; Thom, 'What is a Nation?', in Bhabha (ed.), *Nation and Narration*, p. 19.

33. On George Eliot and the Germans, see Rosemary Ashton, *The German Idea: Four English Writers and the Reception of German Thought 1800–1860* (Cambridge, 1980), pp. 147–77; and Suzanne Graver, *George Eliot and Community: a Study in Social Theory* (Berkeley, CA, 1984). She met Renan in Paris in 1866. See G. S. Haight, *George Eliot: a Biography* (1968; repr. 1992), p. 398. On German and French traditions of nationhood, see Rogers Brubaker, *Citizenship and Nationhood in France and Germany* (Cambridge, MA, 1992); and James Donald, 'The Citizen and the Man about Town' in Stuart Hall and Paul du Gay (eds.), *Questions of Cultural Identity* (1996), pp. 170–90.

34. Cited in M. Walzer, *Regicide and Revolution: Speeches at the Trial of Louis XVI* (Cambridge, 1974), p. 138. On the symbolic significance of the king's death, see Lynn Hunt, *The Family Romance of the French Revolution* (1992).

35. '[S]e sont passés à l'origine de toutes les formations politiques' Renan, 'Qu'est-ce qu'une nation?', in *Oeuvres*, vol. I, p. 891; Thom, 'What is a Nation?', in Bhabha (ed.), *Nation and Narration*, p. 11.

36. Renan, 'Qu'est-ce qu'une nation?', in *Oeuvres*, vol. I, p. 892. See Benedict Anderson, *Imagined Communities*. Cf. Homi Bhabha who suggests the element of performativity in this act of national forgetting. Bhabha, 'DissemiNation: Time, Narrative, and the Margins of the Modern Nation', in Bhabha (ed.), *Nation and Narration*, pp. 291–322, 311. Renan's emphasis on compulsory forgetting is particularly striking at this time of scientific interest in notions of involuntary memory. See Adam Crabtree, *From Mesmer to Freud: Magnetic Sleep and the Roots of Psychological Healing* (New Haven, CT, 1993); and Rick Rylance, *Victorian Psychology and British Culture, 1850–1880* (Oxford, 2000).

37. *The Journals of George Eliot*, ed. Margaret Harris and Judith Johnston, (Cambridge, 1998), pp. 296–8.

38. On Evans, see Valentine Cunningham, *Everywhere Spoken Against: Dissent in the Victorian Novel* (Oxford, 1975), pp. 145–6, 153–5. See also William Mottram, *The True Story of George Eliot: in Relation to Adam Bede* (1905).

39. See Appendix 2 to the World's Classics edition of the novel.

40. *Journals*, p. 296.

41. For instance *Felix Holt* (1866) and *Middlemarch* are both set just before the reform bill of 1832.

42. Given George Eliot's fastidious attention to historical accuracy, it is not clear why she should have shifted the novel backwards in time in this way, although I shall argue that, in terms of the national narrative, 1800 is an auspicious date as that of the Act of Union with Ireland.
43. Chapter 3.
44. Elliott, *Partners in Revolution*, pp. 282–322. See also my 'Infanticide and the Boundaries of Culture, from Hume to Arnold', in Susan Greenfield and Carol Barash (eds.), *Inventing Maternity: Politics, Science and Literature 1660–1865*, (Lexington, KY, 1999), pp. 215–37, 217–19.
45. The Loamshire Militia was based on the Leicestershire Militia which had served in Ireland. George Eliot transcribed details of the celebrations for the Duke of Rutland's majority, from *Gentleman's Magazine* for 1799, as the basis of Arthur's birthday party. It includes a transparency of a medallion of the Duke of Rutland with the following inscriptions: 'Motto: "Hail generous youth!" at the bottom Hibernia receiving the Leicestershire Militia, & presenting them with a wreath of laurel. Motto: "Foremost in Hibernia's cause"'. *A Writer's Notebook*, p. 29.
46. The entry in fact says 'probably in 1839 or 40' (*Journals*, p. 296), although Haight gives early 1839. *George Eliot*, p. 28.
47. They joined the Derby Faith Folk. Cunningham, *Everywhere Spoken Against*, p. 145.
48. *Journals*, p. 296.
49. Mary Voce's testimony is included in *The Life, Character, Behaviour at the Place of Execution and Dying Speech of Mary Voce* (Nottingham, 1802) 'I . . . became intoxicated with a succession of carnal pleasures' and 'in a fit of revenge I sought the deadly poison'. A more conciliatory version which alludes to her poverty is in *A full and particular Account of the Life, Trial and Behaviour of Mary Voce* (Nottingham, 1802). Reprinted in *Adam Bede*, pp. 547–53.
50. *Journals*, p. 73. There is no reference to *The Chimes*, but her entry for 2 January 1858 records reading to George 'the delicious scenes at Tetterby's with the "Moloch of a baby" in the "Haunted Man"', the latest of Dickens's *Christmas Books*.
51. On George Eliot and political reform, see Catherine Gallagher, *The Industrial Reformation of English Fiction* (Chicago, 1985), pp. 219–69.
52. 'Thursday. 22 [October 1857]. *Began my new novel "Adam Bede"'*, *Journals*, p. 70. *The Times* reports trials of child murder cases on 5, 9, 11, 19, and 31 December 1856.
53. There is extensive coverage of Indian infanticide in the final chapter of Ryan's *Infanticide*.
54. On the suppression of *sati*, see esp. Lata Mani, *Contentious Traditions: the Debate on Sati in Colonial India* (Berkeley, CA, 1998).
55. Benjamin Disraeli, *Sybil* (Oxford, 1981), p. 97.
56. See extract from Jonathan Duncan's letter to the Governor General in Council, 2 October 1789, in 'Copy of All Correspondence which has Taken Place on the Subject of Hindoo Infanticide and of All Proceedings of the Indian Government With Regard to that Practice', *Correspondence on Hindoo Infanticide*,

1789–1820 (1824), p. 6. On the suppression of infanticide, see Kanti B. Pakrasi, *Female Infanticide in India* (Calcutta, 1970); Criana Connal, 'Draupadi, Sati, Savitri: The Question of Women's Identity in Colonial Discourse Theory' (D.Phil. thesis, University of Oxford, 1997); Barabara D. Miller, *The Endangered Sex: Neglect of Female Children in Rural North India* (Dehli, 1997); and Lalita Panigrahi, *British Social Policy and Female Infanticide in India* (New Delhi, 1972). Padma Anagol argues, in 'The Emergence of the Female Criminal in India: Infanticide and Survival under the Raj', *History Workshop Journal*, 53 (2002), pp. 73–93, that by the end of the nineteenth century, infanticide had come to be perceived as a woman's crime, rather than a crime provoked by the caste system and the customs of a barbaric people.

57. *Parliamentary Debates*, n.s. 9, 1 May–19 July 1823. See *Correspondence on Hindoo Infanticide* (1824), and two subsequent volumes of *Correspondence Relating to the Practice of Infanticide in India*, published in 1828, and 1843. James Peggs' evangelical work, first published as *Hindoo Infanticide. The Present State of Infanticide in India* (1829), and revised as *The Infanticide's Cry to Britain* 4th edn (1844) draws heavily on the parliamentary correspondence. See also 'Female Infanticide in Central and Western India', in *Calcutta Review* n.s. 1 (May 1844), pp. 372–448: "The Parliamentary Papers on infanticide we are inclined to regard as perhaps the noblest monument which the British Government has yet reared to itself, since it became the Paramount power in India', p. 435.

58. E.g., Charles Raikes, *Notes on the North Western Provinces of India* (1852); J. W. Kaye, *The Administration of the East India Company* (1853); John Cave Browne, *Indian Infanticide, its Origin, Progress and Suppression* (1857); and W. R. Moore, *Report on Female Infanticide* (1859), as well as essays in the periodical press – e.g. *Fraser's*, *Edinburgh Review*, and *Blackwood's Edinburgh Magazine*.

59. Also note Chapman's series on India in *Westminster Review*, in the period in which George Eliot assisted him as editor. Later Lewes's second son studied for the Indian Civil Service; he failed the exams and went to South Africa instead.

60. In some accounts they have also lost their caste. See, e.g., 'Female Infanticide', *Asiatic Journal*, n.s. 3 (Sept–Dec 1830), pp. 164–7.

61. [R. H. Patterson], 'Our Indian Empire', *Blackwood's Edinburgh Magazine* 80 (December 1856), pp. 636–59, 650.

62. Kaye, *Administration*, p. 546; John Wilson, *History of the Suppression of Infanticide in Western India under the Government of Bombay* (Bombay, 1855), p. 430.

63. Legends purporting to narrate the origin of the custom abound in this literature. See, for instance, 'Letter' from A. Walker, 25 Jan 1808 (*Correspondence*, [1828], pp. 31–2): 'a powerful Rajah . . . who had a daughter of singular beauty and accomplishments, desired the Rajgor, or family Brahmin, to affiance her to a prince of desert and rank equal to her own.' But failing to find a suitable husband, the Rajgor tells him to kill her. Eventually he agrees. 'Accordingly the princess was put to death, and female infanticide was from that time

practiced by the Jahrejahs.' Such stories are retold in the literature on infanticide repeatedly, suggesting something of the pleasures of reading about oriental inhumanities. See, for instance, Peggs, *Infanticide's Cry to Britain*, pp. 25–6; or John Campbell, *Narrative of his Operations in the Hill Tracts of Orissa for the Suppression of Human Sacrifices and Female Infanticide* (1861), pp. 78–80.

64. Kaye, *Administration*, p. 546.

65. On British reform policy in India before 1857, see Thomas R. Metcalf, *The Ideology of the Raj* (Cambridge, 1995), ch. 2; Eric Stokes, *The English Utilitarians and India* (Oxford, 1959).

66. On the social mission of English education in British India, see Guari Viswanathan, *Masks of Conquest: Literary Study and British Rule in India* (1989; repr. Delhi, 1998). On the consumption of English literature in India, see also Meenakshi Mukherjee, *Realism and Reality: the Novel and Society in India* (Delhi, 1994).

67. Browne, *Indian Infanticide*, p. 205.

68. Viswanathan, *Masks of Conquest*, p. 86.

69. This annual competition was instituted in 1842, funded by the recently established Indian education fund. See *Correspondence*, (1843), p. 21. The competition – not unlike that for the London Medical Association's Fothergillian medal, won by Ryan – provided a way of inculcating professional ideals among native people. The prize was career advancement either in the East India Company, or as a teacher. The winner in 1848, Cooverjee Rostomjee Mody, assumed an exemplary posture of native self-criticism when he wrote of the 'indefatigable zeal of the British government in this sacred cause... [its] singular conquest over the revolting custom'. Mody, *An Essay on Female Infanticide* (Bombay, 1843), p. 3. See also Bhawoo Dajee, *An Essay on Female Infanticide* (Bombay, 1847).

70. *Correspondence* (1843), p. 45, s.12.

71. Thomas R. Metcalf, *The Aftermath of Revolt: India 1857–1870* (Oxford, 1965); Metcalf, *Ideologies*, pp. 43–52 and passim.,

72. Partha Chatterjee, *The Nation and Its Fragments*, in *The Partha Chatterjee Omnibus* (Delhi, 1999), p. 18: 'The rebels ripped the vest off the face of the colonial power, and for the first time, it was visible in its true form.' See also Bernard S. Cohn, 'Representing Authority in Victorian India', in Eric Hobsbawm and Terence Ranger (eds.), *The Invention of Tradition* (Cambridge, 1983), pp. 165–210. On the moral panic sparked by the Mutiny in Britain, especially in relation to sexual relations, see Lynda Nead, *Myths of Sexuality* (Oxford, 1988), pp. 80–6.

73. Sunday, 6 December 1857, *Journal*, p. 71.

74. Patrick Brantlinger, *Rule of Darkness: British Literature and Imperialism 1830–1914* (Ithaca, NY, 1988), ch. 7; Brijen Kishove Gupta, *India in English Fiction 1800–1970: an Annotated Bibliography* (Metuchen, NJ, 1973).

75. Jenny Sharpe, *Allegories of Empire: the Figure of Woman in the Colonial Text* (Minneapolis, MN, 1993). See especially her discussion of an illustration of the

'Massacre of English Officers and their Wives at Jhansi', from Charles Ball's serial publication, *The History of the Indian Mutiny* (2 vols., 1858).

76. Ball, *History*, vol. 1, p. 252.
77. *Correspondence* (1824), p. 22. On the ambivalence of colonial identity see Homi K. Bhabha, *The Location of Culture* (1994), esp. 'Of Mimicry and Man' (pp. 85–92), and 'Signs Taken for Wonders' (pp. 139–70).
78. Symptomatically, travellers were confused as to whether the absence of women in Indian society was because they were concealed in segregated societies, or more sinisterly because they had been killed at birth – as though secrecy and child murder were interchangeable problems.
79. *Lancet* (10 October 1863), p. 426.
80. This is evident in William Booth's *In Darkest England and the Way Out* (1890), but is apparent in works of social exploration from earlier in the century too. See Peter Keating (ed.), *Into Unknown England, 1866–1913: Selections from the Social Explorers* (Manchester, 1976).
81. Cf. Zizek, 'Fantasy as a Political Category: A Lacanian Approach', in E. Wright and E. Wright (eds.), *Zizek Reader* (Oxford, 1999), pp. 87–101.
82. *Letters of George Eliot* (7 vols., 1954–6), ed. G. S. Haight, vol. 1, pp. 272–3. Cf. Laura C. Berry, *The Child, the State and the Victorian Novel* (Charlottesville, VA, 1999), ch. 4, esp. pp. 149–50.
83. At this early stage in her career, it was important to establish her credentials as a writer of literary worth. Her true identity as a woman and as the mistress of George Henry Lewes, a married man, was dangerously close to breaking, and both factors threatened the reception of her work. In a review essay published in 1856, she had mocked 'lady novelists' for their peculiar brands of 'silliness' – 'the frothy, the prosy, the pious, or the pedantic' (p. 301). 'Silly Novels by Lady Novelists' in *Essays of George Eliot*, ed. Thomas Pinney (1963), pp. 300–24. Yet more damaging, however, would be the consequences of public knowledge of her own position as the mistress of a married man – drawing her into a dangerous confederacy with Hetty, rather than the morally virtuous Dinah. Inserting herself into the English romantic tradition, through affiliation with Wordsworth and Scott, adopting the anonymous narrative voice, as well as the tone of high intellectual and moral seriousness – all might be seen as strategies to conceal her identity. In this light, the choice of child murder as the theme for this novel becomes curiously symptomatic: a novel that tells of Hetty's attempt to conceal the effects of sexual disgrace, by literally burying the evidence, is in itself an attempt to conceal the author's own sexual impropriety. Whether or not one subscribes to the psycho-biographical reading, it is nevertheless the case that the novel's theme of child murder interestingly intersects with its stylistic concerns, and thus also resonates with larger issues of realism in the English novelistic tradition. As it turned out, attempts to conceal her own identity backfired when a clergyman from the Isle of Man named Joseph Liggins claimed to be George Eliot. See Haight, *George Eliot*, pp. 244–5, 280–91. On the psychic costs of her disguise, see Rosemarie Bodenheimer, *The Real Life of Mary Ann Evans* (Ithaca, NY, 1994), ch. 5.

84. Daniel Cottom, *Social Figures: George Eliot, Social History and Literary Representation* (Minneapolis, MN, 1987), pp. 85–90; Elam, *Romancing the Postmodern*. Elam's discussion of George Eliot's vexed relation to romance is complicated by her identification of romance with Scott. Scott for George Eliot, however, had high cultural capital, and was a writer with whom she had every reason to associate. Rather, she wished to dissociate herself from low prestige popular romances, usually by women writers. Ruskin's severe assessment of George Eliot in 1880, as 'the consum[mation] of the English Cockney school', 'a common rail-road station novelist', in 'Fiction Fair and Foul', *Nineteenth Century* (1880–1881), repr. in Carroll (ed.), *Critical Heritage*, pp. 166–7, made in response to *The Mill on the Floss*, was strikingly out of line with other contemporary responses. But it nonetheless reminds us of the thin line that exists between her work and popular melodrama.

85. [George Trevor], 'The Bengal Mutiny', *Blackwood's Edinburgh Magazine*, 82 (September 1857), pp. 372–92.

86. Cf. Williams, *Country and the City*, p. 168.

87. The ideal of the 'Punjab School' of colonial administration in the mid nineteenth century is described by John Beames as 'personal government' in which a magistrate would 'decide cases either sitting on horseback in the village gateway, or under a tree outside the village walls, and write his decision on his knee... and be off to repeat the process in the next village'. See John Beames, *Memoirs of a Bengal Civilian* (1961), pp. 101–3, cited by Metcalf in *Ideologies of the Raj*, p. 38. The magistrate in *Adam Bede* appears for a second time, outside the prison where Hetty is held, and gains admission for Dinah to minister to Hetty in the enclosed space of the prison cell. It is as though Dinah's extreme, outdoor, foreign preaching to strangers that, at the beginning of the novel, inspires the instinctual responses of the villagers, has finally been domesticated into a one-to-one encounter, indoors, and among family members, that is now authorised by the magistrate.

88. Matthew Arnold, *Lectures and Essays in Criticism*, ed. R. H. Super (Ann Arbor, MI, 1962), pp. 258–85, 273.

89. Citations from Arnold, ibid., pp. 272–3. On Wragg's Irishness, cf. Terrence Hawkes, 'The Heimlich Manoeuvre', in *Textual Practice*, 8 (1994), pp. 302–16.

90. Charles Swann, 'No Wragg by Ilissus? A Note on Matthew Arnold's "Wragg is in Custody"', *Victorian Newsletter*, 68 (1985), pp. 21–3; Cynthia Patterson, *The Family in Greek Life* (Cambridge, MA, 1998); and Richard Jenkins, *The Victorians and Ancient Greece* (Oxford, 1980), pp. 161–3.

6 WRAGG'S DAUGHTERS: CHILD MURDER TOWARDS
THE *FIN DE SIÈCLE*

1. Mona Caird, 'Introduction' to *The Morality of Marriage and Other Essays* (1897), p. 16.

2. George K. Behlmer, *Child Abuse and Moral Reform in England, 1870–1908* (Stanford, CA, 1982), pp. 30 and 46. The National Society for the Prevention

Notes to pages 156–160

of Cruelty to Children was preceded by regional associations in Liverpool (1883) and London (1884).

3. New legislation also included the 1872 Infant Life Protection Act that introduced the compulsory registration of child carers and the 1874 Registration Act, for the registration of all births. See Behlmer, *Child Abuse*, pp. 38–43. On the Children's Charter, see pp. 109–10. See also Arnot, 'Infant Death, Child Care and the State'; Behlmer, *The English Home and its Guardians, 1850–1940* (Stanford, CA, 1998); and Rose, *Massacre*. On the ways in which the legislation targeted poor families, see Ellen Ross, *Love and Toil: Motherhood in Outcast London, 1870–1918* (Oxford, 1993). On the representation of state intervention in the family, see Peter Keating, *The Haunted Study: a Social History of the English Novel, 1875–1918* (1989), pp. 152ff., and Berry, *The Child, the State and the Victorian Novel*.

4. On legislative changes see Mary Lyndon Shanley, *Feminism, Marriage and the Law in Victorian England, 1850–1895* (1992); Lee Holcombe, 'Victorian Wives and Property', in Martha Vicinus (ed.), *A Widening Sphere: Changing Roles of Victorian Women* (1980); and Lee Holcombe, *Wives and Property: Reform of the Married Women's Property Law in Nineteenth-Century England* (Oxford, 1983); Barbara Caine, *English Feminism, 1780–1980* (Oxford, 1997), esp. ch. 3 and ch. 4.

5. See Judith Walkowitz, *Prostitution and Victorian Society: Women, Class and the State* (Cambridge, 1980); and Carol Smart, 'Disruptive Bodies and Unruly Sex: the Regulation of Reproduction and Sexuality in the Nineteenth Century', in Smart (ed.), *Regulating Womanhood: Historical Essays on Marriage, Motherhood and Sexuality* (1992), pp. 7–32. On birth control, see below, n. 70.

6. Daniel Pick, *Faces of Degeneration: a European Disorder, c.1848–c.1918* (Cambridge, 1989).

7. On urban degeneration, see Gareth Stedman Jones, *Outcast London* (Oxford, 1971); Zedner, *Women, Crime, and Custody*. On the culture of degeneration, see William Greenslade, *Degeneration, Culture and the Novel, 1880–1940* (Cambridge, 1994).

8. Adrian Desmond and James Moore, *Darwin* (1992), pp. 264–8, 485–99.

9. Anna Davin, 'Imperialism and Motherhood', *History Workshop Journal*, 5 (Spring 1978), pp. 9–65. See also Bernard Semmel, *Imperialism and Social Reform: English Social–Imperial Thought 1895–1914* (1960); Zedner, *Women, Crime and Custody*, ch. 7; Pick, *Faces of Degeneration*, pp. 197ff.; Sally Ledger, *The New Woman* (Manchester, 1996), pp. 62–71; and Antoinette Burton, 'The White Woman's Burden: British Feminists and "The Indian Woman", 1865–1915', in Nupur Chaudhuri and Margaret Stroebel (eds.), *Western Women and Imperialism: Complicity and Resistance* (Bloomington, IN, 1992), pp. 137–8.

10. Gillian Beer, *Darwin's Plots* (1985), pp. 123–45.

11. Darwin, *The Origin of Species*, ed. Gillian Beer (Oxford, 1996), p. 56.

12. On the queen bee as an allegorical representation of maternal virtue at the end of the eighteenth century, see Dror Wahrman, 'On Queen Bees and

Being Queens: A Late Eighteenth-Century Cultural Revolution?', in Jones and Wahrman (eds), *The Age of Cultural Revolutions*, pp. 251–80.

13. Darwin, *Origin of Species*, p. 165.
14. Charles Kingsley's *Water Babies* (1863) brings out clearly the conjunction of Malthusian population control with Darwinian evolution theory. Here the surplus population of the children of the poor are turned into sea creatures. Cf. Gillian Beer, in *Darwin's Plots*, p. 124.
15. See above, Ch. 5.
16. See George W. Stocking, *Victorian Anthropology* (New York, 1987), pp. 164–76.
17. Cf. Sybil Wolfram, *In-Laws and Outlaws: Kinship and Marriage in England* (1987), pp. 169–70.
18. John W. Burrow, *Evolution and Society: a Study in Victorian Social Theory* (Cambridge, 1966), pp. 11, 233–5. See above, Ch. 2.
19. John F. McLennan, *Primitive Marriage* (1865), p. 58.
20. Elman R. Service, *A Century of Controversy: Ethnological Issues from 1860 to 1960* (Orlando, FL, 1985), pp. 4–6; Stocking, *Victorian Anthropology*, pp. 122–4.
21. See reviews in *Athenaeum* (18 March 1865), pp. 376–7, and *Saturday Review* (25 February 1865).
22. For critiques of McLennan, see, e.g., John Lubbock, *The Origin of Civilisation and the Primitive Condition of Man* (1870; Chicago, 1978), pp. 93–4; and Herbert Spencer, *The Principles of Sociology* (2 vols., 1876), vol. 1, pp. 641–60.
23. See Stocking, *Victorian Anthropology*, pp. 200–8; Patricia O'Hara, 'Primitive Marriage, Civilised Marriage: Anthropology, Mythology, and *The Egoist*' in *Victorian Literature and Culture*, 20 (1992), pp. 1–24. On crossovers between evolutionary theory and feminist debates, see Alan P. Barr, 'Evolutionary Science and the Woman Question' in *Victorian Literature and Culture*, 20 (1992), pp. 25–54 and Elizabeth Fee, 'The Sexual Politics of Victorian Anthropology', in Mary S. Hartman (ed.), *Clio's Consciousness Raised: New Perspectives on the History of Women* (New York, 1974) pp. 86–102.
24. Caird, 'The Emancipation of the Family', *Morality of Marriage*, pp. 18–59, pp. 25 passim. She also cites John Lubbock, Julius Lippert, and J. J. Bachofen.
25. Caird, *Morality of Marriage*, pp. 1 and 4.
26. Cf. the arguments of feminist anthropologist, Sarah Hrdy in her recent *Mother Nature: a History of Mothers, Infants, and Natural Selection* (New York, 1999).
27. Caird, *Morality of Marriage*, p. 37.
28. Antoinette Burton, *Burdens of History: British Feminists, Indian Women, and Imperial Culture, 1865–1915* (Chapel Hill, NC, 1994); Anna Davin, 'Imperialism and Motherhood'; and Anne McClintock, *Imperial Leather: Race, Gender, and Sexuality in the Colonial Contest* (New York and London, 1995).
29. Edith Hall, 'Medea and British Legislation', p. 53. She refers to James Robinson Planché's *The Golden Fleece: or, Jason in Colchis and Medea in Corinth*, first performed at Haymarket in 1845, and, as the culmination of the 'tradition', a burlesque influenced by Planché's play, *Jason and Medea: a Ramble after a Colchian*, performed in 1878. See also Fiona Macintosh, 'Medea Transposed: Burlesque and Gender on the Mid-Victorian Stage', and David Gowen,

'*Medea*s on the Archive Database', in Edith Hall *et al.* (eds.), *Medea in Performance 1500–2000* (Oxford, 2000), pp. 75–99, and 232–74.

30. Augusta Webster, *Portraits* (2nd edn, 1870), pp. 1–13.
31. Angela Leighton, *Victorian Women Poets: Writing Against the Heart* (1992), pp. 166–73; Christine Sutphin, 'Augusta Webster', in Abigail Burnham Bloom (ed.), *Nineteenth-Century British Women Writers: a Bibliographical Critical Source Book* (Westport, CT, 2000).
32. 'Medea in Athens', in *Portraits*, pp. 4–5.
33. Rebecca Stott, 'Darwin's Barnacles: Mid-Century Victorian Natural History and the Marine Grotesque', in Roger Luckhurst and Josephine McDonagh (eds.), *Encounters: Transactions between Science and Culture in Nineteenth-Century Britain* (Manchester, 2002), pp. 151–81.
34. 'Medea in Athens', in *Portraits*, pp. 6, 12.
35. Ibid., pp. 1–2, 8, 14.
36. See Ch. 5.
37. The two writers were, of course, known to each other through their writings and mutual associates, and made casual acquaintance at least once, in February 1868. See Haight, *George Eliot*, p. 408.
38. Cf. Gillian Beer, *George Eliot* (Brighton, 1986), pp. 144 and 208.
39. *Felix Holt: the Radical* (Harmondsworth, Penguin, 1995), p. 397.
40. Ibid., p. 23.
41. On evolutionary themes in George Eliot's work, see Beer, *Darwin's Plots*; George Levine, *Darwin and the Novelists: Patterns of Science in Victorian Fiction* (Chicago, 1991); Nancy Paxton, *George Eliot and Herbert Spencer: Feminism, Evolution and the Reconstruction of Gender* (Princeton NJ, 1991); and Sally Shuttleworth, *George Eliot and Nineteenth-Century Science: the Make Believe of a Beginning* (Cambridge, 1984).
42. On Victorian scientific beliefs about the infertility of 'hybrid' races, see Robert J. C. Young, *Colonial Desire: Hybridity in Theory, Culture and Race* (1995), esp. ch. 1.
43. *Daniel Deronda*, ed. Barbara Hardy (Harmondsworth, 1967), pp. 487 and 190.
44. Ibid., at pp. 668, 875, and 882.
45. Cf. Linda Hunt Beckman, *Amy Levy: Her Life and Letters* (Athens, OH, 2000), pp. 112–14; Deborah Epstein Nord, *Walking the Victorian Streets* (Ithaca, NY, 1995), p. 200. Isobel Armstrong links Levy's exploration of racial hatred in this poem to the poet's experience as a lesbian. See *Victorian Poetry: Poetry, Poetics and Politics* (1993), p. 375.
46. Levy, 'Medea', in *A Minor Poet and Other Verse* (2nd edn, 1891), pp. 35–57, n. 53. Levy, like Webster, chooses to call the princess of Corinth Glauce, unlike George Eliot, who opts instead for Creusa. In Euripides's *Medea* she is not given a name, but later writers call her Kreousa (Latin form Creusa) (in origin 'ruling, royal'); others call her Glauke (a colour, or a kind of shining quality). My thanks to Richard Seaford for this.
47. Levy, 'Medea', pp. 48, 51, 53, and 55.
48. Ibid., p. 57.

49. Emily Pfeiffer, 'Outlawed: A Rhyme for the Time', in *Flowers of the Night* (1889), pp. 83, 87–8.
50. Charles Darwin, *The Descent of Man, and Selection in Relation to Sex* (2 vols., 1871; Princeton, NJ, 1981), citations at vol. II, pp. 364–5 and 368 (my emphasis).
51. Ibid., vol. II, pp. 404–5.
52. As in, for instance, Gustave Le Bon, *The Crowd: a Study of the Popular Mind* (1896).
53. Matthew Arnold, *Culture and Anarchy* in *Culture and Anarchy and Other Writings*, ed. Stefan Collini (Cambridge, 1983), citations at pp. 53–211, 100, and 94.
54. Ibid., pp. 175–6.
55. Hypatia Bradlaugh Bonner, *Charles Bradlaugh* (2 vols., 1908), vol. II, p. 28.
56. J. A. Banks and Olive Banks, *Feminism and Family Planning in Victorian England* (Liverpool, 1964), pp. 85–6. On contraception, see also J. Miriam Benn, *Predicaments of Love* (1992); Peter Fryer, *The Birth Controllers* (1965); Angus McLaren, *Birth Control in Nineteenth-Century England* (1978); Richard Allen Soloway, *Birth Control and the Population Question in England, 1877–1930* (Chapel Hill, NC, 1982). On the trial and preceding events, see S. Chandrasekhar, *A Dirty, Filthy Book* (Berkeley, CA, 1979); Roger Manvell, *The Trial of Annie Besant and Charles Bradlaugh* (1976). See also Bonner, *Charles Bradlaugh*, vol. II, pp. 12–38; and Annie Besant, *An Autobiography* (2nd edn, 1893), pp. 206–10.
57. Bonner, *Charles Bradlaugh*, vol. II, p. 17.
58. Lucy Bland, *Banishing the Beast: English Feminism and Sexual Morality, 1885–1914* (1995), p. 202. See also Rosanna Ledbetter, *A History of the Malthusian League 1877–1927* (Columbus, OH, 1976), and Soloway, *Birth Control*, p. 54.
59. Later issued as a single volume, *In the High Court of Justice. Queen's Bench Division, June 18th, 1877. The Queen versus Charles Bradlaugh and Annie Besant* (1877).
60. J. A. Banks and Olive Banks, 'The Bradlaugh-Besant Trial and the English Newspapers', *Population Studies*, 8: 1 (July 1954), pp. 22–34.
61. Darwin was subpoenaed to give evidence in Besant and Bradlaugh's defence at the trial. He refused to attend, pleading ill health, and wrote to Bradlaugh pointing out that his testimony would be of little use to them since he had long been opposed to the use of birth control. Bonner, *Charles Bradlaugh*, vol. II, pp. 23–4; Desmond and Moore, *Darwin*, p. 627.
62. *In the High Court of Justice... Queen vs. Bradlaugh and Besant*, pp. 80–1.
63. Ibid., p. 174.
64. Ibid., p. 91.
65. Ibid., p. 85.
66. *Ibid.*, pp. 92–3. Considerable anxiety focused on overlaying in particular. For debates on this, see Rose, *Massacre*, p. 177.
67. *In the High Court of Justice... Queen vs. Bradlaugh and Besant*, p. 83.
68. Ibid., p. 84.

69. See Banks and Banks, *Feminism and Family Planning*, pp. 92–7.
70. McLaren, *Birth Control in Nineteenth-Century England*, p. 99.
71. *In the High Court of Justice . . . Queen vs. Bradlaugh and Besant*, p. 30.
72. Ibid., p. 76.
73. Shanley, *Feminism, Marriage and the Law*, p. 139.
74. According to Besant, the judge who tried the custody case, Sir George Jessel, had professional scores to settle following the quashing of Bradlaugh and Besant's conviction at the Court of Appeal. On the custody battle and its entanglement in the obscenity trial, see Besant, *Autobiography*, pp. 210–14.
75. Hypatia Bradlaugh, while noting the subsequent estrangement between Besant and her father, nevertheless emphasises Besant's heroism which is always figured around the imminent loss of Mabel. See, e.g., Bonner, *Charles Bradlaugh*, vol. II, p. 19.
76. Bland, *Banishing the Beast*, pp. 222–49.
77. On the double-sided nature of the category of the New Woman, see Ledger, *The New Woman*, esp. ch. 1. See also Ann Ardis, *New Women, New Novels: Feminism and Early Modernism* (New Brunswick, NJ, 1990).
78. Florence Bell and Elizabeth Robbins, *Alan's Wife. A Dramatic Study in Three Scenes. First Acted at the Independent Theatre in London. With an Introduction by William Archer* (1893), p. ix.
79. See *Star* (29 April 1893); *Speaker* (6 May 1893); and *Speaker* (8 July 1893). Cited in Bell and Robbins, *Alan's Wife*, pp. xxx–xxxi.
80. Bell and Robins, *Alan's Wife*, pp. xxxi, xlvi, xlii.
81. Ibid., p. 20.
82. See above, Ch. 2
83. Caird, *Morality of Marriage*, pp. 37–8.
84. Ibid., p. 12.
85. Ledger, *New Woman*, pp. 182–7. See also John Goode, 'Sue Brideshead and the New Woman', in Mary Jacobus (ed.), *Women Writing and Writing About Women* (1979), pp. 100–13 and Penny Boumelha, *Thomas Hardy and Women* (Brighton, 1982).
86. Thomas Hardy, *Jude the Obscure* (Harmondsworth, 1985), citations at pp. 412, 406, and 410.
87. Ibid., p. 440.
88. Ibid., pp. 410–11.

7 ENGLISH BABIES AND IRISH CHANGELINGS

1. Besant, *Autobiography*, pp. 207–14.
2. Ibid., pp. 13 passim.
3. Ibid., pp. 25, and 73–80.
4. On Ireland, modernity, and its ambivalent relations to the discourses of colonialism, see Luke Gibbons, 'Race against Time: Racial Discourse and Irish

History', in *Oxford Literary Review*, special edition, 'Neocolonialism', 13 (1991), pp. 95–117.

5. Richard Kearney, 'Myth and Motherland', in Seamus Deane (ed.), *Ireland's Field Day* (1985), pp. 61–80.

6. Padraic H. Pearse, in *The Field Day Anthology of Irish Writing* ed. Seamus Deane (3 vols., Derry, 1992), vol. II, p. 758. Pearse takes up the figure of child murder in a different way in his polemic on the Irish education system, *The Murder Machine* (1916).

7. Emily Lawless, *With the Wild Geese* (1902), pp. 3–5, lines 1–4, 21–8.

8. See p. 177.

9. Mary Jean Corbett, *Allegories of Union in Irish and English Writing, 1790–1870: Politics, History, and the Family from Edgeworth to Arnold* (New York, 2000), p. 98. The language of contagion was also invoked in discussions of the Act of Union, in 1800, which was sometimes figured as a *cordon sanitaire* to protect Britain and its colonies from European infection. See Tom Dunne, 'Haunted by History: Irish Romantic Writing, 1800–1850', in R. Porter and M. Teich (eds.), *Romanticism in National Context* (Cambridge, 1988), pp. 68–9.

10. Henry Mayhew, *London Labour and the London Poor*, selected and ed. Victor Neuberg (Harmondsworth, 1985), p. 195.

11. See above, Ch. 4.

12. Leerssen, *Remembrance and Imagination*, pp. 159–70.

13. Croker, *Fairy Legends and Traditions of the South of Ireland* (3 vol., 1828), vol. II, p. vi.

14. W. R. Wilde, *Irish Popular Superstitions* (1852; Dublin, 1979), p. 28.

15. Angela Bourke, *The Burning of Bridget Cleary: A True Story* (1999).

16. Cf. Joyce Underwood Monro, 'The Invisible Made Visible: The Fairy Changeling as a Folk Articulation of Failure to Thrive in Infants and Children', and Susan Schoon Eberly, 'Fairies and the Folklore of Disability: Changelings, Hybrids and the Solitary Fairy', in Peter Narváez (ed.), *The Good People: New Fairylore Essays* (New York, 1991), pp. 251–83, and 272–50.

17. Andrew Lang, 'Changelings', *Illustrated London News* (25 May 1895), p. 651.

18. For context, see Pick, *Faces of Degeneration*, pp. 24–6.

19. Bourke, *Burning*, p. 174; and 'Hunting Out the Fairies: E. F. Benson, Oscar Wilde, and the Burning of Bridget Cleary', in Jerusha McCormack, ed., *Wilde the Irish Man* (New Haven, CT, 1998), pp. 36–47.

20. *Spectator* (20 April 1895), p. 533, cited in Bourke, *Burning*, p. 175.

21. Hardy, *Jude the Obscure*, p. 249.

22. See Ch. 4.

23. Ledger, *New Woman*, pp. 187–94; Lyn Pykett, *Engendering Fictions: the English Novel in the Early Twentieth Century* (1995), p. 62. See also Wendell V. Harris, 'John Lane's *Keynotes* Series and the Fiction of the 1890s', *PMLA*, 83 (1968), pp. 1407–13.

24. Hugh Stutfield, 'The Psychology of Feminism', *Blackwood's Edinburgh Magazine*, 161 (1897), pp. 104–17, citations at pp. 109 and 112. See also Stutfield,

'Tommyrotics', *Blackwood's Edinburgh Magazine*, 157 (1895), pp. 833–45; [—], 'She-Notes' by "Borgia Smudgiton", *Punch* 106 (1894), pp. 109, 129; James Ashcroft Noble, 'The Fiction of Sexuality', *Contemporary Review*, 67 (1895), pp. 490–98; Joseph Ashby Sterry, *The New Fiction, a Protest against Sex-Mania and other Papers, by the Philistine* (1895) pp. 85–97; Janet E. Hogarth, 'Literary Degenerates', *Fortnightly Review*, 340 n.s. (April, 1895), pp. 589–92; and review of *Discords* in *Athenaeum* (23 March 1895), p. 375.

25. Laura Marholm Hansson, *Modern Women*, trans. Hermione Ramsden (1896), p. 82.
26. See above, pp. 168–70.
27. Hansson, *Modern Women*, p. 90.
28. George Egerton, *Keynotes and Discords* (1995), p. 159.
29. See George Egerton, *A Leaf from the Yellow Book: the Correspondence of George Egerton*, ed. Terence Devere White (1958), p. 16.
30. Charles A. Read and Katharine Tynan Hawkson (eds.), *The Cabinet of Irish Literature* (4 vols., 1903), vol. IV, p. 310.
31. On Egerton's diasporic Irish identity, see Tina O'Toole, '*Keynotes* from Mill-street, Co. Cork: George Egerton's Transgressive Fictions', *Colby Quarterly*, special issue, 'Irish Women Novelists 1800–1940', ed. Ann Fogarty, 36: 2 (2000), pp. 147–56; and 'Narrating the New Woman: The Feminist Fictions of Sarah Grand and George Egerton' (Ph.D. thesis, National University of Ireland, 2001), p. 249.
32. 'A Keynote to Keynotes', in John Gawsworth [Terence Armstrong], *Ten Contemporaries: Notes Toward their Definitive Biography* (1932), p. 32. These fairy themes are strongly apparent in the lead story of the earlier collection, *Keynotes*, 'A Cross Line'. See Elaine Showalter, *Sexual Anarchy: Gender and Culture at the Fin de Siècle* (1991).
33. Egerton, 'A Keynote to Keynotes', in Gawsworth, *Ten Contemporaries*, p. 58. Cf. Kate McCullough, 'Mapping the *Terra Incognita* of Woman: George Egerton's *Keynotes* (1893) and New Women Fiction', in Barbara Leah Harman and Susan Meyer (eds.), *The New Nineteenth Century: Feminist Readings of Underread Victorian Fiction* (New York, 1996), pp. 205–24.
34. Cf. O'Toole, 'Narrating the New Woman', p. 337.
35. Egerton, *Keynotes and Discords*, p. 144.
36. Sauer, 'Infanticide and Abortion in Nineteenth-Century Britain'.
37. Freud, *Standard Edition*, vol. XVII, pp. 177–204.
38. More recently the Lacanian analyst Serge Leclaire has explored instead the phantasy that a child is being killed – the child in this case being the phantasmatic image of ourselves instilled by our parents. See *A Child is Being Killed: On Primary Narcissism and the Death Drive*, trans. Marie-Claude Hays (Stanford, CA, 1998).
39. On this, and more generally on the anthropomorphic treatment of the foetus, see Barbara Duden, *Disembodying Women: Perspectives of Pregnancy and the Unborn* (Cambridge, MA, 1993), trans. Lee Hoinacki, esp. pp. 73–4.

40. See Nell McCafferty, *A Woman to Blame: the Kerry Babies Case* (Dublin, 1985).
41. See my 'Infanticide and the Nation'.

APPENDIX

1. Knott, *Popular Opposition*, p. 239, and n. 27.
2. R. B. Rose, *Gracchus Babeuf, the First Revolutionary Communist* (1978), pp. 174–8.
3. Dorothy Thompson, *The Chartists: Popular Politics in the Industrial Revolution* (1984; Aldershot, 1986), pp. 165–6.
4. Claeys (ed.), *The Chartist Movement in Britain, 1838–1850* (6 vols., 2001), vol. I, 383–437. Francis Place and Beatrice Webb had already noted the connection between Mudie and the introduction to 'The Book of Murder'. See above, Ch. 4, n. 42.

Select bibliography

Unless otherwise stated all works are published in London.

PRE-1900 SOURCES

MANUSCRIPTS

Huntington Library
    Colman, George, *Preludio*, Larpent MS 565, 2 August 1781.
    Medea and Jason, Larpent MS 565, 2 August 1781.

TRIAL REPORTS

Guildhall Library, London
    Old Bailey Session Papers, 1714–1800

OFFICIAL PAPERS

Correspondence on Hindoo Infanticide, 1789–1820, 1824.
Correspondence Relating to the Practice of Infanticide in India, 1828.
Correspondence Relating to the Practice of Infanticide in India, 1843.
Report from his Majesty's Commissioners for Inquiring into the Administration and Practical Operation of the Poor Laws, 1834.
Report from the Select Committee to Inquire into the Administration of the Relief of the Poor, 3 vols., 1837–8.
Chadwick, Edwin, *Report on the Practice of Interment in Towns*, 1843.
Report from the Select Committee on Friendly Societies Bill, 1854.

OTHER PUBLISHED SOURCES PRE-1900

Alexander, William, *The History of Women, from the Earliest Antiquity to the Present Time*, 2 vols., 1779.
Arnold, Matthew, *Lectures and Essays in Criticism*, ed. R. H. Super, Ann Arbor, MI, 1962.
    Culture and Anarchy and Other Writings, ed. Stefan Collini, Cambridge, 1983.
Awful Disclosures of Maria Monk, (1836).
Ball, Charles, *The History of the Indian Mutiny*, 2 vols., 1858.

Banks, Joseph, *The Endeavour Journal, 1768–1771*, 2 vols., ed. J. C. Beaglehole, Sydney, 1962.

Barbauld, Anna Letitia, *Works of Anna Letitia Barbauld, with a Memoir by L. Aikin*, 2 vols., 1825.

Baxter, G. R. Wythen, *The Book of the Bastiles; or the History of the Working of the New Poor Law*, 1841.

Beames, John, *Memoirs of a Bengal Civilian*, 1961.

Bell, Florence, and Elizabeth Robbins, *Alan's Wife. A Dramatic Study in Three Sections. First Acted at the Independent Theatre in London. With an Introduction by William Archer*, 1893.

Besant, Annie, *The Law of Population: its Consequences, and its Bearing upon Human Conduct and Morals*, 1878.

An Autobiography, 2nd edn, 1893.

Bickerstaffe, Isaac, *Love in a Village: A Comic Opera*, Dublin, 1791.

[Binden, David], *A Scheme for Supplying Industrial Men with Money*... Dublin, 1729.

Blackstone, Sir William, *Commentaries on the Laws of England*, 4 vols., Oxford, 1773.

Blake, William, *The Complete Poetry and Prose*, ed. David V. Erdman, Berkeley, CA, 1982.

Le Bon, Gustave, *The Crowd: a Study of the Popular Mind*, 1896.

Booth, William, *In Darkest England and the Way Out*, 1890.

Browne, Sir John, *A Collection of Tracts Concerning the Present Size of Ireland*, 1729.

Browne, John Cave, *Indian Infanticide, its Origin, Progress and Suppression*, 1857.

Browning, Elizabeth Barrett, *Poems*, 1850.

Burke, Edmuud, *The Writings and Speeches of Edmund Burke*, 9 vols., ed. Paul Langford, Oxford, 1981–2000.

Correspondence, 10 vols., ed. Thomas W. Copeland, Cambridge, 1958–78.

Byron, John, *Byron's Journal of his Circumnavigation 1764–66*, ed. Robert E. Gallagher, Cambridge, 1964.

The Narrative of the Honorable John Byron... *containing an account of the great distresses suffered by himself and companions on the coast of Patagonia from the year 1740 till*... *1746*, 1768.

Caird, Mona, *The Morality of Marriage and Other Essays*, 1897.

Campbell, John, *Narrative of his Operations in the Hill Tracts of Orissa for the Suppression of Human Sacrifices and Female Infanticide*, 1861.

Carlile, Richard, *Every Woman's Book; or What is Love*, 1828.

Carlyle, Thomas, *Works*, Centenary Edition, 30 vols., 1896–9.

Carlyle, Thomas, and Jane Welsh, *Collected Letters of Thomas and Jane Welsh Carlyle*, ed. C. R. Sanders, K. J. Fielding, and others, 29 vols., Edinburgh, 1985.

The Case and Memoirs of the late Rev. Mr. James Hackman, and of his acquaintance with the late Miss Martha Reay: with a commentary on his conviction... *To which is added, a letter to Lord S- and Miss Reay. With an appendix, on the ill-effects of public offices of Justices of the Peace. [With a portrait.]*, 4th edn, 1779.

Case and Memoirs of Miss Martha Ray, 1779.

Celebrated Trials, 5, 1825.

Chadwick, Edwin, 'An Essay on the Means of Insurance against Casualties of Sickness, Decreptitude and Mortality', *Westminster Review*, 18 (Apr. 1828).

The Chartist Movement in Britain, 1838–1850, ed. Gregory Claeys, 6 vols., 2001.

Chénier, M. J., *Oeuvres Complètes*, 8 vols., Paris, 1829.

Child, Francis James, *The English and Scottish Popular Ballads*, 5 vols., 1882; New York, 1957.

Clarkson, Thomas, *The History of the Rise, Progress, and Accomplishment of the Abolition of the African Slave Trade by the British Parliament*, 2 vols., 1808.

Cobbett, William, *Parliamentary History of England*, 1806–12.

Colman, George, the Younger, *Inkle and Yariko*, in Frank Felsenstein (ed.), *English Trader, Indian Maid: Representing Race, Gender and Slavery in the New World: An Inkle and Yarico Reader*, Baltimore, ML, 1999.

Cook, James, *The Journals of Captain Cook on his Voyages of Discovery*, 4 vols., ed. J. C. Beaglehole, 1968–74.

Cottle, Joseph, *Reminiscences of Coleridge and Southey*, 1847.

[Courtenay, John], *An Epistle (Moral and Philosophical) from an Officer at Otaheite to Lady Gr** v* n* r with Notes Critical and Historical*, 1774.

Cowper, William, *The Works of William Cowper*, ed. Rev. T. S. Grimshaw, Boston, 1854.

Croft, Sir Herbert, *Love and Madness: a Story Too True*, 1780.

Croker, Thomas Crofton, *Fairy Legends and Tradition of the South of Ireland*, 3 vols., 1828.

Cummin, William, *The Proofs of Infanticide Considered: Including Dr. Hunter's Tract on Child Murder, with illustrative notes*, 1834.

Dajee, Bhawoo, *An Essay on Female Infanticide*, Bombay, 1847.

Darwin, Charles, *The Origin of Species* (1859), ed. Gillian Beer, Oxford, 1996.
   The Descent of Man, and Selection in Relation to Sex, 2 vols., 1871; Princeton, 1981.

Darwin, Erasmus, *Zoonomia; or the Laws of Organic Life*, 2 vols., 1794–6.

De Quincey, Thomas, *Collected Writings*, ed. David Masson, 14 vols., Edinburgh, 1889–90.

Defoe, Daniel, *Moll Flanders*, 1722.
   Roxana, 1724.
   Some Considerations upon Street Walkers with a Proposal for Lessening the Present Number of Them, 1726.

Dickens, Charles, *Oliver Twist*, 1837–9.
   The Chimes, in *The Christmas Books*, vol. 1, ed. Michael Slater, 1971.
   'Frauds on the Fairies', *Household Words* (1 Oct. 1853).

Disraeli, Benjamin, *Sybil*, 1846.

Doran, John, *Saints and Sinners*, 2 vols., 1868.

Doubleday, Thomas, *The Political Tale of the Tub*, Newcastle-upon-Tyne, 1840.

Egerton, George, *Keynotes; Discords* (1893–4), 1995.

A Leaf from the Yellow Book: the Correspondence of George Egerton, ed. Terence Devere White, 1958.

Eliot, George, *Adam Bede*, ed. and intro. Valentine Cunningham, Oxford, 1996.

Felix Holt, ed. and intro. Linda Mugglestone, Harmondsworth, 1995.

Middlemarch, 1871–2.

Daniel Deronda, ed. and intro. Barbara Hardy, Harmondsworth, 1967.

A Writer's Notebook, 1854–1879, and Uncollected Writings, ed. Joseph Wiesenfarth, Charlottesville, VA, 1984.

Essays of George Eliot, ed. Thomas Pinney, 1963.

The Journals of George Eliot, ed. Margaret Harris and Judith Johnston, Cambridge, 1998.

The George Eliot Letters, 7 vols., ed. G. S. Haight, 1954–6.

An Epistle from Mr Banks, Voyager, Monster-Hunter, and Amoroso to Oberea Queen of Otaheite translated by ABC esq., 1774.

Farr, Samuel, *Elements of Medical Jurisprudence*, 3rd edn, 1815.

'Female Infanticide', *Asiatic Journal*, n.s., 3 (Sept.–Dec. 1830).

Ferguson, Adam, *An Essay on the History of Civil Society* (1767), ed. Fania Oz-Salzberger, Cambridge, 1995.

The Field Day Anthology of Irish Writing, 3 vols., ed. Seamus Deane, Derry, 1992.

Fielding, Henry, *The History of Tom Jones*, 1749.

Fullom, Stephen W., *Poor Law Rhymes: Or Anti-Marcus*, 1839.

Gammage, R. G., *History of the Chartist Movement 1837–1854*, Newcastle, 1894.

Gibbon, Edward, *Decline and Fall of the Roman Empire*, 6 vols., 1788.

Gilbert, Geoffrey, *Law of Evidence*, 1754.

Glover, Richard, *Medea*. 1761.

Godwin, William, *Thoughts Occasioned by the Perusal of Dr Parr's Spital Sermon* (1801), in *Political and Philosophical Writings*, 7 vol., ed. Mark Philp, 1993, vol. II, pp. 163–208.

Memoirs of the Author of A Vindication of the Rights of Woman, 1798.

Enquiry Concerning Population, 1820.

Hall, Charles, *The Effects of Civilization on the People of the European State*, 1805; repr. 1850.

Hansson, Laura Marholm, *Modern Women*, trans. Hermione Ramsden, London, 1896.

Hansard, *Parliamentary Debates*, 1803–91.

Hardy, Thomas, *Jude the Obscure*, Harmondsworth, 1985.

Harrington, James, *Oceana*, 1656.

Hawkesworth, John, *An Account of the Voyages undertaken by the order of his present Majesty for making Discoveries in the Southern Hemisphere, and Successfully performed by Commodore Byron, Captain Wallis, Captain Cateret, and Captain Cook, in the Dolphin, the Swallow, and the Endeavour: drawn up from the Journals which were kept by the several Commanders, and from the papers of Joseph Banks esq.* 3 vols., 1773.

Haywood, Ian (ed.), *Chartist Fiction*, 2 vols., 1999, 2001.

Hazlitt, William, *Complete Works*, 21 vols., ed. P. P. Howe, 1930–4.

Herd, David, *Ancient and Modern Scottish Songs*, 2 vols., Glasgow, 1869.

An Historic Epistle, from Omiah to the Queen of Otaheite; being his remarks on the English Nation, 1775.

Hoare, Prince, *Memoirs of Granville Sharp, Esq.*, 2 vols., 2nd edn, 1878.

Hogarth, Janet E., 'Literary Degenerates', *Fortnightly Review*, n.s., 340 (Apr. 1895), pp. 589–92.

Holyoake, George Jacob, *The Life of J. R. Stephens*, 1881.

Humble, Henry, 'Infanticide, Its Curse and Cure', *The Church and the World: Essays on Questions of the Day*, ed. Rev. Orby Shipley, 1866.

Hume, David, *Philosophical Works*, 4 vols., ed. Thomas Hill Green and Thomas Hodge Grose, Aalen, 1964.

In the High Court of Justice. Queen's Bench Division, June 18th, 1877. The Queen versus Charles Bradlaugh and Annie Besant, etc., 1877.

Johnson, James, *The Scots Musical Museum*, Edinburgh, 1787–1803.

Kant, Immanuel, *Critique of Judgement*, 1790.

Kaye, J. W., *The Administration of the East India Company*, 2nd edn, 1853.

Kierkegaard, S., *Fear and Trembling*, 1843; Princeton, NJ, 1941.

Kingsley, Charles, *Water Babies*, 1863.

Kippis, Andrew, *A Narrative of the Voyages Round the World performed by Capt. James Cook with an account of his life during the previous and intervening period*, 2 vols., 1788.

Lafitau, Jean François, *Moeurs des sauvages ameriquains, comparées aux moeurs des premiers temps*, Paris, 1724.

Lang, Andrew, 'Changelings', *Illustrated London News* (25 May 1895), p. 651.

Lawless, Emily, *With the Wild Geese*, 1902.

The Laws Respecting Women, As they regard their natural rights, or their connections and conduct. . . . Also the Obligation of Parent and Child, 1777.

Levy, Amy, *A Minor Poet and Other Verse*, 2nd edn, 1891.

Locke, John, *Essay Concerning Human Understanding*, 1690.

Lockman, John, *Travels of the Jesuits into Various Parts of the World, compiled from their letters*, 2 vols., 1743.

Lofft, Capel, *Eudosia: or, a Poem on the Universe*, 1781.

Lubbock, John, *The Origin of Civilisation and the Primitive Condition of Man*, Chicago, 1978.

MacDonald, George, *Lillith*, 1895.

MacDonell, John (ed.), *Reports of State Trials, 1820–1858*, n. s., 1888–98.

[MacKarness, Mrs], *Old Jolliffe: Not a Goblin Story, by The Spirit of a Little Bell awakened by 'The Chimes'*, 1845.

McLennan, John F., 'Marriage and Divorce – the Law of England and Scotland', *North British Review*, 35 (1861), pp. 187–218.

'Hill Tribes of India', *North British Review*, 38 (1863), pp. 392–422.

Primitive Marriage, 1865.

Maine, Henry, *Ancient Law*, 1861.

Malthus, T. R., *An Essay on the Principle of Population* (1798), ed. Anthony Flew, Harmondsworth, 1970.

An Essay on the Principle of Population, 2 vols., ed. Patricia James, Cambridge, 1989.

Man, Thomas, *The Benefit of Procreation. Together with Some Few Hints toward the Better Support of Whores and Bastards*, 1739.

Mandeville, Bernard, *The Fable of the Bees*, 2 vols., ed. F. B. Kaye, Oxford, 1924.

A Modest Defence of Public Stews (1724): Augustan Reprint Society Publication No.162, Los Angeles, CA, 1973.

'Marcus', *The Book of Murder*, 1839, repr. in Gregory Claeys (ed.), *The Chartist Movement in Britain, 1838–1850*, 6 vols., 2001, vol. I, pp. 383–437.

An Essay on Populousness, 1838.

On the Possibility of Limiting Populousness, 1838.

Marx, Karl, *Grundrisse: Foundations of the Critique of Political Economy (Rough Draft)*, trans. Martin Nicolaus, Harmondsworth, 1973.

Capital: a Critique of Political Economy, 3 vols., I. trans. Ben Fowkes, II and III trans. David Fernbach, Harmondsworth, 1976–81.

Marx, Karl, and Frederick Engels, 'Manifesto of the German Communist Party', trans. Helen MacFarlane, in *The Red Republican*, 1 (9 Nov. 1850).

Mathias, T. J., *The Pursuits of Literature: a Satirical Poem in Four Dialogues*, 6th edn, 1798.

Mayhew, Henry, *London Labour and the London Poor*, selected and ed. Victor Neuberg, Harmondsworth, 1985.

Meares, John, *Voyages made in the years 1788 and 1789 from China to the North West Coast of America*, 1790.

Millar, John, *Observations Concerning the Distinction of Ranks in Society*, 1771.

Mody, Cooverjee Rostomjee, *An Essay on Female Infanticide*, Bombay, 1843.

Montesquieu, Charles de Secondat, *The Spirit of the Laws*, 1748; Cambridge, 1989.

Moore, George, *Esther Waters*, 1894.

Moore, W. R., *Report on Female Infanticide*, 1859.

Nietzsche, Friedrich, *The Genealogy of Morals*, trans. Douglas Smith, Oxford, 1996.

Noble, James Ashcroft, 'The Fiction of Sexuality', *Contemporary Review*, 67 (1895), pp. 490–8.

Nordau, Max, *Degeneration*, 1895.

Noverre, Charles Edwin, *The Life and Works of the Chevalier Noverre*, 1882.

Omiah's Farewell inscribed to the Ladies of London, 1776.

Otaheite: A Poem, 1774.

Paley, William, *Principles of Moral Philosophy*, 2nd edn, 1786.

The Parliamentary History of England, vols. XVI and XVII, 1765–74.

[Patterson, R. H.], 'Our Indian Empire', *Blackwood's Edinburgh Magazine*, 80 (Dec. 1856), pp. 636–59.

Peggs, James, *Hindoo Infanticide. The Present State of Infanticide in India*, 1829.

The Infanticide's Cry to Britain. The Present State of Infanticide in India, chiefly extracted from Parliamentary Papers. Fourth edition, 1844.

Petty, William, *The Political Anatomy of Ireland*, Shannon, 1970.

Pfeiffer, Emily, *Flowers of the Night*, 1889.

Polwhele, Richard, *The Unsex'd Females: a Poem* (1798), New York, 1974.

[Preston, William], *Seventeen Hundred and Seventy-Seven; or, a Picture of the Manners and Characters of the Age in a Poetical Epistle from a Lady of Quality*, 1777.

Proctor, Bryan Waller, 'The Burial Club, 1839', in *An Autobiographical Fragment and Biographical Notes with Personal Sketches of Contemporaries, Unpublished Lyrics, and Letters of Literary Friends*, 1877.

Procès-verbal de l'Assemblée des Communes et de l'Assemblée Nationale, imprimé par son ordre, 75 vols., Paris, 1789–96.

Raikes, Charles, *Notes on the North Western Provinces of India*, 1852.

[Raynal, Abbé], *A Philosophical and Political History of the Settlement and Trade of the Europeans in the East and West Indies*, 4 vols., trans. J. Justamond, Edinburgh, 1776.

Read, Charles A., and Katherine Tynan Hawkson (eds.), *The Cabinet of Irish Literature*, 4 vols., 1903.

Renan, Ernest, *Oeuvres Complètes*, 10 vols., Paris, 1947.

Richardson, Samuel, *Clarissa*, 1748.

Robison, John, *Proofs of a Conspiracy against all the Religions and Governments of Europe carried on in the Secret Meetings of Freemasons, Illuminati and Reading Societies*, 4th edn, 1798.

Romantic Women Poets, 1788–1848, 2 vols., ed. Andrew Ashfield, Manchester, 1998.

Rousseau, Jean-Jacques, *A Discourse on Inequality*, trans. Maurice Cranston, Harmondsworth, 1984.

   Du Contrat Social, 1762.

Ryan, William Burke, *Infanticide: Its Law, Prevalence, Prevention and History*, 1862.

[Scott, John], *An Epistle from Oberea, Queen of Otaheite to Joseph Banks esq trans. by TQZ, Professor of the Otaheite Language in Dublin . . . and enriched with historical and explanatory notes*, 3rd edn, 1774.

   A Second Letter from Oberea, Queen of Otaheite, to Joseph Banks, tr. From the original brought over by Otaipairoo, envoy extraordinary, with some curious anecdotes of the celebrated foreigner, 1775.

Scott, Walter, *Letters on Demonology and Witchcraft, Addressed to J. G. Lockhart*, 1830.

Seward, Anna, *Elegy on Captain Cook to which is added an Ode to the Sun*, 3rd edn, 1781.

Sharp, Granville, *An English Alphabet for the Use of Foreigners . . . as abridged (for the instruction of Omai) from a former work published in 1767*, 1786.

'She-Notes, by "Borgia Smudgiton"', *Punch*, 106 (1894), pp. 109, 129.

Smith, Adam, *Theory of Moral Sentiments* (1759), ed. D. D. Raphael and A. L. Macfie, Oxford, 1976.

   'Letter to the *Edinburgh Review*' in *Essays on Philosophical Subjects*, ed. W. P. J. Wightman and J. C. Bryce, Oxford, 1980.

   The Wealth of Nations, 1776.

Spencer, Herbert, *The Principles of Sociology*, 2 vols., 1876.

Staunton, Sir George. *An Authentic Account of the Earl of Macartney's Embassy from the King of Great Britain to the Emperor of China*, 2 vols., 1797.

Stephens, Joseph Raynor, *The Political Preacher: an Appeal from the Pulpit on Behalf of the Poor*, 1839.

[Sterry, Joseph Ashby], *The New Fiction, a Protest against Sex-Mania, and other Papers, by the Philistine*, 1894.

Stutfield, Hugh, 'The Psychology of Feminism', *Blackwood's Edinburgh Magazine*, 161 (1897), pp. 104–17.

'Tommyrotics', *Blackwood's Edinburgh Magazine*, 157 (1895), pp. 833–45.

The Sublime: a Reader in British 18th-Century Aesthetic Theory, ed. Andrew Ashfield and Peter De Bolla, Cambridge, 1996.

Swift, Jonathan, *Prose Works*, 14 vols., ed. Herbert Davis, Oxford, 1939–74.

Tennyson, Alfred, *Poems of Tennyson*, Oxford, 1913.

[Trevor, George], 'The Bengal Mutiny', *Blackwood's Edinburgh Magazine*, 82 (Sept. 1857), 372–92.

Vardill, John, *The Distracted Lover*, 1779.

Webster, Augusta, *Portraits*, 2nd edn, 1870.

Wilde, W. R., *Irish Popular Superstitions* (1852), Dublin, 1979.

Wilson, John, *History of the Suppression of Infanticide in Western India under the Government of Bombay*, Bombay, 1855.

Wollstonecraft, Mary, *Works*, 7 vols., ed. Janet Todd and Marilyn Butler, 1989.

Wordsworth, Dorothy, *Journals*, 2 vols., ed. Ernest de Selincourt, 1959.

Wordsworth, William, *Poetical Works*, 5 vols., ed. Ernest de Selincourt, 2nd edn, Oxford, 1952.

The Fourteen Book Prelude, ed. W. J. B Owen, Ithaca, NJ, 1985.

Lyrical Ballads and *Other Poems, 1797–1800*, ed. James Butler and Karen Green, Ithaca, NY, 1992.

Lyrical Ballads, ed. R. L. Brett, and A. R. Jones, 1963.

Wordsworth, William, and Dorothy Wordsworth, *The Letters of William and Dorothy Wordsworth: the Early Years, 1787–1805*, 2nd edn, 7 vols., arranged and edited by Ernest de Selincourt, rev. Chester L. Shaver; vol. 1, rev. Chester L. Shaver, Mary Moorman, and Alan G. Hill, Oxford, 1967–88.

Young, M. J. *Memoirs of Mrs Crouch including a Retrospect of the Stage, During the Years She Performed*, 2 vols., 1806.

NEWSPAPERS AND PERIODICALS PRE-1900

The Alarm Bell, 1839.

Asiatic Journal, 1830.

Athenaeum, 1865, 1895.

Blackwood's Edinburgh Magazine, Edinburgh, 1817–1900.

Calcutta Review, Calcutta, 1844.

Cornhill Magazine, 1881.

Dublin Review 1858.

Evening Post, 1773.

Gentleman's Magazine, 1775–1800.

Lancet, 1855–1865.

Lloyds Evening Post and British Chronicle, 1774.
London Chronicle, 1774.
Morning Chronicle, 1779.
Morning Post, 1779.
Morning Star, 1863.
The National: A Library for the People, 1839.
New Moral World, 1844.
Northern Liberator and Champion, Newcastle-upon-Tyne, 1837–40.
Northern Star, Leeds, 1838–48.
Notes and Queries, 3rd and 4th series, 1863–69.
Pall Mall Gazette, 1866.
Saturday Review, 1865.
The Times, 1788–1900.

POST-1900 SOURCES

Abbott, John Lawrence, *John Hawkesworth: Eighteenth-Century Man of Letters*, Madison, WI, 1982.

Agnew, Jean-Christophe, *Worlds Apart: the Market and the Theatre in Anglo-American Thought, 1550–1750*, Cambridge, 1986.

Alexander, Michael, *Omai, 'Noble Savage'*, 1977.

Altick, Richard, *The Shows of London*, 1978.

Anagol, Padma, 'The Emergence of the Female Criminal in India: Infanticide and Survival under the Raj', *History Workshop Journal*, 53 (2002), pp. 73–93.

Anderson, Benedict, *Imagined Communities*, 1983; rev. 1991.

Andrew, Donna T., *Philanthropy and Police: London Charity in the Eighteenth Century*, Princeton, NJ, 1989.

Ardis, Ann, *New Women, New Novels: Feminism and Early Modernism*, New Brunswick, NJ, 1990.

Ariès, Philippe, *Centuries of Childhood*, Harmondsworth, 1973.

Armstrong, Isobel, *Victorian Poetry: Poetry, Poetics and Politics*, 1993.

Arnot, Margaret L., 'Gender in Focus: Infanticide in England, 1840–1880', Ph.D. thesis, University of Essex, 1994.

   'Infant Death, Child Care and the State: the Baby-Farming Scandal and the First Infant Life Protection Legislation of 1872', *Community and Change*, 9: 2 (1994), pp. 271–311.

Ashton, Rosemary, *The German Idea: Four English Writers and the Reception of German Thought 1800–1860*, Cambridge, 1980.

Averill, James H., 'Wordsworth and "Natural Science": The Poetry of 1798', *Journal of English and Germanic Philology*, 77: 2 (Apr. 1978), pp. 232–46.

Baker, Donald C. 'Tertullian and Swift's "A Modest Proposal"', *Classical Quarterly*, 52 (1957), pp. 219–20.

Banks, J. A., and Olive Banks, 'The Bradlaugh-Besant Trial and the English Newspapers', *Population Studies*, 8: 1 (July 1954), pp. 22–34.

Feminism and Family Planning in Victorian England, Liverpool, 1964.

Barker, Francis, Peter Hume, and Margaret Iverson (eds.), *Cannibalism and the Colonial World*, Cambridge, 1998.

Barker-Benfield, G. J., *The Culture of Sensibility: Sex and Society in Eighteenth-Century Britain*, Chicago, 1992.

Barr, Alan P., 'Evolutionary Science and the Woman Question', *Victorian Literature and Culture*, 20 (1992), pp. 25–54.

Batten Jr., Charles L., *Pleasurable Instruction: Form and Convention in Eighteenth-Century Literature*, Berkeley, CA, 1978.

Beattie, J. M., *Crime and the Courts in England, 1660–1800*, Oxford, 1986.

Beckman, Linda Hunt, *Amy Levy: her Life and Letters*, Athens, OH, 2000.

Beer, Gillian, *Darwin's Plots*, 1985.

George Eliot, Brighton, 1986.

Behlmer, George K., 'Deadly Motherhood: Infanticide and Medical Opinion in Mid-Victorian England', *Journal of the History of Medicine*, 34 (1979), pp. 403–27.

Child Abuse and Moral Reform in England, 1870–1908, Stanford, CA, 1982.

The English Home and its Guardians, 1850–1940, Stanford, CA, 1998.

Bender, John B., *Imagining the Penitentiary: Fiction and the Architecture of Mind in Eighteenth-Century England*, Chicago, IL, 1987.

Benjamin, Walter, *Illuminations*, ed. Hannah Arendt, trans. Harry Zohn, 1970.

Benn, J. Miriam, *Predicaments of Love*, 1992.

Berg, Maxine, and Helen Clifford (eds.), *Consumers and Luxury: Consumer Culture in Europe 1650–1850*, Manchester, 1999.

Bermingham, Ann, and John Brewer (eds.), *The Consumption of Culture 1600–1800: Image, Object, Text*, London and New York, 1995.

Berry, Christopher J., *The Idea of Luxury: a Conceptual and Historical Investigation*, Cambridge, 1994.

Berry, Laura C., *The Child, the State and the Victorian Novel*, Charlottesville, VA, 1999.

Bhabha, Homi K., *The Location of Culture*, 1994.

Bhabha, Homi K. (ed.), *Nation and Narration*, 1990; repr. 1999.

Black, Joel, *The Aesthetics of Murder: a Study in Romantic Literature and Contemporary Culture*, Baltimore, MD, 1991.

Blackburn, Robin, *Overthrow of Colonial Slavery, 1776–1848*, 1988.

Bland, Lucy, *Banishing the Beast: English Feminism and Sexual Morality 1885–1914*, 1995.

Bloom, Abigail Burnham (ed.), *Nineteenth-Century British Women Writers: a Bibliographical Critical Source Book*, Westport, CT, 2000.

Bodenheimer, Rosemarie, *The Real Life of Mary Ann Evans*, Ithaca, NY, 1994.

Bonner, Hypatia Bradlaugh, *Charles Bradlaugh*, 2 vols., 1908.

Boswell, John, *The Kindness of Strangers*, 1988.

Boulton, James T., *The Language of Politics in the Age of Wilkes and Burke*, 1963.

Boumelha, Penny, *Thomas Hardy and Women*, Brighton, 1982.

Bourke, Angela, *The Burning of Bridget Cleary: a True Story*, 1999.

Bowers, Toni, *The Politics of Motherhood: British Writing and Culture 1680–1769*, Cambridge, 1996.

Bown, Nicola, 'Small Enchantments: the Meanings of the Fairy in Victorian Culture', D.Phil. thesis, University of Sussex, 1997.

Fairies in Nineteenth-Century Art and Literature, Cambridge, 2001.

Bradbury, Malcolm, *The History Man*, 2nd edn, 2000.

Brady, Eoin, 'The Petty Concerns of Jonathan Swift: William Petty, Jonathan Swift and the Rational Ideal', MA dissertation, University College Cork, 1995.

Brady, Frank, *James Boswell: the Late Years*, 1984.

Brantlinger, Patrick, *Rule of Darkness: British Literature and Imperialism 1830–1914*, Ithaca, NY, 1988.

Bratton, Jacky, *et al.* (eds.), *Melodrama: Stage, Picture, Screen*, 1994.

Brewer, John, and Roy Porter (eds.), *Consumption and the World of Goods*, 1993.

Briggs, Katherine, *The Fairies of English Tradition and Literature*, 1967; repr. 1989.

Brooks, Peter, *The Melodramatic Imagination: Balzac, Henry James, Melodrama and the Mode of Excess*, 1976; New Haven, CT, 1995.

Brubaker, Rogers, *Citizenship and Nationhood in France and Germany*, Cambridge, MA, 1992.

Burke, Peter, *Popular Culture in Early Modern Europe*, 1978.

Burney, Ian, *Bodies of Evidence*, Baltimore, MD, 1999.

Burrow, John W., *Evolution and Society: a Study in Victorian Social Theory*, Cambridge, 1966.

Burton, Antoinette, *Burdens of History: British Feminists, Indian Women, and Imperial Culture, 1865–1915*, Chapel Hill, NC, 1994.

Butler, Marilyn, 'Revolving in Deep Time: The French Revolution in Narrative', in Keith Hanley and Ray Selden (eds.), *Revolution and English Romanticism: Politics and Rhetoric*, Brighton, 1990, pp. 1–22.

Bynum, W. F., and Roy Porter (eds.), *Companion Encyclopaedia of the History of Medicine*, 2 vols., 1993.

Caine, Barbara, *English Feminism, 1780–1980*, Oxford, 1997.

Carpenter, Andrew, 'Two Possible Sources for Swift's "A Modest Proposal"', *Irish Booklore*, 2 (1992), pp. 147–8.

Carroll, David (ed.), *George Eliot: the Critical Heritage*, 1971.

Chandler, James, *Wordsworth's Second Nature*, Chicago, 1984.

Chandrasekhar, S., *A Dirty, Filthy Book*, Berkeley, CA, 1979.

Chatterjee, Partha, *The Partha Chatterjee Omnibus*, Delhi, 1999.

Chaudhuri, Nupur, and Margaret Stroebel (eds.), *Western Women and Imperialism: Complicity and Resistance*, Bloomington, IN, 1992.

Claeys, Gregory, *Machinery, Money and the Millennium: From Moral Economy to Socialism, 1815–60*, Cambridge, 1987.

Clark, Anna, *The Struggle for the Breeches: Gender and the Making of the British Working Class*, Berkeley and Los Angeles, CA, 1995.

Clark, Thomas Blake, *Omai: First Polynesian Ambassador to England*, San Francisco, CA, 1940.

Clayton, Jay, and Eric Rothstein (eds.), *Influence and Intertextuality in Literary History*, Madison, WI, 1991.

Cockburn, J. S. (ed.), *Crime in England, 1550–1800*, 1977.

Colebourne, Bryan, '"We flea the People and seel their Skins": A Source for a Modest Proposal?', *The Scriblerian and the Kit Cats*, 15: 2 (1983), pp. 132–3.

Colley, Linda, *Britons: Forging the Nation, 1707–1837*, New Haven, CT, 1992.

Connal, Crianna, 'Draupadi, Sati, Savitri: The Question of Women's Identity in Colonial Discourse Theory', D.Phil. thesis, University of Oxford, 1997.

Corbett, Mary Jean, *Allegories of Union in Irish and English Writing, 1790–1870: Politics, History, and the Family from Edgeworth to Arnold*, New York, 2000.

Corti, Lillian, *The Myth of Medea and the Murder of Children*, Westport, CT, 1998.

Cottom, Daniel, *Social Figures: George Eliot, Social History and Literary Representation*, Minneapolis, MN, 1987.

Coveney, Peter, *Poor Monkey: the Child in Literature*, 1957.

Cowherd, Raymond, *Political Economists and the English Poor Laws*, Athens, OH, 1977.

Crabtree, Adam, *From Mesmer to Freud: Magnetic Sleep and the Roots of Psychological Healing*, New Haven, CT, 1993.

Cronin, Richard (ed.), *1798: the Year of the Lyrical Ballads*, 1998.

Crow, Thomas E., *Painters and Public Life in Eighteenth-Century Paris*, New Haven, CT, 1985.

Cullen, L. M., *An Economic History of Ireland Since 1660*, 1978.

Cunningham, Hugh, *The Children of the Poor: Representations of Childhood since the Seventeenth Century*, Oxford, 1991.

Cunningham, Valentine, *Everywhere Spoken Against: Dissent in the Victorian Novel*, Oxford, 1975.

Curtis, T. C., and W. A. Speck, 'The Societies for the Reformation of Manners: Study in the Theory and Practice of Moral Reform', *Literature and History*, 3 (1976), pp. 45–63.

Darnton, Robert, *The Great Cat Massacre and Other Essays in French Cultural History*, Harmondsworth, 1984.

Dart, Gregory, *Rousseau, Robespierre, and English Romanticism*, Cambridge, 1999.

Davin, Anna, 'Imperialism and Motherhood', *History Workshop Journal*, 5 (Spring 1978), pp. 9–65.

Deane, Seamus (ed.), *Ireland's Field Day*, 1985.

De Mause, Lloyd (ed.), *The History of Childhood*, New York, 1974.

Desmond, Adrian, and James Moore, *Darwin*, 1992.

Dickson, P. G. M., *The Financial Revolution in England: a Study in the Development of Public Credit*, 1967.

Digby, Ann, 'Malthus and the Reform of the English Poor Law', in *Malthus and his Time*, ed. Michael Turner, 1986, pp. 157–69.

Dinwiddy, J. R., 'Charles Hall, Early English Socialist', *International Review of Social History*, 21 (1976), pp. 256–76.

Donald, Diana, *The Age of Caricature: Satirical Prints in the Reign of George III*, New Haven, CT, 1996.

Donald, James, 'The Citizen and the Man about Town', in Stuart Hall and Paul du Gay (eds.), *Questions of Cultural Identity*, 1996, pp. 170–90.

Donaldson, Ian, *The Rapes of Lucretia: a Myth and its Transformations*, Oxford, 1972.

Downing, Ben, 'Psalmanazar the Amazing', *Yale Review*, 90: 3 (2002), pp. 46–80.

Driver, Felix, 'Tory Radicalism? Ideology, Strategy and Locality in Popular Politics During the 1830s', *Northern History*, 27 (1991), pp. 120–38.

Power and Pauperism: the Workhouse System, 1834–1884, Cambridge, 1993.

Duden, Barbara, *Disembodying Women: Perspectives of Pregnancy and the Unborn*, trans. Lee Hoinacki, Cambridge, MA, 1993.

Duffy, Michael, *The Englishman and the Foreigner*, Cambridge, 1986.

Dumont, Louis, *From Mandeville to Marx: the Genesis and the Triumph of Economic Ideology*, Chicago, IL, 1977.

Eagleton, Terry, *Criticism and Ideology: a Study in Marxist Form*, 1975; repr. 1998.

Edmond, Rod, *Representing the South Pacific: Colonial Discourse from Cook to Gauguin*, Cambridge, 1997.

Edsall, Nicholas C., *The Anti-Poor Law Movement, 1834–44*, Manchester, 1971.

Edwards, Michael S., *Purge This Realm: a Life of J. R. Stephens*, 1994.

Ehrenpreis, Irvin, *Swift: the Man, his Works and the Age*, 3 vols., 1962–83.

Eigen, Joel, 'Intentionality and Insanity: What the Eighteenth-Century Juror Heard', in William Bynum, Roy Porter, and Michael Shepherd, (eds.), *The Anatomy of Madness: Essays in the History of Psychiatry*, 1985, pp. 34–51.

Elam, Diane, *Romancing the Postmodern*, 1992.

Ellingson, Terry Jay, *The Myth of the Noble Savage*, Berkeley, CA, 2001.

Elliott, Marianne, *Partners in Revolution: the United Irishmen and France*, New Haven, CT, 1982.

Ellis, Markman, *The Politics of Sensibility: Race, Gender and Commerce in the Sentimental Novel*, Cambridge, 1996.

Ellmann, Richard, *Oscar Wilde*, New York, 1988.

Epstein, James A., *Radical Expression: Political Language, Ritual and Symbol in England, 1790–1850*, Oxford, 1994.

Epstein, James A., and Dorothy Thompson (eds.), *The Chartist Experience: Studies in Working-Class Radicalism and Culture, 1830–60*, 1981.

Fabian, Johannes, *Time and the Other: How Anthropology Makes its Objects*, New York, 1983.

Faulkner, Harold Underwood, *Chartism and the Churches: a Study in Democracy*, New York, 1916.

Fee, Elizabeth, 'The Sexual Politics of Victorian Anthropology', in Mary S. Hartman (ed.), *Clio's Consciousness Raised: New Perspectives on the History of Women*, New York, 1974, pp. 86–102.

Ferguson, Frances, *Solitude and the Sublime*, New York, 1992.

Ferguson, Moira, *Subject to Others: British Women Writers and Colonial Slavery, 1670–1834*, New York, 1992.

Ferguson, Oliver W., *Jonathan Swift and Ireland*, Urbana, IL, 1962.

Feugère, Anatole, *Bibliographie Critique de l'Abbé Raynal*, Angoulême, 1922.

Finn, Margot, *After Chartism: Class and Nation in English Radical Politics, 1848–1874*, Cambridge, 1993.

Fliegelman, Jay, *Prodigals and Pilgrims: the American Revolution Against Patriarchal Authority*, Cambridge, 1982.

Forrester, John, *Language and the Origins of Psychoanalysis*, 1980.

Foster, R. F., *Modern Ireland 1600–1988*, 1988.

Foucault, Michel, *Discipline and Punish*, trans. Alan Sheridan, 1977.
  Language, Counter-Memory, Practice, ed. D. Bouchard, trans. Bouchard and S. Simon, Ithaca, NY, 1977.

Francus, Marilyn, 'Monstrous Mothers, Monstrous Societies: Infanticide and the Rule of Law in Restoration and Eighteenth-Century England', *Eighteenth-Century Life*, 21 (1997), pp. 133–56.

Freud, Sigmund, *Standard Edition of the Complete Psychological Works of Sigmund Freud*, 24 vols., ed. James Strachey, 1953–74.

Fryer, Peter, *The Birth Controllers*, 1965.

Gallagher, Catherine, *The Industrial Reformation of English Fiction*, Chicago, 1985.

Gallagher, Catherine, and Stephen Greenblatt (eds.), *Practising New Historicism*, Chicago, IL, 2000.

Gammage, R. G., *History of the Chartist Movement 1837–1854*, Newcastle, 1894.

Garrigan, K. O., (ed.), *Victorian Scandals: Representations of Gender and Class*, Athens, OH, 1992.

Gattrell, V. A. C., *The Hanging Tree: Execution and the English People*, Oxford, 1994.

Gawsworth, John [Terence Armstrong], *Ten Contemporaries: Notes Toward their Definitive Biography*, 1932.

Gibbons, Luke, 'Race against Time: Racial Discourse and Irish History', *Oxford Literary Review*, special edition, 'Neocolonialism', 13 (1991), pp. 95–117.

Gilmartin, Kevin, *Print Politics: the Press and Radical Opposition in Early Nineteenth-Century England*, Cambridge, 1996.

Goldberg, Brian, 'Romantic Professionalism in 1800: Robert Southey, Herbert Croft, and the Letters and Legacy of Thomas Chatterton', *ELH*, 63 (1996), pp. 681–706.

Goldsmith, M. M., *Private Vices, Public Benefits: Bernard Mandeville's Social and Political Thought*, Cambridge, 1985.

Goode, John, 'Sue Bridehead and the New Woman', in Mary Jacobus (ed.), *Women Writing and Writing About Women*, 1979, pp. 100–13.

Gosden, P. H. J. H, *Self-Help: Voluntary Associations in the Nineteenth Century*, 1973.

Gould, Rosemary, 'The History of an Unnatural Act: Infanticide and *Adam Bede*', *Victorian Literature and Culture*, 25 (1997), pp. 263–77.

Gowing, Laura, 'Secret Births and Infanticide in Seventeenth-Century England', *Past and Present*, 156 (Aug. 1997), pp. 87–115.

Graver, Suzanne, *George Eliot and Community: a Study in Social Theory*, Berkeley, CA, 1984.

Gray, Robert, *The Factory Question and Industrial England, 1830–1860*, Cambridge, 1996.

Greenfield, Susan C., and Carol Barash (eds.), *Inventing Maternity: Politics, Science and Literature 1660–1865*, Lexington, KY, 1999.

Greenslade, William, *Degeneration, Culture and the Novel 1880–1940*, Cambridge, 1994.

Groom, Nick, '"With certain grand Cottelisms": Southey and Cottle and the Making of Chatterton's *Works*', (unpublished paper).

Guest, Harriet, *Small Change: Women, Learning, Patriotism, 1750–1820*, Chicago, IL, 2000.

Guest, Ivor, *Ballet of the Enlightenment: the Establishment of the Ballet d'Action in France, 1770–1793*, 1996.

Gupta, Brijen Kishove, *India in English Fiction 1800–1970: an Annotated Bibliography*, Metuchen, NJ, 1973.

Hadley, Elaine, *Melodramatic Tactics: Theatrical Dissent in the English Market Place, 1800–1885*, Stanford, CA, 1995.

Haight, G. S., *George Eliot: a Biography*, 1968; repr. 1992.

Hall, Edith, 'Medea and British Legislation Before the First World War', *Greece and Rome*, 2nd series, 46: 1 (Apr. 1999), pp. 42–77.

Hall, Edith, *et al*. (eds.), *Medea in Performance 1550–2000*, Oxford, 2000.

Hamlin, Christopher, *Public Health and Social Justice in the Age of Chadwick: Britain 1800–1854*, Cambridge, 1998.

Hamlyn, Robin, and Michael Phillips (eds.), *William Blake*, 2000.

Harper, George McClean, *Wordsworth's French Daughter. The Story of her Birth, with Certificates of her Baptism and Marriage*, Princeton, NJ, 1921.

Harris, Wendell V., 'John Lane's *Keynotes* Series and the Fiction of the 1890s', *PMLA*, 83 (1968), pp. 1407–13.

Harth, Philip, 'Introduction', Bernard Mandeville, *Fable of the Bees*, 1989.

Hartle, Paul N., 'A New Source for Swift's "Modest Proposal"', *Swift Studies*, 7 (1992), pp. 97–100.

Hartman, Geoffrey, *Wordsworth's Poetry, 1787–1814*, New Haven, CT, 1964.

Haskell, Thomas L., 'Capitalism and the Origins of Humanitarian Sensibility', *American Historical Review*, 90 (1985), pp. 339–61, 547–66.

Hawkes, Terence, 'The Heimlich Manoeuvre', in *Textual Practice*, 8 (1994), pp. 302–16.

Henriques, Ursula R. Q., *Before the Welfare State: Social Administration in Early Industrial Britain*, 1979.

Higginbotham, Ann R., '"Sin of the Age": Infanticide and Illegitimacy in Victorian Britain', *Victorian Studies*, 32 (1988), pp. 319–35.

Himmelfarb, Gertrude, *The Idea of Poverty*, 1984.

Hobsbawm, Eric, and Terence Ranger (eds.), *The Invention of Tradition*, Cambridge, 1983.

Hoffer, Peter C., and N. E. H. Hull, *Murdering Mothers: Infanticide in England and New England 1558–1803*, New York, 1981.

Hogan, Charles Beecher (ed.), *The London Stage 1660–1800 Part 5*, 3 vols., Carbondale, IL, 1968.

Holcombe, Lee, *Wives and Property: Reform of the Married Women's Property Law in Nineteenth-Century England*, Oxford, 1983.

Homans, Margaret, 'Dinah's Blush, Maggie's Arm: Class, Gender and Sexuality in George Eliot's Early Novels', *Victorian Studies*, 36 (1993), pp. 155–78.

Hrdy, Sarah Blaffer, *Mother Nature: a History of Mothers, Infants, and Natural Selection*, New York, 1999.

Humphries, Jane, 'Protective Legislation, the Capitalist State, and Working-Class Men: the Case of the 1842 Mines Regulation Act', *Feminist Review*, 7 (1981), pp. 1–34.

Hundert, E. G., *Enlightenment's Fable: Bernard Mandeville and the Discovery of Society*, Cambridge, 1994.

Hunt, Lynn, *The Family Romance of the French Revolution*, 1992.

Hunt, Lynn (ed.), *The Invention of Pornography: Obscenity and the Origins of Modernity, 1500–1800*, New York, 1993.

Ignatieff, Michael, *A Just Measure of Pain: the Penitentiary and the Industrial Revolution*, 1978; 1989.

Ignatieff, Michael, and Istvan Hont (eds.), *Wealth and Virtue: the Shaping of Political Economy in the Scottish Enlightenment*, Cambridge, 1983.

Jack, Malcolm, 'One State of Nature: Mandeville and Rousseau', *Journal of the History of Ideas*, 39 (1978), pp. 119–24.

Jackson, Mark, *New-Born Child Murder: Women, Illegitimacy and the Courts in Eighteenth-Century England*, Manchester, 1996.

Jackson, Mark (ed.), *Infanticide: Historical Perspectives on Child Murder and Concealment, 1550–2000*, Aldershot, 2002.

Jacobus, Mary, *Tradition and Experiment in the Lyrical Ballads*, Oxford, 1976.
First Things: The Maternal Imaginary in Literature, Art and Psychoanalysis, New York, 1995.

Jalland, Pat, *Death in the Victorian Family*, Oxford, 1996.

James, Patricia, *'Population' Malthus: his Life and Times*, Cambridge, 1979.

Janowitz, Anne, *Lyric and Labour in the Romantic Tradition*, Cambridge, 1998.

Jenkins, Richard, *The Victorians and Ancient Greece*, Oxford, 1980.

Jesus College Cambridge, *The Malthus Library Catalogue*, 'Preface' by Edward Gray, New York, 1983.

Johnson, James William, 'Tertullian and A Modest Proposal', *Modern Language Notes*, 73 (1958), p. 561.

Johnstone, Kenneth, *The Hidden Wordsworth*, New York, 1997.

Jones, Colin, and Dror Wahrman (eds.), *The Age of Cultural Revolutions: Britain and France, 1750–1820*, Berkeley, CA, 2002.

Jones, Gareth Stedman, *Outcast London*, Oxford, 1971.

Jones, Louis Clark, *The Clubs of the Georgian Rakes*, New York, 1942.

Jones, Vivien, 'Placing Jemima: Women Writers of the 1790s and Eighteenth-Century Prostitution Narratives', *Women's Writing*, 4: 2 (1997), pp. 201–220.

'Scandalous Femininity: Prostitution and Eighteenth-Century Narrative', in Dario Castiglione and Lesley Sharp (eds.), *Shifting the Boundaries: Transformation of the Language of Public and Private in the Eighteenth Century*, Exeter, 1995, pp. 54–70.

Jones, Vivien (ed.), *Women in the Eighteenth Century: Constructions of Femininity*, 1990.

Jordan, Elaine, 'Criminal Conversation: on Mary Wollstonecraft's *The Wrongs of Woman*', *Women's Writing*, 4: 2 (1997), pp. 221–34.

Joyce, Patrick, *Visions of the People: Industrial England and the Question of Class 1848–1914*, Cambridge, 1991.

Karr, David, 'Thoughts that Flash Like Lightening: Thomas Holcroft, Radical Theatre and the Production of Meaning in 1790s London', *Journal of British Studies*, 40: 3 (July 2001), pp. 324–56.

Kaufman, Paul, 'Libraries and Their Users', *Borrowings from the Bristol Library, 1773–1784: a Unique Record of Reading Vogues*, Charlottesville, VA, 1960.

Keating, Peter, *The Haunted Study: a Social History of the English Novel, 1875–1918*, 1989.

Keating, Peter (ed.), *Into Unknown England 1866–1913: Selections from the Social Explorers*, Manchester, 1976.

Keynes, John Maynard, *Essays in Biography*, 1933; repr. 1951.

Kirstein, Lincoln, *Movement and Metaphor: Four Centuries of Ballet*, New York, 1970.

Knelman, Judith, *Twisting in the Wind: the Murderess and the English Press*, Toronto, 1998.

Knott, John, *Popular Opposition to the 1834 New Poor Law*, 1986.

Kowaleski-Wallace, Elizabeth, *Consuming Subjects: Women, Shopping and Business in the Eighteenth Century*, NewYork, 1997.

Kristeva, Julia, *Tales of Love*, trans. Leon S. Roudiez, New York, 1987.

Krueger, Christine L., 'Literary Defences and Medical Prosecutions: Representing Infanticide in Nineteenth-Century Britain', *Victorian Studies*, 40: 2 (Winter 1997), pp. 271–94.

Lamb, Jonathan, 'Circumstances Surrounding the Death of John Hawkesworth', *Eighteenth-Century Life*, 18: 3 (1994), pp. 97–113.

Preserving the Self in the South Seas, 1680–1840, Chicago, IL, 2001.

Landa, Louis A., 'A Modest Proposal and Populousness', *Modern Philology*, 40 (Nov. 1942), pp. 161–70.

Landes, Joan B. *Women and the Public Sphere in the Age of the French Revolution*, Ithaca, NY, 1988.

Landry, Donna, *The Muses of Resistance: Labouring-Class Women's Poetry in Britain, 1739–1796*, Cambridge, 1990.

Langford, Paul, *A Polite and Commercial People: England 1727–1783*, Oxford, 1989.

Laplanche, J. and J.-B. Pontalis, *The Language of Psychoanalysis*, trans. Donald Nicholson-Smith 1973.

Laqueur, Thomas, 'Bodies, Details and the Humanitarian Narrative', in Lynn Hunt (ed.), *The New Cultural History*, Berkeley, CA, 1989, pp. 176–204.

Laslett, Peter, Karla Oosterveen, and Richard M. Smith (eds.), *Bastardy and its Comparative History*, 1980.

Leask, Nigel, *Curiosity and the Aesthetics of Travel Writing 1770–1840; From an Antique Land*, Oxford, 2002.

Leavis, F. R., *The Great Tradition*, 1947; 1973.

Leclaire, Serge, *A Child is Being Killed: On Primary Narcissim and the Death Drive*, trans. Marie-Claude Hays, Stanford, CA, 1998.

Ledbetter, Rosanna, *A History of the Malthusian League 1877–1927*, Columbus, OH, 1976.

Ledger, Sally, *The New Woman*, Manchester, 1996.

Leerssen, Joep, *Mere Irish and Fior-Ghael: Studies in the Idea of Irish Nationality, its Development and Literary Expression prior to the Nineteenth Century*, 1986; Cork, 1996.

   Remembrance and Imagination: Patterns in the Historical and Literary Representation of Ireland in the Nineteenth Century, Cork, 1996.

Lees, Lynn, *The Solidarities of Strangers: the English Poor Laws and the People, 1700–1948*, Cambridge, 1998.

Leighton, Angela, *Victorian Women Poets: Writing Against the Heart*, 1992.

Lein, Clayton D., 'Jonathan Swift and the Population of Ireland,' *Eighteenth-Century Studies*, 8 (1974–5), pp. 431–53.

Lerner, Lawrence, *Angels and Absences: Child Deaths in the Nineteenth Century*, Nashville, 1997.

Lestringant, Frank, *Cannibals: the Discovery and Representation of the Cannibal from Columbus to Jules Verne*, trans. Rosemary Morris, Berkeley, CA, 1997.

Levene, Mark, and Penny Roberts (eds.), *The Massacre in History*, New York and Oxford, 1998.

Levine, George, *Darwin and the Novelists: Patterns of Science in Victorian Fiction*, Chicago, 1991.

Levine, George (ed.), *Cambridge Companion to George Eliot*, Cambridge, 2001.

Liddington, Jill, 'Gender, Authority and Mining in an Industrial Landscape: Anne Lister, 1790–1840', *History Workshop Journal*, 42 (1996), pp. 59–86.

Linebaugh, Peter, *The London Hanged: Crime and Civil Society in the Eighteenth Century*, 1991.

Luckhurst, Roger, and Josephine McDonagh (eds.), *Encounters: Transactions between Science and Culture in Nineteenth-Century Britain*, Manchester, 2002.

Lynham, Deryck, *The Chevalier Noverre, Father of Modern Ballet*, 1950.

McCafferty, Nell, *A Woman to Blame: the Kerry Babies Case*, Dublin, 1985.

McCalman, Iain, *Radical Underworld: Prophets, Revolutionaries, and Pornographers in London, 1795–1840*, Oxford, 1988.

McCarthy, William, 'The Celebrated Academy at Palgrave: A Documentary History of Anna Letitia Barbauld's School', *The Age of Johnson*, 8 (1997), pp. 279–392.

McClintock, Anne, *Imperial Leather: Race, Gender, and Sexuality in the Colonial Contest*, New York, 1995.

McClure, Ruth K., *Coram's Children: the London Foundling Hospital in the Eighteenth Century*, New Haven, CT, 1981.

McCormack, Jerusha (ed.), *Wilde the Irish Man*, New Haven, CT, 1998.

McCullough, Kate, 'Mapping the *Terra Incognita* of Woman: George Egerton's *Keynotes* (1893) and New Women Fiction', in Barbara Leah Harman and Susan Meyer (eds.), *The New Nineteenth Century: Feminist Readings of Underread Victorian Fiction*, New York, 1996, pp. 205–24.

McDonagh, Josephine, 'Do or Die: Problems of Agency and Gender in the Aesthetics of Murder,' *Genders*, 5 (1989), pp. 119–34.

'Infanticide and the Nation: the Case of Caroline Beale', *New Formations*, 32 (1997), 11–21.

'Early Novels', in G. Levine (ed.), *Cambridge Companion to George Eliot*, Cambridge, 2001, pp. 38–56.

'Child Murder in George Eliot's *Adam Bede*: Embedded Histories and Fictional Representation', *Nineteenth-Century Literature*, 56: 2 (2001), pp. 228–59.

McKendrick, Neil, John Brewer, and J. H. Plumb, *The Birth of a Consumer Society: the Commercialisation of Eighteenth-Century England*, 1982.

McLaren, Angus, *Birth Control in Nineteenth-Century England*, 1978.

Reproductive Rituals: the Perception of Fertility in England from the Sixteenth Century to the Nineteenth Century, 1984.

McMinn, Joseph, 'A Weary Patriot: Swift and the Formation of Anglo-Irish Identity', *Eighteenth-Century Ireland*, 2 (1987), pp. 103–13.

Mandler, Peter, *Aristocratic Government in the Age of Reform: Whigs and Liberals, 1830–1852*, Oxford, 1990.

Mani, Lata, *Contentious Traditions: the Debate on Sati in Colonial India*, Berkeley, CA, 1998.

Manvell, Roger, *The Trial of Annie Besant and Charles Bradlaugh*, 1976.

Marshall, David, *The Surprising Effects of Sympathy: Marivaux, Diderot, Rousseau and Mary Shelley*, Chicago, IL, 1988.

Marshall, P. J., and Glyndwr Williams, *The Great Map of Mankind: Perceptions of New Worlds in the Age of Enlightenment*, Cambridge, MA, 1982.

Martelli, George, *Jemmy Twitcher: a Life of the Fourth Earl of Sandwich 1718–1792*, 1962.

Martineau, Jane (ed.), *Victorian Fairy Painting*, exhibition catalogue, 1997.

Mason, Michael, *The Making of Victorian Sexual Attitudes*, Oxford, 1994.

Matus, Jill L., *Unstable Bodies: Victorian Representations of Sexuality and Maternity*, Manchester, 1995.

Mee, John, *Dangerous Enthusiasm: William Blake and the Culture of Radicalism in the 1790s*, Oxford, 1992.

Meek, Ronald L, *Social Science and the Ignoble Savage*, Cambridge, 1976.

Melling, J., and J. Barry (eds.), *Culture in History: Production, Consumption and Value in Historical Perspectives*, Exeter, 1992.

Mellor, Anne K., *Mothers of the Nation: Women's Political Writing in England 1780–1830*, Bloomington, IN, 2000.

Mermin, Dorothy, *Elizabeth Barrett Browning: the Origins of a New Poetry*, Chicago 1989.

Metcalf, Thomas R., *The Aftermath of Revolt: India 1857–1870*, 1965.

The Ideologies of the Raj, Cambridge, 1995.

Midgley, Clare, *Women Against Slavery: the British Campaigns, 1780–1870*, 1992.

Miller, Barbara D., *The Endangered Sex: Neglect of Female Children in Rural North India*, Delhi, 1997.

Mitchell, B. R., and Phyllis Deane, *Abstract of British Historical Statistics*, Cambridge, 1962.

Mitchell, Juliet, and Anne Oakley (eds.), *The Rights and Wrongs of Women*, 1976.

Moorman, Mary, *William Wordsworth: a Biography. The Early Years, 1770–1803*, Oxford, 1957.

Mottram, William, *The True Story of George Eliot: in relation to* Adam Bede, 1905.

Mukherjee, Meenakshi, *Realism and Reality: the Novel and Society in India*, Delhi, 1994.

Mullan, John, *Sentiment and Sociability: the Language of Feeling in the Eighteenth Century*, Oxford, 1988.

Narváez, Peter (ed.), *The Good People: New Fairylore Essays*, New York, 1991.

Nead, Lynda, *Myths of Sexuality*, Oxford, 1988.

'Mapping the Self: Gender, Space and Modernity in Mid-Victorian London', in Roy Porter (ed.), *Rewriting the Self: Histories from the Renaissance to the Present*, 1997, pp. 167–85.

Victorian Babylon, New Haven, CT, 2000.

Newman, Gerald, *The Rise of English Nationalism: a Cultural History, 1740–1830*, New York, 1987.

Nora, Pierre, 'Between Memory and History: *Les Lieux de Mémoire*', trans. Marc Roudebush, *Representations*, 26 (1989), pp. 7–25.

Nord, Deborah Epstein, *Walking the Victorian Streets*, Ithaca, NY, 1995.

Nussbaum, Felicity A., *Torrid Zones: Maternity, Sexuality, and Empire in Eighteenth-Century English Narratives*, Baltimore, ML, 1995.

Obeyesekere, Gananath, *The Apotheosis of Captain Cook: European Mythmaking in the Pacific*, Princeton, NJ, and Hawaii, 1992.

O'Hara, Patricia, 'Primitive Marriage, Civilized Marriage: Anthropology, Mythology, and *The Egoist*', in *Victorian Literature and Culture*, 20 (1992), pp. 1–24.

O'Toole, Tina, '*Keynotes* from Millstreet, Co. Cork: George Egerton's Transgressive Fictions', *Colby Quarterly*, special issue, 'Irish Women Novelists 1800–1940', ed. Ann Fogarty, 36: 2 (2000), pp. 147–56.

'Narrating the New Woman: The Feminist Fictions of Sarah Grand and George Egerton,' Ph.D. thesis, National University of Ireland, 2001.

Orr, Brigid, '"Stifling Pity in a Parent's Breast": Infanticide and Savagery in Late Eighteenth-Century Travel Writing', in Steve Clark (ed.), *Travel Writing and Empire: Postcolonial Theory in Transit*, 1999, pp. 131–46.

Outram, Dorinda, *The Enlightenment*, Cambridge, 1995.

Owen, David, *English Philanthropy, 1660–1960*, Cambridge, MA, 1965.

Owen, W. J. B., '"The Thorn" and the Poet's Intention', *Wordsworth Circle*, 8 (1977).

Packer, Alison, *et al*., *Fairies in Legend and the Arts*, 1980.

Pagden, A. (ed.), *Languages of Politics in Early Modern Europe*, Cambridge, 1987.

Pakrasi, Kanti B., *Female Infanticide in India*, Calcutta, 1970.

Panigrahi, Lalita, *British Social Policy and Female Infanticide in India*, New Delhi, 1972.

Parrish, Stephen, '"The Thorn": Wordsworth's Dramatic Monologue', *ELH*, 24 (1957), pp. 153–64, 160.

    The Art of the Lyrical Ballads, Cambridge, MA, 1973.

Patterson, Cynthia, *The Family in Greek Life*, Cambridge, MA, 1998.

Paulson, Ronald, *Hogarth: His Life, Art, and Times*, 2 vols., New Haven, CT, 1971.

Paxton, Nancy, *George Eliot and Herbert Spencer: Feminism, Evolution and the Reconstruction of Gender*, Princeton, NJ, 1991.

Petchesky, Rosalind Pollack, *Abortion and Woman's Choice: the State, Sexuality and Reproductive Freedom*, 1986.

Phillips, Roderick, *Putting Asunder: a History of Divorce in Western Society*, Cambridge, 1988.

Philp, Mark (ed.), *The French Revolution and Popular British Politics*, Cambridge, 1991.

Pick, Daniel, *Faces of Degeneration: a European Disorder, c.1848–c.1918*, Cambridge, 1989.

Pocock, J. G. A., *The Machiavellian Moment: Florentine Political Thought and the Atlantic Republican Tradition*, Princeton, NJ, 1975.

Pollock, Linda A., *Forgotten Children: Parent–Child Relations from 1500 to 1900*, Cambridge, 1983.

Poovey, Mary, *Making a Social Body: British Cultural Formation, 1830–1864*, Chicago, 1995.

Porter, Roy, and Mikulá Teich (eds.), *Romanticism in National Context*, Cambridge, 1988.

Potter, Tiffany, 'A Colonial Source for Cannibalistic Breeding in Swift's "A Modest Proposal"', *Notes and Queries*, 244, n.s. 46, 3 (1999), pp. 347–8.

Pratt, Mary Louise, *Imperial Eyes: Travel Writing and Transculturation*, 1992.

Prothero, I. J., *Artisans and Politics in Early Nineteenth-Century London: John Gast and his Times*, 1987.

Pykett, Lynn, *Engendering Ficitions: the English Novel in the Early Twentieth Century*, 1995.

Radford, Jean (ed.), *The Progress of Romance: the Politics of Popular Fiction*, 1986.

Radzinowicz, Leon, *History of English Criminal Law and its Administration from 1750*, 4 vols., 1948.

Rawson, Claude, *Order from Confusion Sprung: Studies in Eighteenth-Century Literature from Swift to Cowper*, 1985.

    '"Indians" and Irish: Montaigne, Swift and the Cannibal Question', *Modern Language Quarterly*, 53: 3 (Sept. 1992), pp. 299–364.

    God, Gulliver, and Genocide: Barbarism and the European Imagination, 1492–1945, Oxford, 2001.

Rawson, Elizabeth, *The Spartan Tradition in European Thought*, 1969; Oxford, 1991.

Reed, Mark L., *Wordsworth: the Chronology of the Early Years, 1770–1799*, Cambridge, MA, 1967.

Rennie, Neil, *Far-Fetched Facts: the Literature of Travel and the Idea of the South Seas*, Oxford, 1995.

Richardson, Alan, *Literature, Education and Romanticism: Reading as Social Practice, 1780–1832*, Cambridge, 1994.

Richardson, Ruth, *Death, Dissection, and the Destitute*, 1989.

Robinson, L. L., *The Convict Settlers of Australia*, Melbourne, 1965.

Rodgers, Betsy, *Georgian Chronicle: Mrs Barbauld and her Family*, 1958.

Roe, Nick, *Wordsworth and Coleridge: the Radical Years*, Oxford, 1988.

Rogers, Ben, 'In Praise of Vanity: The Augustinian Analysis of the Benefits of Vice from Port-Royal to Mandeville', D.Phil. thesis, University of Oxford, 1994.

Rogers, Helen, *Women and the People: Authority, Authorship and the Radical Tradition in Nineteenth-Century England*, Aldershot, 2000.

Rose, Jonathan, *The Intellectual Life of the British Working Classes*, New Haven, CT, 2001.

Rose, Lionel, *The Massacre of the Innocents: Infanticide in Great Britain, 1800–1939*, 1986.

Rose, R. B., *Gracchus Babeuf, the First Revolutionary Communist*, 1978.

Rosenfeld, A. H. (ed.), *William Blake: Essays for S. Foster Damon*, Providence, RI, 1969.

Ross, Ellen, *Love and Toil: Motherhood in Outcast London, 1870–1918*, Oxford, 1993.

Rossi, Paolo, *The Dark Abyss of Time: the History of the Earth and the History of Nations from Hooke to Vico*, trans. Lydia G. Cochrane, Chicago, 1984.

Rousseau, G. S. and Roy Porter (eds.), *Sexual Underworlds of the Enlightenment*, Manchester, 1987.

Exoticism in the Enlightenment, Manchester, 1990.

Russell, Gillian, *The Theatres of War: Performance, Politics, and Society, 1793–1815*, Cambridge, 1993.

'Burke's Dagger: Theatricality, Politics and Print Culture', *British Journal for Eighteenth-Century Studies*, 20: 1 (1997), pp. 1–16.

Rylance, Rick, *Victorian Psychology and British Culture, 1850–1880*, Oxford, 2000.

Sahlins, Marshall, *How 'Natives' Think: about Captain Cook, for example*, Chicago, 1995.

Said, Edward, *Orientalism*, 1978; repr., 1985.

The World, the Text and the Critic, 1983.

Sauer, Roger, 'Infanticide and Abortion in Nineteenth-Century Britain', *Population Studies*, 32 (1978), pp. 81–93.

Schulte, Regina, *The Village in Court: Arson, Infanticide, and Poaching in the Court Records of Upper Bavaria 1848–1910*, trans. Barrie Selman, Cambridge, 1994.

Schwarzkopf, Jutta, *Women in the Chartist Movement*, Basingstoke, 1991.

Sedgwick, Eve Kosofsky, *Between Men: English Literature and Male Homosexual Desire*, New York, 1985.

Semmel, Bernard, *Imperialism and Social Reform: English Social–Imperial Thought 1895–1914*, 1960.

Service, Elman R., *A Century of Contoversy: Ethnological Issues from 1860 to 1960*, Orlando, FL, 1985.

Shanley, Mary Lyndon, *Feminism, Marriage and the Law in Victorian England, 1850–1895*, 1992.

Shapiro, Barbara J., *'Beyond Reasonable Doubt' and 'Probable Cause': Historical Perspectives on the Anglo-American Law of Evidence*, Berkeley, CA, 1991.

Sharp, Andrew, *The Discovery of the Pacific Islands*, Oxford, 1960.

Sharpe, Jenny, *Allegories of Empire: the Figure of Woman in the Colonial Text*, Minneapolis, 1993.

Sheets, Paul D., '"'Tis Three Feet Long and Two Feet Wide": Wordsworth's "Thorn" and the Politics of Bathos', *Wordsworth Circle*, 22: 2 (1991), pp. 92–100.

Shepherd, Simon, and Peter Womack, *English Drama: a Cultural History*, Oxford, 1996.

Showalter, Elaine, *Sexual Anarchy: Gender and Culture at the Fin de Siècle*, 1991.

Shuttleworth, Sally, *George Eliot and Nineteenth-Century Science: the Make Believe of a Beginning*, Cambridge, 1984.

Simmel, Georg, *Philosophy of Money*, trans. Tom Bottomore and David Frisby from a first draft by Kaethe Mengelberg, 2nd edn, 1990.

Simpson, David, *Irony and Authority in Romantic Poetry*, 1979.
  Wordsworth and the Figurings of the Real, 1982.

Siskin, Clifford, *The Historicity of Romantic Discourse*, Oxford, 1998.
  The Work of Writing: Literature and Social Change in Britain, 1700–1830, Baltimore, MD, 1998.

Slater, Michael, 'Dickens's Tract for the Times', *Dickens 1970*, 1970, pp. 99–123.

Smart, Carol (ed.), *Regulating Womanhood: Historical Essays on Marriage, Motherhood and Sexuality*, 1992.

Smith, Bernard, *European Vision and the South Pacific*, 2nd edn, New Haven, CT, 1985.

Smith, F. B., *Radical Artisan: William James Linton 1812–97*, Manchester, 1973.

Smith, Roger, *Trial by Medicine: Insanity and Responsibility in Victorian Trials*, Edinburgh, 1981.

Soloway, Richard Allen, *Birth Control and the Population Question in England, 1877–1930*, Chapel Hill, NC, 1982.

Spadafora, David, *The Idea of Progress in Eighteenth-Century Britain*, New Haven, CT, 1990.

Speck, W. A. 'Bernard Mandeville and the Middlesex Grand Jury', *Eighteenth-Century Studies*, 11 (1978), pp. 362–74.
  'The Harlot's Progress in Eighteenth-Century England', *British Journal of Eighteenth-Century Studies*, 3 (1980), pp. 127–39.

Stallybrass, Peter, and Allon White, *The Politics and Poetics of Transgression*, 1986.

Steedman, Carolyn, *Childhood, Culture and Class in Britain: Margaret Macmillan, 1860–1931*, 1990.
  Strange Dislocations: Childhood and the Idea of Human Interiority, 1780–1930, 1995.

'A Weekend with Elektra', *Literature and History*, 6 part 1 (1997), pp. 17–42

Stocking, George W., *Victorian Anthropology*, New York, 1987.

Stokes, Eric, *The English Utilitarians and India*, Oxford, 1959.

Stone, George Winchester (ed.), *The London Stage 1660–1800 Part 4*, 3 vols., Carbondale, IL, 1962.

Stone, Harry, *Dickens and the Invisible World: Fairy Tale, Fantasy, and Novel-Making*, 1979.

Stone, Lawrence, *The Family, Sex and Marriage in England 1500–1800*, 1977.

Road to Divorce: England 1530–1987, Oxford, 1990.

Sussman, Charlotte, *Consuming Anxieties: Consumer Protest, Gender and British Slavery, 1713–1833*, Stanford, CA, 2000.

Sutherland, John, *Was Heathcliff a Murderer?*, Oxford, 1996.

Swann, Charles, 'No Wragg by Ilissus? A Note on Matthew Arnold's "Wragg is in Custody"', *Victorian Newsletter*, 68 (1985), pp. 21–3.

Swann, Karen. '"Martha's Name," or The Scandal of "The Thorn"', in Yopie Prins and Maeera Shreiber (eds.), *Dwelling in Possibility: Women Poets and Critics on Poetry*, Ithaca, NY, 1997, pp. 60–79.

Symonds, Deborah H., *Weep Not for Me: Women, Ballads, and Infanticide in Early Modern Scotland*, Pennsylvania, 1997.

Taylor, Anne, *Annie Besant: a Biography*, Oxford, 1992.

Taylor, Gary, 'Blake's Proverb 67', *Explicator*, 32 (Oct. 1973), p. 8.

Taylor, Jenny Bourne, '"Received, a Blank Child": John Brownlow, Charles Dickens, and the London Foundling Hospital – Archives and Fictions', *Nineteenth-Century Literature* 56: 3 (2001), pp. 293–363.

Thompson, Dorothy, *The Chartists: Popular Politics in the Industrial Revolution*, 1984; Aldershot, 1986.

Tomaselli, Sylvia, 'The Enlightenment Debate on Women', in *History Workshop*, 20 (1985), pp. 101–24.

Traer, James F., *Marriage and the Family in Eighteenth-Century France*, Ithaca, NY, 1980.

Trotter, David, *The English Novel in History 1895–1920*, 1993.

Trumbach, Randolph, 'Erotic Fantasy and Male Libertinism in Enlightenment England', in Lynn Hunt (ed.), *The Invention of Pornography: Obscenity and the Origins of Modernity, 1500–1800*, New York, 1996, pp. 253–82.

Tyson, Gerald P., *Joseph Johnson: a Liberal Publisher*, Iowa, 1979.

Uglow, Jenny, *Hogarth: a Life and a World*, 1997.

Vicinus, Martha (ed.), *A Widening Sphere: Changing Roles of Victorian Women*, 1980.

Vicinus, Martha, '"Helpless and Unfriended": Nineteenth-Century Melodrama', *NLH*, 8: 1 (1981), pp. 127–44.

Viswanathan, Guari, *Masks of Conquest: Literary Study and British Rule in India*, 1989; Delhi, 1998.

Outside the Fold: Conversion, Modernity and Belief, Princeton, NJ, 1998.

Walkowitz, Judith R., *Prostitution and Victorian Society: Women, Class and the State*, Cambridge, 1980.

City of Dreadful Delight: Narratives of Sexual Danger in Late-Victorian London, 1994.

Walzer, M., *Regicide and Revolution: Speeches at the Trial of Louis XVI*, Cambridge, 1974.

Ward, J. T. (ed.), *Popular Movements, c. 1830–1850*, 1970.

Warner, Marina, *Alone of all her Sex: the Myth and Cult of the Virgin Mary*, 1976. *No Go the Bogeyman: Scaring, Lulling and Making Mock*, 1998.

Webb, Beatrice, *English Poor Law History, Part II*, vol. 1, 1963.

Welsh, Alexander, *Strong Representations: Narrative and Circumstantial Evidence in England*, Baltimore, 1992.

Williams, Raymond, *The Country and the City*, 1976.

Winch, Donald, *Riches and Poverty: an Intellectual History of Political Economy in Britain, 1750–1834*, Cambridge, 1996.

Wittkowsky, George, 'Swift's *Modest Proposal*: The Biography of an Early Georgian Pamphlet', *Journal of the History of Ideas*, 4 (1943), pp. 75–109.

Wolfram, Sybil, *In-Laws and Outlaws: Kinship and Marriage in England*, 1987.

Wood, Marcus, *Radical Satire and Print Culture, 1790–1822*, Oxford, 1994.

Wu, Duncan, *Wordsworth's Reading, 1770–1799*, Cambridge, 1993.

Yeo, Eileen, 'Christianity in Chartist Struggle 1838–1842', *Past and Present*, 91 (May 1981), pp. 47–73.

Young, Robert J. C., *Colonial Desire: Hybridity in Theory, Culture and Race*, 1995.

Zedner, Lucia, *Women, Crime, and Custody in Victorian England*, Oxford, 1991.

Zelizer, Viviana A. Rotman, *Pricing the Priceless Child: the Changing Social Value of Children*, 1985; Princeton, NJ, 1994.

Zizek, Slavoj, *Zizek Reader*, ed. E. Wright and E. Wright, Oxford, 1999.

Index

Lightning Source UK Ltd.
Milton Keynes UK
UKHW041510210119
335940UK00001B/185/P